OSWALD CHAMBERS

OSWALD CHAMBERS

THE BEST FROM ALL HIS BOOKS

VOLUME II

CHOSEN AND EDITED BY
HARRY VERPLOEGH

FOREWORD BY
WARREN W. WIERSBE

OLIVER
NELSON

A Division of Thomas Nelson Publishers
Nashville

Published in Nashville, Tennessee, by Oliver-Nelson Books, a division of Thomas Nelson, Inc., Publishers, and distributed in Canada by Lawson Falle, Ltd., Cambridge, Ontario.

Printed in the United States.

ISBN 0-8407-9013-9

1 2 3 4 5 6 - 92 91 90 89

Contents

Foreword

"I shall be buried for a time," said Oswald Chambers, "hidden away in obscurity; then suddenly I shall flame out, do my work, and be gone."

As far as Chambers' personal life was concerned, his prophecy came true; for he was only forty-three years old when he died in 1917. But when it comes to his personal ministry, that is another story; for his work goes right on through the pages of his many books, especially *My Utmost for His Highest*.

God gave Oswald Chambers a penetrating insight into spiritual truth. He also gave him the ability to express that truth in ways that capture our attention and sometimes even shock us, so that we listen to God (not Oswald Chambers) and want to do what He says.

I rejoice that Harry Verploegh has given us a second volume of choice quotations from Oswald Chambers. I have kept the first volume right next to my computer desk, on my shelf of "special tools"; and I refer to it frequently and quote from it often as I write and prepare messages.

But these books are much more than collections of "religious quotations." If you want to do some "blessed browsing," if you want to refresh your heart with vibrant expressions of familiar truths, if you want to learn new truths, then these books are for you.

"You can never give another person that which you have found," Chambers wrote, "but you can make him homesick for what you have." I trust these pages will indeed make us all "homesick" for spiritual reality in Jesus Christ.

WARREN W. WIERSBE

Introduction

Oswald Chambers was remembered as a child for his readiness to pray and his confidence that God would answer his prayers, but it was not until his teenage years that prayer became the working of the miracle of Redemption in him. Chambers was born on July 24, 1874, in Aberdeen, the fourth son of Clarence and Hannah Chambers. Hannah had been raised an Irvingite but became a Baptist under Spurgeon. Oswald's father was pastor of the Crown Terrace Baptist Church in Aberdeen, and later ministered in Stoke-on-Trent, Perth, and London.

As a boy Chambers studied drawing at Sharp's Institute in Perth. After hearing Spurgeon preach in Dulwich, the city where his father retired, Chambers asked to be baptised and began visiting men in the YMCA lodging house. He won an arts scholarship to study abroad from the Art School in South Kensington, but instead took the Arts Course at the University of Edinburgh until he decided at twenty-three to follow the counsel of a number of Scottish men of God, who were aware of his spiritual gifts and encouraged him to accept God's call to the ministry.

He attended the Dunoon Training School, founded by Duncan Mac-Gregor, and within a year became a tutor in philosophy and psychology, taught art, and formed a Browning Society. Chambers beame known at Dunoon as a man of prayer who relied unequivocally on God to supply his needs. He was admired for his love of art and poetry, his radiant disposition, and his generosity to others. At this time he began to speak in open air meetings. He worked in city missions and taught Sunday school.

After seven years of study and teaching, Chambers left Dunoon in 1905. In that same year he met Bishop Juji Nakada, the Japanese evangelist, at a Pentecostal League meeting in Perth. Together these two men, Chambers, long "like a poker," and Nakada, "short like a shovel," planned to stir up the Spirit of God among the Holiness people in an evangelistic tour of America and Japan. Of this tour in 1906–1907, Chambers wrote in his diary that he felt a perfect sense of God's call and leading as one of "the Lord's spoilt bairns" who was being introduced in Brooklyn, Providence, Cincinnati, and Seattle to "choice souls." In considering the evangelist's work he wrote,

> The goodness of God strikes me. People don't know Him, but it is not a wicked ignoring, it is ignorance. The full compassionate love of the Holy Ghost for the crowd is a precious, though intolerable compassion.

During his tour of Japan, Chambers visited the Oriental Mission Bible Society in Tokyo and several interior mission stations. He preached and witnessed the mighty preaching of Nakada.

Upon returning to London via Hong Kong, the Suez, Rome, and Paris, Chambers continued evangelistic work with the League of Prayer and made the acquaintance of the family of the Reverend David Lambert, then a junior minister in Sunderland. Lambert became one of the circle around Gertrude Chambers who later helped publish Chambers' messages, lectures, and prayers and who in the 1970s published a valuable account of Chambers' life and works, *Oswald Chambers: An Unbribed Soul.* David Lambert wrote of the Chambers of this period of evangelistic preaching that

> at the big London meetings he would find an odd corner to be alone with God before speaking in public. Now I know how much preparation there had been in years of discipline, and Christ-following, and strenuous thinking. I did not know it then, yet felt that there was insight and authority and spiritual power far above that of the average minister or missioner.

In the years 1911–1915 preceding his principleship of the Bible Training School near Clapham Common, London, Chambers preached and taught many missions for the League of Prayer in England, Scotland, and Ireland. He began to develop some of the characteristic emphases of his ministry. He stressed the artificiality of man-made religion. He insisted on God's high intention of blessing toward the lowliest and most ordinary Christian who abandons himself or herself in faith to Jesus Christ and makes an absolute commitment to the Word of God. He believed in disciplined study of the humanities as well as of the Bible lest the student learn no method to study God's Word and be forced, in Chambers' terms, to wander aimlessly in it as in a cultivated park. He stressed the importance of seeking a means of applying the experience of sanctification in practical Christian service.

Chambers' own characteristic readiness for God's use is demonstrated in a comment he made to H. Stark upon arriving in Plymouth for meetings: "I hope we shall have a very blessed week-end, Mr. Chambers," said Stark. Chambers replied, "If we behave ourselves, the Lord will help Himself to all He wants from us."

In the spring of 1910 Chambers married Gertrude Hobbs ("Biddy"), the woman who would later use her language skills to publish Oswald Chambers' manuscripts and her notes of his lectures, sermons, and talks after his death, including the devotional classic, *My Utmost for His Highest,* which she compiled.

After their marriage, Mrs. Chambers accompanied Chambers on a four-month mission to the United States. On their return, Chambers settled into his work as Principal of the new nondenominational Bible Training College for the education of home and foreign workers founded in Battersea, London, the center of the League of Prayer. After Chambers' death, student after student wrote of the special features of Chambers' leadership of the school in the five years before he went to the Eastern front as a chaplain for the YMCA. As a teacher Chambers knew instinctively which students could not be forced to change their pet theories and required only his listening ear and patience to develop new understanding and which students needed a devastating but salutary blow to their prejudices and pettinesses. Chambers was a beloved exampled to them of child-like trust in God and self-discipline ("Get out of bed and think about it afterwards" he would advise) and of a rare balance between flexibility and strength in both spiritual and practical matters.

At the outbreak of World War I, Chambers felt a deep and urgent need to exercise his ministry among the British forces but waited patiently for almost nine months for the details to fall into place. Between the fall of 1915 and his death in November 1917, Chambers established two desert mission camps for British troops in Egypt at Zeitoun, nine miles from Cairo and at Ismailia, on the banks of the Suez Canal.

These places of peace in the midst of war preparation were built of native rush mats. The Zeitoun camp included a refreshment marquee for soldiers, a devotional hut for worship services, a smaller hut where Chambers and his assistants conducted Bible classes, a tiny "items" hut where stationery and books were sold, and a dugout. The Chambers family, which now included the tiny Kathleen and their devoted helper, Mary Riley, lived in a bungalow built for them. There they entertained a constant stream of guests. Former students from the Bible Training College assisted Chambers with the administration of the camp activities and the care of souls.

During his two-year ministry in Egypt, Chambers kept a diary where he recorded his early morning thoughts, activities of the day, plans for Bible studies or talks, the responses of his audiences, and encounters with individuals. Sixteen years after his death, extracts from this diary were published with many tributes to his influence on the Mediterranean Expeditionary Forces in *Oswald Chambers: His Life and Work*. With a painter's eye, Chambers repeatedly described the sunrise on the desert, sublime and dazzling with praise to God, a "sealing witness of peace," and at other times a scene of desperate turmoil about which he could be equally delighted:

> This morning is thick with Khamseen wind. As I write, the sky is a most formidable colour, dense lurid copper, and the wind is rampaging with the old antique heat of leagues of desert, not a heat like the sun's heat, but the heat of blinding devastation. . . .

Chambers found his work among the men and the activity of the desert camps constantly invigorating. Of the sunrise near the Suez, he wrote:

> The splendor of these sunrises is unique. . . . All the noises of the camp are stirring and fine, the men are astir at 4 A.M., the stir, the movement of horses, the bugles, the whirr of aeroplanes, all makes this life a real delight to me somehow.

And of an Egyptian noon in July, Chambers noted:

> Sun! I have been considering it. One cannot conceive of such sun unless one has summered in Egypt. It is the only power that makes this land possibly habitable. It is fierce, appallingly so, but fascinating; my own experience is that desert life is productive of intense vitality and energy, not of languor.

Boundless energy and vitality is precisely what Chambers gave to thousands of soldiers from all parts of the Commonwealth who passed through the YMCA mission camps. Living in the discomfort of military bases, their futures uncertain, many afterwards gave tribute to the eloquence and spiritual influence of this gifted man of God. Douglas Downes described Chambers at work in Egypt:

> One of my early memories of Oswald Chambers is that of a lithe figure in khaki, with the eyes of a prophet and the profile of a Savaronola, seated with a group of younger men at a table in the Central YMCA in Cairo. He is telling them in his delightful, sparkling, humorous way that he cannot see the need of so much entertainment stuff to keep the men together of an evening. Out there in his hut at Zeitoun he can get a crowd of Australians night after night attracted by nothing but the message of Redemption.
>
> I went over to Zeitoun, and found the unheard-of thing had come to pass. Men whom no one could accuse of being religious turned up in large numbers on a week-night to hear a religious talk. But it is no ordinary talk, and the man who gives it is no ordinary man. There is no

appeal to the emotions, no cant religious phrases, no anecdotes, just a flow of clear convincing reasoning—stark sincerity, speaking with the authority of deep personal experience; you are brought to the point where the natural man breaks down and where the supernatural must come in to carry you with its confidence right into the presence of God.

Men who visited the mission huts used similar words to describe Chambers' discernment of biblical truth as well as of human need. They mentioned his "penetrating gaze," his keen and alert face, his "canny" understanding of individual men. Many remembered the personal words of comfort Chambers gave them on their departure for front lines in Palestine or France. Others were visited by him while laid aside in hot canvas hospitals. He was for more than one soldier a "detective of the soul, one who has been in intimate fellowship with the unseen." With others who have written of the heightened intensity that war brings to the experience of life, Chambers knew that with many men bound for the front, irresponsible pleasure-seeking would end and stern issues would confront them. He relished the opportunity to speak to them at a time when they would be more open to talk about God and the soul, when the faith of many would be strained. He insisted that in the midst of life-threatening circumstances, a soldier could maintain an unchanging relationship to God through the redemptive work of Christ.

Throughout the period of his chaplaincy Chambers would not allow the disruption, devastation, and death that impinged on his consciousness and crippled many spirits working near the front to undermine his natural buoyancy and confidence in God's sovereignty. He was steadfast in his belief that "the lack of ability and master-mindedness to conduct the war" was an occasion for men to cast themselves on God and find His order in the "haphazard" of ordinary experience or in the midst of an appalling war when hundreds of thousands of men would be battered into eternity.

Chambers was aware, however, that his confidence in God's ends could seem like indifference to the senses of others assaulted by the horror and the contradictions of war. Together with the soldiers who visited the YMCA camps, he probed the meaning of war to men of faith, lecturing boldly on such topics as "Religious Problems Raised by War," "Is Human Sacrifice Redemptive?", "Has History Disproved the Song of the Angels?" (a Christmas talk), and "Does War Create or Reveal Wickedness?" Chambers read other men's attempts to sustain a Christian hope in wartime and was particularly helped by Denny's *War and the Fear of God* and Forsyth's *The Christian Ethics of War*.

At one point in his diary, Chambers recorded his mistaken intuition that the war would end by late 1916. Chambers found that his miscalculation was an indication that "the Holy Spirit must be recognized as the sagacious Ruler in all affairs, and not our astute common sense." In his own experience and in his detailed study of the Old Testament prophets in the last months of his life, Chambers found God's ways inscrutable, but that in the mystery of Redemption.

> God is prepared to run the risk of evil, so to speak, and the Cross is the proof that He Himself has taken the responsibility of its removal.

With many Christians of the Great War period, Chambers looked with amazement, wonder, and tears at the great bravery of the young men who, made of "grand human stuff," withstood the wrath and chaos of war. He prayed that their sacrifices would be acts of worship mirroring the obedience of Christ's painful sacrifice as the means of God's redeeming work. In the last weeks of his life, Chambers meditated on Israel's history as seen through the eyes of the prophets Hosea, Joel, and Amos and considered the spectacle of human evil in his own time. He noted that Amos ascribes to God the power to effect "blasting and mildew and disease and pestilence and error and wrong." He concluded with Amos that all these occurrences are beyond the control of man, that all the consequences are in the "powerful hand of God, and not of blind cause and effect." Again and again Chambers recorded his "joyful detection of God's ruling in the haphazard" in his diary. A month before his death, on a glorious morning when the East was "like a celestial scheme of shot silk" Chambers' heart sprang up to the call of the prophet Amos:

> Seek him that maketh the Pleiades and Orion, and maketh the day dark with night, and turneth the shadow of death into the morning. (Amos 4:8)

In the entries for October 1917, one senses that Chambers had extended himself to the limit of God's requirement. Twice he had to lump diary entries together for lack of opportunity to write. He persuaded Swan, a colleague in the YMCA mission, to lecture on Islam for him. Then in preparation for a mission to Palestine to minister to the wounded and dying for General Allenby, he asked Mrs. Chambers to conduct services and rejoiced in the "lift" of inspiration he felt at those she led. By November 15, 1917, Oswald Chambers was at rest from the intense labor of biblical interpretation and spiritual counsel he fulfilled for the church in the period of the Great War.

It is hoped that this new anthology of excerpts from the Chambers publications will introduce a rising generation of Christians to the profound themes this gifted and faithful teacher explored during his vital ministry in God's joy and under His hand in the second decade of this century.

VIRGINIA VERPLOEGH STEINMETZ

Key to Sources

Quotations are followed by letter codes with numbers that indicate the title of the work from which the extract is taken and the page number on which it appears. For example,

> Beware of being guided by mental or spiritual affinities, let God mix you as He sees fit. SHL. 117

The letters SHL indicate the quotation is taken from *The Servant as His Lord*; the number 117 indicates the quotation is found on page 117 of that work.

Following are the letter codes used in this collection to refer to the works of Oswald Chambers. All the books but one were first published by Christian Literature Crusade in Fort Washington, Pennsylvania. *My Utmost for His Highest* was published by Dodd, Mead & Company, Inc., in New York, New York. The year of publication follows each title.

AUG	*Approved unto God*, 1973
BFB	*Baffled to Fight Better*, 1973
BE	*Biblical Ethics*, 1964
BP	*Biblical Psychology*, 1973
BSG	*Bringing Sons to Glory*, 1973
CD. VOL I	*Christian Discipline*, Vol. I, 1965
CD. VOL II	*Christian Discipline*, Vol. II, 1965
CHI	*Conformed to His Image*, 1971
DI	*Disciples Indeed*, 1960
GW	*God's Workmanship*, 1960
HG	*The Highest Good*, 1965
HGM	*He Shall Glorify Me*, 1965
IWP	*If Thou Wilt Be Perfect*, 1962
IYA	*If Ye Shall Ask*, 1965
LG	*The Love of God*, 1965
MFL	*The Moral Foundations of Life*, 1961

A

ABANDONMENT

Beware of any hesitation to abandon to God. It is the meanest characteristics of our personality that are at work whenever we hesitate, there is some element of self-interest that won't submit to God. CHI. 31

The great aim of the Holy Spirit is to get us abandoned to God. HGM. 78

Jesus Christ always brings us back to one thing—'Stand in right relationship to Me first, then the marvellous doing will be performed in you.' It is a question of abandoning all the time, not of doing. IWP. 115

Abandon to God is of more value than personal holiness. MUH. 52

When we are abandoned to God, He works through us all the time. MUH. 52

The reason some of us are such poor specimens of Christianity is because we have no Almighty Christ. We have Christian attributes and experiences, but there is no abandonment to Jesus Christ. MUH. 58

When a soul abandons to God, God will not abandon it. But let that soul trust its wits and become its own amateur providence and a dexterous muddle will be the result. NKW. 145

. . . what is needed in spiritual matters is reckless abandonment to the Lord Jesus Christ, reckless and uncalculating abandonment, with no reserve anywhere about it; not sad, you cannot be sad if you are abandoned absolutely. PS. 23

The secret of sacramental discipleship is to be so abandoned to the disposition of God in us that He can use us as broken bread and poured out wine for His purpose in the world, even as He broke the life of His own Son to redeem us. RTR. 66

Whenever the call is given for abandon to Jesus Christ, people say it is offensive and out of taste. The counterfeit of abandon is that misleading phrase 'Christian service.' I will spend myself for God, I will do anything and everything but the one thing He asks me to do, viz., give up my right to myself to Him. SHL. 85

ABIDING

In the mystical life the majority of us are hopeless woolgatherers, we have never learned to brood on such subjects as 'abiding in Christ.' MFL. 38

Think of the things that take you out of abiding in Christ—Yes, Lord, just a minute, I have got this to do; Yes, I will abide when once this is finished; when this week is over, it will be all right, I will abide then. *Get a move on;* begin to abide *now.* In the initial stages it is a continual effort until it becomes so much the law of life that you abide in Him unconsciously. Determine to abide in Jesus wherever you are placed. MUH. 166

There is no condition of life in which we cannot abide in Jesus. We have to learn to abide in Him wherever we are placed. OBH. 103

'Severed from Me you can do nothing,' i.e., 'you will not bear My fruit, you will bear something that did not come from Me at all'; but—"Abide in Me," and you will bring forth fruit that testifies to the nature of the vine, fruit whereby the Father is glorified. "The effectual fervent prayer of a righteous man," one who is abiding, "availeth much." OBH. 123

"Abide in Me," says Jesus, in spiritual matters, in money matters, in every one of the matters that make life what it is. RTR. 68

ABILITY

Think of the number of times we say, 'Oh, I can't.' For the good of your own soul, say 'I won't.' To say, 'I can't' enervates the whole life. If we really cannot, God has misled us. Jesus said, "All power is given unto Me"; if He tells us to do something and we cannot, this is simply not true. MFL. 76

We are apt to say that because a man has natural ability, therefore he will make a good Christian. It is not a question of our equipment but of our poverty, not of what we bring with us, but of what God puts into us; not a question of natural virtues of strength of character, knowledge, and experience—all that is of no avail in this matter. The only thing that avails is that we are taken up into the big compelling of God and made His comrades. MUH. 217

Natural ability has nothing to do with fitness for God's salvation, it may have to do with fitness for Christian work, that is a matter of civilisation. PH. 54

ABORTION

Modern tendencies of thought which are working great havoc indicate that a child has not a soul until it is born into this world. The Bible says that body, soul and spirit develop together. This may not appear to the majority of us as being of any importance, but it will do so when we come in contact with the views that are abroad to-day, even amongst some who call themselves Christian teachers, but who are really wolves among the sheep and whose teaching comes from the bottomless pit. BP. 68

'Before I formed thee, I knew thee.' There are pre-natal forces of God at work in a man's life which he may be unconscious of for long enough; but at any moment there may break upon him the sudden consciousness of this incalculable, supernatural surprising power that has got hold of his life before he has got hold of it himself. SSY. 14

ABSTINENCE

Beware of those who teach abstinence from marriage and from meats, they are true neither to God nor man as God made him. SA. 74

ACCOUNTABILITY

Once remove personal accountability to God and you will get immorality, whether it is bestial or not is a matter of accident. BE. 15

The essence of sin is the refusal to recognise that we are accountable to God at all. MFL. 59

ACHIEVEMENT

It is not what a man achieves, but what he believes and strives for that makes him noble and great. NKW. 146

ACTION

The majority of us prefer to get up and ride rather than to 'get up and shove.' It is only the people who 'get out and shove' who really make things go. BFB. 76

Always beware when you can reasonably account to yourself for the action you are about to take, because the source of such clear reasoning is the enthroning of human understanding. It is this element in the personal life of a Christian that fights longest and to the last against the enthronement of Jesus Christ as Lord and Master. OPG. 34

We shall not see Jesus if we sit still, or if we pray and long for Him, but if we go quickly, "there shall ye see Him." Go in your mind, rouse yourself up, indulge no more in reminiscent worship. PH. 126

Are we detached enough from our own spiritual hysterics to wait on God? To wait is not to sit with folded hands, but to learn to do what we are told. These are phases of His ways we rarely recognize. RTR. 46

Always do something you don't need to do for the sake of doing it—it keeps you in moral fighting trim. SA. 94

ACTIVITY/INACTIVITY

The 'practical' craze, anything that is efficient, is the insanity of our day—we must be at it! Do anything at all, but don't take time to sit down and think and pray, that is a waste of time; all that is required is to live right practically. If you are living right practically it is because you have not only experienced new birth, but you are being nourished on the right foundation. HGM. 147

The workable medium is man. God takes as the medium of working the stuff we are made of, and all He requires is for us to be inactive and let Him work. IWP. 64

We put up sighing petitions—'I have tried to be good'; 'I have tried to sanctify myself.' All that is the work of God, and the best thing to do is to stop trying and let God do it. What we have to do, and what God cannot do, is to work out what He has worked in. We try to do God's work for Him, and God has to wait until we are passive enough to let Him work in us. IWP. 65

Do get out of your ears the noisy cries of the Christian world we are in—'Do this and do that.' Never! '*Be* this and that, then I will do through you,' says Jesus. LG. 57

We have to get rid of the plague of the spirit of the religious age in which we live. In Our Lord's life there was none of the press and rush of tremendous activity that we regard so highly, and the disciple is to be as His Master. MUH. 293

To-day the clamour is 'do'; but the great need is to face our souls with God until the sterling stamp and testimony of the life is—"But far be it from me to glory, save in the Cross of our Lord Jesus Christ." We are so taken up with actual happenings that we forget the one fundamental thing, viz., the Cross. Beware of any fascination that takes you away from the centre. PH. 87

To wait upon God is the perfection of activity. PH. 93

The need is not to *do* things, but to *believe*. "What must I *do* to be saved?" "*Believe* on the Lord Jesus Christ, and thou shalt be saved." RTR. 58

The people who are always desperately active are a nuisance; it is through the saints who are one with Him that God is doing things all the time. RTR. 70

God did not create Adam holy, He created him innocent, without self-consciousness (as we understand the word) before God; the one thing Adam was conscious of was God and only of himself in relation to the Being Whose commands he was to fulfil; the main trend of his spirit was towards God. BSG. 10

God created Adam to "have dominion over the fish of the sea, and over the fowl of the air, and over every living thing that moveth upon the earth"; the one thing Adam was not to have dominion over was himself. God was to have dominion over him, and Adam had to partake in his own development by obeying God's rule over him, not his own wisdom. The source of life in Adam was his obedience to God. BSG. 11

Adam, the Federal Head of the human race, was designed by God to take part in his own development, that is, he was intended to turn the natural into the spiritual by a series of choices, which would mean moral progress. CHI. 39

Creation in Christ means that Jesus Christ is able to create us into His own image, not merely re-create us, because what we get in Jesus Christ is something that Adam never had. Adam was created a "son of God," an innocent being with all the possibilities of development before him; God intended him to take part in that development by a series of moral choices whereby the natural life was to be sacrificed to the will of God and turned into a spiritual life. Adam failed to do this. Jesus Christ creates in us not

what was in Adam, He creates in us what He was and is. OBH. 26

Until Adam fell, he was not *interested in* God, he was *one with* God in communion—a man is never interested in that which he is; when Adam fell, he became so appallingly interested in God that he was afraid of Him—"and the man and his wife hid themselves from the presence of the Lord God amongst the trees of the garden." OPG. 6

Adam had the possibility of disobedience, and when temptation came to him producing the dilemma, he deliberately inclined to disobedience, and the disposition to disobey God became the inheritance of the whole of the human race. "Wherefore, as by one man sin entered into the world, and death by sin; and so death passed upon all men, for that all have sinned." PS. 55

The Bible says that God created the Federal Head of the race in His own image; that means that God accepts the responsibility for the human race being put on the wrong track, and the Cross is the proof that He does so. SA. 24

If Adam had not sinned and thereby introduced the heredity of sin into the human race, there is every reason to suppose that the human race would have been transfigured into the real presence of God; but Adam disobeyed, and sin entered in. SA. 46

The Bible does not say that God punished the human race for one man's sin, but that the disposition of sin, i.e., my claim to my right to myself, entered into the human race by one man. SA. 104

ADAM AND EVE

Adam and Eve are not now saying of God's voice, 'Cause me to hear it'; they are hiding from His presence in fear. They have taken individuality, which is the God-created husk of personality, and made it god, and when the Creator, who speaks only in the language of personality, came, they were afraid. It is now self-realization, not God-realization. HGM. 50

Satan 'beguiled' her, meaning by that that there was no clear understanding on her part of the wrong she had done; but "Adam was not beguiled." "He did eat." Adam's sin was the perfect conscious realization of what he was doing. PS. 12

ADAM, FIRST AND SECOND

There are only two Men in the Bible: Adam and Jesus Christ, "with all humanity hanging at their girdles." BSG. 10

When Jesus Christ, the last Adam, came He entered on the same plane as the first Adam, and from that same stage of innocence He worked out the perfect life of holiness that God required, which Adam failed to do. But He had to do more, He had to put the whole human race back, not to where Adam was, but to where Adam had never been, viz., to where He is Himself, an inconceivably higher position. GW. 31

The first Adam, the federal head of the race, swung the race on to the basis of wrath, and Jesus Christ, the Last Adam, swung the human race back on to the basis of love. HGM. 59

According to the Bible, there are only two Men—Adam and Jesus Christ, and God deals with them as the representatives of the human race, not as individuals. PR. 10

The first Adam is called 'the son of God'; the last Adam is *the* Son of God, and we are made *sons* of God by the last Adam. PR. 10

The first Adam and the last Adam are the only two Men according to God's norm, and they both came into this world direct from the hand of God. PR. 10

ADVENT (SECOND)

When Jesus Christ comes again, those who are saved and sanctified will be "changed, in a moment, in the twinkling of an eye"; all disharmony will cease and a new order will begin. BP. 16

The saint alone knows by spiritual intuition that 'He doeth all things well,' he knows that God reigns, and that the clouds are but the dust of his Father's feet and he has no need to fear. He feels assured that these catastrophic occurrences are but incidental, and that a higher peace and a purer character are to be the permanent result. He knows that 'this same Jesus,' who trod this earth with naked feet, 'and wrought with human hands the creeds of creeds,' is coming again, visibly and blessedly coming to earth again, when the petition will be fulfilled, *'Thy kingdom come.'* GW. 88

AFFINITIES

God continually introduces us to people for whom we have no affinity, and unless we are worshipping God, the most natural thing to do is to treat them heartlessly, to give them a text like the jab of a spear, or leave them with a rapped-out counsel of God and go. A heartless Christian must be a terrible grief to Our Lord. MUH. 92

Beware of being guided by mental or spiritual affinities, let God mix you as He sees fit. SHL. 117

Beware of walking in the spiritual life according to your natural affinities. We all have natural affinities—some people we like and others we do not; some people we get on well with and others we do not. Never let those likes and dislikes be the rule of your Christian life. "If we walk in the light, as He is in the light, we have fellowship one with another," i.e., God gives us fellowship with people for whom we have no natural affinity. SSM. 50

AFFLICTION

Stand in the heavenly places in Christ Jesus and when the afflictions come you will praise the Lord, not with a sickly smile but with every bit of you, because you have learned the secret of the eternal weight of glory, and you know that His yoke is easy. LG. 85

AFTERLIFE

Jesus Christ did not use figurative language in talking about the Hereafter. He said: "Let not your heart be troubled"; — "My business is with the Hereafter." Our business is to live a godly life in the present order of things, and not to push out beyond the durations God has placed as limits. SHH. 23

The Bible speaks of "a holy city," "a new earth," and reveals that it is to be brought about by the man who lives his life based on God in all his relationships and does not worry about what he is going to do later. SHH. 40

AGNOSTICISM

All I know of God I have accepted as a revelation, I did not find it out by my head. "Canst thou by searching find out God?" BP. 143

Every Christian unquestionably is mentally agnostic; that is, all we know about God we have accepted by revelation, we did not find it out for ourselves. We did not worry it out by thinking, or work it out by reasoning. BP. 211

Never place an agnostic in the same category as a sceptic. An agnostic is one who says, 'There is more than I know, but I have not found anyone who can tell me about it.' Jesus is never stern with that attitude; but He is stern with the man who objects to a certain way of getting at the truth because he does not like that way. MFL. 21

AGONY

Agony which has God behind it can be turned into triumph; but think of agony in which there is no God, neither in Heaven above nor earth beneath, only the terror of an accusing conscience. No human sympathy can touch that desolation. In all probability the man is to blame for it, and just because he is, no human sympathy can reach him. Anyone can have a fellow-feeling for a poor unfortunate being and can sympathize with him, but who among us can understand agony which goes deeper down than can be put into words? Who but Jesus Christ? BSG. 50

ALONENESS

When God gets us alone by affliction, heartbreak, or temptation, by disappointment, sickness, or by thwarted affection, by a broken friendship, or by a new friendship—when He gets us absolutely alone, and we are dumbfounded, and cannot ask one question, then He begins to expound. MUH. 13

Evil will make a man want to be alone. IYA. 56

AMBITION

Jesus did not put up a child as an ideal, but to show them that ambition has no place whatever in the disposition of a Christian. IWP. 46

Ambition in the spiritual domain is the reaction which refuses to bow its neck to any yoke but the yoke of the Lord Jesus Christ. MFL. 74

It is arduous work to keep the master ambition in front. It means holding one's self to the high ideal year in and year out, not being ambitious to win souls or to establish churches or to have revivals, but being ambitious only to be "accepted of Him." MUH. 77

In natural life we have ambitions and aims which alter as we develop; in the Christian life the goal is given at the beginning, viz., Our Lord Himself. SSY. 110

Ambition means a set purpose for the attainment of our own ideal, and as such it is excluded from the Kingdom of Our Lord. When the disciples asked 'Who then is greatest in the kingdom of heaven?' Jesus called to Him a little child and said—'Except ye become as little children, ye shall in no wise enter into the kingdom of heaven.' The nature of the kingdom of heaven is revealed in the implicit nature of a child, because a child does not work according to a set ambition, he obeys the simple law of his nature. SSY. 112

God grant we may see that the great need of every worker is a first-hand acquaintance with Jesus Christ which puts to death the spirit of ambition. Ambition has murder at its heart; our Lord showed His disciples that ambition is impossible in His kingdom, 'Except ye become as little children, ye shall in no wise enter into the kingdom of heaven.' WG. 103

ANGELS

Read the records in the Bible of angelic appearances, and of the appearances of our Lord after His Resurrection; physical barriers simply did not exist to Him or to them. Physical barriers exist to us because of our nervous system. BP. 198

An angel next in power to God is revealed to be the originator of sin. PS. 10

When we were taught as children that angels watch around our beds it was not a fairy story we were told, but a revelation fact. The angels are there to guard us, and they watch and guard every blood-bought soul. SHL. 29

ANIMALS

The spirit of the brute is part of the spirit of entire nature, and when the brute dies its spirit goes back again into entire nature. The spirit of entire nature is manifestly a creation of God. The spirit in man which holds his soul and body together is entirely different from the spirit of a brute; it is the human spirit which God created when He breathed into man's nostrils the breath of life. BP. 46

ANTAGONISM

It is not antagonism to creeds or points of view, but antagonism encountered *for My sake.* Many of us awaken antagonism by our way of stating things; we have to distinguish between being persecuted for some notion of our own and being persecuted 'for My sake.' We are apt to think only of the bad things as being against Jesus, but it is the refined things, the cultured things, the religious things which are dead against Jesus Christ unless they are loyal to Him. It was the religious people of our Lord's time who withstood Him, not the worldly.   HG. 24

The holiness of God Almighty is Absolute; that is, it knows no development by antagonism.   LG. 95

The law of antagonism runs all through life, physical, moral, mental and spiritual. I am only healthy according to the fighting corpuscles in my blood; when the fighting millions inside get low, I become diseased and after a while I shall be snuffed out. Morally it is the same, we are not born moral, we are born innocent and ignorant; morality is the outcome of fight.   MFL. 74

Life without war is impossible either in nature or in grace. The basis of physical, mental, moral, and spiritual life is antagonism. This is the open fact of life.   MUH. 339

ANXIETY

"Sufficient unto the day is the evil thereof." How much evil has begun to threaten you today? What kind of mean little imps have been looking in and saying; "Now what are you going to do next month—this summer?" "Be anxious for nothing," Jesus says. Look again and think. Keep your mind on the "much more" of your Heavenly Father.   RTR. 83

Jesus declares it to be unreasonable for a disciple to be careful of all that the natural man says we must be careful over. "Behold the fowls of the air: for they sow not, neither do they reap, nor gather into barns; yet your heavenly Father feedeth them. Are ye not much better than they?" . . . "Consider the lilies of the field, how they grow; they toil not, neither do they spin: and yet I say unto you,

that even Solomon in all his glory was not arrayed like one of these." Jesus does not use the illustration of the birds and the flowers by accident, He uses it purposely in order to show the utter unreasonableness from His standpoint of being so anxious about the means of living. Imagine the sparrows and blackbirds and thrushes worrying about their feathers! Jesus says they do not trouble about themselves at all, the thing that makes them what they are is not their thought for themselves, but the thought of the Father in heaven. A bird is a hardworking little creature, but it does not work for its feathers, it obeys the law of its life and becomes what it is. Jesus Christ's argument is that if we concentrate on the life He gives us, we will be perfectly free for all other things because our Father is watching the inner life. We have to maintain obedience to the Holy Spirit, Who is the real principle of our life, and God will supply the 'feathers,' for are we not "much better than they"?   SSM. 68

ARMOUR

"Put on the whole armour of God." If we try to put on the armour without a right relationship to God we shall be like David in Saul's armour; but when we are right with God we find that the armour fits us exactly, because it is God's own nature that is the armour.   OBH. 55

One strong moral man will form a nucleus around which others will gather; and spiritually, if we put on the armour of God and stand true to Him, a whole army of weak-kneed Christians will be strengthened.   OBH. 56

If you have not put on the armour, you will have to fight; but 'having put on the whole armour of God, then *stand.*'   GW. 98

ASCENSION

At His Ascension our Lord became omnipresent, omniscient and omnipotent. This means that all He was in the days of His flesh, all that He was able to impart in the Day of His Resurrection, He is now almighty to bestow without measure on all obedient children of men. BP. 38

On the Mount of Ascension the Transfiguration was completed, and our Lord went back to His primal glory; but He did not go back simply as Son of God: He went back *as Son of Man* as well as Son of God. That means there is freedom of access now for anyone straight to the very throne of God through the Ascension of the Son of Man. LG. 129

ASKING

"Ye shall ask what ye *will*," said Jesus, not what you like, but what your will is in; and we *ask* very few things. BE. 49

"Your Father knoweth what things ye have need of, before ye ask Him." Then why ask? Very evidently our ideas about prayer and Jesus Christ's are not the same. Prayer to Him is not a means of getting things from God, but in order that we may get to know God. IYA. 10

"Ask, and it shall be given you." We grouse before God, and are apologetic or apathetic, but we *ask* very few things; yet what a splendid audacity a child-like child has! and our Lord says, "Except ye . . . become as little children . . ." IYA. 12

Prayer is an effort of will, and Jesus Christ instructs us by using the word 'ask.' "Every one that asketh receiveth." These words are an amazing revelation of the simplicity with which God would

have us pray. The other domains of prayer, the intercession of the Holy Spirit and the intercession of Christ, are nothing to do with us; the effort of our will is to do with us. MFL. 59

The next best thing to do is to ask, if you have not received; to seek, if you have not found; to knock, if the door is not opened to you. OBH. 93

Prayer with most of us is turned into pious platitude, it is a matter of emotion, mystical communion with God. It is no use praying unless we are living as children of God. Then Jesus says— "Everyone that asketh receiveth." RTR. 9

We pray pious blether, our will is not in it, and then we say God does not answer; we never *asked* Him for anything. Asking means that our wills are in what we ask. SSM. 85

ATONEMENT

The marvel of the Atonement is that any man or woman who will make the moral decision that the 'old man' ought to be crucified, and will accept the gift of the Holy Spirit which was manifested in Jesus Christ, will receive the new disposition which introduces him into the kingdom of God, and raises him to sit in heavenly places in Christ Jesus, which surely means a present experience, not a future one. BE. 110

This is the doctrine of the Atonement: "Him who knew no sin" (not sins)— Him who had not the disposition of sin, who refused steadfastly, and to the death on Calvary, to listen to the temptations of the prince of this world, who would not link Himself on with the ruling disposition of humanity, but came to hew a way single-handed through the hard face of sin back to God—"He made to be sin on our behalf; that we might become the righteousness of God in Him." BE. 116

Through the Atonement God deals with the wrong disposition in us, then He gives us the glorious privilege of making our bodies "instruments of righteousness unto God." IWP. 53

The thing that ought to exert the greatest power in our lives is the Atonement. OBH. 120

All the distress and all the sacrifice in the world will never atone for sin. PR. 90

The Atonement means that the whole of the human race has been atoned for, Redemption is complete, and any man can get straight to the throne of God without let or hindrance through the wonder of all that our Lord has done. He is now at the right hand of the Father, not only as Son of God, but as Son of Man. PR. 120

If we have not caught the meaning of the tremendous moral aspect of the Atonement it is because we have never prayed this prayer, 'Search me, O God.' SHL. 50

ATTITUDE

The one attitude of the life is Jesus Christ *first*, *second*, and *third*, and nothing apart from Him. The thing that hinders God's work is not sin, but other claims which are right, but which at a certain point of their rightness conflict with the claims of Jesus Christ. AUG. 33

"Forgetting the things which are behind, and stretching forward to the things which are before . . ." is the only attitude for a saint. PS. 48

AUTHORITY

Authority to be lasting must be of the same order as that of Jesus Christ, not the authority of autocracy or coercion, but the authority of worth, to which all that is worthy in a man bows down. It is only the unworthy in a man that does not bow down to worthy authority. BFB. 86

If I submit to the authority of a Person it must be demonstrated that that Person is greater than I am on the 'worthy' line, the line which is recognized as worthy by the majority of sane humanity; if He is greater there, then I will bow down to His authority at once. BFB. 88

We imagine that if we obey authority we limit ourselves, whereas obedience to authority is not a limitation but a source of power; by obeying we *are* more. BE. 12

Jesus did not teach new things; He taught "as one having authority"—with power to make men into accordance with what He taught. HG. 57

When we begin to usurp authority and say, 'You must' and 'you shall' it is a sure sign that we are out of touch with the supreme Authority. If you are in a position of authority and people are not obeying you, the greatest heartsearching you can have is the realization that the blame does not lie with them, but with you; there is a leakage going on spiritually. Get right with God yourself, and every other one will get in touch with God through you. HGM. 130

The tendency is strong to make the statements of the Bible simpler than God makes them, the reason being that we will not recognize Jesus Christ as the

Authority. It is only when we rely on the Holy Spirit and obey His leadership that the authority of Jesus Christ is recognized.   IWP. 122

The disciple's Lord is the supreme Authority in every relationship of life the disciple is in or can be in.   IWP. 123

The highest authority conceivable for a man is that of a holy character. The holiest character is the Lord Jesus Christ, therefore His statements are never dogmas, they are declarations.   IWP. 123

We find the features of the synagogue of Satan everywhere, but if the disciple will obey, all that power will crumble down as bluff by the marvellous authority of Jesus Christ.   IWP. 125

The characteristic of a saint's life is this bent of obedience, no notion of authority anywhere about it. If we begin to say 'I have been put in this position and I have to exercise authority,' God will soon remove us. When there is steadfast obedience to Jesus, it is the authority of God that comes through and other souls obey at once.   MFL. 128

Either Jesus Christ is the supreme Authority on the human heart, or He is not worth paying any attention to.   MUH. 208

B

BACKSLIDING

Degeneration and backsliding are by no means one and the same. Degeneration begins in almost imperceptible ways; backsliding in the Scriptural use of the term is a distinct forsaking of what I know of God and a deliberate substitution of something other. OPG. 47

The possibility of backsliding is so full of peril that the only safety is to look to Jesus, relying on the Holy Spirit, and never to allow the repose which is a necessity physically to come into the life of the spirit. PS. 48

Always remain alert to the fact that where one man has gone back is exactly where anyone may go back. RTR. 81

In the parable of the two sons some of the elements in the parables of the lost sheep and the lost coin are missed out— the shepherd goes to seek the lost sheep, and the woman searches for the lost coin; but the father does not go to the far country, the son has to leave the pigs and what pigs eat and come back; and if you have backslidden you will have to do the same. SHL. 75

"For My people have committed two evils; they have forsaken Me the fountain of living waters, and hewed them out cisterns, broken cisterns, that can hold no water." Backsliding is twofold, and the term can only be applied to people in this condition. We use the word very loosely, we apply it to people who are degenerating, to people who have

committed sin; but a backslider is neither one nor the other, a backslider is worse than both. He is worse than a person who is degenerating, and worse than a person who has committed sin; he has forsaken God and taken up with something else. WG. 40

Immediately a Christian gets into the way of following his own wise common-sense morality, rather than the dictates of the Spirit of God backing the Word of God, he is on the high road to backsliding. WG. 43

When you come to deal with backsliders, one of the greatest dangers is that they spread their disease more quickly than any other. The presence of one backslider is a peril to a whole community. His or her influence is tenfold worse than a hundred sinners who have never been saved, and the worker for God who begins to deal with a backslider has to learn, first of all, his unutterable powerlessness to touch him. WG. 44

If ever you hear a testimony along this line, 'I was a backslider, but, thank God, I am healed now,' do call a halt in that soul. Backsliding in the Bible is called by words used for the most shocking immorality. Can you imagine anybody who has been guilty of an awful moral crime talking about it in the glib, off-hand way some people talk about backsliding? When a backslider has been reclaimed by God and brought back, when he has returned and has been met by God, the memory of the past is too tremendously humiliating to be mentioned often, and when it is mentioned the atmosphere of the life is one of deep repentance towards God. WG. 47

Never sympathise with a backslider; do all in your power to goad him to return to God. If you cannot do it in words, do it by living in the atmosphere of God and awakening some remembrance of what he once was. WG. 48

BAPTISM

It was at His baptism that the Holy Spirit descended upon Him, and we must never forget that His baptism was a baptism of repentance. It was at His baptism that Jesus Christ definitely took upon Him His vocation, which was to bear away the sin of the world. HGM. 9

Our Lord's vocation, which He accepted at His baptism, was His identification with sin. PR. 51

The baptism of our Lord was an extraordinary spiritual experience to Himself. "And there came a voice from heaven, saying, Thou art my beloved Son, in whom I am well pleased." We have no experience like that; it stands unique. There is only one beloved Son of God; we are sons of God through His Redemption. PR. 52

John knew Who Jesus Christ was, viz., the One Who was to baptise with the Holy Ghost and fire, and yet that One comes to him to be baptised with the baptism of repentance. No wonder John was amazed, and he refused to baptise Jesus until Jesus said, "Suffer it to be so now: for thus it becometh us to fulfil all righteousness." PR. 56

At His Baptism the Son of God as Son of Man, i.e., as the whole human race

rightly related to God, took on Himself the sin of the whole world; that is why He was baptised with John's baptism, which was a baptism of repentance from sin. PR. 85

BEAUTY

The presentation of true Christian experience brings us face to face with spiritual beauty; a beauty which can never be forced or imitated, because it is a manifestation from within of a simple relationship to God that is being worked out all the time. SHL. 66

It is not the passing of the years that matures the life of the Son of God in us, but obedience. As we obey we find that all the power of God is at our disposal, and we too can grow in spiritual beauty. SHL. 67

BELIEF/UNBELIEF

Our Lord's word 'believe' does not refer to an intellectual act, but to a moral act; with our Lord to believe means to commit. "Commit yourself to Me," and it takes a man all he is worth to believe in Jesus Christ. AUG. 114

The Great Life is begun when we believe, belief cannot be pumped up. If we in our hearts believe in Jesus Christ, not *about* Him, but *in* Him, "*He* is all right anyway," it is an evidence that God is at work in our souls. AUG. 115

All our efforts to pump up faith in the word of God is without quickening, without illumination. You reason to yourself and say, 'Now God says this and I am going to believe it,' and you believe it, and re-believe it, and re-re-believe it, and nothing happens, simply because the vital power that makes the words living is not there. BE. 72

Traditional belief has the root of the matter in it, but its form is often archaic. We begin our religious life by believing our beliefs, we accept what we are taught without questioning; then when we come up against things we begin to be critical and we find that however right those beliefs are, they are not right for us because we have not bought them by suffering. BFB. 55

When once you come in contact with Jesus you are not conscious of any effort to believe in Him. DI. 4

If I believe the character of Jesus, am I living up to what I believe? DI. 4

Distortions of belief come because principles are put in the place of Jesus Christ. I must have a personal relationship to Him first, and then let the Holy Spirit apply His teaching. DI. 72

If you deal with people without any faith in Jesus Christ it will crush the very life out of you. If we believe in Jesus Christ, we can face every problem the world holds. HG. 66

To believe that the Lord God omnipotent reigneth and redeemeth is the end of all possible panic, moral, intellectual or spiritual. HG. 104

For a man to believe in the Redemption means that no crime nor terror nor anguish can discourage him, no matter where he is placed. HG. 104

Jesus did not say, 'He that believeth on Me, shall experience the fulness of the blessing of God'; but, 'he that believeth on Me, out of him shall escape everything he receives.' It is a picture of the unfathomable, incalculable benediction which will flow from the one great sovereign source, belief in Jesus. HGM. 18

In the New Testament the emphasis is not on believing, but on receiving. The word "believe" means to commit—a commitment in order to receive. HGM. 28

If you are trying to live up to a standard of belief and find you have not the power to do it, be humble enough to recognize that Jesus Christ knows more about the matter than you do. LG. 111

Never run away with the idea that it does not matter much what we believe or think; it does. What we think and believe, we *are*; not what we say we think and believe, but what we really do think and believe, we are; there is no divorce at all. To believe, in the sense our Lord used the word, is never an intellectual act but a moral act. MFL. 84

A spiritually minded man will never come to you with the demand—"Believe this and that"; but with the demand that you square your life with the standards of Jesus. We are not asked to believe the Bible, but to believe the One Whom the Bible reveals. MUH. 127

I am not saved by believing; I realize I am saved by believing. MUH. 302

No man can believe God unless God is in him. NKW. 66

Many of us use religious jargon, we talk about believing in God, but our actual life proves that we do not really believe one tithe of what we profess. PH. 222

To believe in Jesus means much more than the experience of salvation in any form, it entails a mental and moral commitment to our Lord's view of the world, of the flesh, of the devil, of God, of man, and of the Scriptures. To "believe also in Me" means that we submit our intelligence to Jesus Christ our Lord as He submitted His intelligence to His Father. This does not mean that we do not exercise our reason, but it does mean that we exercise it in submission to Reason Incarnate. PR. 131

Unbelief is the most active thing on earth; it is a fretful, worrying, questioning, annoying, self-centred spirit. To believe is to stop all this and let God work. RTR. 44

The New Testament does not say of Jesus Christ, "This man was God Incarnate, and if you don't believe it you will be damned." The New Testament was written for the confirmation of those who believed He was God Incarnate. SA. 32

. . . the devil likes to deceive us and limit us in our practical belief as to what Jesus Christ can do. There is no limit to what He can do, absolutely none. *'All things are possible to him that believeth.'* Jesus says that faith in Him is omnipotent. God grant we may get hold of this truth. SHL. 31

BELIEVER

It is a mistake to attempt to define what a man must believe before he can be a Christian; his beliefs are the effect of his being a Christian, not the cause of it. CHI. 46

I have no right to say I believe that Jesus is the Son of God unless in my personal life I yield myself to that Eternal Spirit, free from all self-seeking, which became incarnate in Jesus. DI. 1

When a man says he can't believe, don't argue with him on what he doesn't believe but ask him what he does believe, and proceed from that point; disbelief as often arises from temperament as from sin. Every man believes in a good character, then refer to Jesus Christ as the best character in history, and ask him to believe that what He says is likely to be true, and get him to transact business on that. DI. 4

When you come across a believer in Jesus, his very presence alters your outlook. It is not that you have come to someone with amazing intelligence, but that you have come into a sanctuary which is based on a real knowledge of the Redemption. HG. 105

When once a man really believes that the world is redeemed, his belief will manifest itself in every detail, and that is what constitutes the heroism of a believer in Jesus Christ. Our scepticism arises from the fact that we have no experimental knowledge of Redemption. HG. 105

The believer is one who bases all on Jesus Christ's sacrifice, and is so identified with Him that he is made broken bread and poured-out wine in the hands of his Lord. HG. 105

The gift of the Holy Spirit is the impartation of a personal Spirit that blends the historic Son of God and the individual believer into one, and the characteristic of the life is devotion to God, so much so that you don't even know you are devoted to Him until a crisis comes. HGM. 18

BIBLE

The Bible is a world of revelation facts, and when you explain the Bible, take into account all the record of it. The Bible nowhere says we have to believe it is the Word of God before we can be Christians. The Bible is not the Word of

God to me unless I come at it through what Jesus Christ says, it is of no use to me unless I know Him.   AUG. 79

Until the Lord Jesus Christ has been received as the highest and only Authority, Bible explanations are beside the mark because they lack the one efficient seal of the Holy Spirit Who is the only interpreter of the Bible revelation, and the Holy Spirit does not seal Bible interpretation to any man who has not accepted the Lord Jesus Christ as the final Authority for his life, for his mind, and for his whole outlook.   AUG. 110

The Bible is the only Book that throws light on our physical condition, on our soul condition, and on our spiritual condition. In the Bible the sense of smell and sight, etc., are not used as metaphors only; they are identified with the nature of the soul's life. This accounts for what people are apt to call the vulgar teaching of the Bible.   BP. 53

The Holy Spirit exercises a remarkable power in that He will frequently take a text out of its Bible context and put it into the context of our life. We have all had the experience of a verse coming to us right out of its Bible setting and becoming alive in the setting of our own life, and that word becomes a precious, secret possession. See that you keep it a secret possession, don't 'cast your pearls before swine'—those are the strong words of our Lord.   BP. 231

The Bible not only explains God, it explains the world in which we live, it explains not only things that are right, but things that are wrong.   BP. 235

When a man's heart is right with God the mysterious utterances of the Bible are 'spirit and life' to him.   BSG. 42

The only way we can understand the Bible is by personal contact with the Living Word, then the Holy Spirit expounds the literal words to us along the line of personal experience. "The words I speak unto you, they are spirit and they are life."   BSG. 63

A man's attitude to our Lord determines his attitude to the Bible. The 'sayings' of God to a man not born from above are of no moment; to him the Bible is simply a remarkable compilation of literature—"that it is, and nothing more." All the confusion arises from not recognising this. But to the soul born from above, the Bible is the universe of God's revealed will. The Word of God to me is ever according to my spiritual character; it makes clear my responsibility to God as well as my individuality apart from Him   CD. VOL. 1, 15

Beware of the trick of exposition which externalizes Scripture so that we teach but never learn its lessons.   CD. VOL. 2, 19

The Epistles are not the cogitations of men of extraordinary spiritual genius, but the posthumous work of the Ascended Christ and they have therefore a peculiar significance in the programme of Redemption. The Holy Ghost used these men, with all their personal idiosyncrasies, to convey God's message of salvation to the world. Our Lord, so to speak, incarnated Himself in them—the message of God must always be incarnated, but it remains the message *of God*.   CHI. 34

"The Word" is Jesus Himself, therefore we must have an experimental knowledge of Him before we understand the literal words of the Bible.   DI. 6

Bible facts are either revelation facts or nonsense. It depends on me which they are to me.   DI. 6

Our attitude to the Bible is a stupid one; we come to the Bible for proof of God's existence, but the Bible has no meaning for us until we know God does exist. DI. 6

The Bible states and affirms facts for the benefit of those who believe in God; those who don't believe in God can tear it to bits if they choose. DI. 6

People can dispute the words of the Bible as they like, but get a soul in whom the craving for God has come, and the words of the Bible create the new life in him. " . . . *being born again, . . . by the word of God."* DI. 6

If we understood what happens when we use the Word of God, we would use it oftener. The disablement of the devil's power by means of the Word of God conveyed through the lips of a servant of His, is inconceivable. DI. 6

Whenever human nature gets driven to the end of things the Bible is the only Book, and God the only Being, in the world. DI. 7

To read the Bible according to God's providential order in your circumstances is the only way to read it, viz., in the blood and passion of personal life. DI. 8

The Context of the Bible is our Lord Jesus Christ, and personal relationship to Him. The *words* of God and The *Word* of God stand together; to separate them is to render both powerless. Any expounder of the words of God is liable to go off at a tangent if he or she does not remember this stern undeviating standard of exposition, viz., that no individual experience is of the remotest value unless it is up to the standard of The Word of God. GW. 70

Have you ever noticed the vague indefiniteness of the Bible? Unless we are spiritual we shall say, 'I do wish the Bible would talk clearly; why does it not talk as clearly as some little books I have?' If it did, the Bible would be interpretable without any knowledge of God at all. The only way we can understand whether Jesus Christ's teaching of God is by the Spirit that is in Jesus. IWP. 77

Some exceptionally gifted men may derive their conception of God from other sources than the Bible, but all I know of God I have got from the Bible, and those who taught me got what they taught from the Bible. LG. 9

The Bible does not deal with the domain of common-sense facts, we get at those by our senses; the Bible deals with the world of revelation facts which we only get at by faith in God. LG. 23

The mystery of the Bible is that its inspiration was direct from God. MFL. 26

Most of us leave the sweat of brain outside when we come to deal with the Bible. MFL. 77

The New Testament was not written in order to prove that Jesus Christ is the Son of God; but written to confirm the faith of those who believe that Jesus Christ is the Son of God. OBH. 127

The outstanding value of the Bible is that it makes shameful things appear shameful because it never analyses them. OPG. 72

Since Adam, men, individually and collectively, present a muddle morally which has puzzled everyone; the Bible is the only Book that tells us how the moral muddle has been produced, viz. by sin. PS. 69

If you want to find an analysis of every kind of moral and immoral character, the Bible is the place to look for it. PS. 78

We are apt to come to the conclusion that the Bible is tepid. Why, some of the most heroic and drastic thinking is within the covers of the Bible! St. John and St. Paul reconstructed religious thought, quoting from no one; there are no thinkers like them, yet it has been fashionable to belittle them. SHH. 3

All the books of Wisdom in the Bible prove that the only result of sheer thinking on the basis of rationalism is pessimism, fathomlessly profound. SHH. 14

The Bible always emphasises the facts of life as they are. SHH. 48

As long as you live a logical life without realising the deeper depths of your personality, the Bible does not amount to anything; but strike lower down where mathematics and logic are of no account, and you find that Jesus Christ and the Bible tell every time. SHH. 87

The Bible always states the obvious, and we find it to be the thing we have never looked at. Very few of us see the obvious, consequently when it is stated it strikes us as being original. SHH. 125

A remarkable thing about this Book of God is that for every type of human being we come across there is a distinct, clear line laid down here as to the way to apply God's truth to it. The stupid soul, the stubborn soul, the soul that is mentally diseased, the soul that is convicted of sin, the soul with the twisted mind, the sensual soul—everyone of the facts that you meet in your daily walk and business has its counterpart here, and God has a word and a revelation fact

with regard to every life you come across. WG. 13

We must not read the Bible like children. God requires us to read it as men and women, spiritual men and women, I mean. There are things in the Bible that stagger us, things that amaze and terrify; and the worker for God needs to understand not only the terrors of life around, but the terrors of life as God's Book reveals it. WG. 51

BLAME/BLAMELESS

Some of us are so concerned about being blameless before men that we are to be blamed before God. The apostle Paul prays that we may be sanctified and preserved blameless; then it is a matter of absolute indifference what anyone thinks of us, but it is not a matter of indifference what God's Holy Spirit thinks of us. LG. 139

We have to be blameless in all our social relationships before God, but that will not mean that our relations will think us blameless! We can always gauge where we are by the teachings of Jesus Christ. LG. 141

Is it possible to be blameless in our spiritual relationship to Almighty God, to Jesus Christ and to the Holy Ghost? It is not only possible, but God's word tells us that that is what God does. LG. 142

From the moment that God uncovers a point of obstinacy in us and we refuse to let Him deal with it, we begin to be sceptical, to sneer and watch for defects in the lives of others. But when once we yield to Him entirely, He makes us blameless in our personal life, in our practical life, and in our profound life. It is not done by piety, it is wrought in us by the sovereign grace of God, and we have not the slightest desire to trust in ourselves in any degree, but in Him alone. LG. 143

If God can keep you blameless this second, He can do it the next. No wonder Jesus Christ said *"Let not your heart be troubled"!* LG. 144

When a man begins his life with God there are great tracts of his life that he never bothers his head about, but slowly and surely the Spirit of God educates him down to the tiny little scruple. Every crook and cranny of the physical life, every imagination and emotion is perfectly known to God, and He demands that all these be blameless. That brings us to absolute despair unless Jesus Christ can do what He claims He can. PS. 66

'Unblameable' does not mean faultless, but undeserving of censure. SSY. 46

BLESSEDNESS

People want the blessing of God, but they will not stand the probing and the humiliation. AUG. 21

God is never in a hurry; if we wait, we shall see that God is pointing out that we have not been interested in Himself but only in His blessings. The sense of God's blessing is elemental. MUH. 95

People want the blessing of God, but they will not stand the thing that goes straight to the quick. MUH. 354

God will never allow you to hold a spiritual blessing for yourself, it has to be given back to Him that He may make it a blessing to others. If you hoard it, it will turn to spiritual dry rot. If God has blessed you, erect an altar and give the blessing back to God as a love-gift. NKW. 19

The knowledge of the real God is reached when my confidence is placed in God and not in His blessings. NKW. 58

No language can express the ineffable blessedness of the supreme reward that awaits the soul that has taken its supreme climb, proved its supreme love, and entered on its supreme reward. NKW. 129

It is *His* perfections, not ours; His patience, His love, His holiness, His strength—"all spiritual blessings in Christ Jesus." How blind we are! There is a danger with the children of God of getting too familiar with sublime things. We talk so much about these wonderful realities, and forget that we have to exhibit them in our lives. OBH. 35

All the great blessings of God are finished and complete, but they are not mine until I enter into relationship with Him on the basis of His covenant. OPG. 24

We have the notion that it is only when we are pure and holy that God will appear to us; that God's blessing is a sign that we are right with Him. Neither notion is true. Our Lord took care to say that 'God makes His sun to rise on the evil and on the good, and sends His rain on the just and on the unjust'. God's blessings are not to be taken as an indication of the integrity of the character blessed, yet on the other hand the discernment of God's character is determined entirely by the individual character of the person estimating God. OPG. 53

Very few of us are blessed; we lose the blessing immediately we have to wash feet, and all that that symbolises. It takes God Incarnate to do ordinary drudgery and maintain blessedness. The great marvel of the Incarnation is just here. PH. 172

Don't try and find out whether you are a blessing, pay attention to the Source, then out of you will flow rivers of living water that you know nothing about. PH. 240

The true blessedness of the saint is in determinedly making and keeping God first. SSM. 16

BLOOD

The expression 'the blood of Christ' means not only that Christ shed His blood, but that He poured out His very life before God. In the Old Testament the idea of sacrifice is that the blood, which is the life, is poured out to God, its Giver. BE. 60

When the blood is spilt, the soul is gone; when the breath is taken, the soul is gone. The whole life of a man consists physically in his breath and in his blood. The soul in working itself into the blood never fails to impart to it the peculiar character of its own life. This psychologically is brought out very clearly by our Lord's statement, "Except ye eat the flesh of the Son of man, and drink His blood, ye have no life in you." BP. 69

We are apt to look upon the blood of Christ as a kind of magic-working thing, instead of an impartation of His very life. BP. 71

The whole purpose of being born again and being identified with the death of the Lord Jesus is that His blood may flow through our mortal body; then the tempers and the affections and the dispositions which were manifested in the life of the Lord will be manifested in us in some degree. BP. 71

Being cleansed by the blood of Jesus means cleansing to the very heights and depths of our spirit if we walk in the light as God is in the light. IYA. 73

It was not the blood of a martyr, not the blood of goats and calves, that was shed, but "the blood of Christ." The very life of God was shed for the world—"the church of God which He purchased with His own blood." . . . All the perfections of the essential nature of God were in that blood; all the holiest attainments of man were in that blood. PS. 18

BODY

. . . "the time is come that judgment must begin at the house of God." Where is the house of God? My body. AUG. 28

We say we can do what we like with our bodies, we cannot. If I try to satisfy any appetite on the basis of my right to myself, it means there is a spirit of antagonism to Jesus Christ at work in me; if I recognize that my body is the temple of the Holy Ghost, it is a sign that my life is based on the Cross. BE. 68

Man was obviously naked before his disobedience, and the death of his union with God was instantly revealed in his body. BP. 11

. . . from God's standpoint man's chief glory is his body. BP. 50

Immediately we receive the Holy Spirit and are energized by God, we shall find our bodies are the first place of attack for the enemy, because the body has been the centre which ruled the soul and divided it from spiritually intelligent standards; consequently the body is the last 'stake' of Satan. The body is the 'margin of the battle' for you and me. BP. 52

Our present-day 'wise talk' is to push all the teaching of Jesus Christ into a remote domain, but the New Testament drives its teaching straight down to the essential necessity of the physical expression of spiritual life; that just as the bad soul life shows itself in the body, so the good soul life will show itself there too. BP. 71

. . . our body is "the temple of the Holy Ghost," not a thing to be despised. The Bible gives the body a very high place indeed. BP. 166

. . . the chief glory of man is not that he is in the image of God spiritually, but that he is made "of the earth, earthy." This is not man's humiliation but his glory, because through his mortal body is to be manifested the wonderful life and disposition of Jesus Christ. BP. 168

We have to be awake strenuously to the fact that our body is the temple of the Holy Ghost, not only in the spiritual sense, but in the physical sense. When we are born from above we are apt to despise the clay of which we are made. The natural creation and the creation of grace work together, and what we are apt to call the sordid things, labouring with our hands, and eating and drinking, have to be turned into spiritual exercises by obedience, then we shall 'eat and drink, and do all to the glory of God'. HG. 43

It is not what man puts into his body or on his body, but what he brings out of his body, and what he brings out of what he puts on his body, viz. his money, that

reveals what he considers his chief end. HG. 50

God is the Architect of the human body and He is also the Architect of the Body of Christ. There are two Bodies of Christ: the Historic Body and the Mystical Body. The historic Jesus was the habitation of the Holy Ghost, and the Mystic Christ, i.e., the Body of Christ composed of those who have experienced regeneration and sanctification, is likewise the habitation of the Holy Ghost. HGM. 25

The body we have is not sinful in itself; if it were, it would be untrue to say that Jesus Christ was sinless. IWP. 55

As we walk in this body according to the new life that has been imparted to us by the Holy Spirit, we shall find it is no longer mounting up in ecstasy, running and not being weary, but walking with an infinite, steady, uncrushable, indescribable patience until men take knowledge that the Son of God is walking through us again. OBH. 84

"Present your bodies a living sacrifice, holy, acceptable unto God," not 'Present your *all*,' but present your '*body*.' If you obey in this matter of dedication, you can keep your bodily life free from vice and sin. OBH. 110

"Present your bodies . . ." Do not ask God to take your body, but give your body to God. PH. 133

Dust is the finest element in man, because in it the glory of God is to be manifested. The Bible makes much of man's body. The teaching of Christianity on this point has been twisted by the influence of Plato's teaching, which says that a man can only further his moral and spiritual life by despising his body. SHH. 67

When I become a Christian I have exactly the same body as before, but I have to see that my members which were used as 'servants of sin' are now used as 'servants of righteousness.' SHL. 77

Our bodies are not our shame, but our glory, and if we keep them as a temple of the Holy Ghost we shall find that 'the life of Jesus will be manifested in our mortal flesh.' SHL. 78

BODY/SOUL/SPIRIT

When God breathed into man's nostrils the breath of life, man did not become a living God, he became "a living soul." Consequently in man, regenerate or degenerate, there are three aspects—spirit, soul and body. BP. 14

God knows no divorce whatever between the three aspects of a man's nature, spirit, soul and body, they must be at one, and they are at one either in damnation or in salvation. BP. 51

The Bible teaches that it is not the body that breathes, but the soul. The body did not breathe in the beginning before God breathed into man's nostrils the breath of life; so as far as conscious soul life is concerned, it depends on our breathing. All through God's Book the soul life is connected with the breathing; in fact, it is incorporated into our idea of life that when breath is suspended, life is gone. "The soul is departed" is the popular phrase. BP. 69

The soul is the holder of the body and spirit together, and when the spirit goes back to God Who gave it, the soul disappears. In the resurrection there is another body, a body impossible to describe in words, either a glorified body or a damnation body ("... for the hour is coming, in the which all that are in the graves shall hear His voice, and shall come forth; they that have done good, unto the resurrection of life; and they that have done evil, unto the resurrection of damnation"), and instantly the soul is manifested again. BP. 93

Remember, the whole meaning of the soul is to express the spirit, and the struggle of spirit is to get itself expressed in the soul. BP. 245

Do not get the idea of a three-storied building with a vague, mysterious, ethereal upper story called spirit, a middle story called soul, and a lower story called body. We are personality, which shows itself in three phases—spirit, soul, and body. Never think that what energizes the spirit takes time before it gets into the soul and body, it shows itself instantly, from the crown of the head to the soles of the feet. HG. 62

By the Fall man not only died from God, but he fell into disunion with himself; that means it became possible for him to live in one of the three parts of his nature. We want to live a spiritual life, but we forget that that life has to work out in rational expression in our souls; or we want to live a clear life in the soul and forget altogether that we have a body and spirit; or else we want to live the life of a splendid animal and forget altogether the life of the soul and spirit. IWP. 32

When a man is born again of the Spirit of God he is introduced to life with God and union with himself. The one thing essential to the new life is obedience to the Spirit of God Who has energized our spirits; that obedience must be complete in spirit, soul and body. We must not nourish one part of our being apart from the other parts. IWP. 32

Immediately we try to live a spiritual life with God and forget our soul and body, the devil pays attention to our body, and when we pay attention to our body he begins to get at our spirit, until we learn there is only one way to keep right—to live the life hid with Christ in God, then the very life and power of God garrisons all three domains, spirit, soul and body, but it depends on us whether we allow God to do it. IWP. 37

Beware of dividing man up into body, soul and spirit: man *is* body, soul and spirit. Soul has no entity, it depends entirely upon the body, and yet there is a subtle spiritual element in it. Soul is the rational expression of my personal spirit in my body, the way I reason and think and work. MFL. 34

BOOKS

To-day any number of religious books set out to expound Jesus Christ from a philosophical point of view; they are entrancing and apparently helpful, but in reality they do a great deal of harm because instead of helping us to form the mind of Christ and understand His point of view, they serve to confuse our mind. BSG. 66

It is imperative to estimate the danger abroad to-day in books which deal with Christian thinking, particularly those which have the word 'psychology' tacked on; be sure what kind of psychology it is—unless it is the psychology of the Bible it may be the psychology of agnosticism pure and simple; it may sound all right but in the final result it dethrones Jesus Christ. BSG. 68

It is appalling how many books and sermons there are to-day that simply present abstract truths. MFL. 13

Always keep in contact with those books and those people that enlarge your horizon and make it possible for you to stretch yourself mentally. MFL. 92

The books and the men who help us most are not those who teach us, but those who can express for us what we feel inarticulate about. PH. 154

We are apt to wrongly relate ourselves to books and to people. We often hear such remarks as—"The parson is talking over the heads of the men"; or, "The Bible is all very well, but I don't understand it." It is never the thing you understand that does you good, but what is behind what is taught. If it is God's truth, you and I are going to meet it again whether we want to or not. SHH. 65

We should always choose our books as God chooses our friends, just a bit beyond us, so that we have to do our level best to keep up with them. If we choose our own friends, we choose those we can lord it over. SHH. 66

BORN AGAIN

Being born again of the Spirit is an unmistakable work of God, as mysterious as the wind. Beware of the tendency to water down the supernatural in religion. AUG. 47

Being 'born from above' is not a simple easy process; we cannot glide into the Kingdom of God. Common sense reasoning says we ought to be able to merge into the life of God, but according to the Bible, and in actual experience, that is not the order. BE. 45

After being born again a man experiences peace, but it is a militant peace, a peace maintained at the point of war. BE. 78

"Marvel not that I said unto thee, Ye must be"—not developed, not educated, but "born again"—'fundamentally made all over again, before you can see the kingdom of God and enter into it.' HGM. 12

When a man is born again his personality becomes dead to earth as the source of its inspiration and is only alive to God. IWP. 73

The only way we can be born again is by renouncing all other good. The 'old man,' or the man of old, means all the things which have nothing to do with the new life. It does not mean sins, any coward among us will give up wrong things, but will he give up right things? Will we give up the virtues, the principles, the recognition of things that are dearer to the 'Adam' life than the God life? The nature of the 'Adam' disposition in us rebels against sacrificing natural good. Jesus says, 'If you don't sacrifice natural good, you will barter the life I represent.' IWP. 99

We preach to men as if they were conscious of being dying sinners; they are not, they are having a good time, and our talk about being born again is from a domain of which they know nothing. The natural man does not want to be born again. PR. 12

Jesus Christ came into the human race from the outside, and when we are born again, His life comes into us from the outside. PR. 12

The life of Jesus is the life of the normal man of God, but we cannot begin to live it unless we are born from above. PR. 90

Nothing has any power to alter a man save the incoming of the life of Jesus,

and that is the only sign that he is born again. RTR. 86

The natural man does not want to be born again. SHL. 40

If a man's morality is well within his own grasp and he has enough religion to give the right tone to his natural life, to talk about being born again seems utterly needless. SHL. 40

'Marvel not that I said unto thee, Ye must be born again.' The touch that comes is as mysterious as the wind. SHL. 46

A man cannot take in anything he has not begun to think about, consequently until a man is born again what Jesus says does not mean anything to him. SSM. 25

BRAIN

The Bible makes it plain that we can help thoughts of evil; it is Satan's interest to make us think we cannot. God grant the devil may be kept off the brains of the saints! BE. 71

The brain is not a spiritual thing, the brain is a physical thing. Memory is a spiritual thing and exists in the heart; the brain recalls more or less clearly what the heart remembers. BP. 122

Thinking takes place in the heart, not in the brain. BP. 124

The expression of thinking is referred to the brain and the lips because through these organs thinking becomes articulate. BP. 125

It is not sufficient to experience the reality of the Spirit of God within us and His wonderful work; we have to bring our brains into line with our experience so that we can think and understand along Christian lines. It is because so few do think along Christian lines that it is easy for wrong teaching and wrong thinking to come in, especially in connection with the Spirit. BP. 209

As saints our brains ought to be used to systematize and make our own the great revelations given in God's word regarding His purpose for us. HGM. 24

If thinking gives you a headache, it is a sign that you have brains. The brain is not ethereal or mystical, it is purely a machine. The thing that is not mechanical is the power of personality which we call thought. MFL. 19

We are meant to use our brains to express our thought in words, and then to behave according to the way we have thought. A man's spirit only expresses itself as soul by means of words; the brain does not deal with pure thought. No thought is ours until it can be expressed in words. Immediately a thought is expressed in words, it returns to the brain as an idea upon which we can work. MFL. 51

If we are not going to be "conformed to this world; but . . . transformed," we must use our brains. God does the spiritual, powerful part we cannot do; but we have to work it out, and as we do the obeying we prove, i.e., 'make out,' "what is that good, and acceptable, and perfect, will of God." MFL. 80

BROTHERHOOD

When the love of God is shed abroad in our hearts it means that we identify ourselves with God's interest in other people, and God is interested in some strange people! HGM. 41

. . . the ability of a man to help his brother man lies lastingly with God and is not concerned with his aspirations or his education or his attainments. PH. 3

BUSYBODY

The suffering which springs from being "a meddler in other men's matters" (a busy-body) is humiliating to the last degree. A free translation of 1 Thessalonians iv, 11 might well read, "Study to shut up and mind your own business," and among all the texts we hang on our wall let this be one. RTR. 45

C

CAIN

Cain was the first isolated individual; Adam was not an isolated individual. Before the Fall Adam was in relationship with God and with the world; when he was driven out from the Garden he was still in relationship with the world. Cain's sin shattered him into absolute solitariness. BE. 28

The spirit of Cain is jealousy, spite and envy. HGM. 40

Cain's crime is more than murdering his brother, it is a deeper crime within that crime, viz., the putting up of his whole nature against God, and, finally, accusing God for his punishment—'Of course, my sin is unpardonable if You are a holy God, but You are to blame for being a holy God.' OPG. 10

CALVARY

We do not think, and we do not like to think, along Jesus Christ's line, we are told it is old-fashioned and ugly, and so it is; it is awful, it is so awful that it broke God's heart on Calvary. BE. 114

We are all thrilled by high, human, noble pagan sacrifice; it is much more thrilling than Calvary, there is something shameful about that, it is against all human ideas of nobility. The love of God is not in accordance with human standards in any way. LG. 71

Calvary is God's responsibility undertaken and carried through as Redemption. PR. 11

At bottom, sin is red-handed mutiny that requires to be dealt with by the surgery of God—and He dealt with it on Calvary. SHL. 102

CARELESSNESS

Carelessness in spiritual matters is a crime. AUG. 37

CARES

Be careful of anything that is going to deflect your attention from God. It is easier to rely on God in big things than in little things. There is an enormous power in little things to distract our attention from God; that is why our Lord said that "the cares of this world," "the lusts of other things," would choke the word and make it unfruitful. HG. 19

Refuse to be swamped by the cares of this world, cut out non-essentials and continually revise your relationship to God and see that you are concentrated absolutely on Him. SSM. 72

There is something in us that makes us face temptation to sin with vigour and earnestness, but it requires the stout heart that God gives to meet the cares of this life. SSM. 98

CAUSES

To-day we have substituted credal belief for personal belief, and that is why so many are devoted to causes and so few devoted to Jesus Christ. People do not want to be devoted to Jesus, but only to the cause He started. Jesus Christ is a source of deep offence to the educated mind of to-day that does not want Him in any other way than as a Comrade. MUH. 171

CERTAINTY/UNCERTAINTY

Certainty is the mark of the common-sense life: gracious uncertainty is the mark of the spiritual life. To be certain of God means that we are uncertain in all our ways, we do not know what a day may bring forth. This is generally said with a sigh of sadness, it should be rather an expression of breathless expectation. We are uncertain of the next step, but we are certain of God. Immediately we abandon to God, and do the duty that lies nearest, He packs our life with surprises all the time. MUH. 120

CHANCE

The circumstances of a saint's life are ordained of God. In the life of a saint there is no such thing as chance. God by His providence brings you into circumstances that you cannot understand at all, but the Spirit of God understands. MUH. 312

Nothing happens by chance to a saint, no matter how haphazard it seems. It is the order of God, and the experience of new birth means that we are able to discern the order of God. PR. 33

"One of the most immutable things on earth is mutability." Your life and mine is a bundle of chance. SHH. 17

CHANGE

We can change the world without when we change the recording instrument within. Commit sin, and I defy you to see anything beautiful without; fall in love, and you will see beauty in everything. SA. 47

Jesus Christ is the One Who can transmute everything we come across. SHH. 10

CHARACTER

The discernment of God's truth and the development of character go together. AUG. 35

If excellence of character is made the test, the grace of God is "made void," because a man can develop an amazing perfection of character without a spark of the grace of God. If we put a saint or a good man as the standard, we blind ourselves to ourselves, personal vanity makes us do it; there is no room for personal vanity when the standard is seen to be God Himself. DI. 32

Character is always revealed in crises. GW. 10

If you find your spiritual character is disappointing you, you are not developing a family likeness to Jesus Christ, it is because there is no inner reality. HGM. 110

The Holy Spirit will glorify Jesus only, consequently the interpretation of the Bible and of human life depends entirely on how we understand the character of Jesus Christ. IWP. 122

We are apt to think that everything that happens to us is to be turned into useful teaching; it is to be turned into something better than teaching, viz. into character. LG. 52

God has to hide from us what He does until by personal character we get to the place where He can reveal it. MUH. 87

No man is born either naturally or supernaturally with character, he has to make character. MUH. 167

Jesus Christ does not make us original characters, He makes our characters replicas of His own; consequently, argues the Spirit of God, when men see us, they will not say, 'What wonderful, original, extraordinary characters.' No, none of that rubbish! They will say, 'How marvellous God must be to take poor pieces of human stuff like those men, and turn them into the image of Jesus Christ!' ". . . which things the angels desire to look into." OBH. 28

Spiritual character is only made by standing loyal to God's character no matter what distress the trial of faith brings. OPG. 18

A man is what he is in the dark. PH. 76

Holiness is the balance between my disposition and the laws of God as expressed in Jesus Christ, and if I have enough spiritual fighting capacity I shall produce a character that is like Jesus Christ's. SA. 94

Disposition is the set of my mind; character is the whole trend of my life, not what I do occasionally. Character is what we make; disposition is what we are born with. We make our characters out of the disposition we have, and when we are born again we get a new disposition, the disposition of the Son of God. We cannot imitate the disposition of Jesus Christ; it is either there or it isn't. SA. 102

In the natural world I am born with an heredity for which I am not responsible, and I have a disposition through that heredity; but I have not a character through heredity. God gives disposition, but never character. SA. 109

. . . the man who has attained a sagacious character during life is like a most refreshing, soothing, healing ointment. SHH. 78

God will put the disposition of His Son, Holy Spirit, into any man who asks, then on that basis man has to work out a holy character. "*Work out* your own salvation with fear and trembling; for it is God which *worketh in* you. . . ." SHH. 94

A man's character tells over his head all the time. SHH. 139

Character is made by things done steadily and persistently, not by the exceptional or spasmodic, that is something God mourns over—"your goodness is as a morning cloud, . . ." SSM. 76

CHASTITY

Chastity is undesirable if I want to be a beast; but no holiness or rectitude of character is impossible; it is simply undesirable if I prefer the other way. SHH. 105

You cannot have holiness without a chaste physical life. WG. 104

CHERUBIM

The cherubim are an Old Testament figure of the Mystical Body of Christ. BP. 233

The cherubim are not like anything in heaven above or in the earth beneath, but like something which is now being made, viz., the Mystical Body of Christ. This is prefigured in Genesis; when Adam and Eve were driven out of the garden of Eden there was placed "at the east of the garden of Eden Cherubims, and a flaming sword which turned every

way, to keep the way of the tree of life."
BP. 233

The cherubim are the guardians into the holiest of all, and when the Mystical Body of Christ is complete, all the 'machinery' of this earth will be moved and directed by the Spirit of God. BP. 234

CHILD

A child's life has no dates, it is free, silent, dateless. A child's life ought to be a child's life, full of simplicity. BSG. 15

May God have mercy on the parents who develop precocity in a child! What happens physically in children who show amazing signs of wisdom is that the grey matter of the brain is being used as quickly as it is formed. Precocity is something that ought to be checked. We are apt to place our faith on the years when we are in the making, whereas lives ought to be allowed to develop along a right line to the point of reliability. BSG. 18

The child-heart is open to any and all avenues; an angel would no more surprise it than a man. In dreams, in visions, in visible and invisible ways, God can talk and reveal Himself to a child; but this profound yet simple way is lost for ever immediately we lose the open, childlike nature. CD. VOL. 1, 7

When a child knows it has done something wrong and you want him to say he is sorry, the natural inclination of the child is stubbornly to refuse to say he *is* sorry; but until he does say so, there is no emancipation for him on to a higher level in his own life. This is the key to the way we are built all through; it is true not only in a child's life but in the moral domain, and emphatically true in the spiritual domain. PH. 208

As we bring the child mind to what Jesus says about things, we will begin to manifest the miracle of an undisturbed heart. In the Cross our Lord deals with everything that keeps a man's heart disturbed. PH. 222

CHOICE

After we are sanctified we have the same body, but it is ruled by a new disposition, and we have to sacrifice our natural life to God even as Jesus did, so that we make the natural life spiritual by a series of direct moral choices. IWP. 55

God does not make us holy in the sense of character; He makes us holy in the sense of innocence, and we have to turn that innocence into holy character by a series of moral choices. These choices are continually in antagonism to the entrenchments of our natural life, the things which erect themselves as ramparts against the knowledge of God. MUH. 252

God never removes from us the power of stepping aside; we can step aside any moment we like. OBH. 17

There is an inspiration in choosing to do wrong, it means a simplification of the life. Immediately you choose to do wrong you are not only conscious that you are without excuse, you become brazenly fixed in the wrong; that is the characteristic of the devil. OPG. 14

Our choice is indelibly marked for time and eternity. What we decide makes our destiny, not what we have felt, nor what we have been moved to do, or inspired to see, but what we decide to do in a given crisis, it is that which makes or mars us. PS. 44

CHRIST

The number of insidious and beautiful writers and speakers to-day whose final net result will be found to be anti-Christ, is truly alarming. The writers I mean are those who examine psychologically the Person of our Lord on the ground of facts discoverable in unregenerate human consciousness, and effectually dissolve away the Person of Jesus Christ so marvellously revealed in the New Testament. AUG. 105

Jesus Christ, as Representative Man, accepted the responsibility of exhibiting on the human plane the absolute holiness of God; He lived up to God's standard in every detail of holy living and holy speaking and holy working, and His claim is that through the Atonement He can put us in the place where we can do the same. BE. 11

The only way we can explain Jesus Christ is the way He explains Himself—and He never explains Himself away. Why did Jesus Christ live and die? The Scriptures reveal that He lived and died and rose again that we might be readjusted to the Godhead, i.e., that we might be delivered from sin and be brought back into the relationship of favour with God. If we teach that Jesus Christ cannot deliver from sin we shall end in nothing short of blasphemy. BP. 36

The Person of Jesus Christ revealed in the New Testament is unique—God-Man. In Him we deal with God as Man, the God-Man, the Representative of the whole human race in one Person. BSG. 9

A great many of the books written on what is called 'the Psychology of Jesus' are an attempt to understand the Person of Jesus through an understanding of ourselves. That is fatally misleading because Jesus Christ does not begin where we begin. BSG. 9

There was no ambiguity in Our Lord's mind as to Who He was, or as to the meaning of the step He was taking; He was no longer maturing, He was mature. He is not manifested here as our Example, but as God Incarnate for one purpose—to be identified with the sin of the world and to bear it away. BSG. 24

The Jesus who saves our souls and identifies us with Himself is 'this same Jesus' who went to sleep as a Babe on His mother's bosom; and it is 'this same Jesus,' the almighty, powerful Christ, with all power in heaven and on earth, who is at work in the world to-day by His Spirit. BSG. 72

When the flatteries, the eulogies, the enthusiasms and the extravagances regarding Jesus Christ have become enshrined sentiments in poetry and music and eloquence, they pass, like fleeting things of mist, coloured but for a moment by reflected splendours from the Son of God, and our Lord's own words come with the sublime staying of the simple gentleness of God: "I AM THE WAY, AND THE TRUTH, AND THE LIFE." CD. VOL. 1, 11

Jesus Christ is the normal Man, the Man according to God's standard, and God demands of us the very holiness He exhibited. CHI. 60

Our Lord was brought up so much in ordinary surroundings that the religious people of His day said that He was "a gluttonous man, and a wine-bibber." His life was unassuming in its naturalness. HG. 45

A healthy-hided moral man does not want Jesus Christ; a ritualist does not want Jesus Christ; a rationalist does not want Jesus Christ. It is along this line we begin to understand why Jesus said, "I am not come to call the righteous," i.e. the whole and the healthy, "but sinners to repentance." 'I am come to those who mourn, to those who are afflicted, to those who are in a condition of insatiable thirst.' HG. 54

When Jesus Christ came near men, He convicted them of sin, but He convicted them also of this, that they could be like He was if they would only come to Him. HG. 80

Jesus Christ is the One who upsets the humanitarian reign. That is why in certain moods of individual as well as national experience, Jesus Christ is considered the enemy of mankind. "Think not that I am come to send peace on earth: I came not to send peace, but a sword." HGM. 61

Jesus Christ is not only Saviour, He is King, and He has the right to exact anything and everything from us at His own discretion. HGM. 129

Many who knew Our Lord while He was on earth saw nothing in Him; only after their disposition had been altered did they realize Who He was. Our Lord lived so ordinary a life that no one noticed Him. LG. 43

Jesus Christ is at work in ways we cannot tabulate; lives are being drawn to Him in a thousand and one incalculable ways; an atmosphere is being created, seeds are being sown, and men are being drawn nearer to the point where they will see Him. LG. 105

Jesus Christ—He is the Truth; He is the Honourable One; He is the Just One; He is the Pure One; He is the altogether Lovely One; He is the only One of Good

Report. No matter where we start from, we will always come back to Jesus Christ. MFL. 91

Jesus Christ effaced the Godhead in Himself so effectually that men without the Spirit of God despised Him. No one without the Spirit of God, or apart from a sudden revelation from God, ever saw the true Self of Jesus while He was on earth. He was "as a root out of a dry ground," thoroughly disadvantaged in the eyes of everyone not convicted of sin. MFL. 104

There is an aspect of Jesus that chills the heart of a disciple to the core and makes the whole spiritual life gasp for breath. This strange Being with His face "set like a flint" and His striding determination, strikes terror into me. He is no longer Counsellor and Comrade, He is taken up with a point of view I know nothing about, and I am amazed at Him. At first I was confident that I understood Him, but now I am not so sure. I begin to realize there is a distance between Jesus Christ and me; I can no longer be familiar with Him. He is ahead of me and He never turns round; I have no idea where He is going, and the goal has become strangely far off. MUH. 75

Our Lord never pleaded, He never cajoled, He never entrapped; He simply spoke the sternest words mortal ears ever listened to, and then left it alone. MUH. 230

We have to get out into faith in Jesus Christ continually; not a prayer meeting Jesus Christ, nor a book Jesus Christ, but the New Testament Jesus Christ, Who is God Incarnate, and Who ought to strike us to His feet as dead. MUH. 318

Our Lord was not a recluse nor an ascetic, He did not cut Himself off from society, but He was inwardly disconnected all the time. He was not aloof, but He lived in another world. He was so much in the ordinary world that the religious people of His day called Him a glutton and a wine-bibber. MUH. 332

Jesus Christ was born *into* this world, not *from* it. He did not evolve out of history; He came into history from the outside. Jesus Christ is not the best human being, He is a Being Who cannot be accounted for by the human race at all. MUH. 360

It was never from His right to Himself that our Lord Jesus Christ spoke; He never thought from His right to Himself; that is, He never thought or spoke from His bodily conditions or the condition of His circumstances. We do talk from our right to ourselves, from the condition of our bodies, from our personal possessions; these are the things we all reason from naturally. They are the things the Son of God never reasoned from; He thought and spoke always from His Father; that is, He expressed the thought of God in light. When we are sanctified, the Spirit of God will enable us to do the same. As we go on with God we shall find that we see things in quite a different way, we see them with the eyes of Jesus Christ. OBH. 46

Jesus Christ is *Saviour* and *Lord* in experience, and *Lord* and *Saviour* in discernment. OBH. 88

Jesus Christ is not a Being with two personalities; He is Son of God (the exact expression of Almighty God), and Son of Man (the presentation of God's normal man). As Son of God, He reveals what God is like; as Son of Man, He mirrors what the human race will be like on the basis of Redemption—a perfect oneness between God and man. PR. 13

Never allow the thought that Jesus Christ stands with us against God out of pity and compassion; that He became a curse for us out of sympathy with us. Jesus Christ became a curse for us by the Divine decree. MUH. 326

We do not know Jesus Christ by knowing ourselves; to think we do is a modern fallacy. "No man knoweth the Son but the Father; neither knoweth any man the Father, save the Son, and he to whomsoever the Son will reveal Him." PR. 28

According to the revelation of the Bible, our Lord is not to be looked upon as an individual Man, but as the One Who represents the whole human race. PR. 73

Jesus Christ does not produce heaven and peace and delight straight off, He produces pain and misery and conviction and upset, and a man says, 'If that is all He came to do, then I wish He had never come.' But this is not all He came to do: He came to bring us into a supernatural union with His Father. PR. 122

Watch the tendency abroad to-day; people want to get rid of Jesus Christ, they cannot prove that He did not live, or that He was not a remarkable Man; but they set to work to dissolve Him by analysis, to say He was not really God Incarnate. Jesus Christ always upsets the calculations of humanity; that is what made Voltaire say 'Crucify the wretch, stamp Him and His crazy tale out,' because He was the stumbling-block to all the reasonings of men. PS. 73

Jesus Christ is the One Who has the power to impart His own innate spiritual life, viz. Holy Spirit, to unholy men, and develop them until they are like Himself. That is why the devil hates Jesus Christ, and why he tries to make men calculate without Him. PS. 74

Jesus Christ stands for all that a man should be, and to the saints He stands for all that God is. PS. 74

There is only one God for the Christian, and He is Jesus Christ. SA. 15

Jesus Christ, the second Adam, the second Federal Head of the race, entered into this order of things as Adam did, straight from the hand of God; and He took part in His own development until it reached its climax, and He was transfigured. SA. 46

If Jesus Christ has done no mighty works for me it is either because I don't believe He can, or I don't want Him to. I may say—"Oh yes, I believe Jesus Christ will give me the Holy Spirit"; but I am not prepared for Him to do it, I don't want Him to. Will you launch out on what Jesus says? If you will, you will find that God is as good as His word. SSH. 92

Jesus Christ did not come to found religion, nor did He come to found civilisation, they were both here before He came; He came to make us spiritually real in every domain. In Jesus Christ there was nothing secular and sacred, it was all real, and He makes His disciples like Himself. SSM. 49

If we want to know the universal sovereignty of Christ, we must get into solitude with Him. It is not sufficient for someone else to tell us about Him; we must perceive with our own eyes Who He is, we must know Him for ourselves. SSY. 133

We adapt the New Testament to suit our own ideas; consequently we look on Jesus Christ as One Who assists us in our enterprises. The New Testament idea is that Jesus Christ is the absolute Lord over His disciples. SSY. 138

If Jesus Christ cannot deliver from sin, if He cannot adjust us perfectly to God as He says He can, if He cannot fill us with the Holy Ghost until there is nothing that can ever appeal again in sin or the world or the flesh, then He has misled us. But blessed be the Name of God, He can! He can so purify, so indwell, so merge with Himself, that only the things that appeal to Him appeal to you, to all other appeals there is the sentence of death, you have nothing to answer. GW. 24

CHRIST, DEATH OF

The death of Jesus was not a satisfaction paid to the justice of God—a hideous statement which the Bible nowhere makes. The death of Jesus was an exact revelation of the justice of God. When we read of the sacrifice of Jesus Christ, it is the sacrifice of God also. " . . . God was in Christ reconciling the world unto Himself." BSG. 78

The only one who can reckon he is 'dead indeed unto sin' is the one who has been through identification with the death of Jesus; when he has been through that moral transaction he will find he is enabled to live according to it; but if I try the 'reckoning' business without having gone through identification with the death of Jesus, I shall find myself deceived; there is no reality. When I can say, 'I have been crucified with Christ,' a new page of consciousness opens before me, I find there are new powers in me, I am able now to fulfil the commands of God, able to do what I never could do before, I am free from the old bondage, the old limitations; and the gateway to this new life is the death of Jesus. GW. 86

That Christ died for me, therefore I go scot free, is never taught in the New Testament. What *is* taught in the New Testament is that 'He died for all." MUH. 303

We are acceptable with God not because we have obeyed, or because we have promised to give up things, but because of the death of Christ, and in no other way. MUH. 303

The modern view of the death of Jesus is that He died for our sins out of sympathy. The New Testament view is that He bore our sin not by sympathy, but by identification. He was *made to be sin.* Our sins are removed because of the death of Jesus, and the explanation of His death is His obedience to His Father, not His sympathy with us. MUH. 303

The Death of Jesus Christ is the performance in history of the very Mind of God. There is no room for looking on Jesus Christ as a martyr; His death was not something that happened to Him which might have been prevented: His death was the very reason why He came. MUH. 326

By the death of the Son of Man upon the Cross, the door is opened for any individual to go straight into the presence of God; and by the Resurrection our Lord can impart to us His own life. PR. 111

The death of Jesus not only gives us remission from our sins, it enables us to assimilate the very nature of Jesus until in every detail of our lives we are like Him. PS. 17

The death of Jesus reaches away down underneath the deepest sin human nature ever committed. PS. 18

The height and depth of our salvation are only measured by God Almighty on His throne and Jesus Christ in the heart of hell. The most devout among us are too flippant about this great subject of the death of Jesus Christ. PS. 18

The offering of Jesus is not pathetic in the tiniest degree; it is beyond all pathos. PS. 19

Identification with the death of Jesus Christ means identification *with* Him to the death of everything that never was in Him. RTR. 29

. . . when once we see that the New Testament emphasizes Jesus Christ's death, not His life, that it is by virtue of His death we enter into His life, then we find that His teaching is for the life He puts in. SA. 40

Our Lord is not foreseeing with the vision of a highly sensitive nature that His life must end in disaster, He states over and over again that He came on purpose to die. 'From that time began Jesus to shew unto his disciples, how that he must go unto Jerusalem, and suffer many things of the elders and chief priests and scribes, and be killed, and the third day be raised up.' SSY. 110

CHRIST, MIND OF

To have the mind of Christ means that we are willing to obey the dictates of the Holy Spirit through the physical machines of our brains and bodies till our living bears a likeness to Jesus. BE. 97

How are we to form the mind of Christ? By letting His Spirit imbue our spirit, our thinking, our reasoning faculties, then we shall begin to reason as Jesus did, until slowly and surely the very Spirit that fed the life of Jesus will feed the life of our soul. IYA. 74

"Let this mind be in you, which was also in Christ Jesus . . ." That is a command. God does not give us the mind of Christ, He gives us the Spirit of Christ, and we have to see that the Spirit of Christ in us works through our brains in contact with actual life and that we form His mind. Jesus Christ did not become humbled—"He humbled Himself." LG. 71

Most of us baulk forming the mind of Christ; we do not object to being delivered from sin and hell, but we do object to giving up the energy of our minds to form the mind of Christ. MFL. 49

The Holy Spirit represents the actual working of God in a man, and He enables us to form the mind of Christ if we will. MFL. 49

We construct the mind of Christ in the same way as we construct the natural mind, viz., by the way our disposition reacts when we come in contact with external things. MFL. 49

When the Spirit of God touches us, we are responsible for forming the mind of Christ. God does the wonderful indwelling part, but we have to do the expressing, and when once we understand how God has made us, it becomes not at all difficult to do it. MFL. 78

Every power of our being is no longer to be used at the dictates of our right to ourselves, but to be subordinated to the Spirit of God in us Who will enable us to form the mind of Christ. MFL. 102

The moment we obey the light the Spirit of God brings, the mind of Jesus is formed in us in that particular, and we begin to reason as He reasons; but if we debate and go back to our old way of reasoning we grieve the Spirit of God. OBH. 78

We have to keep our soul fit to form the mind of Christ. OBH. 78

CHRISTIAN

Human strength and earnestness cannot make a man a Christian any more than they can make him an angel; he must receive something from God, and that is what Jesus Christ calls 'being born from above.' AUG. 78

You can always tell whether Christians are spiritually minded by their attitude to the supernatural. BP. 91

In the final issue Christian principles are found to be antichrist, i.e., an authority other than Christ Himself. CHI. 29

We are apt to have a disproportionate view of a Christian because we look only at the exceptions. The exceptions stand out *as* exceptions. The extraordinary conversions and phenomenal experiences are magnificent specimen studies of what happens in the life of everyone, but not one in a million has an experience such as the Apostle Paul had. The majority of us are unnoticed and unnoticeable people. LG. 35

The secret of the Christian is that he knows the absolute Deity of Jesus Christ. LG. 118

If I find it hard to be a Christian it is a sign that I need the awakening of new birth. Only a spiritually ignorant person tries to be a Christian. MFL. 21

The outstanding characteristic of a Christian is this unveiled frankness before God so that the life becomes a mirror for other lives. By being filled with the Spirit we are transformed, and by beholding we become mirrors. You always know when a man has been beholding the glory of the Lord, you feel in your inner spirit that he is the mirror of the Lord's own character.   MUH. 23

A Christian is one who trusts the wits and the wisdom of God, and not his own wits.   MUH. 218

The most seriously minded Christian is the one who has just become a Christian; the mature saint is just like a young child, absolutely simple and joyful and gay.   PH. 185

Until a man is born again, he cannot think as a Christian.   PR. 98

The New Testament view of a Christian is that he is one in whom the Son of God has been revealed, and prayer deals with the nourishment of that life.   RTR. 43

A Christian is to be consistent only to the life of the Son of God in him, not consistent to hard and fast creeds. Men pour themselves into creeds, and God Almighty has to blast them out of their prejudices before they become devoted to Jesus Christ.   SSM. 44

A missionary and a Christian ought to be one and the same, and a Christian is one who is united to his Lord by a living union of character.   SSY. 118

CHRISTIANITY

The whole point of vital Christianity is not the refusal to face things, but a matter of personal relationship, . . .   BFB. 40

Men have tried to get at the truth of Christianity head-first, which is like saying you must think how you will live before you are born. We instantly see the absurdity of that, and yet we expect to reason out the Christian life before we

have been born into the realm of Jesus Christ. "Except a man be born again, he cannot see the kingdom of God."   BFB. 102

Christianity is personal, therefore it is un-individual. An individual remains definitely segregated from every other individual; when you come to the teaching of Our Lord there is no individuality in that sense at all, but only personality, "that they may be *one.*"   BE. 31

God's idea is that individual Christians should become identified with His purpose for the world. When Christianity becomes over-organized and denominational it is incapable of fulfilling our Lord's commission; it doesn't 'feed His sheep,' it can't.   DI. 36

Christianity is not a clean heart empty, which means a collapse sooner or later, but a life passionately full of personal devotion to Jesus Christ, and a determined identification with His interests in other men.   HGM. 34

Once let that man realize that Christianity is not a decision for Christ, but a complete surrender to let Him take the lordship, and Jesus will appear to him. He will do more, He will put into him a totally new heredity, the heredity that was in Himself. That is the amazement of regeneration.   HGM. 37

Christianity is a personal relationship which works spontaneously by 'the moral originality of the Holy Ghost,' there is a perfect gaiety of delight.
HGM. 113

The great curse of modern Christianity is that people will not be careless about things they have no right to be careful about, and they will not let God make them careful about their relationship to Him.   IWP. 67

The essence of Christianity is not a creed or a doctrine, but an illumination that emancipates us—'I see Who Jesus is.' It is always a surprise, never an intellectual conception. LG. 118

The passion of Christianity is that I deliberately sign away my own rights and become a bond-slave of Jesus Christ. MUH. 308

We are not introduced to Christianity by explanations, but we must labour at the exposition of Christianity until we satisfactorily unfold it through God's grace and our own effort. NKW. 23

Many of us think that God wants us to give up things; we make Christianity the great apotheosis of giving up! NKW. 124

Jesus Christ comes to the central part of a man's life, and the bedrock of Christianity is that Jesus Christ has done something for me I could not do for myself. PH. 61

We have made Christianity to mean the saving of our skins. PH. 226

Christian Psychology is based on the knowledge of the Lord Jesus Christ, not on the knowledge of ourselves. PR. 9

Christianity means staking ourselves on the honour of Jesus; His honour means that He will see us through time, death and eternity. RTR. 41

Jesus Christ's view is that the Christian religion has been tried and abandoned, but never been tried and failed. SA. 27

Jesus Christ said—"You call Me Master and Lord, but you don't do what I say." That is the gist of the failure of Christianity; it has been tried and abandoned because it has been found difficult; but it has never failed when it has been tried and gone on with honourably. There is no problem or difficulty that stretches before a man for which adherence to Jesus Christ will not give him the line of solution. SA. 73

CHRISTIAN LIFE

The Christian life is stamped all through with impossibility. Human nature cannot come anywhere near Jesus Christ's demands, and any rational being facing those demands honestly, says, 'It can't be done, apart from a miracle.' Exactly. In our modern Christianity there is no miracle; it is—'You must pray more'; 'you must give up this and that'—anything and everything but the need to be born into a totally new kingdom. BE. 30

The stedfast habit of the Christian life is the effacement of self, letting Jesus work through us without let or hindrance as the Father worked through Him. BSG. 43

God never allows a Christian to carry on his life in sections—so much time for study and meditation and so much for actual work; the whole life, spirit, soul and body must progress together. IWP. 36

The severest discipline of a Christian's life is to learn how to keep "beholding as in a glass the glory of the Lord." MUH. 23

If we are going to live as disciples of Jesus, we have to remember that all noble things are difficult. The Christian life is gloriously difficult, but the difficulty of it does not make us faint and cave in, it rouses us up to overcome. MUH. 189

. . . there is one definite aim in every Christian life, and that aim is not ours, it is God's. PH. 177

The characteristics that Jesus Christ exhibited in His human life are to be exhibited in the Christian. PR. 18

The secret of a Christian's life is that the supernatural is made natural by the grace of God. The way it is worked out in expression is not in having times of communion with God, but in the practical details of life. SSM. 53

In the beginning of the Christian life it seems easier to drift and to say 'I can't,' but when once we do put on His yoke, we find, blessed be the Name of God, that we have chosen the easiest way after all. Happiness and joy attend, but they are not our aim, our aim is the Lord Jesus Christ, and God showers the hundredfold more on us all the way along. SSM. 97

The whole meaning of the Christian life from Our Lord's standpoint is to be ready for Him. SSY. 34

We do not start with our idea of what the Christian life should be, we start with Christ, and we end with Christ. Our aims in natural life continually alter as we develop, but development in the Christian life is an increasing manifestation of Jesus Christ. SSY. 110

. . . you cannot develop your own Christian life unless it is there. The advice given that if you work for God you develop your own life often means that if you work for God you get right yourself; you do not, you have to be right with God first. WG. 20

"The majority of Christian people are always washing and mending their nets; but when Jesus Christ comes along, He tells them to launch out and let them down; it is the only way to catch fish." God grant we may see the aptness of Jesus Christ's words, "I will make you fishers of men." WG. 85

CHRISTIAN SCIENCE

Christian Science is a specimen of the way people garrison themselves around within a little world of their own. The teaching of Christian Science makes its followers deny that there are such things as sin and disease and death—they are all imagination; and they shut themselves in a little world of their own and say, 'It is so easy to believe in the goodness of God'; of course it is! But let the house of their creed be taken and battered in by the gales of God; let them be driven out of the little enclosures of their preconceived notions, out into the big indifferent world, driven clean out to face the facts of sin and disease and death, and where does their belief in the goodness of God go? It cannot stand the test. GW. 92

The modern name for the worship of physical health is Christian Science. The great error of the healthy-minded cult is that it ignores a man's moral and spiritual life. PS. 76

CHRIST IN US

'Christ in me' means ultimately 'me' altogether in Christ. That is, 'Christ in me' means that I am willing to let Christ 'grow in me.' The obverse side of 'Christ in me' is 'me in Christ'; it is an incorporation. GW. 64

We are invited, we are commanded and pleaded with, to believe the gospel of the grace of God, which is, "Christ in you, the hope of glory." OBH. 19

It is not power to live like Jesus; it is Christ living in us, and it is His life that is seen, but it is only seen as by faith we walk in the light. OBH. 22

"When it pleased God . . . to reveal His Son in me." You in your shop, you in your office, you in your home, say that in your own heart—'The Son of God revealed *in me!*' That is sanctification. OBH. 45

Thank God for experiences, for the power to be enchanted, but this is the thing that tells—"Christ in you." PH. 175

CHURCH

The Church of Jesus Christ . . . seeking favour in the eyes of the world, seeking signs and wonders, and Christ stands without the door knocking. BSG. 41

The most fundamental heresies which split the Christian Church are those build on what Jesus Christ can do instead of on Himself. Wreckage in spiritual experience always follows. DI. 3

The gifts of the Spirit are not for individual exaltation, but for the good of the whole Body of Christ. The Body of Christ is an organism, not an organization. How patient God is in forming the Body of Christ. HGM. 11

According to our Lord, the bedrock of membership in the Christian Church is a personal revelation from God as to Who Jesus is, and a public declaration of it. LG. 127

The personal Holy Spirit builds us up into the body of Christ. All that Jesus Christ came to do is made ours experimentally by the Holy Spirit, and all His gifts are for the good of the whole body, not for individual exaltation. LG. 131

The Church ceases to be a spiritual society when it is on the look-out for the development of its own organization. MUH. 194

The Church is the new Spirit-baptized Humanity based on the Redemption of Jesus Christ. SA. 18

CIRCUMSTANCES

Never allow that your circumstances exonerate you from obeying any of the commands of Jesus. BE. 59

There are circumstances in life which make us know that Satan's sneer is pretty near the mark. I love God as long as He blesses me, saves my soul and puts me right for heaven; but supposing He should see fit to let the worst things happen to me, would I say, "Go on, do it" and love Him still? CHI. 111

God seems to have a delightful way of upsetting things which we have calculated on without Him. We get into places and circumstances He never chose, and suddenly they are shaken and we find we have been calculating on them without God; He has not entered in as a living factor. GW. 80

"In my distress . . ." There are elements in our circumstances if we are children of God that can only be described by the word *'distress'*; it would be untruthful to say it was otherwise. HG. 9

Where you look for God, He does not appear; where you do not look for Him, there He is—a trick of the weather, a letter, and suddenly you are face to face with the best thing you ever met. HGM. 32

It is not faith to believe that God is making things work together for good unless we are up against things that are ostensibly working for bad. HGM. 32

God's order comes to us in the ordinary haphazard circumstances of life, and when we are in touch with Him the sacrament of His presence comes in the common elements of Nature and ordinary people. HGM. 32

Jesus Christ, by the Spirit of God, always keeps us on top of our circumstances. IYA. 15

There is no such thing as chance in the life of a saint, and we shall find that God by His providence brings our bodies into circumstances that we cannot understand a bit, but the Spirit of God understands; He is bringing us into places and among people and under conditions in order that the intercession of the Holy Spirit in us may take a particular line. Do not, therefore, suddenly put your hand in front of the circumstances and say, 'No, I am going to be my own amateur providence, I am going to watch this and guard that.' IYA. 107

Never allow to yourself that you could not help this or that; and never say you reach anywhere *in spite of* circumstances; we all attain *because* of circumstances and no other way. MFL. 95

It is impossible for Christ to be where you are, that is why He has put you there. You have to put on the new man in the actual circumstances you are in and manifest Him. NKW. 41

God does not further our spiritual life in spite of our circumstances, but in and by our circumstances. The whole purpose of God is to make the ideal faith actually real in the lives of His servants. God is working for His highest purpose until it and man's highest good become one. NKW. 113

Don't loaf along like a strayed poet on the fringes of God's providence; the Almighty has got you in hand, leave yourself alone and trust in Him. Half the sentimental pious folks that strew the coasts of emotional religious life are there because we will engineer our own circumstances. NKW. 133

We have to be for God's purpose, and God cannot explain His purpose until it happens. God's omniscience, God's order, and God's opportunity in my individual life all work together, and Jesus Christ enters into my life just at the point of the haphazard circumstances I am in. NKW. 133

Remember, we go through nothing that God does not know about. OBH. 82

. . . all the grace of God is ours without let or hindrance through the Lord Jesus, and He is ready to tax the last grain of sand and the remotest star to bless us. What does it matter if circumstances are hard? Why shouldn't they be! We are the ones who ought to be able to stand them. OBH. 86

. . . if you have seen God face to face your circumstances will never arouse any panic in you. OPG. 64

The saint recognises in all the ordinary circumstances of his life the hand of God and the rule of God, and Jesus says we cannot do that unless we are born from above. PR. 33

The circumstances of our Lord were anything but ideal, they were full of difficulties. Perhaps ours are the same, and we have to watch that we remain true to the life of the Son of God in us, not true to our own aims and ends. There is always a danger of mistaking our own aim and end for the aim of the life of God in us. PR. 43

The life of the Son of God in us is brought into the same kind of circumstances that the historic life of Jesus Christ was brought into, and what was true of Him will be true also of His life in us. PR. 45

The more complicated the actual conditions are, the more delightfully joyful it is to see God open up His way through. RTR. 24

If God has made your cup sweet, drink it with grace; if He has made it bitter, drink it in communion with Him. RTR. 49

It is one thing to go through a crisis grandly, and another thing to go through every day glorifying God when nobody is paying any attention to you. RTR. 51

CIVILIZATION

Civilization and its amenities are made possible by Christianity, but they are not Christianity, and it is these amenities which ensnare and devastate in the time in which we live, and if we by unspiritual self-indulgence have been living our life in the externals, we shall be caught by this crisis and whirled into confusion. CD. VOL. 1, 115

God engineers us out of our sequestered places and brings us into elemental conditions, and we get a taste of what the world is like because of the disobedience of man. We realize then that our hold on God has been a civilized hold, we have not really believed in Him at all. HGM. 92

The first civilization was founded by a murderer, and the whole basis of civilized life is a vast, complicated, more or less gilded-over system of murder. We find it more conducive to human welfare not to murder men outright, we do it by a system of competition. It is ingrained in our thinking that competition and rivalry are essential to the carrying on of civilized life; that is why Jesus Christ's statements seem wild and ridiculous. They are the statements either of a madman or of God Incarnate. OPG. 13

The conditions of our civilised life today ought to be realised more keenly by the Christian than by the natural man, but we must see that the worship of God is put on the throne and not our human wits. PR. 65

The evidence of Christianity is not the good works that go on in the world; these are the outcome of the good there is in human nature, which still holds remnants of what God designed it to be. There is much that is admirable in the civilisation of the world, but there is no promise in it. The natural virtues exhaust themselves; they do not develop. PR. 65

The manipulation of civilised life has not resulted in the development of the tillage of the land, but in the building up of treasure, and it is not only the miser who grabs. SHH. 63

The birds of civilization come and lodge in the branches of the spiritual tree and men say 'Now this is what is to be!' and they have not seen God's purpose at all. If we do not see God's purpose we shall continually be misled by externals. SSY. 80

From the very beginning God's work has seemed a forlorn hope, as if He were being worsted; and all the arguments seem to be in favour of working on other lines—the line of education, of healing, and of civilization. These are the 'birds' which come and lodge in the branches, and men are saying that the present manifestation of civilization is the outcome of Christianity. 'This,' they say, 'is Christianity, this is the real thing, these educational forces, these healing and civilizing forces. This is what missions ought to be doing, not going off on the line of personal sanctification or of devotion to Jesus; we have grown out of all that. We must devote ourselves to the things we can see; we must educate and train these benighted races and introduce our wider, better views, and in that way the Kingdom of God will come in.' This is not God's way. God will bring in His Kingdom in His own way. Jesus says that in this dispensation 'the kingdom of God is within you without observation.' All these forces of civilization have been allowed to lodge in the branches of the spiritual tree of Christianity, whilst the Life that makes them possible is not recognized. They receive shelter from that which they are not themselves, and men's eyes are blinded to the real issue. It is astounding how far away men will get when once they leave the humble stand of a life hid with Christ in God. SSY. 117

CLEVERNESS

Never choose a text, let the text choose you. Cleverness is the ability to do things better than anyone else. Always hide that light under a bushel. The Holy Ghost is never clever. AUG. 41

CLOUDS

Thank God, when clouds are around the saint knows that they are but the dust of the Father's feet, and when the shadows are dark and terrible and the soul seems to fear externally as it enters the cloud, he finds "no man any more, save Jesus only with themselves." IYA. 80

It is an insult to-day to tell some men and women to cheer up. One of the most shallow petty things that can be said is that "every cloud has a silver lining." There are some clouds that are black all through. SA. 17

COERCION

There is something so natural and yet so supernatural about Jesus. We never read that Jesus button-holed anybody. HGM. 141

Our Lord was never impatient. He simply planted seed thoughts in their minds and surrounded them with the atmosphere of His own life. He did not attempt to convince them, but left mistakes to correct themselves, because He knew that eventually the truth would bear fruit in their lives. How differently we would have acted! We get impatient and take men by the scruff of the neck and say: 'You must believe this and that.' LG. 107

There is only one Lord of men, the Lord Jesus Christ, and yet He never insists upon His authority; He never says 'Thou shalt'; He takes the patient course with us, as He did with the early disciples. LG. 126

Our Lord never once used signs and wonders to get a man off his guard and then say, 'Now believe in Me.' Jesus Christ never coerced anybody, He never used supernatural powers or the apparatus of revival; He refused to stagger human wits into submitting to Him, He always put the case to a man in cold blood, 'Take time and consider what you are doing.' PB. 66

God never coerces a man, he has to take God's way by his own moral choice; we reverse the order and demand of God that He does our work. SHL. 99

Our Lord never pleaded, He never cajoled, He never entrapped; He simply spoke the sternest words mortal ears ever heard, and then left it alone. Our Lord has a perfect understanding that when once His word is heard, it will bear fruit sooner or later. SSY. 137

COMMANDS/COMMANDMENTS

The Ten Commandments were not given with any consideration for human ability or inability to keep them; they are the revelation of God's demands made of men and women who had declared that if God would make His law known, they would keep it. "And all the people answered together, and said, All that the Lord hath spoken we will do." BE. 7

The commandments of God exhibit not His consideration for man, but His authoritative demands of man. BE. 15

No man can keep Jesus Christ's commandments unless God has done a radical work in his heart; but if He has, this is the practical, commonsense proof—he keeps the commandments of Jesus. BP. 132

No natural man is free to keep the commandments of God, he is utterly unable to unless he is born again of the Holy Spirit. Freedom means ability to keep the law; every kind of freedom has to be earned. BSG. 21

The commands of God are enablings. HGM. 30

The argument that the keeping of certain commandments is not essential to salvation is such a mean, beggarly line of argument that it need scarcely be mentioned. If my love for God is so faint and poor that I will only do what is abso-

lutely essential and not what it is my privilege to do, it is then that I deserve not only to be 'least in the kingdom of heaven,' but not to be in it at all. HGM. 136

The Bible reveals that when the Holy Spirit has come into us, every command of God is an enabling. PR. 90

If the commands of Jesus Christ in our life clash with the most sacred relationships on earth, it must be instant obedience to Him. PR. 93

COMMITMENT

Personal contact with Jesus alters everything. Be stupid enough to come and commit yourself to what He says. The attitude of coming is that the will resolutely lets go of everything and deliberately commits all to Him. MUH. 163

COMMONPLACE

The things that Jesus did were of the most menial and commonplace order, and this is an indication that it takes all God's power in me to do the most commonplace things in His way. MUH. 255

Times of feasting reveal a man's master like nothing else in human life, and it is in those times that Our Lord reveals Himself to be Master. My treatment of Jesus Christ is shown in the way I eat and drink, I am either a glutton and put Jesus Christ to shame, or else I am an ascetic and refuse to have fellowship with Him in eating and drinking; but when I become a humble saint I reveal Him all the time in the ordinary common ways of life. NKW. 74

A life with presence, i.e., an uncommon spirit, redeems any situation from the commonplace. It may be cleaning boots, doing house work, walking in the street, any ordinary thing at all, but immediately it is touched by a man or woman with presence it ceases to be commonplace. OPG. 70

Our Lord took words that were despised and transfigured their meaning; He did things that were commonplace and sordid and ordinary and transfigured them. Our Lord was the unconscious light in the midst of the most ordinary circumstances conceivable. RTR. 84

COMMON SENSE

The God I infer by my common sense has no power over me at all. DI. 12

If I enthrone common sense as God, there are great regions of my life in which I do not countenance God. HG. 37

Whenever we read anything that is very plain in our Lord's words, we either say that we cannot understand it or that it has another meaning. Common sense is the best gift we have, but it must be under the dominant rule of God. We enthrone common sense, we do not enthrone God. HG. 86

The Bible speaks about the Redemption, viz., what God has done for the human race, not about what we can get at by our common sense. HGM. 63

The danger with us is that we want to water down the things that Jesus says and make them mean something in accordance with common sense; if it were only common sense, it was not worth while for Him to say it. The things Jesus says about prayer are supernatural revelations. MUH. 147

Common sense is not faith, and faith is not common sense; they stand in the re-

lation of the natural and the spiritual; of impulse and inspiration. Nothing Jesus Christ ever said is common sense, it is revelation sense, and it reaches the shores where common sense fails. MUH. 304

To be guided by common sense alone is fanatical; both common sense and faith have to be brought into relation to God. NKW. 135

The reason we know so little about God's wisdom is that we will only trust Him as far as we can work things out according to our own reasonable common-sense. OPG. 35

The Lord Jesus Christ is not a common-sense fact, that is, we do not understand Him by means of our common sense. PR. 19

The Bible does not deal in common-sense facts; the natural universe deals in common-sense facts, and we get at these by our senses. The Bible deals with revelation facts, facts we cannot get at by our common sense, facts we may be pleased to make light of by our common sense. PR. 20

In order to get scientific knowledge we must use our common sense; but if we are going to know the facts with which Jesus Christ deals, the facts which He says belong to the Kingdom of God, we must have them revealed to us. 'Marvel not that I say unto you, You must be born again before you can come into contact with the domain in which I live.' PR. 20

Common sense does not reveal Jesus Christ; to common sense He is nothing more than a Nazarene carpenter who lived twenty centuries ago. No natural man can know Jesus Christ. PR. 21

Higher criticism, so called, works on the lines of common sense, consequently when it deals with our Lord (Whose highest sense is not common sense, but Deity), He has to be explained away, His Person is 'dissolved by analysis.' PR. 21

If we take the common-sense universe and discard the revelation of Jesus Christ we make what He says foolishness, because He talks from the universe of revelation all the time. Jesus Christ lived in the revelation world which we do not see, and until we get into His world we do not understand His teaching at all. In Him we find that the universe of revelation and the universe of common-sense were made one, and if ever they are to be one in us it can only be by receiving the heredity of Jesus, viz., Holy Spirit. SSM. 48

COMPROMISE

In the temptation of our Lord the compromise for good ends is pictured, 'Don't be so stern against sin; compromise judiciously with evil and You will easily win Your Kingship of men.' When we become rightly related to God our intellect is apt to say exactly the same thing, 'Don't be narrow; don't be so pronounced against worldliness, you will upset your friends.' Well, upset them, but never upset the main thing that God is after. There is always the tendency to compromise and we have to be roused up to recognize it. We have to walk in very narrow paths before God can trust us to walk in the wide ones. We have to be limited before we can be unlimited. MFL. 124

The Bible nowhere teaches us to be uncompromising in our opinions. Jesus did not say, 'Leap for joy when men separate you from their company for the sake of your convictions;' He said, 'Leap for joy

when men cast out your name as evil, *for the Son of Man's sake.'* I may be such a pig-headed cross-patch, and have such determined notions of my own, that no one can live with me. That is not suffering for the Son of Man's sake, it is suffering for my own sake. MFL. 124

"The Kingdom of God is within you"— uncompromisingly within you. We must never compromise with the kingdoms of this world; the temptation the devil presents is that we should compromise. We recognise his temptation in the teaching which proclaims that there is no such thing as the devil and no such place as hell; much that is called sin is a mere defect; men and women are like poor babes lost in the wood; just be kind and gentle with them; talk about the Fatherhood of God, about Universalism and Brotherhood, the kindness of Providence and the nobility of man. PR. 70

CONCEIT

Conceit means my own point of view and I don't care what anyone else says. "Be not wise in your own conceits," says Paul. . . . Conceit makes the way God deals with me personally the binding standard for others. AUG. 42

CONCENTRATION

There are far more people interested in consecration than concentration. It is easier to fuss around at work than to worship; easier to pay attention to details, to say our prayers or conduct a meeting, than to concentrate on God. AUG. 86

Concentration on the part of a Christian is of more importance than consecration. BE. 21

When we are concentrated on God we enter on a life of revelation, we begin to penetrate and discover things.   HGM. 72

We have to learn to bring "every thought into captivity to the obedience of Christ"; to 'stay our imagination' on God. This can only be done by concentration, by fixing our thoughts and our imagination deliberately on God.
MFL. 79

God gives us the Holy Spirit not only for holy living but for holy thinking, and we are held responsible if we do not think concentratedly along the right lines. To concentrate with our mind fixed on one trend of things is never easy to begin with. There never is a time when we cannot begin to concentrate.   MFL. 80

"Be ye not unwise, but understanding what the will of the Lord is." We have to use the same power of concentration spiritually as we do naturally.   MFL. 80

Narrow all your interests until the attitude of mind and heart and body is concentration on Jesus Christ. "Look unto Me."   MUH. 22

The golden rule for your life and mine is this concentrated keeping of the life open towards God. Let everything else—work, clothes, food, everything on earth—go by the board, saving that one thing.   MUH. 23

You no more need a holiday from spiritual concentration than your heart needs a holiday from beating.   MUH. 106

Jesus says that there is only one way to develop spiritually, and that is by concentration on God. "Do not bother about being of use to others; believe on Me"—pay attention to the Source, and out of you will flow rivers of living water.   MUH. 139

Soul is my personal spirit as it reasons, and thinks, and looks at things; I have to call my powers together and concentrate on God. It is possible to concentrate and yet not concentrate on God.   PH. 92

The one dominating abandon of the life is concentration on God, consequently every other carefulness is careless in comparison.   SSM. 67

Our Lord teaches that the one great secret of the spiritual life is concentration on God and His purposes. We talk a lot about concentration, but it ends in sentimentalism because there is nothing definite about it. Consecration ought to mean the definite yielding of ourselves over as saved souls to Jesus and concentrating on that.   SSM. 73

CONDEMNATION

The whole human race is condemned to salvation by the Cross of our Lord.   PR. 50

God nowhere holds a man responsible for having the heredity of sin; the condemnation begins when a man sees and understands that God can deliver him from the heredity of sin and he refuses to let Him do it; at that moment he begins to get the seal of damnation.   PR. 50

Jesus Christ never says that a man is damned because he is a sinner; the condemnation is when a man sees what Jesus Christ came to do and will not let Him do it.   RTR. 60

This is the condemnation, that the Light, Jesus Christ, has come into the world, and I prefer darkness, i.e., my own point of view.   SA. 49

CONDUCT

The seemliness of Christian conduct is not consistent adherence to a mere principle of peace, but standing true to Jesus Christ.   CD. VOL. 1, 117

If our best obedience, our most spotless moral walking, our most earnest prayers, are offered to God in the very least measure as the ground of our acceptance by Him, it is a fatal denial of the Atonement.   CHI. 80

How impatient we are in dealing with other people! Our actions imply that we think God is asleep, until God brings us to the place where we come on them from above.   DI. 40

All my devotion is an insult to God unless every bit of my practical life squares with Jesus Christ's demands.   DI. 72

The word *walk* breathes character, it is the symbol for seemly behaviour.   HG. 42

Our conduct before men will be judged by whether we walk in the seemliness of sanctity before God. That means conduct according to the highest we know, and the striking thing is that the highest we know is God Himself.   HG. 42

It is righteous behaviour that brings blessing on others, and the heart of faith sees that God is working things out well.   HG. 45

Others are doing things which to you would be walking in craftiness, but it may not be so with them: God has given you another standpoint.   MUH. 259

What any man has ever done, any man can do if he does not watch.   NKW. 85

CONFESSION

The Bible tests all experience, all truth, all authority, by our Lord Himself and our relationship to Him personally; it is

the confession of conduct. '. . . he that confesseth Me before men,' said Jesus; the word 'confess' means literally that every bit of my bodily life speaks the same truth as our Lord exhibited in the flesh.   GW. 71

Beware of having anything that makes your mind accept an excuse for yourself. I can step out of darkness into the light—when God is willing? No, when I am willing. 'I do want to be in living communion with God'; I don't, if I did, I could be there in one second; the reason I am not there is that I won't confess, I won't submit to God's condemnation of the thing. Immediately confession is made the Atonement of Our Lord steps in with its supernatural efficacy.   HGM. 133

Confession is not for the sake of other people, but for our own sake. Confession means we have trusted God for this thing and we believe on the ground of His word that the work is done. We realize by confessing that we have no one saving God to stand by us.   OBH. 126

Nothing can act as an atonement for wrong saving an absolutely clean confession to God. To walk in the light with nothing folded up is our conscientious part, then God will do the rest.   OPG. 58

If I say with my self what I believe and confess it with my mouth, I am lifted into the domain of that thing.   PH. 209

If a child is to be taken out of his sulky mood he has to go across the disinclination of his reserve and *say* something; and this is true of all moral and spiritual life.   PH. 209

Jesus said, "Everyone therefore who shall confess *Me* before men . . ." and it tests a man for all he is worth to confess

Jesus Christ, because the confession has to be made in the set he belongs to and esteems.   SHH. 83

No man can confess Jesus Christ without realising the cost to others; if he states this, he rebukes them.   SHH. 83

Jesus never used the word *testify*; He used a much more searching word—*confess*. "Whosoever therefore shall confess Me before men, . . ." The test of goodness is confession by doing the will of God. 'If you do not confess Me before men,' says Jesus, 'neither will your heavenly Father confess you.'   SSM. 105

Notice the emphasis that the New Testament places on 'confessing,' on 'preaching,' and on 'testifying,' all expressive of this perfect finish for God. And notice too that it is this characteristic that Satan attacks. He is at the back of the movement abroad to-day which advocates living a holy life, but 'don't talk about it.'   SSY. 107

CONFIDENCE

We won't walk before God because we are not confident in Him, and the proof that we are not confident in God is that occasionally we get into the sulks. If you are walking with God it is impossible to be in the sulks. Never have the idea that you have disobeyed when you know you have not, the reason you say so is because you are not walking in the permanent light of faith.   NKW. 60

It is nonsense to imagine that God expects me to discern all that is clear to His own mind, all He asks of me is to maintain perfect confidence in Himself. Faith springs from the indwelling of the life of God in me.   OPG. 37

The great object of the enemy of our souls is to make us fling away our confidence in God; to do this is nothing less than spiritual suicide.   OPG. 57

God expects His children to be so confident in Him that in a crisis they are the ones upon whom He can rely.   PH. 39

There is no more glorious opportunity than the day in which we live for proving in personal life and in every way that we are confident in God.   PH. 41

CONFLICT

A worldly man has no carnality; he is not conscious of any conflict between the Spirit and his flesh; when he is born again the conflict begins, and there is a disclosure of the carnal mind, which is *'enmity against God.'* No man knows he has that enemy on the inside until he receives the Holy Spirit.   BE. 79

It is a great deal easier to fight than to stand; but spiritually our conflict is not so much a fight as a standing on guard—"having done all, *to stand."* When we are in a frenzy, we attack; when we are strong, we stand to overcome.   OBH. 55

Jesus Christ came to fit men to fight, He came to make the lame, the halt, the paralysed, the all but sin-damned, into terrors to the prince of this world.   SHL. 9

If there is one thing an unsaved man is incapable of doing, it is fighting against the awful powers of sin. He can fight in the physical realm because he has the spirit of lust; but Paul warns that 'our wrestling is not against flesh and blood, but against . . . the spiritual hosts of wickedness in the heavenly places.' No man is a match for that warfare unless he is saved by God's grace.   SHL. 9

The conflict for the Christian is not a conflict with sin, but a conflict over the natural life being turned into the spiritual life. SSM. 63

CONFUSION

There are times in spiritual life when there is confusion, and it is no way out to say that there ought not to be confusion. It is not a question of right and wrong, but a question of God taking you by a way which in the meantime you do not understand, and it is only by going through the confusion that you will get at what God wants. MUH. 256

CONQUERORS

"Wherefore take unto you the whole armour of God"—not to fight, but to stand. We are not told to attack, to storm the forts of darkness; we are told to stand, unpanicky and unbudged, more than conquerors. A conqueror is one who fights and wins, a 'more than conqueror' is one who easily and powerfully overcomes. The struggle is not against flesh and blood, it is against principalities and powers. We cannot touch them by intellect or organisation, by courage or foresight or forethought, we cannot touch them at all unless we are based on the Redemption. IYA. 31

If we attempt to take a holiday, the next time we want to pray it is a struggle because the enemy has gained a victory all round, darkness has come down and spiritual wickedness in high places has enfolded us. If we have to fight, it is because we have disobeyed; we ought to be more than conquerors. IYA. 32

No power on earth or in hell can conquer the Spirit of God in a human spirit, it is an inner unconquerableness.
MUH. 105

We cannot be *more than* conquerors if there is nothing to fight! Our Lord Himself and the Spirit of God in the Epistles make it very clear that everything that is not of God will try its best to kill His life out of us; yet instead of doing that it makes us all the stronger. SHL. 18

The love of God in Christ Jesus is such that He can take the most unfit man— unfit to survive, unfit to fight, unfit to face moral issues—and make him not only fit to survive and to fight, but fit to face the biggest moral issues and the strongest power of Satan, and come off more than conqueror. The love of God in Christ Jesus through the mighty Atonement is such that it can do this for the feeblest, the most sinful man, if he will hand himself over to God. SHL. 19

CONSCIENCE

Another standard of authority is that of conscience, or 'the inner light'—what Socrates called 'the presiding daemon,' an un-get-at-able, indefinable spirit which gives liberty or check to whatever a man feels impelled to do. BE. 13

Every man has a conscience, although every man does not know God. BE. 14

Conscience is the 'eye of the soul,' and the orbit of conscience, that marvellous recorder, is the heart. BP. 143

Probably the best illustration of conscience is the human eye. The eye records what it looks at, and conscience may be pictured as the eye of the soul recording what it looks at, and, like the eye, it will always record exactly what it is turned towards. BP. 194

My conscience makes me know what I ought to do, but it does not empower me to do it. "For that which I do I allow not;

for what I would, that do I not; but what I hate, that do I." DL. 26

We are never told to walk in the light of conscience, but to walk in the light of the Lord. HG. 16

After a great spiritual crisis a man's conscience looks out towards God in a new light, the light which Jesus Christ throws upon God, and he has to walk in that light and bring his bodily life into harmony with what his conscience records. MFL. 121

Conscience is that faculty in me which attaches itself to the highest that I know, and tells me what the highest I know demands that I do. It is the eye of the soul which looks out either towards God or towards what it regards as the highest, and therefore conscience records differently in different people. MUH. 134

If the voice of God does not correspond with what conscience says, I need pay no attention to it; but when it says the same thing as conscience, I must either obey or be damned in that particular. NKW. 53

If conscience were the voice of God it would be the most contradictory voice human ears ever listened to. Conscience is the eye of the soul; and how it records depends entirely upon the light thrown upon God. OBH. 67

If I am in the habit of steadily and persistently facing myself with God, my conscience will always introduce God's perfect law to me; the question then is will I do what my conscience makes me understand clearly I should do? OBH. 67

We avoid forming a sensitive conscience when we say—'Oh well, God cannot expect me to do this thing, He has not told

me to do it.' How do we expect God to tell us? The word is "not in heaven . . . neither is it beyond the sea . . . but the word is very nigh unto thee, in thy mouth, and in thy heart, that thou mayest do it." OBH. 68

Can God readjust a seared conscience and make it sensitive again? He can, and it is done by the vicarious Atonement of our Lord. "How much more shall the blood of Christ . . . purge your conscience from dead works to serve the living God?" OBH. 71

'If only God would not be so holy as my conscience tells me He is.' It is a mixed-up certainty, I know I am not right with God and I don't want to be—and yet I do. OPG. 8

Intellectually, we are inclined to ignore sin. The one element in man that does not ignore sin is conscience. The Holy Spirit deals with conscience first, not with intellect or emotions. PR. 122

The greatest problems of conscience are not the wrong things we have done, but wrong relationships. PS. 21

Conscience is the standard by which men and women are to be judged until they have been brought into contact with the Lord Jesus Christ. PS. 43

Conscience is the internal perception of God's moral law. Have you ever been convicted of sin by conscience through the Spirit of God? If you have, you know this—that God dare not forgive you and be God. PS. 65

"Conscience is the innate law in human nature whereby man knows he is known." SA. 44

When a man gets rightly adjusted to God his conscience staggers him, and his reason condemns him from all standpoints. SA. 44

The phrase "Conscience can be educated" is a truth that is half an error. Strictly speaking, conscience cannot be educated; what is altered and educated is a man's reasoning on what his conscience records. SA. 44

It is not sufficient for a Christian to walk in the light of his conscience; he must walk in a sterner light, in the light of the Lord. SA. 48

Conscience will always record God whenever it has been faced by God. SA. 49

CONSCIOUSNESS

The thing that hurts Jesus is asking Him to give us experiences—'I want to be conscious of God's presence.' Get rid of the morbid idea of consciousness, be so completely in Jesus that His presence is salvation continually. GW. 26

When we are being initiated into a new experience we are conscious of it, but any sane person is much too wise to mistake consciousness of life for life itself. It is only the initial stages of new experiences which produce consciousness of themselves, and if we hug the consciousness of God's blessings and of His presence we become spiritual sentimentalists. God began to introduce us to life, and we would not go through with it. HG. 110

Most of us live on the borders of consciousness—consciously serving, consciously devoted to God. All this is immature, it is not the real life yet. . . . MUH. 320

God only manifests Himself *in* His children, consequently others see the manifestation, the child of God does not. You say, 'I am not conscious of God's blessing now'—thank God! 'I am not conscious now of the touches of God'—thank God! 'I am not conscious now that God is answering my prayers'—thank God! If you are conscious of these things it means you have put yourself outside God. "That the life also of Jesus might be made manifest in our mortal flesh"—'I am not conscious that His life is being manifested,' you say, but if you are a saint it surely is. OBH. 66

The rarest asset to a godly life is to be practically conscientious in every situation. OPG. 70

At the beginning of the spiritual life the consciousness of God is so wonderful that we are apt to imagine our communion with God depends upon our being conscious of His presence. Then when God begins to withdraw us into Himself, and things become mysterious, we lose our faith and get into the dark, and say—'I must have backslidden,' and yet we know we have not, all we know is that we have lost our consciousness of God's presence. PH. 103

We are much more than we are conscious of being. Our Lord said the Holy Spirit would bring back into our conscious mind the things He had said. We never forget a thing although often we cannot recall it; we hear it and it goes into the unconscious mind. Things go on in our unconscious minds that we know nothing about, and at any second they may burst up into our conscious life and perturb us. The Spirit of God enters into a man below the threshold of his consciousness. SA. 103

We are much more than we are conscious of, and if Jesus Christ only came

to alter our conscious life, then the Redemption is 'much ado about nothing.'
SHL. 53

only asks us to do the thing we are perfectly fitted to do by grace, and the cross will always come along that line.   SSY. 108

CONSECRATION

You cannot consecrate yourself *and* your friends. If at the altar your heart imagines that loving arms are still around you, and that together, lovers as lovers, and friends as friends, can enter through this mighty gate of supreme Sanctification, it is a fond dream, doomed to disillusionment. Alone! Relinquish all! You cannot consecrate your children, your wife, your lover, your friend, your father, your mother or your own life as yours. You must abandon all and fling yourself on God as a mere conscious being, and unperplexed, seeking you'll find Him.
CD. VOL. 2, 88

All ecstasies and experiences, all inner voices and revelations and dreams, must be tested by the pure outer light of Jesus Christ and His word. By looking to Him we are changed into the same image from glory to glory, when consecration has been made a definite transaction.
CD. VOL. 2, 95

You cannot consecrate what is not yours.   IWP. 44

We must never allow anything to interfere with the consecration of our spiritual energy. Consecration is our part, sanctification is God's part; and we have deliberately to determine to be interested only in that which God is interested.   MUH. 332

The idea that we have to consecrate our gifts to God is a dangerous one. We cannot consecrate what is not ours. We have to consecrate ourselves, and leave our gifts alone. God does not ask us to do the thing that is easy to us naturally; He

CONSISTENCY/INCONSISTENCY

There never was a more inconsistent Being on this earth than Our Lord, but He was never inconsistent to His Father.
MUH. 319

CONTENTMENT

When I wish I was somewhere else I am not doing my duty to God where I am. I am wool-gathering, fooling with my own soul; if I am God's child I have no business to be distracted. If I keep myself from covetousness, content with the things I have, I remain within the frontiers of God. If I have the spirit of covetousness in my heart I have no right to say, 'The Lord is my helper'—He is not, He is my destroyer. I have no right to say I am content and yet have a mood that is not contented.   HG. 30

If I am ill-tempered, set on some change of circumstances, I find God is not supporting me at all; I have worried myself outside the moral frontier where He works and my soul won't sing; there is no joy in God, no peace in believing.
HG. 30

As long as we remain within the moral frontiers of God, watching our hearts lest we give way to ill-content, to covetousness, or self-pity, the things which take us outside God's frontier, then God says, *"I will in no wise fail thee, neither will I in any wise forsake thee."*   HG. 32

CONVERSION

We may be converted, but obviously we have too often *not* become as little children.   CD. VOL. 2, 17

'Except ye be converted, and become as little children . . .' is true for all the days of the saintly life, we have continually to turn to God. NKW. 51

I have to convert my natural life continually into submission to the Spirit of God in me, otherwise I shall produce the divorce which ends in hell. NKW. 52

The attitude of continuous conversion is the only right attitude towards the natural life, and it is the one thing we object to. NKW. 51

To call conversion new birth is an impoverishment. Because a man who has lived in sin stops sinning, it is no sign that he is born from above. NKW. 59

CONVICTIONS

If you remain true to Jesus Christ there are times when you will have to go through your convictions and out the outer side, and most of us shrink from such a step because it means going alone. The 'camp' means the religious set you belong to; the set you do not belong to does not matter to you. BFB. 73

It is easier to be true to our convictions than to Jesus Christ, because if we are going to be true to Him our convictions will need to be altered. DI. 1

The way our heart is hardened is by sticking to our convictions instead of to Christ. Look back at your life with God and you will find that He has made havoc of your convictions, and now the one thing that looms larger and larger is Jesus Christ and Him only, God and God only. GW. 37

The word 'convict' means moral conviction, not logical conviction. When the Holy Spirit is come, He will convict a man with a power of moral conviction beyond the possibility of getting away from it. HG. 107

It is not our business to convince other people, that is the insistence of a merely intellectual, unspiritual life. The Spirit of God will do the convicting when we are in relationship where we simply convey God's word. IWP. 66

Beware of making a fetish of consistency to convictions instead of developing your faith in God. 'I shall never do that'—in all probability you will have to if you are a saint. NKW. 144

God's Book never tells us to walk in the light of convictions, but in the light of the Lord. SSM. 101

Never discard a conviction; if it is important enough for the Spirit of God to have brought it to your mind, that is the thing He is detecting. SSY. 45

COST

Jesus Christ has counted the cost. Men are not going to laugh at Him at last and say—"This man began to build, and was not able to finish." MUH. 128

COVETOUSNESS

What is true of Adam is true of every man and woman, and "not all mankind could amend his fall, or bring him back from going astray." This inheritance of covetousness is the very essence of the Fall, and no praying and no power of man, single or banded together, can ever avail to touch it; the only thing that can touch it is the great Atonement of our Lord Jesus Christ. IWP. 23

Never lay the flattering unction to your soul that because you are not covetous for money or worldly possessions, you are not covetous for anything. The fuss and distress of owning anything is the last remnant of the disposition of sin. Jesus Christ possessed nothing for Himself. IWP. 26

CREATION

God did not create man by direct fiat; He moulded him by His own deliberate power. BP. 13

God did not create man as a puppet to please a despotic idea of His own, He created us out of the superabundant flow of overflowing love and goodness, He created us susceptible of all the blessedness which He had ordained for us. He 'thought' us in the rapture of His own great heart, and lo, we are! Created in the image of God were we, innocent of evil, of great God-like capacities. LG. 10

"We are the offspring of God." But the creator-power in Jesus Christ is vested in a more marvellous way even than when God created the world through Him for He has that in Himself whereby He can create His own image. God created the world and everything that was made through the Son, and "that which hath been made was life in Him"; therefore just as God created the world through Him, the Son is able to create His own image in anyone and everyone. Have we ever thought of Jesus as the marvellous Being Who can create in us His own image? OBH. 25

The matter of God's creation is a satisfaction to God, and when we come to know God by His Spirit we are as delighted with His creation as He is Himself. OPG. 2

"If any man is in Christ Jesus," his nervous system will prove that he is "a new creature," and the material world will appear to him as a new creation because he is now seeing it as the mirror of God's thought. SA. 45

CREED

A creed means the ordered exposition of the Christian faith, an attempt to explain the faith you have, not the thing that gives you the Christian faith. It is the most mature effort of the human intellect on the inside, not on the outside. The churches make the blunder when they put the creed as the test on the outside, and they produce parrots who mimic the thing. AUG. 82

The religious pose is based, not on a personal relationship to God, but on adherence to a creed. Immediately we mistake God for a creed, or Jesus Christ for a form of belief, we begin to patronise what we do not understand. BFB. 59

If I become a devotee of a creed I cannot see God unless He comes along my line. BFB. 97

People accept creeds, but they will not accept the holy standards of Jesus Christ's teaching. BE. 56

Our creeds teach us to believe in the Holy Spirit: the New Testament says we must receive Him. LG. 114

The counterfeit of true spirituality is that produced by creeds. PH. 154

CRITICISM

A critic must be removed from what he criticises. Before a man can criticise a work of art or a piece of music, his information must be complete, he must stand away from what he criticises as superior to it. No human being can ever take that attitude to another human being; if he does he puts himself in the wrong position and grieves the Holy Spirit. SSM. 76

A man who is continually criticised becomes good for nothing, the effect of criticism knocks all the gumption and power out of him. SSM. 76

The temper of mind that makes us lynx-eyed in seeing where others are wrong does not do them any good, because the effect of our criticism is to paralyse their powers, which proves that the criticism was not of the Holy Ghost; we have put ourselves into the position of a superior person. SSM. 77

Jesus says a disciple can never stand away from another life and criticise it, therefore He advocates an uncritical temper, "Judge not." Beware of anything that puts you in the place of the superior person. SSM. 77

When the Holy Spirit reveals something of the nature of sin and unbelief in another, His purpose is not to make us feel the smug satisfaction of a critical spectator, 'Well, thank God, I am not like that'; but to make us so lay hold of God for that one that God enables him to turn away from the wrong thing. SSM. 77

Our Lord allows no room for criticism in the spiritual life, but He does allow room for discernment and discrimination. SSM. 78

The Holy Ghost works through the saints unbeknown to them, He works through them as light. If this is not understood, you will think the preacher is criticising you all the time. He is not; it is the Holy Spirit in the preacher discerning the wrong in you. SSM. 81

CROSS

The Cross of Christ is the Self-revelation of God, the exhibition of the essential nature of the Godhead. AUG. 57

The Cross is the expression of the very heart of God, and when my eyes are opened I see that Jesus Christ has made the basis of life Redemptive, and it cost Him everything to do it. BE. 61

My aim is not to be the saving of my own soul, getting myself put right for heaven, but battling to the death for what the Cross of Christ stands for. BE. 67

The Resurrection and glorification through the Ascension are understandable only by the Cross. BSG. 49

The Cross of Christ pronounced final and irrevocable judgement against the prince of this world. GW 129

The cross is the gift of Jesus to His disciples and it can only bear one aspect: 'I am not my own.' HG. 99

It is a slander to the Cross of Christ to say we believe in Jesus and please ourselves all the time, choosing our own way. HG. 99

Steady contemplation of the Passion of our Lord will 'do to death' everything that is not of God. It is only after a long while of going on with God and steady contemplation of the Cross that we begin to understand its meaning. IWP. 60

Will you let Jesus take the sense of the heroic right out of you? will you let Him make you see yourself as He sees you until for one moment you stand before the Cross and say, "Nothing in my hands I bring"? How many of us are there to-day? Talk about getting people to hear that, they won't have it! Jesus says they won't. No crowd on earth will ever listen to that, and if under some pretence you get them and preach the Cross of Christ they will turn with a snubbing offence from the whole thing as they did in Our Lord's day. IWP. 103

The Cross is a triumph for *the Son of Man*; any and every man has freedom of access straight to the throne of God by right of what our Lord accomplished through His death on the Cross. MFL. 106

There is nothing more certain in Time or Eternity than what Jesus Christ did on the Cross: He switched the whole of the human race back into a right relationship with God. He made Redemption the basis of human life, that is, He made a way for every son of man to get into communion with God. MUH. 97

The Cross of Jesus is the revelation of God's judgment on sin. Never tolerate the idea of martyrdom about the Cross of Jesus Christ. The Cross was a superb triumph in which the foundations of hell were shaken. MUH. 97

The Cross is not the cross of a man but the Cross of God, and the Cross of God can never be realized in human experience. The Cross is the exhibition of the nature of God, the gateway whereby any individual of the human race can enter into union with God. When we get to the Cross, we do not go through it; we abide in the life to which the Cross is the gateway. MUH. 97

Re-state to yourself what you believe, then do away with as much of it as possible, and get back to the bedrock of the Cross of Christ. In external history the Cross is an infinitesimal thing; from the Bible point of view it is of more impor-

tance than all the empires of the world. MUH. 330

In holiness movements and spiritual experience meetings the concentration is apt to be put not on the Cross of Christ, but on the effects of the Cross. MUH. 331

The one thing we have to do is to exhibit Jesus Christ crucified, to lift Him up all the time. Every doctrine that is not imbedded in the Cross of Jesus will lead astray. MUH. 355

Very few of us have any understanding of the reason why Jesus Christ died. If sympathy is all that human beings need, then the Cross of Christ is a farce, there was no need for it. What the world needs is not "a little bit of love," but a surgical operation. MUH. 355

The New Testament emphasises the death of Christ because the Cross is the Centre that reveals the very heart of God. PH. 136

Our Lord is absolutely sure that as representative Man before God He will get the whole human race through, in spite of everything the devil can do, and the Cross is an absolute triumph. PR. 94

The Cross is not the cross of a man but the Cross of God, and the Cross of God can never be realised in human experience. PR. 99

The Cross of Jesus is the revelation of God's judgment on sin. It is not the cross of a martyr; it is the substitution of Jesus for sinful humanity. PR. 100

The Cross did not *happen* to Jesus, He came on purpose for it. The whole purpose of the Incarnation is the Cross— "the Lamb slain from the foundation of the world." PR. 100

Our cross is what we hold before the world, viz., the fact that we are sanctified to do nothing but God's will. We have given away our right to ourselves for ever, and the cross we take up is a sign in heaven, on earth and to hell, that we are His and our own no longer. PR. 102

We are apt to imagine that the cross we have to carry means the ordinary troubles and trials of life, but we must have these whether we are Christians or not. Neither is our cross suffering for conscience' sake. Our cross is something that comes only with the peculiar relationship of a disciple to Jesus Christ; it is the evidence that we have denied our right to ourselves. PR. 102

The Cross of Jesus Christ is the point where God and sinful man merge with a crash, and the way to life is opened; but the crash in on the heart of God. SA. 38

The cross is the deliberate recognition of what our personal self is for, viz., to be given to Jesus, and we take up that cross daily and prove we are no longer our own. SHL. 85

CRUCIFIXION

To be 'crucified with Christ' means that in obedience to the Spirit granted to me at regeneration, I eagerly and willingly go to the Cross and crucify self-realization for ever. BE. 88

Crucifixion means death. BP. 261

"He was *crucified through weakness*"— the strongest Being Who ever trod this earth, because He knew what He could do and did not do it. "He saved others, Himself He cannot save." BSG. 32

At the wall of the world stands God with His arms outstretched; and when a man or woman is driven there, the consolations of Jesus Christ are given. SA. 17

CURIOSITY

To be curious about another person's affairs is an impertinence and is never Christian. NKW. 145

This is a day of intolerant inquisitiveness. Men will not wait for the slow, steady, majestic way of the Son of God; they try to enter in by this door and that door. PH. 85

Scientific knowledge, which is systematised common sense, is based on intense intellectual curiosity. Curiosity in the natural world is right, not wrong, and if we are not intellectually curious we shall never know anything, God never encourages laziness. PR. 20

When the Holy Spirit comes in He makes us know that there are things we must remain ignorant of. Beware of entering into competition with the Holy Spirit. When we become curious and pry where we have no business to pry, we are eating of the fruit of the tree of which God said, 'Ye shall not eat of it.' SHL. 56

D

DAMNATION

The revelation the Bible makes is not that men are getting worse, but that men are damnable—consequently they are saveable; the system of things he lives in may get worse, but a man can't be worse than damnable. OPG. 14

I seal myself with damnation when I see the Light, Jesus Christ, and prefer my own standpoint. SA. 24

. . . the Bible nowhere says that men are damned; the Bible says that men are damnable. There is always the possibility of damnation in any life, always the possibility of disobedience; but, thank God, there is also always the possibility of being made 'more than conqueror.' The possibilities of life are awful. SHL. 26

Jesus Christ spoke rugged truth, He was never ambiguous, and He says it is better to be maimed than damned, better to enter into life lame in man's sight and lovely in God's than to be lovely in man's sight and lame in God's. SSM. 35

DARKNESS

A darkened heart is a terrible thing, because a darkened heart may make a man peaceful. BP. 139

'Darkness' is my own point of view, my prejudices and preconceived determinations; if the Spirit of God agrees with these, well and good; if not, I shall go my own way. BP. 221

Oh, the unspeakable benediction of the "treasures of darkness"! But for the night in the natural world we should know nothing of moon or stars, or of all the incommunicable thoughtfulness of the midnight. So spiritually it is not the days of sunshine and splendour and liberty and light that leave their lasting and indelible effect upon the soul but those nights of the Spirit in which, shadowed by God's hand, hidden in the dark cleft of some rock in a weary land, He lets the splendours of the outskirts of Himself pass before our gaze. It is such moments as these that insulate the soul from all worldliness and keep it in an 'other-worldliness' while carrying on work for the Lord and communion with Him in this present evil world. PH. 13

If things are dark to us spiritually, it is because there is something we will not do. Intellectual darkness comes because of ignorance; spiritual darkness comes because of something I do not intend to obey. SSM. 67

DEATH

By the term 'Death' is meant that the body crumbles back into dust, the soul disappears, and the spirit goes back to God Who gave it. BP. 25

To look for death to make me holy is to make out that death, which is 'the last enemy,' is going to do what the Atonement cannot do. GW. 54

Had Adam done so, the members of the human race would have gone on developing until they were transfigured into the presence of God; there would have been no death. PR. 11

If I do not put to death the things in me that are not of God, they will put to death the things that are of God. SA. 111

Remember, there is death, and there is worse than death—sin and tragedy and the possibility of terrible evil. SHH. 79

We have so taken for granted the comfort that Jesus Christ brings in the hour of death that we forget the awful condition of men apart from that revelation. SHL. 24

We know nothing about the mystery of death apart from what Jesus Christ tells us; but blessed be the Name of God, what He tells us makes us more than conquerors, so that we can shout the victory through the darkest valley of the shadow that ever a human being can go through. SHL. 24

The Bible reveals that death is inevitable—'and so death passed upon all men.' 'It is appointed unto men once to die.' Repeat that over to yourself. It is appointed to every one of us that we are going to cease to be as we are now, and the place that knows us now shall know us no more. We may shirk it, we may ignore it, we may be so full of robust health and spirits that the thought of death never enters, but it is inevitable. SHL. 25

DEBATE

If you debate for a second when God has spoken, it is all up. Never try and realize more clearly and say, 'I wonder if that is the Lord?' 'I wonder if He did speak?' Be reckless immediately, fling it all out to Him, and you will suddenly find it is the Lord, and that He has nourishment already prepared for you; and you may also find that He has a very searching thing to say to you. GW. 58

God never debates or argues. HG. 116

The battle comes when we begin to debate instead of obeying. We have to obey and leave all consequences with God. MFL. 31

Never debate when the Holy Spirit brings back a word of Jesus Christ. PR. 34

When I want to debate about doing what I know to be supremely right I am not in touch with God. RTR. 52

Human authority always insists on obedience; Our Lord never does. He makes His standard very clear, and if the relation of the spirit within me is that of love to Him, then I do all He says without any hesitation. If I begin to hesitate and to debate, it is because I love someone else in competition with Him, viz., myself. SSY. 87

DEBT/DEBTOR

As long as there is a human being who does not know Jesus Christ, I am his debtor until he does. RTR. 31

Thank God, when He has saved us, He does give us something to do, some way of expressing our gratitude to Him. He gives us a great noble sense of spiritual honour, the realization that we are debtors to every man because of the Redemption of Jesus Christ. The sense of our debt to Jesus is so overwhelming that we are passionately concerned for that brother, that friend, those unsaved nations; in relation to them we are the bondslaves of Jesus. SSY. 23

I realize with joy that I cannot live my own life; I am a debtor to Christ, and as such I can only realize the fulfilment of His purposes in my life. To realize this sense of spiritual honour means I am spoilt for this age, for this life, spoilt from every standpoint but this one, that I can disciple men and women to the Lord Jesus. SSY. 23

DELIVERANCE

. . . if you are not delivered from any particular element of sin, the reason is either you don't believe God can deliver you or you don't want Him to. Immediately you want Him to deliver you, the power of God is yours and it is done, not presently, but now, and the manifestation is wonderful. BE. 69

If Jesus Christ can keep me walking on the top of the waves, He can keep me underneath them. GW. 57

God does not deliver us gradually, but suddenly, it is a perfect deliverance, a complete emancipation. When the deliverance is realized, it is realized altogether, from the crown of your head to the sole of your foot, and your devotion to God is on account of that deliverance. It is a good thing to begin prayer with praising God for His attributes, and for the way those attributes have been brought to bear on our personal salvation. Let your mind soak in the deliverance of God, and then praise Him for them. HG. 26

Why our Lord said that self-pity was of the devil is that self-pity will prevent us appreciating God's deliverance. HG. 27

When we begin to say 'Why has this happened to me?' 'Why does poverty begin to come to me?' 'Why should this difficulty come, this upset?' it means that we are more concerned about getting our own way than in esteeming the marvellous deliverance God has wrought. HG. 27

When it comes to deliverance from sin, it is not a question of going to God to ask Him to deliver us from sin, it is a question of accepting His deliverance. If we forget that, we take the Lord out of the Atonement and make it an abstract statement and instantly do the Pharisaic dodge of putting burdens on people that they cannot bear. IYA. 85

DEPRAVITY

It is entire rightness with Jesus Christ alone that prevents elemental depravity working in the heart and out into deeds. If I trust Jesus Christ's diagnosis and hand over the keeping of my heart to Him, I need never know in conscious experience what depravity is, but if I trust in my innocent ignorance I am likely one of these days to turn a corner and find that what He said is true. OPG. 15

Instead of its being a sign of good taste, it is a sign of shocking unbelief when men won't face what Jesus Christ has put so plainly, so unmistakably plainly, so brutally plainly at times, about the human heart. OPG. 15

. . . if our desires and our thinking do not spring from the basis of a determined recognition of God, we are depraved, no matter what our experience spiritually. OPG. 16

DESIRE

The remarkable thing about the 'universe of desire' is that at any second it may alter. Every now and again a tumult comes into a man's life and alters what he desires. BE. 18

You see someone set on a line you know to be wrong, but remember, at any second the universe of his desire may change. To remember this will bring a tremendous hopefulness and cure us of our unbelief about any life. BE. 19

Desire is what you determine in your mind and settle in your heart and set yourself towards as good, and that is the thing God will fulfil if you delight in Him—that is the condition. BE. 49

I want to ask a very personal question— How much do you want to be delivered from? You say, 'I want to be delivered from wrong-doing'—then you don't need to come to Jesus Christ. 'I want to walk in the right way according to the judgement of men'—then you don't need Jesus Christ. But some heart cries out—'I want, God knows I want, that Jesus Christ should do in me all He said He would do.' How many of us 'want' like that? God grant that this 'want' may increase until it swamps every other desire of heart and life. GW. 22

When we are detached from things on the inside the fury of desire burns itself out. HGM. 111

DESPAIR

The basis of things is not reasonable, but wild and tragic, and to face things as they are brings a man to the ordeal of despair. BFB. 12

There is no son of man that need despair, Jesus Christ can reproduce His saving work in any and every man, blessed be the Name of God! BSG. 14

Despair is always the gateway of faith. HG. 76

To face ourselves with the standards of Jesus produces not delight, but despair to begin with; but immediately we get to despair we are willing to come to Jesus as paupers and to receive from Him. Despair is the initial gateway to delight in faith. SSY. 64

DESTINY

Our Christian destiny is to fulfil "the high calling of God in Christ Jesus." When a soul comes face to face with God, the eternal Redemption of the Lord Jesus is concentrated in that little microcosm of an individual life, and through the pinhole of that one life other people can see the whole landscape of God's purpose. HG. 105

Jesus Christ makes human destiny depend entirely upon a man's relationship to Himself. LG. 127

The majority of us keep taking in and forget altogether that somehow we must work out what we take in: we cannot elude our destiny, which is practical. MFL. 50

Our destiny as spiritual men and women is the same as our destiny as natural men and women, viz., practical, from which destiny there is no escape. MFL. 51

Beware of the fanaticism of self-denial, it will lead to error lasting in its effects. When we go off on that line we become devoted to our interpretation of our destiny. Destiny is never abstract. The destiny of a human being is vested in personal relationship to God. NKW. 48

Our destination is to be as God, that is what we are here to become, and in Jesus Christ we do become so. NKW. 58

God's destiny for a life will be fulfilled though the details of the fulfilment are determined by the individual. OPG. 38

No human being has a destiny like His; no human being can be a Saviour. There is only one Saviour, the Lord Jesus Christ, and the profundity of His agony has to do with the fulfilling of His destiny. PR. 85

Our destiny as His disciples is to be in fellowship with God as Jesus was. PR. 89

Our destiny is to work out what God works in. It is not that our eternal salvation depends upon our doing it, but our value to God does, and also our position in the Kingdom of God. PR. 91

DESTITUTION

Our Lord begins where we would never begin, at the point of human destitution. The greatest blessing a man ever gets from God is the realization that if he is going to enter into His Kingdom it must be through the door of destitution. Naturally we do not want to begin there, that is why the appeal of Jesus is of no use until we come face to face with realities; then the only One worth listening to is the Lord. We learn to welcome the patience of Jesus only when we get to the point of human destitution. It is not that God *will not* do anything for us until we get there, but that He *cannot*.
HGM. 16

When we come to the place of destitution spiritually we find the Lord waiting, and saying, "If any man thirst, let him come unto Me, and drink." There are hundreds at the place of destitution and they don't know what they want.
HGM. 16

The bedrock in Jesus Christ's kingdom is poverty, not possession; not decisions for Christ, but a sense of absolute futility—'I can't begin to do it.' That is the entrance; and it does take us a long while to believe we are poor. It is at the point of destitution that the bounty of God can be given. HGM. 17

When a man knows his destitution, knows he cannot get hold of God, cannot be the things he longs to be, he begins to realize what it was Jesus Christ came to do, viz., to supply what he really lacks. HGM. 108

To be willingly poor for God is to strip myself of all things for the sake of Jesus Christ. IWP. 58

DESTRUCTION

You will never find in the Bible that things are destroyed for the sake of destruction. Human beings destroy for the sake of destruction, and so does the devil; God never does, He destroys the wrong and the evil for one purpose only, the deliverance of the good. PS. 24

Our Lord reveals Himself as the destroyer of all peace and happiness and of ignorance, wherever these are the cloke for sin. PS. 24

It sounds a startling and amazing thing to say that Jesus did not come to send peace, but He said He did not. The one thing Jesus Christ is after is the destruction of everything that would hinder the emancipation of men. PS. 24

I can easily say I am not convicted of sin; but immediately I stand face to face with Jesus Christ I know the difference between Him and myself; I have no cloke and no excuse, and if I refuse to allow the Lord to deliver me from all that

He reveals, I shall be destroyed with the thing He came to destroy. "To this end was the Son of God manifested, that He might destroy the works of the devil." PS. 25

Sin must be destroyed, not corrected; it is the destruction of something in order to lead to emancipation. PS. 27

DETERMINATION

Determination means to fix the form of our choice, and God demands that we use this power when we pray. The majority of us waste our time in mere impulses in prayer. BP. 107

The marvel of the goodness of God is that He does so much for us; if we would only meet with physical obedience what God does for us spiritually, the whole of our body would be under such control that we should apprehend His meaning when He speaks. It is not a question of learning a thing outside but of determination inside. MFL. 80

DEVIL

The devil is the antagonist of God: Satan is the result of a relationship set up between man and the devil. BE. 62

"Resist the devil," not attack him. BSG. 29

Having "suffered being tempted" He knows how terrific are the onslaughts of the devil against human nature unaided; He has been there, therefore He can be touched with the feeling of our infirmities. CHI. 99

The downward look of eternal life is manifested by Our Lord—a fearless, clear-eyed, understanding look at sin, at death, and at the devil,—that is the un-mistakable characteristic of the downward look of our Lord. The devil's counterfeit is no sin, no hell and no judgment. HG. 112

In the Bible the devil is represented as the antagonist of Deity; Satan represents the self-interest of humanity. Our Lord's words "Get thee hence, Satan" refer to the interests of humanity in conflict with God's interests. HGM. 60

Jesus Christ never applied the words "children of the devil" to ordinary sinners, He applied them to religious disbelievers. IWP. 27

The devil is a bully, but he cannot stand for a second before God. IYA. 32

'I have asked God to bring out in me the graces of the Spirit, but every time the devil seems to get the better of me.' What you are calling 'the devil' is the very thing God is using to manifest the graces of the Spirit in you. LG. 97

The devil does not tempt us to do wrong things; he tries to make us lose what God has put into us by regeneration, the possibility of being of value to God. When we are born from above the central citadel of the devil's attack is the same in us as it was in our Lord—viz., to do God's will in our own way. PR. 63

Everything the devil does, God overreaches to serve His own purpose. RTR. 38

DEVOTION

Many of us only know devotee-ness to a creed, to a phase of evangelical truth, very few know anything about personal devotion to Jesus. HGM. 141

One life wholly devoted to God is of more value to God than one hundred lives simply awakened by His Spirit. MUH. 115

If the closest relationships of life clash with the claims of Jesus Christ, He says it must be instant obedience to Himself. Discipleship means personal, passionate devotion to a Person, Our Lord Jesus Christ. MUH. 184

There is a difference between devotion to a Person and devotion to principles or to a cause. Our Lord never proclaimed a cause; He proclaimed personal devotion to Himself. MUH. 184

If you are rightly devoted to Jesus Christ, you have reached the sublime height where no one thinks of noticing you, all that is noticed is that the power of God comes through all the time. NKW. 131

It is essential to go through a crisis with God which costs you something, otherwise your devotional life is not worth anything. You cannot be profoundly moved by nothing, or by doctrine; you can only be profoundly moved by devotion. NKW. 136

Anywhere the man who is devoted to Jesus Christ goes, Jesus Christ is there with him. RTR. 40

God engineers everything; wherever He puts us, our one great aim is to pour out a wholehearted devotion to Him in that particular work. "Whatsoever thy hand findeth to do, do it with thy might." RTR. 47

DIFFICULTY

Nothing is ever attained in the natural world without difficulty and the same thing applies in the spiritual world. BSG. 19

The bigger the difficulty, the more amazing is your profit to Jesus Christ as you draw on His supernatural grace. MFL. 74

DISCERNMENT

The characteristic of a man without the Spirit of God is that he has no power of perception, he cannot perceive God at work in the ordinary occurrences. The marvellous, uncrushable characteristic of a saint is that he does discern God. BP. 111

God never gives us discernment of what is wrong for us to criticize it, but that we might intercede. HG. 21

Discernment is the power to interpret what we see and hear. IWP. 42

The one great characteristic of being born from above is that I know Who Jesus is. It is a discernment; something has happened on the inside, the surgery of events has opened my eyes. LG. 117

Once let me obey God and I shall discern that I have no right to an attitude of mind to anyone other than His attitude. If I am determined to know the teaching of Jesus Christ at all costs, I must act on the intention that is stirred in me to do God's will, however humiliating it may be; and if I do, I shall discern. MFL. 25

Don't begin to work from your carnal suspicions—how many people mistake carnal suspicions for spiritual discernment! If God gives you a spirit of discernment, it is all right, there are times when He does, but I would like to warn you—never ask God to give you discernment. I have heard people ask God to give them the spirit of discernment, and I have felt constrained to say, 'Lord, lead that soul not into temptation.' WG. 55

DISCIPLE

To 'go forth unto Him without the camp, bearing His reproach,' does not mean going outside the worldly crowd; it means being put outside the religious crowd you belong to. One of the most poignant bits of suffering for a disciple comes along that line. BFB. 73

. . . it is only to the soul disciplined by suffering, by loneliness, and by Divine guidance, that "our Father's feet" appear among the dusty clouds. CD. VOL. 1, 49

You say you are called to be a missionary, a minister, a Christian worker: you are called to be a disciple of Jesus Christ, other things are *etceteras*. GW. 96

. . . a disciple is committed to much more than belief in Jesus; he is committed to his Lord's view of the world, of men, of God and of sin. HG. 64

If we were to estimate ourselves from our Lord's standpoint, very few of us would be considered disciples. HG. 71

If you are a disciple, be loyal to Him; that means you will have to choke off any number of things that might fritter you away from the one Centre. IWP. 125

To-day, as in the days of His flesh, men are being drawn to Jesus by their dominating sincerity, but human sincerity is not enough to make a man a disciple of Jesus Christ. LG. 109

The first thing a man needs is to be born into the Kingdom of God by receiving the Holy Spirit, and then slowly and surely be turned into a disciple. LG. 112

Our Lord never sent the disciples out on the ground that He had done something for them, but only on the ground that they had seen Him. LG. 115

The disciples did not understand what Jesus taught them in the days of His flesh; but His teaching took on new meaning when once they received the Holy Spirit. LG. 125

Our Lord's making of a disciple is supernatural. He does not build on any natural capacity at all. God does not ask us to do the things that are easy to us naturally; He only asks us to do the things we are perfectly fitted to do by His grace, and the cross will come along that line always. MUH. 269

If we are to be disciples of Jesus, we must be made disciples supernaturally; as long as we have the dead set purpose of being disciples we may be sure we are not. *"I have chosen you."* That is the way the grace of God begins. It is a constraint we cannot get away from; we can disobey it, but we cannot generate it. The drawing is done by the supernatural grace of God, and we never can trace where His work begins. MUH. 269

A disciple is one who has nothing but the new name written all over him; self-interest and pride have been erased entirely. OBH. 103

The one mark of a disciple is moral originality. The Spirit of God is a well of water in the disciple, perennially fresh. OBH. 104

Our Lord's last command was not—'Go and save men,' but—"Go and make disciples," we cannot make disciples of others unless we are disciples ourselves. PH. 132

The disciple realises that his Lord's honour is at stake in his life, not his own honour. PR. 106

The secret of a disciple is personal devotion to a personal Lord, and a man is open to the same charge as Jesus was, viz., that of inconsistency, but Jesus Christ was never inconsistent to God. SSM. 44

To be a disciple means to be a believer in Jesus—one who has given up his right to himself to the ownership of Christ. 'You must possess My nature in yourselves,' says Jesus, 'then go and preach in My Name'—in My nature. SSY. 146

The sovereign preference of the disciple's person must be for the Person of the Lord Jesus over every other preference. This preference for Him is first and last against all competition. SSY. 158

DISCIPLESHIP

Whenever Our Lord talked about discipleship He prefaced it with an 'IF,' never with an emphatic assertion 'You must.' Discipleship carries an option with it. AUG. 49

When we are young a hurricane or thunderstorm impresses us as being very powerful, yet the strength of a rock is infinitely greater than that of a hurricane. The same is true with regard to discipleship. The strength there is not the strength of activity but the strength of *being*. AUG. 123

The secret of discipleship is the Cross of Our Lord Jesus Christ. BSG. 23

To make disciples, then, we must have been made disciples ourselves. There is no royal road to sainthood and discipleship. The way of the Cross is the only way. We see God only from a pure heart, never from an able intellect. CD. VOL. 2, 113

One life straight through to God on the ground of discipleship is more satisfactory in His sight than numbers who are saved but go no further. CHI. 18

We never become disciples in crowds or even in twos; discipleship is always a personal matter. HGM. 124

There is no room in Our Lord's conception of discipleship for a disciple to say, 'Now, Lord, I am going to serve You.' That does not come into His idea of discipleship. It is not that we work for God, but that God works through us; He uses us as He likes, He allots our work where He chooses, and we learn obedience, even as our Lord did. HGM. 126

The call to discipleship comes as mysteriously as being born from above; once a man hears it, it profoundly alters everything. It is like the call of the sea, the call of the mountains, not everyone hears these calls, only those who have the nature of the sea or the mountains— and then only if they pay attention to the call. To hear the call of God or the call to discipleship necessitates education in understanding and discernment. HGM. 141

. . . the conditions of discipleship are not the conditions for salvation. We are perfectly at liberty to say, 'No, thank you, I am much obliged for being delivered from hell, very thankful to escape the abominations of sin, but when it comes to these conditions it is rather too much; I have my own interests in life, my own possessions.' IWP. 118

The first step to sacramental discipleship is the crowning of Jesus as Lord. PH. 137

Following Jesus Christ is a risk absolutely; we must yield right over to Him, and that is where our infidelity comes in, we will not trust what we cannot see, we will not believe what we cannot trace, then it is all up with our discipleship. SSM. 71

"If ye love Me, ye will keep My commandments." Jesus makes this the test of discipleship. The motto over our side of the gate of life is—'All God's commands I can obey.' SSM. 96

Discipleship is built not on natural affinities but entirely on the supernatural grace of God. The one characteristic of discipleship is likeness to Jesus Christ. SSY. 66

DISCIPLINE

God seems to delight to stir up our nests; it is not the devil who does it, but God; this is curiously unrecognized on our part. HG. 7

Our convictions and conscientious relationships have continually to be enlarged, and that is where the discipline of spiritual life comes in. HGM. 76

The discipline of negatives is the hardest discipline in the spiritual life, and if you are going through it you ought to shout 'Hallelujah,' for it is a sign that God is getting your mind and heart where the mind and heart of Jesus Christ was. IWP. 44

It is never God's will for us to be dummies or babies spiritually, it is God's will for us to be sons and daughters of God, but He does not prevent us paying the price of being sons and daughters. He makes us sons and daughters potentially, and then sends us out to be sons and daughters actually. IYA. 89

The sanctified saint is one who has disciplined the body into perfect obedience to the dictates of the Spirit of God, consequently his body does with the greatest of ease whatever God wants him to do. MFL. 39

The one thing for which we are all being disciplined is to know that God is real. As soon as God becomes real, other people become shadows. Nothing that other saints do or say can ever perturb the one who is built on God. MUH. 19

Jesus did not say that everyone must cut off the right hand, but—If your right hand offends you in your walk with Me, cut it off. There are many things that are perfectly legitimate, but if you are going to concentrate on God you cannot do them. Your right hand is one of the best things you have, but, says Jesus, if it hinders you in following His precepts, cut it off. This line of discipline is the sternest one that ever struck mankind. MUH. 181

We can all see God in exceptional things, but it requires the culture of spiritual discipline to see God in every detail. MUH. 319

God will not discipline us, we must discipline ourselves. God will not bring every thought and imagination into captivity; we have to do it. MUH. 323

God disciplines us by disappointment. Life may have been going on like a torrent, then suddenly down comes a barrier of disappointment, until slowly we learn that the disappointment was His appointment. PH. 84

The delays of Jesus discipline us while they continually tantalise us. PH. 219

It may be that in our inner life Jesus is teaching us by the disciplining force of His delays. 'I expected God to answer my prayer, but He has not.' He is bringing us to the place where by obedience we shall see what it is He is after. PH. 221

The reason for the need of discipline is that our bodies have been used by the wrong disposition, and when the new disposition is put in the old physical case is not taken away, it is left there for us to discipline and turn into an obedient servant to the new disposition. SSM. 35

When Jesus Christ has altered our disposition, we have to bring our body into harmony with the new disposition, and cause it to exercise the new disposition, and this can only be done by stern discipline, discipline which will mean cutting off a great many things for the sake of our spiritual life. SSM. 37

DISCIPLING

We don't go in for making disciples today, it takes too long; we are all for passionate evangelism—taken up with adding to the statistics of "saved souls," adding to denominational membership, taken up with the things which show splendid success. Jesus Christ took the long, long trail—"If any man will be My disciple, let him deny himself"—"Take time to make up your mind." CHI. 18

If I have been obeying the command of Jesus to 'go and make disciples,' I know what they want; they want Him. We are so interested in our own spiritual riches that souls that are white unto harvest are all around us and we don't reap one for Him. HGM. 17

Discipling is our work. When God's great redemptive work has issued in lives in salvation and sanctification, then the work of the worker begins. It is then that we find the meaning of being 'workers together with Him.' LG. 91

God saves men; we are sent out to present Jesus Christ and His Cross, and to disciple the souls He saves. The reason we do not make disciples is that we are not disciples ourselves, we are out for our own ends. SSY. 51

'Make disciples of all the nations.' That cannot be done unless Jesus Christ is Who He says He is. SSY. 160

There is no respect of persons with God, no respect of nations with God—here, there, anywhere and everywhere, wherever God likes to stir up your nest and fling you, disciple all the nations. WG. 88

DISCOURAGEMENT

Discouragement is disenchanted self-love, and self-love may be love of devotion to Jesus. My devotion to Jesus must altogether efface my consciousness of devotion to Him. GW. 79

If you are going through disenchantment, remember that is not the end, the end is the life which exhibits the spirit of Jesus—"I delight to do Thy will, O My God." HGM. 113

Discouragement is 'disenchanted egotism.' PH. 236

If you are going through a period of discouragement there is a big personal enlargement ahead. We have the stride of Divine Healing, of Sanctification, of the Second Coming; all these are right, but the stride of God is never anything less than union with Himself. PH. 236

If once a man knows in his own life that God can do what Jesus Christ said He could, he can never be put in the place where he will be discouraged. He may be put in the heart of the vilest and most terrible phases of heathenism, but he can never be discouraged, nor can he be defiled, because he has the very nature of God in him and he is kept like the light, unsullied. SSY. 78

We cannot be discouraged if we belong to Him, for it was said of Him—'he shall not fail nor be discouraged.' SSY. 170

DISILLUSIONMENT

If we get taken up with salvation or with holiness or Divine healing instead of with Jesus Christ, we will be disillusioned. HGM. 110

We pin our faith to a plan of salvation that can be expressed in words and we glory in it, then we begin to find it does not work and a curious disillusionment begins. HGM. 110

If I am taken up with the created things and forget Jesus Christ I shall find that things disappoint and I get disillusioned. HGM. 111

DISPOSITION

Jesus Christ makes no allowance for heroic moods; He judges us by the diligently applied bent of our disposition. BE. 21

The natural man is not in distress, not conscious of any disharmony in himself; he is not "in trouble as other men," and is quite content with being once-born; the things Jesus Christ stands for have no meaning for the natural man. The Bible refers to this disposition as one of darkness—". . . being darkened in their understanding." BE. 76

The Bible does not deal with sin as a disease; it does not deal with the outcome of sin, it deals with the disposition of sin itself. The disposition of sin is what our

Lord continually faced, and it is this disposition that the Atonement removes. BE. 116

Jesus Christ is our Saviour because He saves us from sin, radically altering the ruling disposition. Anyone who has been in contact with the Lord when He alters the ruling disposition knows it, and so do others. BE. 117

. . . through the Atonement there is perfect readjustment to God, perfect forgiveness, and the gift of a totally new disposition which will manifest itself in the physical life just as the old disposition did. BE. 117

To make the removal of the wrong disposition mean that God removes our *human nature* is absurd. God does remove the wrong disposition, but He does not alter our human nature. We have the same body, the same eyes, the same imperfect brain and nervous system, but Paul argues—you used to use this body as an obedient slave to the wrong disposition, now use it as an obedient slave to the new disposition. BP. 262

Jesus Christ came to do what no man can do for himself, viz., alter his disposition. HGM. 13

The disposition in us is either implanted naturally through the first Adam, or implanted supernaturally through the last Adam by regeneration and sanctification. IWP. 53

Jesus Christ gives the power of His own disposition to carry us through if we are willing to obey. That is why He is apparently so merciless to those of us who have received the Holy Spirit, because He makes His demand according to His disposition, not according to our natural disposition. LG. 121

The reason the Incarnation and the Atonement are not credible to some people is that their disposition is unregenerated. MFL. 24

When Our Lord faced men with all the forces of evil in them, and men who were clean living and moral and upright, He did not pay any attention to the moral degradation of the one or to the moral attainment of the other; He looked at something we do not see, viz., the disposition. MUH. 279

The disposition of sin is not immorality and wrong-doing, but the disposition of self-realization—I am my own god. This disposition may work out in decorous morality or in indecorous immorality, but it has the one basis, my claim to my right to myself. MUH. 279

Our destiny is determined by our disposition. Our Lord's destiny was determined by His disposition. Our destiny is preordained, but we are free to choose which disposition we will be ruled by. We cannot alter our disposition, but we can choose to let God alter it. If our disposition is to be altered, it must be altered by the Creator, and He will introduce us into a totally new realm by the miracle of His sovereign grace. Redemption means that Jesus Christ can give us a new disposition. At regeneration the Holy Spirit puts in us a totally new disposition, and as we obey that disposition the life of the Son of God will be manifested in our mortal flesh. PR. 88

The disposition of a man determines the way he will decide when the crisis comes, but the only One Who knows the disposition other than the man himself is God. PS. 45

The unaltered, natural disposition of a man is called by our Lord 'darkness,'

that means prejudice against the light. PS. 44

The natural is not sinful, neither is it spiritual; the ruling disposition of my personality makes it either sinful or spiritual. SHL. 83

Beware of refining away the radical aspect of our Lord's teaching by saying that God puts something in to counteract the wrong disposition—that is a compromise. Jesus never teaches us to curb and suppress the wrong disposition; He gives us a totally new disposition, He alters the mainspring of action. Our Lord's teaching can be interpreted only by the new Spirit which He puts in; it can never be taken as a series of rules and regulations. SSM. 29

A man cannot imitate the disposition of Jesus Christ: it is either there, or it is not. When the Son of God is formed in me, He is formed in my human nature, and I have to put on the new man in accordance with His life and obey Him; then His disposition will work out all the time. SSM. 29

DOCTRINE

Doctrine is expounded not by our intelligence, not by our searching, but by the indwelling of a completely new Spirit imparted to us by the Lord Jesus Christ. BE. 104

To be devoted to doctrines will twist us away from the Centre; devotion to Jesus Christ relates our doctrines to the one Centre, Jesus Christ. BSG. 64

The test of all doctrine is, does it produce a likeness to Jesus Christ? The final test is how a man's thinking works out in his life. BSG. 70

... don't try to be consistent to a doctrine or a creed, the Lord Jesus is the only One to whom you have to be consistent. GW. 111

Many have begun well but have gone off on doctrine, all their energy is spent furthering a cause, Jesus Christ is not the dominating ruler. NKW. 119

In dealing with all implicit things, such as love, there is a danger of being sentimentally consistent to a doctrine or an idea while the actual life is ignored; we forget that we have to live in this world as human beings. OPG. 43

Consistency in doctrine ought to work out into expression in actual life, otherwise it produces the humbug in us; we have the jargon of the real thing, but actually we are not there. OPG. 43

Anything that makes a man keep up a posture is not real; e.g., it is not true to say that an understanding of the doctrine of sanctification will lead you into the experience: doctrinal exposition comes after the experience in order to bring the actual life into perfect harmony with the marvel of the work of God's grace. OPG. 43

Never pin your faith to a doctrine or to anyone else's statement, get hold of God's Book, and you will find that your spiritual character determines exactly how God deals with you personally. PS. 79

DOOR

Have you been trying to make prayer, or faith, or the Bible, or experience, the Door? These may be ornaments about the Door, but the Door is the Lord Jesus Himself. Be absolutely loyal to Him. GW. 111

Learn to enter in by the Door until it becomes the ordinary attitude of your life and you will find pasture without hunting for it, it is there. It is never a confined place, but always a door. The world, the flesh and the devil cannot imprison you, it is a life of absolute freedom. GW. 112

The door is opened wide by a God of holiness and love, and any and every man can enter in through that door, if he will. "I am the way." Jesus Christ is the exclusive Way to the Father. IWP. 127

The door is always open to God until I shut it. God never shuts it; I shut it, then I lose the key and say, 'It's all up; whatever I do now God is entirely to blame.' OPG. 12

We enter into the life of Jesus by means of His death, that is our only door of entrance. We may try and batter through some other way if we choose—through Bethlehem, through the teachings of Jesus, but we cannot get in. Those ways in would produce frauds and humbugs. PR. 25

At His Ascension our Lord enters Heaven and keeps the door open for humanity. His Cross is the door for every member of the human race to enter into the life of God. PR. 118

DOUBT

A man ceases to be an honest doubter the moment he refuses one way of getting at the truth because he does not like that way. BSG. 61

If a man refuses to try the way Jesus Christ puts before him, he ceases from that second to be an honest doubter; he must try it and put Jesus Christ's teaching to the proof. A man cannot say he is an honest intellectual doubter if he refuses one way of getting at the truth; that is mental immorality. MFL. 21

How can anyone who is identified with Jesus Christ suffer from doubt or fear! It ought to be an absolute paeon of perfectly irrepressible, triumphant belief. MUH. 318

When you really see Jesus, I defy you to doubt Him. MUH. 359

To refuse to try a line Jesus Christ points out because I do not like it, shuts my mouth as an honest doubter. I must try it and see if it works. SA. 34

Some people seem to think it is an amazingly clever thing to doubt Jesus Christ; it is an evil thing. Whenever the evil personality of unbelief asked the Lord anything, He never answered; but when the heart cries out, He answers immediately. SHL. 59

DUTY

It is never your duty to go the second mile, to give up your possessions or property to someone else, but Jesus says if we are His disciples, that is what we will do. BE. 26

'No! equal duties, but not equal rights.' We all have equal duties to perform towards God, but not equal rights. BP. 203

. . . if you are a disciple of Jesus Christ, you will always do more than your duty, you will always be doing something equivalent to 'going the second mile.' People say, 'What a fool you are!' BP. 204

Once we become rightly related to God, duty will never be a disagreeable thing of which we have to say with a sigh, 'Oh, well, I must do my duty.' Duty is the daughter of God. MFL. 90

The direction of duty lies not in doing things for God, but in doing what God tells us to do, and God's order comes to us in the haphazard moments. We do not make the haphazard moments, God is the arranger of the haphazard. The direction of duty is loyalty to God in our present circumstances. NKW. 119

We know very little about devotion to Jesus Christ. We know about devotion to right and to duty, but none of that is saintly, it is purely natural. My sense of duty and of right can never be God's. If I can state what my duty is, I have become my god in that particular. There is only One Who knows what my duty is as a Christian, and that is God. NKW. 140

Be renewed in the spirit of your mind, says Paul, not that you may do your duty, but that you may make out what God's will is. NKW. 140

As God's children we are never told to walk in the light of conscience or of a sense of duty; we are told to walk in the light of the Lord. PH. 114

E

EARNESTNESS

Earnestness in prayer is often put in the place of right relationship to God.
SHH. 137

Prayer is never heard on the ground of earnestness, but only on the ground of the Redemption. SHH. 137

Most of us make the blunder of depending upon our own earnestness and not on God at all, it is confidence in Jesus that tells. SSM. 59

God is never impressed by our earnestness; we are not heard because we are in earnest, but on the ground of Redemption only. We have "boldness to enter into the holiest *by the blood of Jesus,*" and by no other way. SSM. 60

EARTH

In God's sight the land has rights just as human beings have, and many of the theories which are being advanced today go back to God's original prescription for the land. BE. 24

The world and the earth are not the same; the world represents the societies of men on God's earth, and they do as they like; the earth remains God's. "Blessed are the meek: for they shall inherit the earth." The meek bide God's time. BE. 37

Earth is man's domain, but the Bible talks about a 'hereafter' without the sin and iniquity, "a new heaven and a new earth." We are going to be here, marvellously redeemed, in this wonderful place which God made very beautiful, and which has been played havoc with by sin. LG. 27

"The first man is of the earth, earthy." This is man's glory, not his shame, because it is in a creature made of the earth that God is going to manifest His glory. We are apt to think that being made of the earth is our humiliation, but it is the very point that is made much of in God's word. PR. 12

To Jesus the earth was His Father's house, and His Father's concerns possessed His imagination. PR. 46

Sin, according to the Bible, is man taking his right to himself, and thereby he lost his lordship over the air and earth and sea. The only Being who ever walked this earth and was Lord of earth and air and sea as God designed man to be, was Jesus Christ. SA. 115

ECSTASY

Esctasy is a word applied to states of mind marked by temporary mental aberration and altered consciousness, a state in which a man is taken out of his ordinary setting into an extraordinary state where he sees and hears things apart from the bodily organs. Remember, this power may be for good or bad. A necromancer can take a man's personality right out of his bodily setting and put him into another setting where he sees

73

and hears altogether apart from his body. BP. 255

Never give way to spiritual ecstasy unless there is a chance of working it out rationally, check it every time. IWP. 33

Ecstasy of spirit leads to external ritual in the rational life, and makes the bodily life spend its time in dreaming. IWP. 35

Beware of being carried off into any kind of spiritual ecstasy either in private or in public. There is nothing about ecstasy in [this verse]: "Thou shalt love the Lord thy God with all thy heart"— the sovereign preference of our personality for God. IWP. 89

The security of the position into which God brings His saints is such that the life is maintained without ecstasy. There is no place for ecstasy and manifestations in a normal healthy spiritual life. MFL. 32

There are certain phases of the life of faith which look so much like cant and humbug that we are apt to grieve God's Spirit by our religious respectability in regard to them, and ecstasy is just one of those phases. An ecstasied man is one whose state of mind is marked by mental alienation from his surroundings, and his very consciousness is altered into excessive joy. These states are open gateways for God or for the devil. NKW. 68

Ecstasy is not a state in which to live; keep your ecstatic times dark. You have no business to show the depths to anyone but yourself and God. NKW. 68

Every time we have transacted business with God on His covenant and have let go entirely on God, there is no sense of merit in it, no human ingredient at all, but such a complete overwhelming sense of being a creation of God's that we are transfigured by peace and joy. NKW. 70

EDUCATION

There are no experts in spiritual matters as there are in scientific matters. The spiritual expert is never so consciously because the very nature of spiritual instruction is that it is unconscious of itself; it is the life of a child, manifesting obedience, not ostentation. "Whosoever therefore shall humble himself as this little child, the same is greatest in the kingdom of heaven." BFB. 45

Education is for the purpose of behaviour, and habits are the stuff out of which behaviour is formed. BE. 57

As we go in the spiritual life the Spirit of God educates us down to the scruple, that is, He applies the commandments of God to all the ramifications of our being. HGM. 135

In every civilised country we are told that if we will educate the people and give them better surroundings, we shall produce better characters. Such talk and such theories stir aspirations, but they do not work out well in reality. The kingdom within must be adjusted first before education can have its true use. To educate an unregenerate man is but to increase the possibility of cultured degradation. No one would wish to belittle the lofty attainments of education and culture, but we must realise we have to put them in their high, mighty, second place. Their relationship in human life is second, not first. PH. 3

EGOISM

Of egoism only good things can be said. It is that system of thinking which makes the human personality the centre. The thinking that starts from all kinds of abstractions is contrary to the Bible. The Bible way of thinking brings us right straight down to man as the centre. That which puts man right and keeps man right is the revelation we have in God's Book. BP. 151

Everything in the Bible is related to man, to his salvation, to his sanctification, to his keeping, etc. Any system of thinking which has man for its centre and as its aim and purpose is rightly called Egoism. BP. 152

ELECTION (PREDESTINATION)

The call of God is not for the special few, it is for everyone. Whether or not I hear God's call depends upon the state of my ears; and what I hear depends upon my disposition. "Many are called but few are chosen," that is, few prove themselves the chosen ones. MUH. 14

"I have chosen you." Keep that note of greatness in your creed. It is not that you have got God but that He has got you. MUH. 299

'Ye did not choose me, but I chose you.' That is always the way the grace of God begins to work, it is a constraint we cannot get away from. We can disobey it, but we cannot generate it. The drawing power is the supernatural grace of God, and we can never trace where that work begins. We have to choose to obey, and He does all the rest. SSY. 64

The connection between the election of God and human free will is confusing to our Gentile type of mind, but the connection was an essential element underlying all Hebrew thought. The predestinations of God cannot be experienced by individuals of their own free

choice; but when we are born again, the fact that we do choose what has been predestined of God comes to us as a revelation. The rationalist says it is absurd to imagine that the purposes of Almighty God are furthered by an individual life, but it is true. God's predestinations are the voluntary choosing of the sanctified soul. SSY. 102

EMANCIPATION

Emancipation means deliverance while I am in the flesh, not counteraction or suppression; it may begin in counteraction, but blessed be God, emancipation is possible here and now. BP. 261

Emancipation does not remove the possibility of disobedience; if it did, we should cease to be human beings. BP. 261

We have been dealing with the emancipation of spirit from slavery of sin, now we come to the Bible teaching that the spirit can operate through our senses, so that we can express in our lives that we are delivered; no 'reckoning' or hoodwinking ourselves, no pretending we are emancipated when we are not, but the manifestation through every cell of our bodies that God has done what we testify with our mouth He has done. BP. 262

When any sinful man accepts morally the verdict of God on sin in the cross of Christ, he becomes emancipated. PS. 74

A moral decision is different from a mental decision, which may be largely sentiment. A moral decision means— 'My God, I accept Thy verdict against sin on the cross of Jesus Christ, and I want the disposition of sin in me identified with His death'—immediately a man gets there, all that we understand by the Holy Ghost working in His tremendous power through the Redemption takes place, and the emancipation of humanity is furthered. PS. 74

EMOTION

Very often you will find that God paralyses your emotional nature and allows you to feel nothing, it is a sure sign that He is guiding, because your life has been too full of emotions you have not been working out. BE. 73

The sovereign emotions are guided and controlled by love, but bear in mind that love in its highest moral meaning is the preference of one person for another person. A Christian's love is personal passionate devotion to Jesus Christ, and he learns to grip on the threshold of his mind as in a vice every sentiment awakened by wrong emotions. BE. 73

God holds the saints responsible for emotions they have not got and ought to have as well as for the emotions they have allowed which they ought not to have allowed. BE. 73

If we indulge in inordinate affection, anger, anxiety, God holds us responsible; but He also insists that we have to be passionately filled with the right emotions. The emotional life of a Christian is to be measured by the exalted energy exhibited in the life of our Lord. BE. 73

If we have no emotional life, then we have disobeyed God. "Be filled with the Spirit"; it is as impossible to be filled with the Spirit and be free from emotion as it is for a man to be filled with wine and not show it. BE. 74

We must be thrilled, and if human nature does not get its thrills from the right place, it will take them from the wrong. Enthusiasm means, to use the phrase of a German mystic, 'intoxicated with God,' filled to overflowing with God; no spasmodic spirituality about us, but a perennial source of freshness, making us a delight to our Lord, and a channel of blessing to all with whom we come in contact. GW. 68

Emotion is not simply an overplus of feeling, it is life lived at white-heat, a state of wonder. HG. 33

It is easier to be swayed by emotions than to live a life shot through with the Holy Spirit, a life in which Jesus is glorified. LG. 121

A sentimentalist is one who delights to have high and devout emotions stirred whilst reading in an arm-chair, or in a prayer meeting, but he never translates his emotions into action. MFL. 13

. . . a sentimentalist is usually callous, self-centred and selfish, because the emotions he likes to have stirred do not cost him anything, and when he comes across the same things in the domain where things are real and not sentimental, the revenge comes along the line of selfishness and meanness, which is always the aftermath of an unfulfilled emotion. MFL. 13

The higher the emotion, the purer the desire, the viler is the revenge in the moral character unless the emotion is worked out on its right level. MFL. 14

Always do something along the line of the emotion that has been stirred; if you do not, it will corrupt that which was good before. The curbing of the outward action revenges itself in a meaner disposition on the inside, and the higher the religious emotion, the more appalling is the reaction unless it is worked out on its own level. MFL. 14

Every emotion must express itself, and if it is not expressed on the right level, it will react on a lower level; and the higher the emotion, the more degraded the level on which it will react. MFL. 56

You have no business to harbour an emotion the outcome of which you can see to be bad; if it is an emotion to be generous, then *be* generous, or the emotion will react and make you a selfish brute. SA. 72

ENEMY

We are apt to forget that the enemy is unseen and that he is supernatural. GW. 98

The enemies of the Cross of Christ, whom Paul characterizes so strongly, and does it weeping, are those who represent the type of things that attract far more than Jesus Christ. IWP. 102

We have not to wait for some great onslaught of the enemy, he is here all the time and he is wily. The secret of the sacred struggle for prayer lies in the fact that we must stand in the armour of God, practising what God would have us do, then we can hold the position of prayer against all the attacks of the devil. IYA. 33

Never try to be right with an abstract enemy, but get right with the enemy you have got. It is easy to talk about loving the heathen; never go off on the abstract. The direction of Divine living is that I have to be as kind to others as God has been to me, not the others I have not met, but those I have met. PH. 66

It is never wise to under-estimate an enemy. We look upon the enemy of our souls as a conquered foe; so he is, but only to God, not to us. RTR. 58

The love of God is manifested in that He laid down His life for His enemies, something no man can do. SA. 16

. . . the fundamental revelation of the New Testament is that God redeemed the whole human race when they were spitting in His face, as it were. SA. 16

Jesus Christ makes us flesh-and-blood dreadnoughts. Not all the power of the enemy can fuss or turn aside the soul that is related to God through the Atonement. SHL. 28

The love of God is revealed in that He laid down His life for His enemies, and Jesus tells us to love our fellow-men as God has loved us. SSM. 51

"I say unto you, Love your enemies." Jesus does not say, 'Love every one.' The Bible never speaks vaguely, it always speaks definitely. People speak about loving 'mankind,' and loving 'the heathen'; Jesus says, "Love your enemies." Our Lord does not say, '*Bless* your enemies,' He says, '*Love* your enemies.' He does not say, '*Love* them that curse you'; He says, '*Bless* them that curse you.' '*Do good* to them that hate you,'—not *bless* them. He does not say, '*Do good* to them that despitefully use you'; He says, '*Pray* for them that despitefully use you.' Each one of these commands is stamped with sheer impossibility to the natural man. If we reverse the order Jesus has given it can be done with strain, but kept in His order I defy any man on earth to be able to do it unless he has been regenerated by God the Holy Ghost. SSM. 52

ENVIRONMENT

There is a difference between circumstances and environment. We cannot control our circumstances, but we are

the deciders of our own environment.
NKW. 21

Environment is the element in our circumstances which fits the disposition. A man convicted of sin and a man in love may be in the same external circumstances, but the environment of the one is totally different from that of the other. NKW. 21

Our environment depends upon our personal reaction to circumstances. 'Circumstances over which I have no control' is a perfectly true phrase, but it must never be made to mean that we cannot control ourselves in those circumstances. NKW. 21

EUCHARIST

The ordinance of the Lord's Supper is not a memorial of One Who has gone, but of One Who is always here. PS. 30

EVIL

Every now and again when you look at life from a certain angle it seems as if evil and wrong and legalized iniquity are having it all their own way and you feel that everything must go to pieces; but it doesn't, around it is the sovereignty of God, 'Hitherto shalt thou come, but no further.' Blessed be the Name of God, evil shall not ultimately triumph!
GW. 101

"If ye then being evil . . . ". Jesus Christ is made to teach the opposite of this by modern teachers; they make out that He taught the goodness of human nature.
HG. 87

It is not only necessary to have an experience of God's grace, we must have a body of beliefs alive with the Spirit of Jesus, then when we have learned to see

men as He sees them, there is no form of disease or anguish or devilishness that can belch up in human life that can disturb our confidence in Him; if it does disturb us, it is because we don't know Him. HG. 88

Note what causes you the deepest concern before God. Does social evil produce a deeper concern than the fact that people do not believe on Jesus Christ? It was not social evil that brought Jesus Christ down from heaven, it was the great primal sin of independence of God that brought God's Son to Calvary.
HG. 107

EVOLUTION

Evolution means a gradual working out or development. There is a difference between natural evolution and spiritual evolution: in natural evolution we do not know the final goal; in spiritual evolution the goal is given before the start—". . . till we all come in the unity of the faith . . . unto a perfect man, unto the measure of the stature of the fulness of Christ." BE. 42

Devotion to the ephemeral scientific doctrine of evolution is responsible for the endeavour to make out that the Bible means a period of years instead of a solar day. The particular unparabolic use of the term "morning and evening" in Genesis distinctly indicates a solar day. BP. 7

God's order is seen in the first and the last; the middle is the record of man's attempt to arrange things in his own way. Man is to be again in the image of God, not by evolution, but by Redemption.
CHI. 15

When Thought is young, life looks simple, so does History, and man's explanation is correspondingly simple and glib. 'Evolution' is the name given in our day to this young and ill-considered outlook—it is all a simple and obvious method of growth and development; to talk about the Fall is absurd, and any conception that does not recognize that the world is getting better, is discarded. GW. 88

People talk about the evolution of the race. The writers of to-day seem to be incapable of a profound understanding of history, they write glibly about the way the race is developing, where are their eyes and their reading of human life as it is? We are not evolving and developing in any sense to justify what is known as evolution. We have developed in certain domains but not in all. We are nowhere near the massive, profound intellectual grasp of the men who lived before Christ was born. What brain to-day can come near Plato, or Socrates? And yet people say we are developing and getting better, and we are laying the flattering unction to our souls that we have left Jesus Christ and His ideas twenty centuries behind. No wonder Jesus said that if we stand by Him and take His point of view, men will hate us as they hated Him. HG. 65

The New Testament does not say that the human race is evolving, but that the human race is a magnificent ruin of what it was designed to be. SA. 14

EXAMPLE

In presenting the life of Jesus Christ we are not presenting an example, but an historic Fact essential to our soul's salvation. BSG. 46

When the testimony and the 'Hallelujah' are followed by the following of His steps in example, then comes the tre-

mendous flow of the power of God wherever you go. GW. 97

Our Lord builds His deepest teaching on the instinct of emulation. When His Spirit comes in He makes me desire not to be inferior to Him Who called me. Our example is not a good man, not even a good Christian man, but God Himself. By the grace of God I have to emulate my Father in heaven. "Be ye therefore perfect, even as your Father which is in heaven is perfect." MFL. 71

It is easy to put up our Lord as an Example, but according to the New Testament He is much more. He is the Redeemer, One who can reproduce His own life in us. PR. 18

Jesus Christ did not live and die to be our Example only, but that He might put us in the place where He is by means of His wonderful Atonement. Reverence your own body and soul and spirit for this one purpose, and reverence everyone else's, for the same purpose. SHL. 77

Woven into our Lord's Divine rule of life is His reference to our Example. Our Example is not a good man, not even a good Christian man, but God Himself. We do not allow the big surprise of this to lay hold of us sufficiently. Jesus nowhere says, 'Follow the best example you have, follow Christians, watch those who love Me and follow them'; He says, 'Follow your Father which is in heaven'—that you may be good men? That you may be lovable to all men? No, 'that ye may be the children of your Father which is in heaven,' and that implies a strong family likeness to Jesus Christ. SSM. 51

EXPECTATION

When once expectation is killed out of the heart, we can scarcely walk, the feet become as lead, the very life and power goes, the nerves and everything begin to fall into decay. The true nature of a man's heart according to the Bible is that of expectation and hope. MFL. 47

When our Lord sympathises with the heart broken by sin or sorrow, He binds it up and makes it a new heart, and the expectation of that heart ever after is from God. MFL. 47

The expectation of the heart must be based on this certainty: "In all the world there is none but thee, my God, there is none but thee." Until the human heart rests there, every other relationship in life is precarious and will end in heartbreak. MFL. 47

There are unexpected issues in life; unexpected joys when we looked for sorrow, and sorrow when we expected joy, until we learn to say 'all my expectations are from Thee.' PH. 84

EXPERIENCE

Experience is the gateway through which salvation comes into our conscious life, the evidence of a right relationship to Jesus Christ. Never preach experience, preach the great thought of God that lies behind. People stagnate because they never get beyond the image of their experiences into the life of God which transcends all experience. Jesus Christ Himself is the Revelation, and all our experiences must be traced back to Him and kept there. AUG. 47

The standard for Christian experience is not the experience of another Christian, but God Himself. "Be ye therefore perfect, even as your Father which is in heaven is perfect." 'If you are My disciple,' says Jesus, 'the standard by which

you are to measure your experiences as a regenerated saint is the character of God.' BFB. 89

. . . there are facts revealed in God's Book which are not common to our experience, and a great moment is reached in the mental life when our minds are opened to the fact that there are states of experience, either for good or bad, about which the majority of us know nothing. It is easy to ridicule these experiences, but ridicule may be a sign of ignorance; it may simply mean—I know everything that everybody can experience, and if a man says he has seen things I have not seen, then I take him to be a fool and laugh at him. It is I who am the fool. BP. 254

We must distinguish between the revelation of Redemption and the experience of regeneration. We don't *experience* life; we are alive. We don't *experience* Redemption; we experience the life of God coming into our human nature, and immediately the life of God comes in it produces a surface of consciousness, but Redemption means a great deal more than a man is conscious of. CHI. 9

Experiences are apt to be exalted out of all due measure whereas they are but the outward manifestation of the oneness with God made possible for us in Christ Jesus. DI. 17

Get into the habit of chasing yourself out of the sickly morbid experiences that are not based on having been with Jesus; they are not only valueless, but excessively dangerous. DI. 13

The great bedrock of Christian experience is the outside fact of the Resurrection made inwardly real by the incoming of the Holy Spirit. DI. 17

Our identity with Jesus Christ is immediately practical or not at all, that is, the new identity must manifest itself in our mortal flesh otherwise we can easily hoax ourselves into delusions. Being "made the righteousness of God in Him" is the most powerfully practical experience in a human life.   DI. 17

My experience of salvation never constitutes me an expounder of the Atonement. I am always apt to take my experience for an inclusive interpretation instead of its being merely a gateway for *me* into salvation.   DI. 18

We continually want to present our understanding of how God has worked in our own experience, consequently we confuse people. Present Jesus Christ, lift Him up, and the Holy Spirit will do in them what He has done in you.   DI. 18

Beware of making your religious experiences a cloak for a lack of reality.   DI. 19

Would to God we got finished once for all with the experience of being adjusted to God, and let Him send us forth into vicarious service for Him!   DI. 19

Our Lord makes no divisions such as conversion, regeneration, sanctification, He presents the truth in nugget form and the apostles beat out the nuggets into negotiable gold, it is in their writings that we have the stages of experience worked out.   HGM. 16

I do not *experience* God; I relate all my experiences to the revelation of God which Jesus Christ has made.   HGM. 147

The experiences of salvation and sanctification spring from the perfect Source, and it is this that gives the devil his chance to come as an angel of light and make us seek experiences instead of Christ.   IWP. 11

Satan does not tempt saints to tell lies or to steal or drink, he does not come to them in that way; he comes along the line of their experiences, he seeks to separate Christian experience from the Lord Jesus and make us want to hug a certain type of experience for ourselves.   IWP. 11

To those who have had no spiritual experience it sounds absurd to talk about being one with God in Christ, absurd to talk about being guided by the Spirit, they are impatient with it; of course they are, they must be made part of the Perfect (i.e. be born from above) before they can understand the language of the Perfect in experience.   IWP. 12

We need to receive the Holy Spirit, not only for Christian experience but to bring us into perfect union with God.   IWP. 13

Beware of the subtle danger that gets hold of our spiritual life when we trust in our experience. Experience is absolutely nothing if it is not the gateway only to a relationship. The experience of sanctification is not the slightest atom of use unless it has enabled me to realize that that experience means a totally new relationship.   IWP. 85

If we think only along the line of our experience we become censorious, not humble. Sanctification is the gateway to a sanctified life, not to boasting about an experience.   MFL. 103

There are phases of God's truth that cannot be experienced, and as long as we stay in the narrow grooves of our experience we shall never become God-like, but specialists of certain doctrines—

Christian oddities. We have to be specialists in devotion to Jesus Christ and in nothing else. MFL. 110

One of the touchstones of experience is—Has God altered the thing that matters? If you still hanker after the old things, it is absurd to talk about being born from above, you are juggling with yourself. MUH. 317

Whenever there is the experience of fag or weariness or degradation, you may be certain you have done one of two things—either you have disregarded a law of nature, or you have deliberately got out of touch with God. NKW. 37

When the Bible records facts of experience, look in your own experience for the answer; when the Bible reveals standards of revelation, look to God, not to experience. NKW. 89

'I can live beautifully in my own little religious bandbox.' That is not Christian experience. We have to face the whole of life as it is, and to face it fearlessly. OBH. 92

The difficulty of Christian experience is never in the initial stages. Experience is a gateway, not an end. OBH. 93

Beware of any experience that does not wed itself to the words of Jesus. Experience is simply the doorway into the great revelation of Jesus Christ. OBH. 121

Experience is never the ground of our confidence; experience is the opening of the door to a new life which must be continued in. Some of us are continually having doors opened, but we will not go through them. *Don't slack off,* keep on with the thing which you have learned. OBH. 125

The Holy Ghost working in me does not produce wonderful experiences that make people say 'What a wonderful life that man lives'; the Holy Ghost working in me makes me a passionate, devoted, absorbed lover of the Lord Jesus Christ. PH. 30

Experience is a gateway to understanding, not an end in itself. PH. 82

God wants to get us into the place where He holds absolutely, and experiences never bother us. Oh, the relief of it! The burden gone, the effort gone, no conscious experience left, because Jesus Christ is All and in All. PH. 83

The average preaching of the Gospel deals mainly with the scenic cases, with people who have gone through exceptional experiences. None of the early disciples had had these exceptional experiences; they saw in Jesus Christ what they had never seen before—a Man from another realm, and they began to long after what He stood for. PR. 12

We so continually run down the revelations of the New Testament to the level of our own experience. That is wrong; we must let God lift up our experience to the standard of His word. PR. 52

We must beware of estimating God's salvation by our experience of it. Our experience is a mere indication in conscious life of an almighty salvation which goes far beyond anything we ever can experience. SHL. 54

Never push an experience you have had into a principle by which to guide others. SSY. 59

EXPRESSION

The value of a spiritual teacher is that he expresses for us what we have been trying to express for ourselves but could not. Whenever a person or a book expresses for us what we have been trying to express for ourselves, we feel unspeakably grateful, and in this way we learn how to express for ourselves. BP. 247

Tribulation will teach us how to express things, our circumstances will teach us, temptations of the devil will teach us, difficult things will teach us. All these things will develop the power of expression until we become responsible in expression of the Spirit of God as Jesus Christ was the responsible expression of the mind of God Almighty. BP. 247

Beware of saying there is no difference in the external life of a person who is born again and one who is sanctified. It is untrue to revelation and to experience alike; there is a tremendous difference. The spirit in a born again person does not express itself in the flesh in the same degree that it does when the point of sanctification has been reached, because the body has not yet learned obedience to God. BP. 249

Expression is always unconscious. "His name shall be in their foreheads"— where everyone can see it saving the man himself. PH. 173

There is a snare in being able to talk about God's truth easily because frequently that is where it ends. If we can express the truth well, the danger is that we do not go on to know more. Most of us can talk piously, we have the practice but not the power. SSM. 39

EXTRAVAGANCE

When we begin to try to economize, God puts dry rot in us instantly. I don't care what line the economy takes, it produces dry rot. When we have the lavish hand, there is munificence at once. "There is that scattereth, and increaseth yet more; and there is that withholdeth more than is meet, but it tendeth only to want." HG. 40

Extravagance is the only line for the religious man. We do not believe this to begin with, we are so completely reasonable and common sense, consequently we base everything on self-realisation instead of on Christ-realisation. SHH. 142

Our attitude is that if we are extravagant a rainy day will come for which we have not laid up. You cannot lay up for a rainy day and justify it in the light of Jesus Christ's teaching. SHH. 143

F

FACTS

Facing facts as they are produces despair, not frenzy, but real downright despair, and God never blames a man for despair. BFB. 12

Face facts. Very few of us will face facts, we prefer our fictions. Our Lord teaches us to look things full in the face and He says: 'When you hear of wars and disturbances, do not be scared.' It is the most natural thing in the world to be scared. There is no natural heart of man or woman that is not scared by these things, and the evidence that God's grace is at work amongst us is that we do not get terrified. CD VOL. 1, 110

God does not thunder His truth into our ears, our attitude of mind must be submissive to revelation facts. Each one of us brings certain prejudices, civilized pre-judgments, which greatly hinder our understanding of revelation facts. DI. 6

You cannot deal with facts as you like, you may object to them, but a fact is a fact, whether a common-sense fact or a revelation fact. DI. 19

Facts in the natural domain have to be accepted, and facts in the revelation domain have to be accepted; our explanation of facts is always open to alteration, but you cannot alter facts. The Bible does not simply explain to us the greatest number of facts, it is the only ground of understanding *all* the facts, that is, it puts into the hand of the Spirit-born the key to the explanation of all mysteries. GW. 70

We must distinguish between an accurate fact and a truthful fact. The devil, sin, disease, spiritualism, are all accurate facts, but they are not truthful facts. MFL. 85

You never get at God by blinking facts, but only by naming Him in the facts; whether they are devilish or not, say, 'Lord, I thank Thee that Thou art here.' OPG. 33

The Bible is the universe of revelation facts; the natural world is the universe of common-sense facts, and our means of communication with the two universes is totally different. PR. 20

When we come to the universe of the Bible, the revelation facts about God, intellectual curiosity is not of the slightest use. Our senses are no good here, we cannot find out God by searching. We may have inferences from our common-sense thinking which we call God, but these are mere abstractions. We can only get at the facts that are revealed in the Bible by faith. PR. 20

Jesus Christ is a revelation fact, sin is another, the devil is another, the Holy Spirit is another. Not one of these is a common-sense fact. If a man were merely a common-sense individual, he could do very well without God. PR. 20

The domain in which Jesus Christ lives is the domain of Bible facts. PR. 20

You cannot prove facts; you have to swallow them. PS. 77

It is much easier not to look at the facts of life but to take an intellectual view which acts as a searchlight, and has the tyranny of an idea or an intuition. A man's intellectual view reveals what it does and no more, everything looks simple in the light of it; but when we come to the daylight of facts we shall find something that knocks the bottom board out of all our calculations. SHH. 124

FAITH

Many of us have no faith in God at all, but only faith in what He has done for us, and when these things are not apparent we lose our faith and say, 'Why should this happen to Me?' BFB. 101

The basis of spiritual construction is implicit faith in Jesus Christ. If I stake all on His astute Mind I will find I have struck bedrock. The majority of us only believe in Jesus Christ as far as we can see by our own wits. BE. 49

"Faith claims the whole man and all that God's grace can make him," just as it claimed the whole of our Lord's life. CHI. 51

You may ask for faith to further orders, but you will never have faith apart from Jesus Christ. CHI. 60

Faith means that I commit myself to Jesus, project myself absolutely on to Him, sink or swim—and you do both, you sink out of yourself and swim into Him. CHI. 60

In the face of problems as they are, we see in Jesus Christ an exhibition of where our faith is to be placed, viz., in a God whose ways we do not understand. DI. 12

To think of what Jesus is to us always encourages our faith; if we begin with our obedience, our faith gets paralysed. GW. 13

We make it hard for people—'Do this and that,' and they obey and nothing happens. We have left out altogether the receiving of Christ Jesus the Lord; personal relationship to Jesus Christ first, then faith comes naturally. GW. 15

If my faith in the Redemptive work of Christ does not react in a practical life which manifests it, the reason is a wrong temper of mind in me. HG. 101

Nowadays the tendency is to switch away from "the righteousness which is of God by faith," and to put the emphasis on doing things. You cannot do anything at all that does not become, in the rugged language of Isaiah, "as filthy rags," if it is divorced from living faith in Jesus Christ. If we have the tiniest hankering after believing we can be justified by what we have done, we are on the wrong side of the Cross. HG. 108

It is in the sphere of humiliation that we find our true worth to God, and that is where our faithfulness has to be manifested. LG. 54

No one is surprised over what God does when once he has faith in Him. LG. 149

Faith gets us into the middle, which is God and God's purpose. MFL. 64

The life of faith is not a life of mounting up with wings, but a life of walking and not fainting. It is not a question of sanctification; but of something infinitely further on than sanctification, of faith that has been tried and proved and has stood the test. MUH. 79

Believe steadfastly on Him and all you come up against will develop your faith. MUH. 242

Faith is unutterable trust in God, trust which never dreams that he will not stand by us. MUH. 242

Every time you venture out in the life of faith, you will find something in your common-sense circumstances that flatly contradicts your faith. Common sense is not faith, and faith is not common sense; they stand in the relation of the natural and the spiritual. MUH. 242

Faith in antagonism to common sense is fanaticism, and common sense in antagonism to faith is rationalism. The life of faith brings the two into a right relation. MUH. 304

Faith in the Bible is faith in God against everything that contradicts Him—I will remain true to God's character whatever He may do. "Though He slay me, yet will I trust Him"—this is the most sublime utterance of faith in the whole of the Bible. MUH. 305

We have the idea that God rewards us for our faith, it may be so in the initial stages, but we do not earn anything by faith, faith brings us into right relationship with God and gives God His opportunity. God has frequently to knock the bottom board out of your experience if you are a saint in order to get you into contact with Himself. God wants you to understand that it is a life of *faith*, not a life of sentimental enjoyment of His blessings. MUH. 305

Faith by its very nature must be tried, and the real trial of faith is not that we find it difficult to trust God, but that God's character has to be cleared in our own minds. MUH. 305

Faith that is sure of itself is not faith; faith that is sure of God is the only faith there is. MUH. 356

Faith never knows where it is being led, it knows and loves the One Who is leading. It is a life of *faith*, not of intelligence and reason, but a life of knowing Who is making me 'go.' NKW. 11

Until we get through all the shivering wisdom that will not venture out on God, we will never know all that is involved in the life of faith. NKW. 13

If we are going to live a life of faith, we must rest nowhere until we see God and know Him in spite of all apparent contradictions. NKW. 13

We must remember that faith in God always demands a concession from us personally. NKW. 17

There is nothing more heroic than to have faith in God when you can see so many better things in which to have faith. NKW. 45

The sure sign that we have no faith in God is that we have no faith in the supernatural. NKW. 66

Weak faith chooses the visible things instead of enduring as seeing Him Who is invisible, and slowly and surely such faith settles down between mammon and righteousness. NKW. 82

Faith in antagonism to common sense is fanaticism, and common sense in antagonism to faith is rationalism. The life of faith brings the two into right relationship. No one can solve the difficulty of making them one for me, I must do it for myself, and I can only solve it by life not by thinking, just as the natural can only be made spiritual in life, not in thinking. NKW. 107

... faith must prove itself by the inward concession of its dearest objects, and in this way be purified from all traditional and fanatical ideas and misconceptions. NKW. 112

We are apt to say that religion is religion, and business is business; but there is no cleavage in the life of faith. NKW. 136

The whole discipline of the life of faith is to make the ideal visions of faith and the actual performance of life one in personal possession. Only one Being can enable us to make the ideal and the actual one in personal life, viz., the Holy Spirit. NKW. 142

If we have been born from above of the Spirit of God, the deep craving of our hearts is to be as holy as Jesus Christ, and just as we took the first step in salvation by faith, so we take the next step by faith. OBH. 19

There is no such thing as a *venture* of faith, only a determined *walk with God* by faith. OPG. 19

I don't believe God unless He will give me something in my hand whereby I may know I have it, then I say, 'Now I believe.' There is no faith there. "*Look unto Me*, and be ye saved," God says. OPG. 25

If you stick stedfastly, not to your faith, but to the One Who gives you the faith, there is a time coming when your whole way of being impressed, and your reasoning, will be made clear to your own satisfaction. PH. 206

Faith is more than an attitude of mind, faith is the complete, passionate, earnest trust of our whole nature in the Gospel of God's grace as it is presented

in the Life and Death and Resurrection of our Lord Jesus Christ. RTR. 35

If we have faith at all it must be faith in Almighty God; when He has said a thing, He will perform it; we have to remain steadfastly obedient to Him. RTR. 39

Bank your faith in God, do the duty that lies nearest and "damn the consequences." SHH. 74

If you stand true to your faith in God, there will be situations in which you will come across extortioners, cunning, crafty people, who use their wits instead of worshipping God, and you will appear a fool. Are you prepared to appear a fool for Christ's sake? SHH. 83

Most of us are pagans in a crisis; we think and act like pagans, only one out of a hundred is daring enough to bank his faith in the character of God. SSM. 67

FAITH, TRIAL OF

Fortitude in trial comes from having the long view of God. No matter how closely I am imprisoned by poverty, or tribulation, I see "the land that is very far off," and there is no drudgery on earth that is not turned Divine by the very sight. CHI. 86

Faith must be tried, and it is the trial of faith that is precious. If you are fainthearted, it is a sign you won't play the game, you are fit for neither God nor man because you will face nothing. NKW. 36

Faith is not logical, it works on the line of life and by its very nature must be tried. Never confound the trial of faith with the ordinary discipline of life. Much that we call the trial of our faith is

the inevitable result of being alive.
NKW. 117

When we have become rightly related to God, it is the trial of our faith that is precious. OBH. 21

When we go through the trial of faith we gain so much wealth in our heavenly banking account, and the more we go through the trial of faith the wealthier we become in the heavenly regions. OBH. 103

To walk with God means the perpetual realization of the nature of faith, viz., that it must be tried or it is mere fancy; faith un-tried has no character-value for the individual. OPG. 18

There is nothing akin to faith in the natural world, defiant pluck and courage is not faith; it is the *trial* of faith that is "much more precious than of gold," and the trial of faith is never without the essentials of temptation. OPG. 18

It is the trial of our faith that is precious. 'Hang in' to Jesus Christ against all odds until He turns your spiritual beliefs into real possessions. PH. 44

The thing that is precious in the sight of God is faith that has been tried. Tried faith is spendable; it is so much wealth stored up in heaven, and the more we go through the trial of our faith, the wealthier we become in the heavenly regions. PH. 83

Faith must be tried or it is not faith, faith is not mathematics nor reason. Scriptural faith is not to be illustrated by the faith we exhibit in our common-sense life, it is trust in the character of One we have never seen, in the integrity of Jesus Christ, and it must be tried.
PH. 204

It is a great thing to see physical pluck, and greater still to see moral pluck, but the greatest to see of all is spiritual pluck, to see a man who will stand true to the integrity of Jesus Christ no matter what he is going through. PH. 205

FALL

In thinking about the world we are apt to overlook the greatest factor of all from the Bible standpoint, viz., that man belongs to a fallen race. In our intellectual conceptions the Fall has no place at all; the human race is looked upon as a crowd of innocent babes in the wood.
BE. 33

The Bible indicates that everything which partakes of the curse through the Fall will be restored by God's mighty Redemption; nothing will be lost. BP. 45

FANATICISM

A fanatic is one who entrenches himself in invincible ignorance. BFB. 41

If a man has never gone through a spell of fanaticism it is because he is not prepared to cut off anything in order to get at reality. It is essential to be maimed for a while in order to develop our life with God. HGM. 111

Fanaticism is the insane sign of a sane relationship to God in its initial working. The joy of the incoming grace of God always makes us fanatical. IWP. 105

What the world calls fanaticism is the entrance into Life. SSM. 55

We are so afraid of being fanatical; would to God we were as afraid of being 'fushionless.' We should a thousand times rather be fanatical in the beginning than poor 'fushionless' creatures all our lives, limp and useless. SSM. 55

Always make allowances for people when they first enter into Life, they have to enter on the fanatical line. The danger is lest they stay too long in the stage of fanaticism. When fanaticism steps over the bounds, it becomes spiritual lunacy. SSM. 55

FASTING

If I want to see the Face of God I must fast from other things and concentrate on God. HGM. 112

Fasting means concentration. SSM. 61

FATE

No man has a fate portioned out to him; a man's disposition makes what people call his fate. HG. 32

Fate means stoical resignation to an unknown force. NKW. 13

FEAR

The greatest fear a Christian has is not a personal fear, but the fear that his Hero won't get through, that God will not be able to clear His character. BFB. 14

There is no need to fear, if we keep within the moral frontiers of God we can say boldly, "The Lord is my helper." HG. 31

The remarkable thing about fearing God is that when you fear God you fear nothing else, whereas if you do not fear God you fear everything else. HG. 42

There is never any fear for the life that is hid with Christ in God, but there is not only fear, but terrible danger, for the life unguarded by God. IWP. 41

"Perfect love casteth out fear," but to say "therefore will we not fear, though the earth be removed . . ." is only possible when the love of God is having its way. RTR. 62

. . . we all know men who say they are not afraid, but the very fact that they say it, proves they are. SSM. 42

FEELING

If you are living a life right with God, you will have feeling, most emphatically so, but you will never run the risk of basing your faith on feelings. BE. 70

By Redeemed Experience is meant eternal life manifested in the fleeting moments of temporal life. What is *not* meant is the consciousness of feeling good, or the consciousness of the presence of God. If we mistake these feelings for eternal life, we shall be disillusioned sooner or later. HG. 110

Watch every time you get to a tight feeling spiritually, to a dry feeling rationally, to a hindered feeling physically, it is the Spirit of God's quiet warning that you should repair to the heavenly places in Christ Jesus. IWP. 40

FELLOWSHIP

"If we walk in the light, as God is in the light," we have fellowship with everyone else who is in the light. BE. 31

In the discipline of fellowship God always makes us go first as apprentices. He gives us comrades and leaders and guides whom we depend upon up to a certain stage, then there comes the experience of going alone. GW. 122

Until we get into fellowship with God His suggestions are no good to us. When people are intimate with one another suggestions convey more than words, and when God gets us into oneness with Himself we recognize His suggestions. NKW. 125

The fellowship of the disciples is based not on natural affinities of taste but on fellowship in the Holy Ghost, a fellowship that is constrained and enthralled by the love and communion of our Lord and Saviour Jesus Christ. PH. 12

FOLLOWING

We are not called to follow in all the footsteps of the saints, but only in so far as they followed their Lord. The great meaning of following is that we imitate as children, not as monkeys. LG. 62

It does sound vague to say 'be followers of God,' but when we realize that Jesus Christ is the life of God, then we know where we are. He is the One Whom we have to imitate and follow, but we must first of all be born again and receive His Spirit, and then walk in the Spirit. LG. 62

If Jesus Christ is the life of God and we have to follow Him, we must find out what His joy was. It certainly was not happiness. LG. 63

We do not know where our 'Jerusalem' is, but we have to go up to it, and the only way to go up to it is not by trying to find out where it is, but by being followers of God's life. LG. 68

We are to follow Jesus Christ down here in the actual world where there is any amount of impurity, but we have this hope, that "we shall be like Him," consequently we purify ourselves. LG. 72

When Jesus Christ says 'Follow Me,' He never says to where, the consequences must be left entirely to Him. NKW. 12

FORGETTING

The surest test of maturity is the power to look back without blinking anything. When we look back we get either hopelessly despairing or hopelessly conceited. The difference between the natural backward look and the spiritual backward look is in what we forget. Forgetting in the natural domain is the outcome of vanity—the only things I intend to remember are those in which I figure as being a very fine person! Forgetting in the spiritual domain is the gift of God. The Spirit of God never allows us to forget what we have been, but He does make us forget what we have attained to, which is quite unnatural. The surest sign that you are growing in mature appreciation of your salvation is that as you look back you never think now of the things you used to bank on before. CHI. 86

Forgetting in the Divine mind is an attribute, in the human mind it is a defect, consequently God never illustrates His Divine forgetfulness by human pictures, but by pictures taken from His own creation—'As far as east is from the west, so far hath He removed our transgressions from us.' 'I have blotted out, as a thick cloud, thy transgressions, . . .' The reason God never uses the human illustration is that a human being is incapable of forgiving as God does until he is made like God through regeneration. GW. 10

FORGIVENESS

Forgiveness is the Divine miracle of grace. AUG. 47

Have we ever contemplated the amazing fact that God through the Death of Jesus Christ forgives us for every wrong we have ever done, not because we are sorry, but out of His sheer mercy? God's forgiveness is only natural in the supernatural domain.   AUG. 47

There is no such thing as God overlooking sin, therefore if He does forgive there must be a reason that justifies Him in doing so.   BE. 32

A man has to clear the conscience of God in forgiving him.   BE. 63

The forgiveness of a child of God is not placed on the ground of the Atonement of our Lord, but on the ground that the child of God shows the same forgiveness to his fellows that God his Father has shown to him.   CD. VOL. 2, 28

The marvel of conviction of sin, of forgiveness, and of the holiness of God are so interwoven that the only forgiven man is the holy man. If God in forgiving me does not turn me into the standard of the Forgiver, to talk about being saved from hell and made right for heaven is a juggling trick to get rid of the responsibility of seeing that my life justifies God in forgiving me.   CHI. 26

When once a man receives the humiliating conviction that he has broken God's law, and is willing to accept on God's terms the gift of forgiveness and of a new life, he will find he is brought to the place where he can live a holy life in order to vindicate God in forgiving him. This is evangelical repentance, and it is fundamentally different from the reformation which springs from remorse awakened by an overweening self-respect.   GW. 85

We reason in this way: 'God is so loving that I know He will forgive me.' God is so holy that it is much more likely He will say I must be damned.   HG. 105

God can forgive a man anything but despair that He can forgive him.   HGM. 65

Repentance means that we recognize the need for forgiveness—'hands up, I know it.'   HGM. 101

When God forgives a man He gives him the heredity of His own Son, and there is no man on earth but can be presented 'perfect in Christ Jesus.' Then on the ground of the Redemption, it is up to me to live as a son of God.   HGM. 102

Jesus Christ did not say '*because* we forgive our debtors,' but "*as* we forgive our debtors," that is, as children of God we are forgiven not on the ground of Redemption, but on the ground that we show the same forgiveness to our fellows that God has shown to us. 'For if ye forgive men their trespasses, your heavenly Father will also forgive you: but if ye forgive not men their trespasses, neither will your Father forgive your trespasses."   HGM. 102

God's method in forgiveness is exactly the method of our forgiveness, and is according to our human sense of justice.   HGM. 103

We may forgive easily, because we are shallow, but when we are deeply roused, we cannot forgive unless our sense of justice is satisfied.   HGM. 103

. . . the forgiveness of God does not work unless we turn; it cannot, any more than it does according to human justice.   HGM. 104

It would be an immoral thing to forgive a man who did not say he was sorry. If a man sins against you and you go to him and point out that he has done wrong— if he hears you, then you can forgive him; but if he is obstinate you can do nothing; you cannot say 'I forgive you,' you must bring him to a sense of justice. HGM. 104

I cannot forgive my enemies and remain just unless they cease to be my enemies and give proof of their sorrow, which must be expressed in repentance. I have to remain stedfastly true to God's justice. There are times when it would be easier to say 'Oh well, it does not matter, I forgive you,' but Jesus insists that the uttermost farthing must be paid. HGM. 104

The love of God is based on justice and holiness, and I must forgive on the same basis. HGM. 104

The distinctive thing about Christianity is forgiveness, not sanctification or my holiness, but forgiveness—the greatest miracle God ever performs through the Redemption. HGM. 105

By means of the Redemption God undertakes to deal with a man's past, and He does it in two ways—first, He forgives it, and then He makes it a wonderful culture for the future. HGM. 105

Forgiveness means not merely that a man is saved from sin and made right for heaven—no man would accept forgiveness on such a level; forgiveness means that I am saved from sinning and put into the Redeemer to grow up into His image. HGM. 105

Forgiveness is the miracle of grace; it is impossible for human beings to forgive, and it is because we do not see this that we misunderstand the revelation of forgiveness. HGM. 105

When God says 'Don't do that any more,' He instils into me the power that enables me not to do it any more, and the power comes by right of what Jesus Christ did on the Cross. That is the unspeakable wonder of the forgiveness of God, and when we become rightly related to God, we are to have the same relationship to our fellow men that God has to us. "And be ye kind one to another, tenderhearted, forgiving one another, even as God for Christ's sake hath forgiven you." HGM. 105

Beware of the pleasant view of the Fatherhood of God—God is so kind and loving that of course He will forgive us. That sentiment has no place whatever in the New Testament. The only ground on which God can forgive us is the tremendous tragedy of the Cross of Christ; to put forgiveness on any other ground is unconscious blasphemy. The only ground on which God can forgive sin and reinstate us in His favour is through the Cross of Christ, and in no other way. MUH. 325

When once you realize all that *it cost God to forgive you*, you will be held as in a vice, constrained by the love of God. MUH. 325

If God does forgive sin, it is because of the Death of Christ. God could forgive men in no other way than by the death of His Son, and Jesus is exalted to be Saviour because of His death. MUH. 326

Never build your preaching of forgiveness on the fact that God is our Father and He will forgive us because He loves us. It is untrue to Jesus Christ's revelation of God; it makes the Cross unnecessary, and the Redemption "much ado about nothing." MUH. 326

If God were to forgive me my sin without its being atoned for, I should have a greater sense of justice than God. PH. 183

Forgiveness does not mean merely that I am saved from sin and made right for heaven; forgiveness means that I am forgiven into a recreated relationship to God. PH. 184

When God forgives, He never casts up at us the mean, miserable things we have done. "I have blotted out, as a thick cloud, thy transgressions, and, as a cloud, thy sins." A cloud cannot be seen when it is gone. PH. 224

I have no right to say that I believe in forgiveness as an attribute of God if in my own heart I cherish an unforgiving temper. The forgiveness of God is the test by which I myself am judged. RTR. 38

If I am forgiven without being altered by the forgiveness, forgiveness is a damage to me and a sign of the unmitigated weakness of God. SA. 19

Jesus Christ's revelation is the forgiveness of God, and the tremendous miracle of Redemption is that God turns me, the unholy one, into the standard of Himself, the Forgiver, by the miracle of putting into me a new disposition. The question up to me is—"Do I want Him to do it?" SA. 19

The great thing up to God is that in forgiving me He has to give me the heredity of His Son. God Himself has answered the problem of sin and there is no man on earth but can be presented "perfect in Christ Jesus." SA. 28

God's conscience means He has to forgive completely and finally redeem the human race. SA. 28

The point about Christian forgiveness is not that God puts snow over a dung-heap, but that He turns a man into the standard of the Forgiver. SA. 28

FREEDOM/LICENSE

If you have taken on you the vows of God, never be surprised at the misery and turmoil that come every time you turn aside. Other people may do a certain thing and prosper, but you cannot, and God will take care you do not. There is always one fact more known only to God. AUG. 68

True liberty is the ability earned by practice to do the right thing. There is no such thing as a gift of freedom; freedom must be earned. BE. 25

Spiritually, liberty means the ability to fulfil the law of God, and it establishes the rights of other people. BE. 25

We are called to present liberty of conscience, not liberty of view. If we are free with the liberty of Christ, others will be brought into that same liberty—the liberty of realizing the dominance of Jesus Christ. MUH. 127

License is the rebellion against all law— 'I will do what I like and care for no one'; liberty is the ability to perform the law, there is no independence of God in my make-up. SSM. 34

FREE WILL

Our Lord's attitude to the human will is not that frequently presented to-day; He never says that a man must make vows and decisions. 'Decisions for Christ' fail, not because men are not in earnest, but because the bedrock of Christianity is left out. The bedrock of Christianity is not strength of will, but the realization of my inability to decide: if I am ever going to be what Jesus Christ wants me to be, He must come in and do it, I am an abject pauper morally and spiritually. Fundamental free will is never possible, if it were our vowing would be omnipotent, we could do as we liked. GW. 141

The only thing that gives a personality freedom of will is the salvation of Jesus Christ. IWP. 91

The subject of human free will is apt to be either understated or overstated. No man has the power to act an act of pure, unadulterated, free will. God is the only Being Who can act with absolute free will. MFL. 27

The Bible reveals that man is free to choose, but it nowhere teaches that man is fundamentally free. MFL. 27

Man is free to choose in so far as no human force can constrain him against his will. MFL. 27

When the Holy Spirit comes into a man, He brings His own generating will power and makes a man free in will. MFL. 28

Will simply means the whole nature active, and when the Holy Spirit comes in and energizes a man's will, he is able to do what he never could do before, viz., he is able to do God's will. MFL. 28

Within certain limits we have the power to choose, for instance, a man has the power to refuse to be born again, but no man has absolute free will. There comes a time when the human will must yield allegiance to a force greater than itself. PR. 89

FRETTING

Fretting springs from a determination to get our own way. MUH. 186

FRIEND

There is always an intangible something which makes a friend, it is not what he does, but what he is. BFB. 65

The friendships and gifts of the world are perfectly sincere, but the saint soon realizes that these friendships and gifts are embarrassing and hindering if he is to remain loyal to God. NKW. 28

Never confound 'Saviour' with 'friend,' Our Lord said 'Ye are My friends' to His disciples, not to sinners. NKW. 72

When once the relationship of being the friends of Jesus is understood, we shall be called upon to exhibit to everyone we meet the love He has shown to us. Watch the kind of people God brings across your path, you will find it is His way of picturing to you the kind of person you have been to Him. OBH. 109

There is a time in spiritual life when God does not seem to be a friend. Everything was clear and easily marked and understood for a while, but now we find ourselves in a condition of darkness and desolation. PH. 95

"Greater love hath no man than this, that a man lay down his life for his friends," has nothing to do with Christianity; an atheist will do this, or a blackguard, or a Christian; there is nothing divine about it, it is the great stuff that human nature is made of. SA. 16

FRUIT

The way to test men, Jesus says, is "by their fruit." We say that the fruit of the Spirit has altogether to do with the spiritual, but the Bible reveals that the spiritual must show itself in the physical. BP. 51

The fruit of pseudo-evangelism is different from "the fruit of the Spirit." DI. 25

The seed is the word of God, and no word of God is ever fruitless. If I know that the sowing is going to bring forth fruit, I am blessed in the drudgery. Drudgery is never blessed, but drudgery can be enlightened." HG. 36

Our Lord tells us to judge the preacher or the teacher "by his fruits." Fruit is not the salvation of souls, that is God's work; fruit is "the fruit of the Spirit," love, joy, peace, etc. LG. 46

The way Jesus dealt with the disciples is the way He deals with us. He surrounded the disciples with an atmosphere of His own life and put in seed thoughts, that is, He stated His truth, and left it to come to fruition. LG. 124

The fruit of the Spirit is the exact expression of the disposition of Jesus. PH. 173

We cannot pretend to have the fruit of the Spirit if we have not; we cannot be hypocritical over it. PH. 173

Jesus tells His disciples to test preachers and teachers by their fruit. There are two tests—one is the fruit in the life of the preacher, and the other is the fruit of the doctrine. The fruit of a man's own life may be perfectly beautiful, and at the same time he may be teaching a doctrine which, if logically worked out, would produce the devil's fruit in other lives. It is easy to be captivated by a beautiful life and to argue that therefore what that life teaches must be right. Jesus says, 'Be careful, test your teacher by his fruit.' The other side is just as true, a man may be teaching beautiful truths and have magnificent doctrine while the fruit in his own life is rotten. We say that if a man lives a beautiful life, his doctrine must be right; not necessarily so, says Jesus. Then again we say because a man teaches the right thing, therefore his life must be right; not necessarily so, says Jesus. Test the doctrine by its fruit, and test the teacher by his fruit. SSM. 98

The way fruit remains is by prayer. Our Lord puts prayer as the means to fruit-producing and fruit-abiding work; but, remember, it is prayer based on His agony, not on our agony.
SSY. 126

G

If we are ever going to come anywhere near understanding what our Lord's agony in the Garden of Gethsemane represents, we have to get beyond the small ideas of our particular religious experiences and be brought to see sin as God sees it—"For He hath made *Him to be sin* for us, *who knew no sin;* that we might be made the righteousness of God in Him." DI. 65

It was not the death on the cross that Jesus feared in Gethsemane; He stated most emphatically that He came on purpose to die. In Gethsemane He feared lest He might not get through as Son of Man. He would get through as Son of God—Satan could not touch Him there; but Satan's onslaught was that He would get through as an isolated Figure only; and that would mean that He could be no Saviour. MUH. 96

Our Lord, as Son of Man, has been through the depths of His agony in Gethsemane, and He has won at every point. He has won for the bodies of men, He has won for the minds and souls of men and for the spirits of men; everything that makes up a human personality is redeemed absolutely, and no matter whether a man be a vile sinner or as clean as the rich young ruler, he can enter into the marvellous life with God through the way made by the Son of Man. PR. 94

Consecrating natural gifts is popular but a snare. AUG. 89

'I have the gift of a voice and I will consecrate it to God and sing "Always, only, for my King."' If a man or woman is devoted to God, they can sing anything with the blessing of God; but if they are not right they may sing "Take my life," and serve the devil in doing it. It is not the external things that tell, but the ruling disposition. There is no indication in God's Word that we should consecrate natural gifts, although we find many such indications in hymns. The only thing we can consecrate is our bodies. If we consecrate them to God, He takes them. AUG. 90

If you feel remarkably generous, then be generous at once, act it out; if you don't, it will react and make you mean. BE. 73

We have to distinguish between acquiring and receiving. We *acquire* habits of prayer and Bible reading, and we *receive* our salvation, we *receive* the Holy Spirit, we *receive* the grace of God. We give more attention to the things we acquire; all God pays attention to is what we receive. Those things we receive can never be taken from us because God holds those who receive His gifts. DI. 25

The idea of receiving anything as a gift from God is staggeringly original; we imagine we have to earn things by prayer and obedience. HGM. 14

The Gift of God is the Son of God; the gift from the Gift of God is the Holy Spirit. HGM. 15

. . . the only sign that a particular gift comes from the risen Christ is that it edifies the Church. Nothing else is of any account, no flights of imagination, no spiritual fancies, only one thing is of account, viz., the building up of men and women in the knowledge of the Lord. HGM. 26

The majority of us are not in the place where God can give us 'the hundredfold more.' We say, "A bird in the hand is worth two in the bush," while God is wanting to give us the bush with all the birds in it! It is necessary to be detached from things and then come back to them in a right relationship. HGM. 111

We have to get rid altogether of the idea that our gifts are ours, they are not, gifts are gifts, and we have to be so given over to God that we never think of our gifts, then God can let His own life flow through us. IWP. 44

Gifts are *gifts*, not graces. IWP. 44

The continual demand to consecrate our gifts to God is the devil's counterfeit for sanctification. MFL. 106

When a man is born again, he knows that it is because he has received something as a gift from Almighty God and not because of his own decision. MUH. 10

We have the notion that we can consecrate our gifts to God. You cannot consecrate what is not yours; there is only one thing you can consecrate to God, and that is your right to yourself. If you will give God your right to yourself, He will make a holy experiment out of you. God's experiments always succeed. MUH. 165

We have to realize that we cannot earn or win anything from God; we must either receive it as a gift or do without it. The greatest blessing spiritually is the knowledge that we are destitute; until we get there Our Lord is powerless. He can do nothing for us if we think we are sufficient of ourselves, we have to enter into His Kingdom through the door of destitution. As long as we are rich, possessed of anything in the way of pride or independence, God cannot do anything for us. It is only when we get hungry spiritually that we receive the Holy Spirit. MUH. 333

What do we do to earn a gift? Nothing; we take it. If we have the slightest remnant of thinking we can earn it, we will never take it; if we are quite certain we do not deserve it, we will take it. OBH. 22

The only thing I can give to God is 'my right to myself.' If I will give God that, He will make a holy experiment out of me, and God's experiments always succeed. OBH. 104

There is always an amazed surprise when we find what God brings with Him when He comes, He brings everything! OPG. 41

Watch your motive for giving presents; it is a good way of discerning what a mean sneak you are capable of being. The giving of presents is one of the touchstones of character. If your relationship with God is not right in your present-giving, you will find there is an abomination of self-interest in it somewhere, even though you do it out of a warm-hearted impulse; there is a serpent-insinuation in it. It creeps into all our charity unless the life is right with God. OPG. 59

God and His promises are eternal. "The gift *of God* is eternal life." PH. 76

The right to ourselves is the only thing we have to give to God. We cannot give our natural possessions, because they have been given to us. If we had not our right to ourselves by God's creation of us, we should have nothing to give, and consequently could not be held responsible. PR. 102

. . . our reason for giving is not to be because men deserve it, but because Christ tells us to give. SHH. 141

As long as we have something to give, we must give. How does civilisation argue? "Does this man deserve that I should give to him?" "If I give that man money, I know what he will do with it." Jesus Christ says, *"Give to him that asketh thee,"* not because he deserves it, but *"because I tell you to."* SHH. 141

The greatest motive in all giving is Jesus Christ's command. SSM. 47

. . . in our Lord's day the Pharisees made a tremendous show of giving; they gave from a play-acting motive, that they might "have glory of men." They would put their money in the boxes in the women's court of the Temple with a great clang which sounded like a trumpet. Jesus tells us not to give in that way, with the motive to be seen of men, to be known as a generous giver, for "Verily I say unto you, They have their reward," that is all there is to it. SSM. 56

The kindness and the generosity of God is known when once we come under the shadow of His hand. We may kick if we like or fume, and the fingers hurt; but when we stop kicking, the fingers caress. SSY. 109

GLOSSALALIA

"For if I pray in an unknown tongue, my spirit prayeth, but my understanding is unfruitful . . ." The question of tongues here is not a question of foreign languages, but what is called 'glossalalia,' i.e., spiritual gibberish, nothing intelligible in it. Such phrases as 'Hallelujah!' and 'Glory be to God!' come about in this way. Just as a baby 'blethers' for expression before its human spirit has worked through its soul, so a soul when being born of the Holy Ghost is apt to be carried away with emotional ecstasy. Try and understand a baby's blether, you cannot, unless you are its mother, then possibly you may. BP. 264

'If you don't watch what you are doing, this will produce disgraceful mockery among the nations. If they come into your meetings and see you jabbering, you will give an occasion to the enemy to blaspheme'. In the modern Tongues movement the responsibility is with the teachers. May God have mercy on them! BP. 265

"When the day of Pentecost was fully come . . . they were all filled with the Holy Ghost, and began to speak with other tongues, as the Spirit gave them utterance." This was not 'glossalalia,' it was the gift of new language. BP. 266

GOD

Is the essential nature of Deity omniscience, omnipotence and omnipresence? The essential nature of Deity is holiness, and the power of God is proved in His becoming a Baby. That is the staggering proposition the Bible gives—God became the weakest thing we know. AUG. 81

The term 'the Fatherhood' of God is rarely used nowadays in the New Testament sense, it is only used in the sense of God as Creator, not in the sense that Jesus Christ used it; the consequence is great havoc is produced in our Lord's teaching. If God is our Father by creation in the sense Jesus says He is by the experience of regeneration, then the Atonement is nonsense. BE. 103

God is the only Being who can afford to be misunderstood; we cannot, Job could not, but God can. BFB. 28

If God is only a creed or a statement of religious belief, then He is not real . . . BFB. 36

The revelation given by Jesus Christ of God is not the revelation of Almighty God, but of the essential nature of Deity—unutterable humility and moral purity, utterly worthy in every detail of actual life. BFB. 98

God is a Person, and He expresses the peculiar stamp of His Person in all that He creates. When we have the Spirit of God and are forming a responsible intelligence spiritually, we begin to think God's thoughts after Him and to see His meaning, not by our natural intelligence, but by the Spirit of God. BP. 249

The first sign of the dethronement of God is the apparent absence of the devil and the peaceful propaganda that is spread abroad. The great cry to-day is 'Be broad; accommodate yourself with evil so diplomatically that the line of demarcation is gone. Run up the white flag, say to the prince of this world, "We have been too puritanical in the past, there has been too clear a division between us, now we will go arm-in-arm."' BSG. 33

I know no other God in Time or Eternity than Jesus Christ; I have accepted all I know of God on the authority of the revelation He gave of Him. CHI. 46

God's ways are "past finding out!" We often state the character of God in terms of brutal harshness while our motive is to glorify Him. DI. 12

Never attempt to explain God to an exasperated soul, because you cannot. Don't take the part of Job's friends and say you can explain the whole thing; if you think you can, you are very shallow. You have to take on the attitude of vicarious waiting till God brings the light. DI. 13

Never accept an explanation of any of God's ways which involves what you would scorn as false and unfair in a man. DI. 16

If I enthrone anything other than God in my life, God retires and lets the other god do what it can. HG. 29

Any interest that would induce me away from the shadow of the Almighty is to be treated as a snare. Resolutely treat no one seriously but God. "The Lord is *my* rock, and *my* fortress, and *my* deliverer, *my* God, *my* strong rock . . . *my* shield, and the horn of *my* salvation, *my* high tower." Note the 'my's' here, and laugh at everything in the nature of misgiving for ever after! HG. 114

My conception of God must embrace the whole of my life. HGM. 108

When I see the Lord truly I see Him as God of my whole being; if He is only God in sections of me, He is not God at all. HGM. 108

We look for God to manifest Himself to His children: God only manifests Himself *in* His children. MUH. 112

The revelation of God in the Old Testament is that of a working God. No other religion presents God either as diligent or as suffering, but as an all-in-all principle, ruling in lofty disdain. NKW. 118

Six days God laboured, *thinking* Creation, until, as He thought, so it was. OPG. 3

It is one thing to deceive other people, but you have to get up very early if you want to take in God! OPG. 48

God wants us to realise His sovereignty. We are apt to tie God up in His own laws and allow Him no free will. We say we know what God will do, and suddenly He upsets all our calculations by working in unprecedented ways; just when we expected He would do a certain thing, He did the opposite. PH. 84

"I shall not be greatly moved." God lifts us up and poises us in Himself as surely as He has established the stars. PH. 94

God is never in a hurry. PH. 231

God Almighty became the weakest thing in His own creation, a Baby. PR. 47

If God is first, you know you can never think of anything He will forget. RTR. 44

God is the controller of History. SHL. 91

'Lo, I am with you all the days.' He is the one Who is surrounding us, listening and sympathising and encouraging. Our audience is God, not God's people, but God Himself. The saint who realizes that can never be discouraged, no matter where he goes. SSY. 38

We are apt to talk sentimental nonsense about the Universal Fatherhood of God; to knock the bottom board out of Redemption by saying that God is love and of course He will forgive sin. When the

Holy Spirit comes, He makes us know that God is *holy* love, and therefore He cannot forgive sin apart from the Atonement; He would contradict His own nature if He did. SSY. 144

GOD AND MAN

The Bible reveals that man's calling is to stand before God and develop by obedience from the lowest point of conscious innocence to the highest reach of conscious holiness, with no intermediaries. This is man's calling as God created him, and that is why God will never leave us alone until the blaze and pain of His fire has burned us as pure as He is Himself. BE. 111

Only by being re-created and readjusted to God through the Atonement of our Lord Jesus Christ can we understand the marvellous unity between God and man for which God destined man. BE. 113

There is no subject more intimately interesting to modern people than man's relationship to man; but men get impatient when they are told that the first requirement is that they should love God first and foremost. "The first of all the commandments is, . . . thou shalt love the Lord thy God with all thy heart, and with all thy soul, and with all thy mind, and with all thy strength: this is the first commandment." BE. 124

The Bible says that the spirit of a man goes back to God. This does not imply that man's spirit is absorbed into God; but that man's spirit goes back to God with the characteristics on it for either judgment or praise. BP. 46

God breathed into man that which, going forth from God and entering into man, became the spirit of man, that spirit is essentially man's spirit, and never ceases to be man's spirit. BSG. 74

When I realize that there is something between God and me, it is at the peril of my soul I don't stop everything and get it put right. Immediately a thing makes itself conscious to me, it has no business there. CHI. 74

Man was not so created as to be able to reach the goal by drawing the required power from his own resources, he needed the aid of continual communications of life from God, and the reason of our Lord's coming was in order that the normal development of man, which sin had interrupted, might begin afresh. GW. 31

Man was created to be the friend and lover of God and for no other end, and until he realizes this he will go through turmoil and upset. Human nature must rise to its own Source, the bosom of God, and Jesus Christ by His Redemption brings it back there. GW. 40

Never trust (in the fundamental meaning of the word) any other saving Jesus Christ. That will mean you will never be unkind to anybody on the face of the earth, whether it be a degraded criminal or an upright moral man, because you have learned that the only thing to depend on in a man is what God has done in him. HG. 66

One great thing to notice is that God's order comes to us in the haphazard. We try to plan our ways and work things out for ourselves, but they go wrong because there are more facts than we know; whereas if we just go on with the days as they come, we find that God's order comes to us in that apparently haphazard way. HGM. 31

If you want to know God's original design for man, you see it in Jesus Christ; He was easily Master of the life on the earth, in the air and in the sea, not as God, but as Man; it was the human in Jesus that was master. HGM. 60

We try to help God help Himself to us; we have to get out of the way and God will help Himself to our lives in every detail. IWP. 47

God is "longsuffering to you-ward." At present He is giving men opportunity to try every line they like in individual life as well as in the life of the nations at large. Some things have not been tried yet, and if God were to cut us off short we would say, 'If You had left us a bit longer we could have realised our ideal of society and national life.' God is allowing us to prove to the hilt that it cannot be done in any other way than Jesus Christ said, viz., by a personal relationship to God through Jesus Christ Who is *God and Man—One.* LG. 31

God will do everything I cannot do, but He will do nothing He has constructed me to do. MFL. 35

The only Being Who understands us is the Being Who made us. It is a tremendous emancipation to get rid of every kind of self-consideration and learn to heed only one thing, the relationship between God and ourselves. MFL. 63

Never say—God must do this thing. He must not; God will fulfil His own word. You have no business to dictate to Him, you have to remain true to God and when His word is fulfilled, you will know He has fulfilled it because it is a supernatural fulfilment. NKW. 49

God is a perplexing Being to man because He is never in the wrong, and through the process of allowing every bit of man's wrongdoing to appear right at the time, He proves Himself right ultimately. Beware of the conception that God has to use His wits to keep Himself from being outwitted by man and the devil. NKW. 55

God never hastens and He never tarries. He works His plans out in His own way, and we either lie like clogs on His hands or we assist Him by being as clay in the hands of the potter. NKW. 58

Don't only make room for God, but believe that God has room enough for you. NKW. 66

God cannot come to me in my way, He can only come in His own way—in ways man would never dream of looking for Him. NKW. 98

God is a consuming fire. He will hold and hurt cruelly, and we may cry out to Him to let us go, but He will not let us go. God loves us too much to let us go, and He will burn and burn until there is nothing left but the purity that is as pure as He is—unless we determine to side with the impure and become as reprobate silver. OBH. 38

Men are apt to cry to God to stop—'If only God would leave me alone!' God never will. His passionate, inexorable love never allows Him to leave men alone, and with His children He will shake everything that can be shaken till there is nothing that can be shaken any more; then will abide the consuming fire of God until the life is changed into the same image from glory to glory, and men see that strong family likeness to Jesus that can never be mistaken. OBH. 38

God cannot do certain things without the co-operation of man. We continually ask, 'Why doesn't God do the thing instead of waiting for me?' He cannot. It is the same problem as the difference between God's order and His permissive will. His permissive will allows the devil to do his worst and allows me to sin as I choose, until I choose to resist the devil, quit sinning, and come to God in the right relationship of a covenant with Him through Jesus Christ. OPG. 24

Man has to go out of himself in his covenant with God as God goes out of Himself in His covenant with man. It is a question of faith in God. OPG. 24

The Second Man is the Son of God historically manifested, and the prophecy of what the human race is going to be. In Him we deal with God as Man, the God-Man, the Representative of the whole human race in one Person. PR. 13

God is long-suffering; He is giving us ample opportunity to try whatever line we like both in individual and in national life, but the Bible reveals that in the final end of all things, men will confess that God's purpose and His judgment are right. We must disabuse our minds of the idea that God sits like a Judge on a throne and batters humanity into shape. He is sometimes presented in that way, not intentionally, but simply because the majority of people have forgotten the principle laid down by Jesus, that "there is nothing covered that shall not be revealed; and hid, that shall not be known"; and that in the end, God's judgments will be made utterly plain and clear, and men will agree that they are right. Meantime, God is giving humanity and the devil ample opportunity to try and prove that His purposes and His judgments are wrong. PS. 68

The standard of Christianity is not that of a man, but of God; and unless God can put His Spirit into a man, that standard can never be reached. SHH. 133

Although you know that the best of men are but the best of men, it is part of moral calibre to hold true to the highest you know, and to remember that "there is none good save one, even God." SHH. 135

Man is dust and divinity. "And the Lord God formed man of the dust of the ground, and breathed into his nostrils the breath of life." SHH. 152

It is a marvellous moment in a man's life when he knows he is explored by God. SHL. 47

"I am come . . . to fulfil." An amazing word! Our shoes ought to be off our feet and every common-sense mood stripped from our minds when we hear Jesus Christ speak. In Him we deal with God as man, the God-Man, the Representative of the whole human race in one Person. The men of His day traced their religious pedigree back to the constitution of God, and this young Nazarene Carpenter says, '*I* am the constitution of God'; consequently to them He was a blasphemer. SSM. 21

We have to learn that God is not meant for us, it is we who are meant for God. SSY. 166

Jesus Christ does satisfy the last aching abyss of the human heart, but that must never lead to thinking of God the Father, God the Son, and God the Holy Ghost as an Almighty arrangement for satisfying us. '*Know ye not that . . . ye are not your own!*' It is this realization that is wrought in us by the Holy Ghost. SSY. 166

GOD, CALL OF

If you only know what God can do your talk is altogether of that, a logical exposition of doctrine, but if you have heard God's call you will always keep to the one centre, the Person of the Lord Jesus Christ. DI. 10

You can never fag the life out of the one whose service springs from listening to the voice of God, its inspiration is drawn not from human sympathy, but from God Himself. DI. 10

One man or woman called of God is worth a hundred who have elected to work for God. DI. 10

The call of God is difficult to state, it is implicit, not explicit. The call of God does not come to everyone, it comes only to the man who has the nature of God in him. For every man who is true to the call of God, there are many who are true to the call of a creed or doctrinal evangelism. GW. 134

We need trained ears to hear. One man may hear the call of God and another hear nothing; it depends on what goes on within the man, not outside him. HGM. 107

The first thing that impresses us about the call of God is that it comes to the whole man, not to one part of him. The majority of us are godly in streaks, spiritual in sections; it takes a long time to locate us altogether to the call of God. HGM. 108

The majority of us have no ear for anything but ourselves, we cannot hear a thing God says. To be brought into the zone of the call of God is to be profoundly altered. MUH. 16

When once the call of God comes, begin to go and never stop going. MUH. 271

We make calls out of our own spiritual consecration, but when we get right with God He brushes all these aside, and rivets us with a pain that is terrific to one thing we never dreamed of, and for one radiant flashing moment we see what He is after, and we say—"Here am I, send me." MUH. 274

The call of God embarrasses us because of two things—it presents us with sealed orders, and urges us to a vast venture. NKW. 11

When God calls us He does not tell us along the line of our natural senses what to expect; God's call is a command that *asks* us, that means there is always a possibility of refusal on our part. NKW. 11

It cannot be definitely stated what the call of God is to, because it is a call into comradeship with God Himself for His own purposes, and the test of faith is to believe that God knows what He is after. NKW. 12

The call is God's idea, not our idea, and only on looking back over the path of obedience do we realize what is the idea of God; God sanctifies memory. When we hear the call of God it is not for us to dispute with God, and arrange to obey Him if He will expound the meaning of His call to us. NKW. 12

As long as we insist on having the call expounded to us, we will never obey; but when we obey it is expounded, and in looking back there comes a chuckle of confidence—'He doeth all things well.' NKW. 12

We have nothing to do with what will happen if we obey, we have to abandon to God's call in unconditional surrender and smilingly wash our hands of the consequences. NKW. 13

Arguers against obeying the call of God will arise in the shape of country and kindred, and if you listen to them you will soon dull your ears to God's call and become the dullest, most commonplace Christian imaginable, because you have no courage in your faith; you have seen and heard, but have not gone on. If you accept sympathy from those who have not heard the call of God, it will so blunt your own sense of His call that you become useless to Him. NKW. 14

It is not sin or disobedience only that keeps us from obeying the call of God, but the good, right, natural things that make us hesitate. The natural can only be transformed into the spiritual by obedience, and the beginnings of God's life in a man or woman cut directly across the will of nature. NKW. 16

The discernment of God's call does not come in every moment of life, but only in rare moments; the moments Our Lord spoke of as 'the light.' We have to remain true to what we see in those moments; if we do not, we will put back God's purpose in our life. The undercurrent of regret arises when we confer with those who have not heard the call of God, and if we listen to them we get into darkness. NKW. 118

The call of God is a call in accordance with the nature of God, not in accordance with my idea of God. NKW. 127

You hear the call of God and realize what He wants, then you begin to find reasons why you should not obey Him. Well, obey Him, because away in some other part of the world there are other circumstances being worked by God, and if you say—'I shan't, I wasn't made for this,' you get out of touch with God. Your 'goings' are not according to your mind, but according to God's mind. Remain true at all costs to what God is doing with you and don't ask why He is doing it. NKW. 132

When the call of Jesus Christ comes, it comes to *you*, it cannot come to your father or your mother, or to your wife, or to your own self-interest; it comes entirely to your personal life. Instantly the clamour begins. Father and mother say No, the claims of my own life say No; Jesus Christ says Yes. Think—could Jesus Christ's call mean that I hurt my father and mother irrevocably? Certainly it could not; then if I obey Him, even though it looks like bringing the sword and the upset into lives, in the final wind-up God will bring His widsom out perfectly, and I shall find that every one of those human relationships have been brought in in the wake of my obedience. The point is—will I trust God, or lean to my own convictions? NKW. 133

The call of God is a call according to the nature of God; where we go in obedience to that call depends entirely on the providential circumstances which God engineers, and is not of any moment. The danger is to fit the call of God into the idea of our own discernment and say, 'God called me *there.*' If we say so and stick to it, then it is good-bye to the development of the life of God in us. We have deliberately shifted the ground of His call to fit our own conception of what He wants. PR. 43

When God calls us He never gives security; He gives us a knowledge of Himself. SHL. 108

'Obedience to Your call would mean I should get into difficulties with my home, my father, my mother, and I cannot possibly be the means of bringing suffering on them.' Jesus says, 'If you are going to be My disciples, you must be prepared to.' God knows what it costs them, and what it costs you to allow it. SHL. 110

When we speak of a call we nearly always leave out one essential feature, viz.: the nature of the one who calls. We speak of the call of the sea, the call of the mountains, the call of the great ice barriers. These calls are heard by a few only because the call is the expression of the nature from which the call comes, and can only be heard by those who are attuned to that nature. SSY. 9

The call of God is essentially expressive of the nature of God, it is His own voice. SSY. 9

Very few of us hear the call of God because we are not in the place to answer; the call does not communicate because we have not the nature of the One Who is calling. SSY. 9

The call of God is not the echo of my nature, but expressive of God's nature. SSY. 10

There are strands of the call of God providentially at work that you know and no one else does. It is the threading of God's voice for you on some particular line, and it is no use to consult anyone else about it, or to say that other people are dull because they do not hear it. SSY. 10

The call of God is not a call to any particular service, although my interpretation of the call may be; the call to service is the echo of my identification with God. SSY. 12

We are apt to forget the mystic, supernatural touch of God which comes with His call. If a man can tell you how the call of God came to him and all about it, it is questionable whether he ever had the call. The call to be a professional man may come in that explicit way, but the call of God is much more supernatural. ssy. 14

The realization of the call of God in a man's life may come as with a sudden thunder-clap or by a gradual dawning, but in whatever way it comes, it comes with the undercurrent of the supernatural, almost the uncanny; it is always accompanied with a glow—something that cannot be put into words. ssy. 14

The moment that the consciousness of the call of God dawns on us, we know that it is not a choice of our own at all; the consciousness is that of being held by a power we do not fully know. *'I have chosen him.'* ssy. 15

If the call of God is there, it is not within the power of untoward things to turn you. Your heart remains, not untouched by them, but unbroken, and you are surprised at yourself—'Why didn't I go under here, and there?" *'I called thee.'* ssy. 17

We try to make calls out of our own spiritual consecration, but when we are put right with God, He blights all our sentimental convictions and devotional calls. He brushes them all aside, and rivets us with a passion that is terrific to one thing we had never dreamed of, and in the condition of real communion with God, we overhear Him saying: 'Whom shall I send, and who will go for us?' and for one radiant, flashing moment we see what God wants, and say in conscious freedom—'Here am I, send me.' ssy. 17

It is always well to go back to the foundation truths revealed in God's word regarding what He expects of the man or woman who wishes to be what He wants. 'Called to be saints,' that is what God expects. ssy. 26

When once the call of God comes, begin to go and never stop going, no matter how many delightful resting places there may be on the way.

Christ's call is 'Follow Me.' Our attitude ought to be—'Lord, if it be thou, bid me come unto thee,' and Jesus will say *'Come.'* ssy. 54

'Come, follow me,' not, Find out the way, but—Come. You cannot come if there is any remnant of the wrong disposition in you, because you are sure to want to direct God. 'Come unto Me,' these words were spoken to men who had felt the appeal of the Highest, the aspiration, the longing, the master passion to be perfect—'Come unto Me, and I will rest you, stay you, poise you; take my yoke on you and learn of Me, and you will discover rest all along the way.' ssy. 61

The call of the sea, the call of the mountains, the call of the wild—all these calls are perfectly in accord with the nature of the caller, not necessarily in accord with the nature of the one who listens. Everyone does not hear the call of the sea, only the one who has the nature of the sea in him hears it. The call of the mountains does not come to everyone, only to the one who has the nature of the mountains in him. Likewise the call of God does not come to everyone, it comes only to those who have the nature of God in them. The call of Jesus Christ does not come to everyone, only to those who have His nature. ssy. 162

GOD, COMMUNION WITH

It is not a haphazard thing, but in the constitution of God, that there are certain times of the day when it not only seems easier, but it *is* easier, to meet God. HGM. 87

Nights and days of prayer and waiting on God may be a curse to our souls and an occasion for Satan. So always remember that the times we have in communion with God must be worked out in the soul and in the body. IWP. 33

Jesus Christ was a Man among men, a Man living in unsullied communion with God. That is the kind of man He expects us to be through His regeneration of us. PR. 44

GOD, FACE OF

There *is* a dark line in God's face, but what we do know about Him is so full of peace and joy that we can wait for His interpretation. DI. 13

Jesus Christ is to us the faithful Face of God. PR. 138

The Face of God is the Lord Jesus Christ. PR. 138

If there is a dark line in God's face to us, the solution does not lie in saying what is not true to fact, but in bowing our heads and waiting; the explanation is not yet. All that is dark and obscure just now will one day be as radiantly and joyously clear as the truth about God we already know. No wonder our Lord's counsel is, 'Fear not!' SSY. 109

GOD, GLORY OF

"And the glory which Thou gavest Me I have given them." The glory of our Lord was the glory of a holy life, and that is what He gives to us. He gives us the gift of holiness . . . IYA. 57

We have the idea that God is going to do some exceptional thing, that He is preparing and fitting us for some extraordinary thing by and bye, but as we go on in grace we find that God is glorifying Himself here and now, in the present minute. If we have God's say-so behind us, the most amazing strength comes, and we learn to sing in the ordinary days and ways. MUH. 156

. . . when we are born again, we ought to know exactly why His life is born into us—for the glory of God. PR. 46

Jesus Christ, Son of God and Son of Man, is not a mere individual, He is the One Who represents the whole human race. In order to see the human race as God intends it to be, look at the life of Jesus; and by the Redemption the human race is to be brought there. When the human race is actually there, Jesus Christ as Son of Man ceases to be and becomes absolute Deity again. The Son becomes subject to the Father, and God remains all in all. Our Lord's prayer is answered. "And now, O Father, glorify Thou Me with Thine own self with the glory which I had with Thee before the world was." That glory is to be in God. PR. 135

The glory of Jesus was not an external thing; He effaced the Godhead in Himself so effectually that men without the Spirit of God despised Him. His glory was the glory of actual holiness. PR. 135

This is the glory of the saint here and now—the glory of actual holiness manifested in actual life. Whether it comes out in eating and drinking or in preaching, it must show in every detail straight through until the whole limit actually manifests the complete new life. PR. 136

'I want those whom Thou hast given Me,' says Jesus, 'to behold My glory.' What is His glory? "The glory which I had with Thee before the world was," and our perpetual glory is not only that we are saved and sanctified and redeemed and lifted into the glory of unspeakable things as the result of our Lord's Redemption, but something other—we shall see God face to face, an inconceivable beatific vision. This is what Jesus Christ has prayed for His saints. This is not the glory we have here, but the glory we are going to have, the glory of beholding His glory. PR. 138

GOD, IMAGE OF

God is sometimes referred to as the sun, but the sun is never stated to be made in the image of God, although there are illustrations of God in God's Book drawn from the sun. But nowhere is it stated that God made the sun in His own image. BP. 13

The angels can manifest the image of God only in bodiless spirits; only one being can manifest God on this earth, and that is man. BP. 16

We are never told to be like the unique Being the Lord Jesus Christ who came into the world as God Incarnate to put away sin, but when sin has been put away through the Atonement, we are to be conformed to His image. BSG. 44

"GOD IS LOVE"

What a rest comes when the love of God has been shed abroad in my heart by the Holy Spirit! I realize that God is love, not loving, but love, something infinitely greater than loving, consequently He has to be very stern. BP. 135

"God is love." The Bible does not say that God is loving, but that God is love. The phrase 'the lovingkindness of God' is frequently used, but when the nature of God is revealed, the Bible does not say God is a loving Being, it says, "God is love." BP. 217

God is Love. No one but God could have revealed *that* to the world, for men, and we all indeed, see nothing but its contradiction in our own limited world of experience. It needs but little imagination to construe the life of hundreds of this great city's inhabitants into a vehement laughter at such a declaration as 'God is love.' LG. 7

. . . oh the sublimity of the Abraham-like faith that dares to place the centre of its life and confidence and action and hope in an unseen and apparently unknown God, saying, 'God is love,' in spite of all appearances to the contrary; saying, "Though He slay me, yet will I trust in Him." Such faith is counted to a man for righteousness. LG. 7

Though it is too difficult, nay impossible, to trace that God is love by mere unaided human intellect, it is not impossible to the intuitions of faith. LG. 13

God is Love—one brief sentence, you can print it on a ring: it is the Gospel. A time is coming when the whole round world will know that God reigns and that God is Love, when hell and heaven, life and death, sin and salvation, will be read and understood aright at last. LG. 14

That God is love is a revelation. PH. 64

GOD, LOVE FOR

Love is the sovereign preference of my person for another person, and we may be astonished to realize that love springs from a voluntary choice. Love for God does not spring naturally out of the human heart; but it is open to us to choose whether we will have the love of God imparted to us by the Holy Spirit. BP. 119

The highest love is not natural to the human heart. Naturally, we do not love God, we mistrust Him. BP. 133

The natural man does not like God's commands; he will not have them, he covers them over and ignores them. Jesus said that the first commandment is: "Thou shalt love the Lord thy God with all thy heart, and with all thy soul, and with all thy mind and with all thy strength." Men put the second commandment first: "Thou shalt love thy neighbor as thyself." The great cry today is 'love for mankind.' The great cry of Jesus is 'love for God first,' and this love, the highest love, the supreme, passionate devotion of the life, springs from the inner centre. BP. 135

It is pathetic the number of people who are piously trying to make their poor human hearts love God! The Holy Spirit sheds abroad in my heart, not the power to love God, but the very nature of God; and the nature of God coming into me makes me part of God's consciousness, not God part of my consciousness. I am unconscious of God because I have been taken up into His consciousness. BP. 217

Ask yourself what sort of conception you have of loving God. The majority of us have a bloodless idea, an impersonal, ethereal, vague abstraction, called 'love to God.' Read Jesus Christ's conception; He mentions relationships of the closest, most personal, most passionate order, and says that our love for Him must be closer and more personal than any of those. IWP. 84

The only way to love God with all our soul is to give up our lives for His sake, not give our lives to God, that is an elemental point, but when that has been done, after our lives have been given to God, we ought to lay them down for God. IWP. 85

To love God with all our mind we have to 'soar above created things, and penetrate into the uncreated good,' viz., God. When the Spirit of God begins to deal on this side of things we shall feel at sea, if we are not spiritual, as to what is meant; when we are spiritual we feel with our hearts, not with our heads—'Yes, I begin to see what it means.' IWP. 86

If we try to prove to God how much we love Him, it is a sure sign that we do not love Him. The evidence of our love for Him is the absolute spontaneity of our love, it comes naturally. MUH. 21

The springs of love are in God, not in us. It is absurd to look for the love of God in our hearts naturally, it is only there when it has been shed abroad in our hearts by the Holy Spirit. MUH. 121

When a disciple is dominated by his love to Jesus Christ, he is not always conscious of Him. It is absurd to think that we have to be conscious all the time of the one we love most. The one we are conscious of is the one we do not love most. A child is not conscious all the time of his love for his mother; it is the crisis that produces the consciousness. When we are getting into the throes of love, we are conscious of it because we are not in love yet. SSY. 158

GOD, LOVE OF

The love of God is the great mainspring, and by our voluntary choice we can have that love shed abroad in our hearts, then unless hindered by disobedience, it will go on to develop into the perfect love described in 1 Cor. xiii. BP. 119

". . . the love of God is shed abroad in our hearts by the Holy Ghost which is given unto us." This does not mean that when we receive the Holy Spirit He enables us to have the capacity for loving God, but that He sheds abroad in our hearts *the love of God*, a much more fundamental and marvellous thing. BP. 217

There is nothing on earth like the love of God when once it breaks on the soul, it may break at a midnight or a dawn, but always as a great surprise, and we begin to experience the uniting of our whole being with the nature of God. CHI. 88

"Keep yourselves in the love of God," says Jude, that is keep your soul open not only to the fact that God loves you, but that He is *in* you, in you sufficiently to manifest His perfect love in every condition in which you can find yourself as you rely upon Him. CHI. 89

God grant we may not only experience the indwelling of the love of God in our hearts, but go on to a hearty abandon to that love so that God can pour it out through us for His redemptive purposes for the world. He broke the life of His own Son to redeem us, and now He wants to use our lives as a sacrament to nourish others. CHI. 91

The love of God rakes the very bottom of hell, and from the depths of sin and suffering brings sons and daughters to God. HG. 120

When the love of God is realized by me, the sovereign preference of my person for God enables Him to manifest *His* purpose in me. HG. 121

To realize the dimensions of the love of God, its breadth, and length, and depth, and height, will serve to drive home to us the reality of God's love, and the result of our belief in that love will be that no question will ever profoundly vex our minds, no sorrow overwhelm our spirits, because our heart is at rest in God, just as the heart of our Lord was at rest in His Father. This does not mean that our faith will not be tested; if it is faith, it must be tested, but, profoundly speaking, it will be supremely easy to believe in God. HG. 121

The love of God gives us a new method of seeing Nature. His voice is on the rolling air, we see Him in the rising sun, and in the setting He is fair; in the singing of the birds, in the love of human hearts, the voice of God is in all. Had we but ears to hear the stars singing, to catch the glorious pealing anthem of praise echoing from the hills of immortality by the heavenly hosts! LG. 10

The love of God is not revealed by intellectual discernment, it is a spiritual revelation. LG. 15

"Keep yourselves in the love of God," not 'keep on loving God,' none can do that. When once you have understood the truth about your own heart's sinfulness, think not again of it, but look at the great, vast, illimitable magnificence of the love of God. LG. 19

The foundation of God's love is holiness—"without which no man shall see the Lord." God's love then must be the justification of His holiness. LG. 22

The love of God is going to embrace everyone and everything in the sovereign preference of His person, which is for His Son. God purposes that everyone of us shall partake of the very essential nature of Jesus Christ and stand in complete union with Himself, even as Jesus did. LG. 32

The love of God is not to be looked for in justice, right, truth, and purity; the love of God *is* Jesus Christ. LG. 69

God's love seems so strange to our natural conceptions that it has to be commended, i.e. recommended, to us before we see anything in it. It is only when we have been awakened by conviction to the sin and anarchy of our hearts against God that we realise the measure of His love toward us, even "while we were yet sinners." "The Son of God, Who loved me, and gave Himself for *me*"—Paul never lost the wonder of that love. OBH. 59

The revelation comes home to me that God has loved me to the end of all my meanness and my sin, my self-seeking and my wrong motives; and now this is the corresponding revelation—that I have to love others as God has loved me. God will bring around us any number of people we cannot respect, and we have to exhibit the love of God to them as He has exhibited it to us. OBH. 59

It is significant to note that whenever the Bible uses terms such as 'repent,' 'remember,' 'forsake,' 'love,' in connection with God, their human meaning does not apply, e.g., the love of God can only be illustrated by the character of God. OPG. 22

Not until we realise that there is something tragic at the basis of human life

shall we recognise the love of God. PH. 65

When the love of God is in me I must learn how to let it express itself; I must educate myself in the matter; it takes time. "Acquire your soul with patience," says Jesus. PH. 67

The only way in which the Kingdom of God can be established is by the love of God as revealed in the Cross of Jesus Christ, not by the lovingkindness of a backboneless being without justice or righteousness or truth. The background of God's love is holiness. His is not a compromising love, and the Kingdom of our Lord can only be brought in by means of His love at work in regeneration. PR. 69

We have to form the mind of Christ until we are absorbed with Him and take no account of the evil done to us. No love on earth can do this but only the love of God. RTR. 44

God has loved me to the end of all my sinfulness, of all my self-will, all my stiff-neckedness, all my pride, all my self-interest; now He says—"love one another, as I have loved you." I am to show to my fellow men the same love that God showed me. That is Christianity in practical working order. RTR. 46

The love of God in Christ Jesus is such that He can take the most unfit man— unfit to survive, unfit to fight, unfit to face moral issues—and make him not only fit to survive and to fight, but fit to face the biggest moral issues and the strongest power of Satan, and come off more than conqueror. RTR. 55

It does not matter where a man may get to in the way of tribulation or anguish, none of it can wedge in between and separate him from the love of God in Christ Jesus. RTR. 61

To most of us it is a matter of moonshine whether Jesus Christ lived or died or did anything at all; God has to "recommend" His love to us. It is only when we come to our wits' ends, or reap a distress, or feel the first twinge of damnation and are knocked out of our complacent mental agility over things, that we recognise the love of God. SHH. 28

God sends His rough weather and His smooth weather, but we pay no attention to either because we are taken up only with the one central thing—the love of God in Christ Jesus. SHL. 23

The marvel of the Divine love is that God exhibits His love not only to good people but to bad people. SSM. 50

It is the great patient love of God that gives the warning. "The way of transgressors is hard." Go behind that statement in your imagination and see the love of God. God is amazingly tender, but the way of transgressors cannot be made easy. God has made it difficult to go wrong, especially for His children. SSM. 93

The first mighty name for the consolations of the way is love—'that the love wherewith thou lovedst me may be in them.' It is the Holy Ghost Who brings this consolation. He sheds abroad the love of God in our hearts, the nature of God as exhibited in Jesus, with its impenetrable reserves. No human being can pump up what is not there. The consolation of love is not that of exquisite human understanding, it is the real nature of God holding the individual life in effectual rectitude and effectual communion in the face of anything that may ever come. SSY. 98

GOD, PRESENCE OF

If we try to drown God's presence in the depths of iniquity, it is there; if we go to the heights and speculate, it is there—insisting, wooing, drawing; the hand of Christ knocking at the door, for one purpose, to get in. The Spirit of God is everywhere, would that men would yield to Him! BE. 101

What are you haunted by? You will say—By nothing, but we are all haunted by something, generally by ourselves, or, if we are Christians, by our experience. The Psalmist says we are to be haunted by God. The abiding consciousness of the life is to be God, not thinking about Him. The whole of our life inside and out is to be absolutely haunted by the presence of God. MUH. 154

To the thought of the saints God is never far enough away to think about them, there is no separation; He thinks them. PH. 104

God will consume and shake, and shake and consume, till there is nothing more to be consumed, but only Himself—incandescent with the presence of God. PS. 67

God is never away off somewhere else; He is always *there*. RTR. 58

If we look for God in the physical domain we shall see Him nowhere; if we look for Him in the kingdom on the inside, in the moral relationships, we shall find Him all the time. SHL. 101

GOD, VOICE OF

Never make the mistake of thinking that God speaks unmistakably clearly; He speaks in the gentlest of whispers, so unutterably quiet that it is not easy to hear Him. We only realize His voice more clearly by recklessness. GW. 58

God always speaks quietly, and if you try to catch an echo of His voice you will never hear it. When the moment comes and you hear, as it were from someone else, 'It is the Lord,' recklessly abandon immediately. If you say, 'I thought it was God's voice,' but you did not recklessly obey, you will find it has gone and you will have to wait now. GW. 58

There are many ways of "following the Lamb whithersoever He goeth" because we know His voice. His voice has no tone of self-realization in it, nor of sin, but only the tone of the Holy Ghost. His voice is essentially simple; it is "a still, small voice," totally unlike any other voice. The Lord is not in the wind, not in the earthquake or in the fire, but only in "a sound of gentle stillness." HGM. 51

There are no panics intellectual or moral. What a lot of panicky sparrows we are, the majority of us. We chatter and tweet under God's eaves until we cannot hear His voice at all—until we learn the wonderful life and music of the Lord Jesus telling us that our heavenly Father is the God of the sparrows, and by the marvellous transformation of grace He can turn the sparrows into His nightingales that can sing through every night of sorrow. A sparrow cannot sing through a night of sorrow, and no soul can sing through a night of sorrow unless it has learned to be silent unto God—one look, one thought about my Father in heaven, and it is all right. IWP. 91

Every word God has spoken will be absolutely fulfilled; to climb down from that confidence is to be disloyal to God. OPG. 23

There is always the danger of becoming a fanatical adherent to what God has said instead of adhering to God who said it. OPG. 23

If I am 'in Christ' the angels of God are always ascending and descending on my behalf, and the voice that speaks is the voice of God. OPG. 40

A disciple must be careful not to talk in the darkness; the listening ear is to be his characteristic, not listening to the voice of sympathising fellow disciples, or to the voice of self-pity, but listening only to the voice of the Lord. PH. 11

The voice of the Lord listened to in darkness is so entrancing that the finest of earth's voices are never afterwards mistaken for the voice of the Lord. PH. 12

To silence the voice of God is damnation in time; eternal damnation is that for ever. "God answereth me no more." PS. 46

The Holy Spirit's voice is as gentle as a zephyr, the merest check; when you hear it do you say, 'But that is only a tiny detail, the Holy Spirit cannot mean that, it is much too trivial a thing'? The Holy Spirit does mean that, and at the risk of being thought fanatical you must obey. SSM. 110

To be brought within the zone of God's voice is to be profoundly altered. SSY. 10

The life given by God is capable of immediately hearing the voice of God's own nature. Unless the nature of God comes into you, said Jesus to Nicodemus, you cannot understand Him; but if His nature comes into you, of course you will hear Him. SSY. 11

'Grieve not the Spirit.' He does not come with a voice like thunder, with strong emphatic utterance—that may come ultimately; but at the beginning His voice is as gentle as a zephyr. At the same time it carries an imperative compulsion—we know the voice must be obeyed. SSY. 44

GOD, WILL OF

One of the dangers of fanaticism is to accept disaster as God's appointment, as part of His design. It is not God's design, but His permissive will. There is a vital moral difference between God's order and His permissive will. BFB. 13

One of the subtlest snares is the idea that we are here to live a holy life of our own, with our eyes fixed on our own whiteness; we are here to carry out God's will as Jesus carried it out. Jesus carried out the will of God as the Saviour of the world; we are to carry out His will as saints. BSG. 27

Inestimable damage is done when the will of God is made an external law to be obeyed by conscious grasp. The will of God is apprehended by an almost unconscious impelling of the indwelling Holy Spirit. CD. VOL. 2, 105

The characteristic of our Lord's life was submission to His Father, not the crushing down of His own will to His Father's, but the love-agreement of His will with His Father's—'I am here for one thing only, to do Thy will, and I delight to do it.' MFL. 114

The complete life is the life of a child. When I am consciously conscious, there is something wrong. It is the sick man who knows what health is. The child of God is not conscious of the will of God because he *is* the will of God. When

there has been the slightest deviation from the will of God, we begin to ask—What is Thy will? MUH. 233

The remarkable thing about the life of Our Lord was not that He was eager to do God's will, but that He was *obedient* to do it. He never put His fingers across the threads of His Father's providential order for Him and gave a tug saying—'Now I will help You,' and pulled the thing right out of His Father's hands. He simply obeyed, leaving His Father's wisdom to arrange all for Him. We rush in and say—I see what God wants and I will do it, and we wound our own souls and injure other lives. NKW. 49

Doing the will of God is instantaneously continuous. Am I doing the will of God *now*? NKW. 69

Doing God's will is never hard. The only thing that is hard is *not* doing His will. OBH. 130

All the forces of nature and of grace are at the back of the man who does God's will because in obedience we let God have His amazing way with us. OBH. 130

If some of us were taken to be specimens of doing God's will, we should be sorry recommendations! OBH. 130

When we say "Thy will be done," do we say it with a sigh? If so, we have never realized that the character of God is holy love; nothing can ever happen outside His purposeful will. RTR. 37

God's permissive will is the means whereby His sons and daughters are to be manifested. We are not to be like jelly-fish saying—"It's the Lord's will." We have not to put up a fight before God, not to wrestle with God, but to wrestle before God with things. RTR. 49

The difference between a man with the Spirit of God and a man without, is that the one does the will of God by deliberate, delighted choice; the other does the will of God without knowing what he is doing, kicking and rebelling. RTR. 77

Jesus Christ gives the vision of God, God's order; but He also gives us God's permissive will. God's order, according to Jesus Christ, is no sin, no sickness, no limitation, no evil, and no wrong: His permissive will allows these things, and I have to get at God's order through His permissive will by an effort of my own. SA. 89

God's order is—no sin, no sickness, no devil, no war: His permissive will is things as they are. SHH. 7

Our Lord's first obedience was not to the needs of men, not to the consideration of where He would be most useful, but to the will of His Father. 'Lo, I am come to do thy will, O God.' SSY. 95

GOD, WORD OF

The only way the words of God can be understood is by contact with the Word of God. The connection between our Lord Himself, who is the Word, and His spoken words is so close that to divorce them is fatal. "The words that I speak unto you, they are spirit, and they are life." BE. 122

If I have disobeyed, the Word of God is dried up, there is "no open vision." Immediately I obey the Word is poured in. DI. 8

Watch every time the Word of God is made a sacrament to you through someone else, it will make you re-tune your ears to His Word. DI. 8

Just as the words of God and The Word of God are the counterpart of each other, so the commandments of our Lord and the conduct of His saints are the counterpart of each other; if they are not, then we are 'none of His.' GW. 71

As in the beginning God's word was the creative fiat, and that word's witness to itself satisfied God, so the work of Christ in a disciple witnesses to Him; it is the Living Word speaking the words, "the words that I speak unto you, they are spirit and they are life." OPG. 3

It is not my faith laying hold of the word, but the life in the word laying hold on me and faith is as natural as breathing, and I say, 'Why, bless God, I *know* that is true!' OPG. 3

No one is ever the same after listening to the word of God, you cannot be; you may imagine you have paid no attention to it, and yet months after maybe a crisis arises and suddenly the word of God comes and grips you by the throat, so to speak, and awakens all the terrors of hell in your life, and you say, 'Wherever did that word come from?' Years ago, months ago, weeks ago, it sank straight into our unconscious mind, God knew it was there though you did not, and it did its damaging work, and now it has suddenly come to light. PS. 26

God says that His word shall not return unto Him void—the abiding success of the word of God! PS. 26

The word of God is never without power, and as a servant or handmaid of God you have nothing whatever to do with whether people dislike and reject the word of God, or 'purr' over it. See you preach it no matter what they think of you, that is a matter of absolute indifference, sooner or later the effect of that word will be manifested. The great snare is to seek acceptance with the people we talk to, to give people only what they want; we have no business to wish to be acceptable to the people we teach. PS. 26

"Study to show thyself approved"—unto the saints? No, "unto God." I have never known a man or woman who taught God's word to be always acceptable to other people. PS. 26

Sow the Word of God, and everyone who listens will get to God. If you sow vows, resolutions, aspirations, emotions, you will reap nothing but exhaustion, '. . . and ye shall sow your seed in vain, for your enemies shall eat it'; but sow the Word of God, and as sure as God is God, it will bring forth fruit. SHL. 114

'Build up your character bit by bit by attention to My words,' says Jesus, then when the supreme crisis comes, you will stand like a rock. SSM. 109

Our Lord says that His word was not His own, but His Father's. Jesus never spoke from His right to Himself. 'The words that I say unto you, I speak not from myself.' Jesus Christ is the Word of God in His own Person; He spoke the words of God with a human tongue, and He has given to His disciples the words the Father gave to Him. The disciple has not only to speak the words of God with his tongue, but to bear the evidence of being a word of the Son, as Jesus was the Word of God. SSY. 96

. . . there is a wrong use of God's word and a right one. The wrong use is this sort of thing—someone comes to you, and you cast about in your mind what sort of man he is, then hurl a text at him like a projectile, either in prayer or in talking as you deal with him. That is a use of the word of God that kills your own soul and the souls of the people you deal with. The Spirit of God is not in that. Jesus said, "The words I speak unto you, they are spirit, and they are life." "Who also hath made us able ministers of the new testament; not of the letter, but of the spirit: for the letter killeth, but the spirit giveth life." Do remember to keep your soul in unsullied touch with the directions of the Spirit. WG. 16

Never drag down the word of God to anybody's understanding. Hammer at it, keep at it, and drive at it, till the laziness is taken out of people's hearts and brains and bodies, and they are willing to face what this Book has to say about their condition, and face it with the sterling earnestness they use to see what the newspapers have to say when they are on the hunt for a new situation. God grant we may learn the imperativeness of getting at what the word of God has to say about our particular need, then perhaps we will begin to understand why we have that need. WG. 78

"The words that I speak unto you, they are spirit, and they are life." The word of God is "a lamp" and "a light," but when people get off on the 'stupid' lines, it is all instincts, impressions, vague ideas— "ever learning, and never able to come to the knowledge of the truth." Then is the time when men of reprobate mind creep in and lead astray. WG. 79

Take heed to yourself, take heed how you read, and above all don't argue. Have you learned this, Christian worker, that when any soul begins to discuss the baptism with the Holy Spirit, it is time you got out of the way? They have a controversy with the Holy Ghost, not with you. 'Sanctification' is not a man's term; it is God's: 'the baptism with the Holy Ghost' is not man's conception, it is

God's, and when a soul begins to argue on these matters, remember, worker for God, it is the Holy Spirit they are arguing with, the Word of God they are haggling about. God grant we may not hinder those who are battling their way slowly into the light. WG. 98

GOD, WRATH OF

The love of God and the wrath of God are obverse sides of the same thing, like two sides of a coin. The wrath of God is as positive as His love. God cannot be in agreement with sin. When a man is severed from God the basis of his moral life is chaos and wrath, not because God is angry, like a Moloch, it is His constitution of things. CHI. 14

The wrath of God abides all the time a man persists in the way that leads away from God; the second he turns, he is faced with His love. Wrath is the dark line in God's face, and is expressive of His hatred of sin. CHI. 14

Jesus Christ came right straight down into the very depths of wrath, He clothed Himself with the humanity of the race that had fallen and could not lift itself, and in His own Person He annihilated the wrath until there is "no condemnation," no touch of the wrath of God, on those who are "in Christ Jesus." CHI. 15

When we speak of the wrath of God we must not picture Him as an angry sultan on the throne of heaven, bringing a lash about people when they do what He does not want. There is no element of personal vindictiveness in God. It is rather that God's constitution of things is such that when a man becomes severed from God his life tumbles into turmoil and confusion, into agony and distress, it is hell at once, and he will

never get out of it unless he turns to God; immediately he turns, chaos is turned into cosmos, wrath into love, distress into peace. CHI. 67

GOOD AND EVIL

The primal curse of God was on Adam when he ate the fruit of the tree of knowledge of good and evil. Adam was intended to know good and evil, but not by eating of the fruit of the tree; God wanted him to know good and evil in the way Jesus Christ knew it, viz., by simple obedience to His Father. BFB. 34

Knowledge of evil broadens a man's mind, makes him tolerant, but paralyses his action. Knowledge of good broadens a man's mind, makes him intolerant of all sin, and shows itself in intense activity. A bad man, an evil-minded man, is amazingly tolerant of everything and everyone, no matter whether they are good or bad, Christian or not, but his power of action is paralysed entirely; he is tolerant of everything—the devil, the flesh, the world, sin, and everything else. BP. 57

The most staggering thing about Jesus Christ is that He makes human destiny depend not on goodness or badness, not on things done or not done, but on Who we say He is. IWP. 116

God put man in the garden with the tree of knowledge of good and evil, and said, "Ye shall not eat of it." God did not say they were not to know good and evil, but that they were not to know good and evil by eating of the tree. They were intended to know evil in the way Jesus Christ knew it, viz., by contrast with good. They did eat of the tree, consequently the human race knows good by contrast with evil. Adam knew evil positively and good negatively, and none of us knows the order God intended. SA. 71

Jesus Christ knew evil negatively by positively knowing good; He never ate of the tree, and when a man is reborn of the Spirit of God that is the order. SA. 72

To say that "sin is nothing but the shadow of good" is not true. Evil, according to the Bible, is the shadow of good, but sin is positive defiance. You can be educated by evil, but not by sin. Sin is the positive disposition in me that has to be removed; evil is the negative thing outside me. SA. 105

The knowledge of evil that came through the Fall gives a man a broad mind, but instead of instigating him to action it paralyses his action. Men and women whose minds are poisoned by gross experience of evil are marvellously generous with regard to other people's sins; they argue in this way—'To know all is to pardon all.' Every bit of their broadmindedness paralyses their power to *do* anything. They know good only by contrast with evil, which is the exact opposite of God's order. SHL. 65

If we know good only by contrast with evil, we shall have the devilishness of the serpent through gross experience. But when we know good and evil in the way Jesus Christ knew them, all our subtle wisdom is on the side of the good and our dove-like nature is towards evil. SHL. 69

GOOD/BETTER/BEST

Good things will always be the bane of the spiritual life until they are wedded to and lost in the best. When God begins with us He gives us good things, He showers them down. IWP. 77

The great enemy of the life of faith in God is not sin, but the good which is not good enough. The good is always the enemy of the best. MUH. 146

In the spiritual life we do not go from good to better, and from better to best; because there is only One to Whom we go, and that One is The Best, viz., God Himself. There can be no such thing as God's second best. NKW. 47

In seeking the Best we soon find that our enemy is our good things, not our bad. The things that keep us back from God's best are not sin and imperfection, but the things that are right and good and noble from the natural standpoint. NKW. 47

Very few of us debate with the sordid and the wrong, but we do debate with the good; and the higher up we go in the scale of the natural virtues, the more intense is the opposition to Jesus Christ, which is in inverse ratio to what one would naturally imagine. NKW. 47

It is the *good* that hates the *best*. It is not only sin that produces the havoc in life, but the natural determination to 'boss the show' for God and everyone else. NKW. 50

It is the things that are right and noble and good from the natural standpoint that keep us back from God's best. To discern that the natural virtues antagonize surrender to God, is to begin to see where the battle lies. It is going to cost the natural everything, not something. NKW. 105

"And if thy right hand offend thee, cut it off, and cast it from thee: for it is profitable for thee that one of thy members should perish, and not that thy whole body should be cast into hell." What does that mean? It means absolute un-flinching sternness in dealing with the right things in yourself that are not the best. "The good is the enemy of the best" in every man, not the bad, but the good that is not good enough. Your right hand is not a bad thing, it is one of the best things you have, but Jesus says if it offends you in developing your spiritual life, and hinders you in following His precepts, cut it off and cast it from you. SSM. 35

GOODNESS

If being in the presence of a good man or woman does not produce a reaction towards goodness in me, I am in a bad way. CHI. 25

Fits of goodness may often be seen in a base character, indicating a capacity to be noble; but apart from that, all kinds of natures are conscious of moments of unusual power and insight and excellence. These moments are wonderful and delightful episodes in both intellectual and spiritual life, yet they nearly always leave the nature with a reaction. Such emotion is no more real goodness than a dewdrop is a diamond or a meteor a star. GW. 67

One might almost say that our every effort to be good and our every effort to be holy is a sure sign that we are neither good nor holy. A child makes no effort to be the daughter or son of its parents, and a child of God born of the Spirit makes no conscious effort to be good or to be holy; but just as a child trying to imitate someone else's mother is bound to fail, so the natural man trying to imitate God is bound to fail. GW. 67

It is never my sense of goodness that brings me into touch with God, but my sense of unworthiness: 'Woe is me! for I am undone'—that brings me into the presence of God at once. HGM. 108

There is only one Being to whom the term 'good' can be applied, and that is the Perfect Being, the term cannot be applied to good men. IWP. 9

We will deal treacherously with the Bible records if we are not soaked in the revelation that God only is good. We will put the saints on the throne, not God. There is only one unshakable goodness, and that is God. It takes time to get there because we will cling to things and to people. Those of us who ought to be princes and princesses with God cling to the shows of God's goodness instead of God Himself. IWP. 31

The best of men and women are but the best of men and women, the only good is God, and Jesus Christ always brings the soul face to face with God, and that is the one great thought we have to be soaked with. IWP. 31

The expression of Christian character is not good doing, but God-likeness. If the Spirit of God has transformed you within, you will exhibit Divine characteristics in your life, not good human characteristics. God's life in us expresses itself as *God's* life, not as human life trying to be godly. MUH. 264

Very few of us debate with the sordid and evil and wrong, but we do debate with the good. It is the good that hates the best, and the higher up you get in the scale of the natural virtues, the more intense is the opposition to Jesus Christ. MUH. 344

One of the greatest demands of God on the human spirit is to believe that God is good when His providence seems to prohibit the fulfilment of what He has promised. NKW. 97

Get rid of the idea that you must do good things, and remember what Jesus says, 'If you believe on Me, out of you will flow rivers of living water.' PH. 67

"The fruit of the Spirit is in all goodness and righteousness and truth." Some of us have goodness only in spots. SSM. 88

GOSPEL

What is needed to-day is not a new gospel, but live men and women who can re-state the Gospel of the Son of God in terms that will reach the very heart of our problems. AUG. 16

Never water down or minimise the mighty Gospel of God by considering that people may be misled by certain statements. Present the Gospel in all its fullness and God will guard His own truth. AUG. 40

The Gospel of the New Testament is based on the absoluteness of revelation, we cannot get it by our common sense. If a man is to be saved it must be from outside, God never pumps up anything from within. AUG. 45

The Gospel of Jesus Christ awakens an intense craving and an equally intense resentment. AUG. 46

When people say, 'Preach us the simple Gospel,' what they mean is, 'Preach us the thing we have always heard, the thing that keeps us sound asleep, we don't want to see things differently'; then the sooner the Spirit of God sends a thrust through their stagnant minds the better. BE. 40

We preach to men as if they were conscious of being dying sinners, they are not, they are having a good time, and all our talk about the need to be born again is from a domain they know nothing about; because some men try to drown unhappiness in worldly pleasures it does not follow all are like that. BE. 76

A gospel based on preconceived notions is merely an irritant. BFB. 32

The natural heart, we cannot repeat it too often, does not want the Gospel. BP. 134

That the natural heart of man does not want the Gospel of God is proved by the resentment of the heart against the working of the Spirit of God, 'No, I don't object to being forgiven, I don't mind being guided and blessed, but it is too much of a radical surrender to ask me to give up my right to myself and allow the Spirit of God to have absolute control of my heart.' BP. 135

The greatest number of men are moral, not immoral; a clean moral life which is sufficient for itself apart from God— that is the evidence of the guarding of Satan, and we all know as workers for God the difficulty, the almost insuperable difficulty, there is in presenting the Gospel to a good-living worldling, not because his mind is obtuse or because he is insensitive, but because he is supernaturally guarded by a 'fully armed strong man.' GW. 100

It is not a new gospel we need, that is the jargon of the hour; it is the old gospel put in terms that fit the present-day need, and for one man or one book that does that there are hundreds who tell us that what we want is a new gospel. What we want is men who have the grace of their Lord to face the present-day problems with the old Gospel. HG. 58

The Gospel of the grace of God awakens an intense longing in human souls and an equally intense resentment, because the revelation which it brings is not palatable. There is a certain pride in man that will give and give, but to come and accept is another thing. I will give my life to martyrdom, I will give myself in consecration, I will do anything, but do not humiliate me to the level of the most hell-deserving sinner and tell me that all I have to do is to accept the gift of salvation through Jesus Christ. MUH. 333

The Gospel of Jesus Christ always forces an issue of will. MUH. 358

The gospel is not so much good news to man as good news about God. "And to preach it with no fine rhetoric." PH. 135

The Gospels always present truth in 'nugget' form, and if we want to know the stages of evangelical experience, we must go to the Epistles which beat out into negotiable gold the nuggets of truth presented by our Lord. PR. 24

The temptation to win and woo men is the most subtle of all, and it is a line that commends itself to us naturally. But you cannot win and woo a mutiny; it is absolutely impossible. You cannot win and woo the man who, when he recognises the rule of God, detests it. The Gospel of Jesus Christ always marks the line of demarcation, His attitude all through is one of sternness, there must be no compromise. PR. 69

. . . the Gospel message is that we can be born from above the second we want to. PR. 122

The Gospel does not present what the natural man wants but what he needs, and the Gospel awakens an intense resentment as well as an intense craving. SHL. 40

As long as we speak winsomely about the 'meek and gentle Jesus,' and the beautiful ideas the Holy Spirit produces when He comes in, people are captivated, but that is not the Gospel. The Gospel does away with any other ground to stand on than that of the Atonement. Speak about the peace of heaven and the joy of the Lord, and men will listen to you; but tell them that the Holy Spirit has to come in and turn out their claim to their right to themselves, and instantly there is resentment—'I can do what I like with my body; I can go where I choose.' SHL. 72

We are not sent to develop the races, we are sent to preach the Gospel to every creature because Our Lord has commanded it, *and for no other reason.* God's purpose is at the back of the whole thing, and His purpose is revealed by His Spirit to sanctified souls only. SSY. 120

GRACE

We are apt to mistake the sovereign works of grace in salvation and sanctification as being final—they are only beginnings. BSG. 15

There is no condescension in grace, a sinner is never afraid of Jesus . . . HGM. 14

To build on the fundamental work of God's grace and ignore the fact that we have to work it out in a mechanical life produces humbugs, those who make a divorce between the mysterious life and the practical life. BE. 56

The one great problem in spiritual life is whether we are going to put God's grace into practice. God won't do the mechanical; He created us to do that; but we can only do it while we draw on the mysterious realm of His divine grace. BE. 57

. . . purity in God's children is not the outcome of obedience to His law, but the result of the supernatural work of His grace. "*I* will cleanse you'; '*I* will give you a new heart'; '*I* will put My Spirit within you, and cause you to walk in My statutes'; '*I* will do it all.' GW. 75

The grace of God makes us honest with ourselves. We must be humorous enough to see the shallow tricks we all have, no matter what our profession of Christianity. We are so altogether perverse that God Almighty had to come and save us! NKW. 89

God not only gives me supernatural grace, but He is in me to will and to do of His good pleasure, and that means I can do all that God's will and my conscience indicate I should do. OBH. 130

Grace is the overflowing immeasurable favour of God; God cannot withhold, the only thing that keeps back His grace and favour is our sin and perversity. OPG. 18

If we are saved by the grace of God it means not only that we are delivered from perdition, but that we are a new creation. The condemnation is to know a thing and not work it out. PH. 62

We have the notion at first that when we are saved and sanctified by God's supernatural grace, He does not require us to do anything, but it is only then that He begins to require anything of us. PR. 75

Never forget for one moment that you are what you are by the grace of God. If you are not what you are by the grace of God, then may God have mercy on you! Everything we are that is not through the grace of God will be a dead clog on us. PS. 22

The miracle of the grace of God is that He can make the past as though it had never been. RTR. 33

The grace of God which comes through Jesus Christ is revealed in that God laid down His life for His enemies. SA. 16

Jesus Christ came to make the great laws of God incarnate in human life; that is the miracle of God's grace. We are to be written epistles, "known and read of all men." There is no allowance whatever in the New Testament for the man who says he is saved by grace but who does not produce the graceful goods. Jesus Christ by His Redemption can make our actual life in keeping with our religious profession. SSM. 90

GREATNESS

We all recognize human trappings; only one in a thousand recognizes human greatness. We bow not to greatness, but to the trappings of money and of birth. If I bow because I must, I am a conventional fraud; if I bow because I recognize true greatness, it is a sign that I am being emancipated. The greatest humiliation for a Christian is to recognize that he has ignored true greatness because it was without trappings. If the Pharisees had been reverent towards true greatness, they would not have treated the Nazarene Carpenter as they did. NKW. 136

The lives of great men leave us with a sense of our own littleness which paralyses us in our effort to be anything else. PH. 1

We have not been told to follow in all the footsteps of the mountain-like characters, but in the footsteps of their faith, because their faith is in a Person. PH. 2

The Bible indicates that a man always falls on his strongest point. Abraham, the man of faith, fell through unbelief; Moses, the meek man, fell through losing his temper; Elijah, the courageous man, fell through losing heart; and Solomon, the most colossally wise, wealthy, luxurious, superb king, fell through grovelling, sensual idolatry. SHH. 8

GROWTH

If my mind and heart and spirit is getting fixed with one Figure only, the Lord Jesus Christ, and other people and other ideas are fading, then I am growing in grace. AUG. 33

We grow exactly like our spirit. If that spirit is the spirit of man, we shall grow further and further away from the image of God; but if we have the Spirit of God within, we shall grow more and more "into the same image from glory to glory." BP. 249

The spirit is soul expressing itself in the body. The body has an enormous influence on the soul, and the soul on the body. When the body is developing into manhood or womanhood there is a sudden awakening of the soul to religious influences, and it is always a dangerous time. What is looked upon as evidence of the grace of God at work is merely the opening up of the soul in the process of development. BSG. 17

When a man is born from above, the life of the Son of God begins in him, and he can either starve that life or nourish it. IYA. 10

Most of us develop our Christianity along the line of our temperament, not along the line of God. MUH. 295

One of the best things for your spiritual welfare is to keep recounting the wonders God has done for you, record them in a book; mark the passage in your Bible and continually refer to it, keep it fresh in your mind. PH. 47

There is another element in this new life which is often overlooked, viz., that it is unconscious in its growth. When Jesus said "Consider the lilies of the field, how they grow," He was referring to the new life in us. If we make His words apply to the natural life only, we make Him appear foolish. If we are born of God and are obeying Him, the unconscious life is forming in us just where we are. God knows exactly the kind of garden to put His lilies in, and they grow and take form unconsciously. PR. 39

The new life is in Him, and we have to remember that it grows like the lily. The right atmosphere for the new life to grow in is exactly where our natural life is placed. PR. 40

The new life must go on and take form unconsciously. God is looking after it, He knows exactly the kind of nourishment as well as the kind of disintegration that is necessary. Be careful that you do not bury the new life, or put it into circumstances where it cannot grow. A lily can only grow in the surroundings that suit it, and in the same way God engineers the circumstances that are best fitted for the development of the life of His Son in us. PR. 40

Most of us want something to show for what we do. We are not interested in God's life in us, but only in our life in God. We are not after the development of the unconscious life of the Son of God in us, but after the 'small change' which enables us to say, 'I did this and that.' The life of the Son of God grows feebler in a life of that order. PR. 41

Where we are actually is the Almighty's business, not ours. "Consider the lilies." Our Lord knows what to do with His own lilies; if we try to transplant them they will die. We are in such a desperate hurry, but it is in the unrecorded years, the times we are apt to think are of no account, that we are developing most for the value of the Son of God. PR. 41

The majority of us so harp on the ordinary evangelical line that we thank God for saving us and then leave the thing alone. We cannot grow *into* holiness, but we must grow *in* it. PR. 51

Thank God there is a pain attached to being saved, the pain of growing until we come to maturity where we can do the work of a son or daughter of God. PS. 29

When we lie like fallow ground, God puts in new seeds and the harvest is the ripe fruit of God; otherwise it is ripe fruit of naturalness only. Lying fallow is always the secret of spiritual growth. RTR. 13

We have to keep in the light as God is in the light and the grace of God will supply supernatural life all the time. Thank God there is no end to His grace if we will keep in the humble place. The overflowing grace of God has no limits, and we have to set no limits to it, but "grow in grace, and in the knowledge of our Lord and Saviour Jesus Christ." RTR. 69

We grow spiritually by obeying God through the words of Jesus being made spirit and life to us, and by paying attention to where we are, not to whether we are growing or not. We grow spiritually as our Lord grew physically, by a life of simple, unobtrusive obedience. SHL. 67

We have to nourish the life of the Son of God in us, and we do it by bringing our natural life into accordance with His life and transforming it into a spiritual life by obedience. SHL. 68

There is only one way to develop spiritually, and that is by concentrating on God. Don't bother about whether you are growing in grace or whether you are being of use to others, but believe on Jesus and out of you will flow rivers of living water. SSM. 69

"Consider the lilies of the field, how they grow"—they simply *are*. Take the sea and the air, the sun, the stars and the moon, they all *are*, and what a ministration they exert! So often we mar God's designed influence through us by our self-conscious effort to be consistent and useful. It seems unreasonable to expect a man to consider the lilies, yet that is the only way he can grow in grace. SSM. 69

How are you to grow in the knowledge of God? By remaining where you are, and by remembering that your Father knows where you are and the circumstances you are in. Keep concentrated on Him and you will grow spiritually as the lily. SSM. 70

How many people are born into the world by taking thought? The springs of natural life cannot be got at by the reasoning of common-sense, and when you deal with the life of God in your soul, Jesus says, 'Remember that your growth in grace does not depend on your watching it, but on your concentration on your Father in heaven.' SSM. 70

Notice the difference between the illustrations we use in talking of spiritual growth and the illustrations Jesus uses. We take our illustrations from engineering enterprises, from motor-cars and aeroplanes, *et cetera*, things that compel our attention. Jesus Christ took His illustrations from His Father's handiwork, from sparrows and flowers, things that none of us dream of noticing; we are all breathless and passionate and in a hurry. We may think till all is blue, but Jesus says you cannot add one inch to your height in that way. We cannot possibly develop spiritually in any way other than the way He tells us, viz., by concentration on God. SSM. 70

GRUDGING

. . . if there is the tiniest grudge in our spirit against another, from that second, spiritual penetration into the knowledge of God will cease. PH. 219

When you are thinking of the grudge you owe someone, let the Spirit of God bring back to your mind how you have treated God. RTR. 70

GUIDANCE

Divine guidance by the Word indicates a profound and personal preparation of heart. God's sayings are sealed to every soul saving as they are opened by the indwelling Spirit of God. CD. VOL. 1, 17

To search for a word of God to suit one's case is never Divine guidance, but guidance by human caprice and inclination. CD. VOL. 1, 18

Jesus Christ is the only One who has not only been on this earth, but beyond it, consequently He alone is our guide. HGM. 81

It seems so ridiculous and so conceited to say that God Almighty is our Father and that He is looking after our affairs; but looked at from the position in which Jesus places us we find it is a marvellous revelation of truth. MFL. 32

Never run before God's guidance. If there is the slightest doubt, then He is not guiding. Whenever there is doubt— *don't*. MUH. 4

God never guides presently, but always now. Realize that the Lord is here *now*, and the emancipation is immediate. MUH. 112

There are times of crisis when we must wait on God, but they are rare. It is the abortion of piety to ask God to guide us here and there, of course He will! Such asking is not real. Remember our Lord's injunction—'Except ye become as little children.' NKW. 143

Jesus guides us by making us His friends. SSY. 69

H

HABIT

In the most superficial matters put yourself under control, your own control. Be as scrupulously punctual in your private habits as you would be in a Government office.   DI. 67

Before any habit is formed you must put yourself under mechanical laws of obedience, and the higher the emotion started by the Spirit of God, the keener must be the determination to commit yourself.   DI. 69

Habit is a mechanical process of which we have ceased to become conscious. The basis of habit is always physical. A habit forms a pathway in the material stuff of the brain, and as we persist in thinking along a certain line we hand over a tremendous amount to the machine and do things without thinking.   MFL. 19

We infect the places we live in by our ruling habit.   MFL. 19

The sentimental type of Christian is the sighing, tear-flowing, beginning-over-again Christian who always has to go to prayer meetings, always has to be stirred up, or to be soothed and put in bandages, because he has never formed the habit of obedience to the Spirit of God.   MFL. 39

Anything and everything is possible in the way of habits. Habits form a pathway in the material stuff of the brain. We cannot form a habit without thinking about it; but when once the pathway in the brain is formed we can do a thing easily without thinking about it. For instance, we were not born with the ready-made habit of dressing ourselves, we had to form that habit. If we persist in using our bodies in a certain way, alterations will take place in the make-up of the brain. Spiritually we have to learn to form habits on the basis of the grace of God.   MFL. 77

In physical life we do best those things we have habitually learned to do, and the same is true in mental and spiritual life. We do not come into the world knowing how to do anything; all we do we have acquired by habit. Remember, habit is purely mechanical.   MFL. 93

The forming of a new habit is difficult until you get into the way of doing the thing, then everything you meet with aids you in developing along the right line. It is good practice to sit down for five minutes and do nothing; in that way you will soon discover how little control you have over yourself.   MFL. 96

In forming a new habit it is vitally important to insist on bringing the body under control first. Paul says, 'I maul and master my body, in case, after preaching to other people, I am disqualified myself.'   MFL. 96

Your god may be your little Christian habit, the habit of prayer at stated times, or the habit of Bible reading. Watch how your Father will upset those times if you begin to worship your habit instead of what the habit symbolizes—I can't do that just now, I am praying; it is my hour with God. No, it is your hour with your habit. MUH. 133

Every habit is purely mechanical, and whenever we form a habit it makes a material difference in the brain. The material of the brain alters very slowly, but it does alter, and by repeatedly doing a thing a groove is formed in the material of the brain so that it becomes easier to do it again, until at last we become unconscious of doing it. SSM. 38

If once your nerves are in the habit of doing a thing physically, you will do it every time, until you break the habit deliberately; and the same is true spiritually . . . Jesus Christ demands of the man who trusts in Him the same reckless sporting spirit that the natural man exhibits in his life. SSM. 71

HAPPINESS

Happiness is no standard for men and women because happiness depends on my being determinedly ignorant of God and His demands. BE. 14

Happiness is the characteristic of a child, and God condemns us for taking happiness out of a child's life; but as men and women we should have done with happiness long ago, we should be facing the stern issues of life, knowing that the grace of God is sufficient for every problem the devil can present. BP. 116

When a man is happy, he cannot pull a long face, he may try to, but it is the face of a clown; when he is happy inside he shows it on the outside. If you hear a Christian with a sad face saying, 'Oh, I am so full of the joy of the Lord,' well, you know it is not true. If I am full of the joy of the Lord, it will pour out of every cell of my body. BP. 262

HATRED

God loves the world so much that he hates with a perfect hatred the thing that is twisting men away from Him. BP. 120

Hatred is the supreme detestation of one personality for another, and the other person ought to be the devil. BP. 120

Jesus . . . our love for Him is to be so intense that every other relationship is 'hatred' in comparison if it should conflict with His claims. BP. 169

If we are foolish enough in the eyes of the world to order our life according to the rule of the kingdom of heaven, the only virtue will be, says Jesus, that men will hate you as they hated Me. HG. 54

"If any man come to Me, and hate not . . . he cannot be My disciple." The word 'hate' sounds harsh, and yet it is uttered by the most human of human beings because Jesus was Divine; there was never a human breast that beat with more tenderness than Jesus Christ's. The word 'hate' is used as a vehement protest against the pleas to which human nature is only too ready to give a hearing. If we judge our Lord by a standard of humanity that does not recognize God, we have to put a black mark against certain things He said. One such mark would come in connection with His words to His mother at Cana, "Woman, what have I to do with thee?" Another would come in connection with John the Baptist; instead of Jesus going and taking His forerunner out of prison, He simply sends a message to him through His disciples—"Go your way and tell John . . . and blessed is he, whosoever shall not be offended in Me." IWP. 107

"If any man come to Me, and hate not . . . , *he cannot be My disciple.*" Our Lord implies that the only men and women He will use in His building enterprises are those who love Him personally, passionately and devotedly beyond any of the closest ties on earth. The conditions are stern, but they are glorious. MUH. 128

Jesus Christ hates the wrong in man, and Calvary is the estimate of His hatred. MUH. 326

"Be not hasty in thy spirit to be angry." Anger nearly always covers up a thing that is wrong. SHH. 89

HEALING

When the soul is perplexed—and it certainly will be if we are going on with God, because we are a mark for Satan—and the sudden onslaught comes, as it did in the life of Job, we cry, 'Heal me because I am in pain,' but there is no answer. Then we cry, 'Heal me, not because I am in pain, but because my soul is perplexed; I cannot see any way out of it or why this thing should be'; still no answer; then at last we cry, 'Heal me, O Lord, not because of my pain, nor because my soul is sick, but for Thy mercies' sake.' Then we have the answer, "The Lord hath heard my supplication." The surroundings of the soul, the scenes which arise from our doings, do produce perplexity in the soul. The soul cannot be separated from the body, and bodily perplexities produce difficulties in the soul, and these difficulties go inward and at times intrude right to the very throne of God in the heart. BP. 88

In every case of healing by God it comes through a child-like trust in Jesus Christ. IMP. 36

The one thing Jesus Christ did when He came in contact with lunacy was to heal it, and the greatest work of the devil is that he is producing lunacy in the name of God all over the world in the spiritual realm, making people who did know God go off on tangents. What did Jesus say? ". . . so as to lead astray, if possible, even the elect." IWP. 89

The Redemption of our Lord Jesus Christ mirrored in the Atonement embraces everything. Sin, sickness, limitation and death are all done away with in Redemption; but we have to remember the Atonement works under God's dispensational sovereignty. It is not a question of whether God will sovereignly permit us to be delivered from sin in this dispensation, it is His distinct expressive will that we should be delivered. When it comes to the question of sickness and limitation, it is not a question of whether we will agree with God's will, but whether God's sovereignty is active—that predispensational efficacy of the Atonement on our behalf just now. IYA. 85

That God does give wonderful gifts of the Atonement before their dispensation is clear, there are innumerable cases of healing, but if I make that the ground on which God must work, I intercede no longer, I cannot, I become a dictator to God. When anyone is sick, I do not pray, I say, 'They have no business to be sick,' and that means I have destroyed altogether my contact with God. IYA. 86

There are cases recorded in the Bible, and in our own day, of people who have been marvellously healed, for what purpose? For us to imitate them? Never, but in order that we might discern what lies behind, viz., the individual relationship to a personal God. PS. 77

HEALTH

There is no such thing as pain in the mass, pain is individual; nobody can feel more pain than the acme of nerves will give, and the more physical expression there is in pain, the less pain there is. It is by refusing to estimate things in their right light that we misunderstand the direction of pain. BP. 117

Instead of the Bible belittling the laws of health and bodily uprightness and cleanliness, it insists on these by implication far more than modern science does by explicit statement. BP. 167

If we are going to follow Jesus, we must do to death infirmity-sins. God cannot do it, we have to do it ourselves. Satan takes occasion of the frailty of the bodily temple and says, 'Now you know you cannot do that, you are so infirm, you cannot concentrate your mind,' etc. Never allow bodily infirmities to hinder you obeying the commands of Jesus. IWP. 53

Physical health is a delight because it is an exact balance between our physical life and outer circumstances. Disease means that outer circumstances are getting too much for the vital force on the inside. Morally it is the same. OBH. 102

Health is simply the balance of our bodily life with external circumstances, anything that upsets the equilibrium on the inside upsets the bodily equilibrium on the outside, consequently when a man is convicted of sin, his 'beauty consumes away like a moth.' PR. 14

For a man to make health his god is to put himself merely at the head of the brute creation. PS. 77

Health means the balance between my physical life and external nature, and is maintained purely by a sufficient fighting vitality within against things outside. Health is equilibrium maintained through a terrific power of fight. Disease means that the harmony of health is gone, and a sign that the fighting corpuscles are getting weak. The things which keep you going when you are alive, disintegrate you when you are dead. Everything that is not my physical life is designed to put me to death, but if I have enough fighting power I produce the balance of health. The same is true in my moral life. SA. 93

. . . "if any would not work, neither should he eat." There are plenty of folks who eat but don't work, and they suffer for it. If we are physically healthy, the benefit of the food we eat corresponds to the work we do, and the same is true in mental, moral and spiritual health. SHH. 64

One word about the physical condition of people. There is a threshold to our nerves, that is, a place where the nerves begin to record. Some people's nerves do not record things as quickly as others. Some people have what is called the 'misery' threshold of nerves, the threshold where the nerves begin to record is much lower down than it is in other people. Take it in connection with sound, some people can sleep in a tremendous racket, noise makes not the slightest difference to them. The ear gathers up vibrations, and only when those vibrations are quick enough do we hear. If the threshold of our hearing were lower, we should hear anything that makes waves in the atmosphere, we should hear the flowers grow, everything that grows makes a motion in the atmosphere. The majority of us have a threshold that is high up, and we cannot hear unless there is sufficient vibration in the atmosphere. Get a nervous system where the threshold of nerves is low, and life is an abject torture to that one wherever he goes. What is the good of telling him to cheer up? There is a bigger problem there than we can touch. That one is in contact with forces which the majority of us know nothing about; he is tortured by things we never hear, tortured by things we never feel. Such people take a very gloomy view of life; they cannot help it. WG. 61

In dealing with sick souls, we must remember the Master's way, how He went to the root of the matter. Hear Him as He said, time and again when one was brought to Him for physical healing, "thy sins be forgiven thee." Dig out the "root of bitterness," then there can be no fruit to sour the life and set the nerves on edge. WG. 64

. . . if you are a worker for Jesus Christ, He will open your eyes wide to the fact that sin and misery and anguish are not imaginary, they are real. Anguish is as real as joy; fired, jangled and tortured nerves are as real as nerves in order. Low threshold nerves, where everything is an exquisite misery, are as real as high threshold nerves where nothing is misery. WG. 65

HEARING

Once a week at least read the Sermon on the Mount and see how much you have hearkened to it—"Love your enemies, bless them that curse you"; we do not listen to it because we do not want to. OBH. 54

When we *hear* a thing is not necessarily when it is spoken, but when we are in a state to listen to it and to understand. Our Lord's statements seem to be so

simple and gentle, and they slip unobserved into the subconscious mind. Then something happens in our circumstances, and up comes one of these words into our consciousness and we *hear* it for the first time, and it makes us reel with amazement. SSY. 60

I will always hear what I listen for, and the ruling disposition of the soul determines what I listen for, just as the ruling disposition either keeps the eyes from beholding vanity or makes them behold nothing else. When Jesus Christ alters our disposition, He gives us the power to hear as He hears. BP. 74

"He that hath ear to hear, let him hear." Before we can hear certain things, we must be trained. Our disposition determines what we listen for; and when Jesus alters the disposition, He gives us the power to hear as He hears. OBH. 54

HEART

A man never believes what Jesus Christ says about the human heart until the Holy Ghost gives him the startling revelation of the truth of His diagnosis. AUG. 48

If once Jesus Christ is clear to the vision of the heart, everything else is simple. AUG. 111

Jesus Christ does not simply say, 'Thou shalt not do certain things'; He demands that we have such a condition of heart that we never even think of doing them, every thought and imagination of heart and mind is to be unblameable in the sight of God. BE. 9

The heart is the exchange and mart; our words and expressions are simply the coins we use, but the 'shop' resides in the heart, the emporium where all the goods are, and that is what God sees but no man can see. BP. 102

Pain exists in the heart and nowhere else. BP. 116

The real spiritual powers of a man reside in the heart, which is the centre of the physical life, of the soul life, and of the spiritual life. BP. 125

The heart is the first thing to live in physical birth and in spiritual birth. It is a wonderful thing that God can cleanse and purify the thinking of our hearts. BP. 125

Remember the two alternatives: our heart may be the centre of the Divine rule making us one with God's thoughts and purposes, or it may be the centre of the devil's rule making us one with the prince of this world, the being who hates God, one with the natural life which barters the spiritual. BP. 137

. . . "God hardened Pharaoh's heart." This must not be interpreted to mean that God hardened a man's heart and then condemned him for being hard. It means rather that God's laws, being God's laws, do not alter, and that if any man refuses to obey God's law he will be hardened away from God, and that by God's own decree. No man's destiny is made for him, he makes his own; but the imperative necessity that a man must make his own destiny is of God. BP. 139

The heart never dies, it is as immortal as God's Spirit because it is the centre of man's spirit. Memory never dies, mind never dies; our bodily machine dies, and the manifestation of our heart and life in the body dies, but the heart never dies. BP. 140

The tiniest bit of sin is an indication of the vast corruption that is in the human heart. CHI. 71

The Bible term "heart" is best understood if we simply say 'me,' it is the central citadel of a man's personality. MFL. 113

There is only one Being Who can satisfy the last aching abyss of the human heart, and that is the Lord Jesus Christ. MUH. 212

The discovery of the desperate recesses in the human heart is the greatest evidence of the need for the Redemption. OPG. 72

Jesus Christ is the Master of the human soul, He knows what is in the human heart, and He has no illusions about any man. PH. 51

The human heart must have satisfaction, but there is only one Being Who can satisfy the last aching abyss of the human heart, and that is our Lord Jesus Christ. PH. 52

"My peace I give unto you, let not your heart be troubled," i.e., see that your heart does not get disturbed out of its relationship to Me. SA. 99

"The sacrifices of God are a broken spirit." When my heart is broken, the husk of individual relationship is merged into a personal relationship, and I find that God rehabilitates everything, i.e., He puts things back into their right fittings in me. SHH. 31

Jesus Christ has undertaken through His Redemption to put into us a heart so pure that God Almighty can see nothing to censure in it, and the Holy Spirit searches us not only to make us know the possibilities of iniquity in our heart, but to make us 'unblameable in holiness in His sight.' SHL. 48

Jesus Christ is either the supreme Authority on the human heart or He is not worth listening to, and He said: 'For from within, out of the heart of men, proceed . . .' and then comes that very ugly catalogue. Jesus did not say, 'Into the human heart these things are injected,' but, 'from within, out of the heart of men all these evil things proceed.' If we trust our innocent ignorance to secure us, it is likely that as life goes on there will come a burst-up from underneath into our conscious life which will reveal to us that we are uncommonly like what Jesus Christ said. SHL. 63

HEAVEN

"We look for new heavens and a new earth"; nowadays people have got tired of the preaching about a future heaven and they have gone to the other extreme and deal only with what is called the practical, consequently they rob themselves of the unfathomable joy of knowing that everything God has said will come to pass. BE. 36

The Redemption covers more than men and women, it covers the whole earth; everything that has been marred by sin and the devil has been completely redeemed by Jesus Christ. ". . . new heavens and a new earth, wherein dwelleth righteousness." BE. 37

When I asked God to give me the Holy Spirit, He did so, and what a transformation took place! Life became heaven on earth after being hell on earth. LG. 118

There is no heaven with a little corner of hell in it. God is determined to make you pure and holy and right; He will not allow you to escape for one moment from the scrutiny of the Holy Spirit. MUH. 183

We are lifted up into that inviolable place that cannot be defiled, and Paul states that God can raise us up there *now*, and that the wonder of sitting in the heavenly places in Christ Jesus is to be manifested in our lives while we are here on earth. OBH. 32

We must have in our minds that by "heavenly places" is meant all that Jesus Christ was when He was down here, and all that He is revealed to be now by the Word; and God raises us up to sit together with Him there. There is ample time and ample room to grow in the heavenly places. OBH. 33

The marvellous characteristic of the Spirit of God in you and me when we are raised up to the heavenly places in Christ Jesus is that we look to the Creator, and see that the marvellous Being Who made the world and upholds all things by the word of His power is the One Who keeps us in every particular. OBH. 33

Jesus Christ tells us to take the lessons of our lives from the things men never look at—"Consider the lilies"; "Behold the fowls of the air." How often do we look at clouds, or grass, at sparrows, or flowers? Why, we have no time to look at them, we are in the rush of things—it is absurd to sit dreaming about sparrows and trees and clouds! Thank God, when He raises us to the heavenly places, He manifests in us the very mind that was in Christ Jesus, unhasting and unresting, calm, steady, and strong. OBH. 33

Jesus warns the disciple never to be afraid of the contempt of the world when he possesses spiritual discernment. Those who are in the heavenly places see God's counsels in what to the wisdom of the world is arrogant stupidity. OBH. 36

'I would be all right,' we say, 'if God saved me and took me straight to heaven.' That is exactly what He will do! "We will come unto him and make Our abode with him"—the Triune God abiding with the saint. OBH. 103

HELL

. . . hell is God; if there were no God, there would be no hell. BE. 86

If we only believe in Jesus because He delivers us from hell, we will forsake Him in two seconds if He crosses our purposes or goes contrary to our personal disposition of mind. PH. 229

Every man has power to go to hell because by nature man's will is towards self-realisation. SHH. 118

. . . there is an *Angelic Hell*; there is no other place for fallen angels. SHL. 29

It is never stated that God has provided a place for men who will not come to Him; it is implied with solemn warning that the only place they can go to is that 'prepared for the devil and his angels.' SHL. 29

HEREDITY

Unless Jesus Christ can put a totally new heredity into us, there is no use asking us to think about the wonderful life He lived. The revelation made by the Redemption is that God can put into us a new disposition whereby we can live a totally new life. PR. 80

Heredity is a bigger problem than I can cope with; but if I will receive the gift of the Holy Spirit on the basis of Christ's Redemption, He enables me to work out that Redemption in my experience. SA. 70

I will ask God to make my work fine and clean; He won't do it, it is not His job. God's job is to alter my heredity, I cannot alter that; but when my heredity is altered, I have to manifest my altered heredity in actual circumstances. SA. 89

The Holy Spirit in a Christian wars against the old heredity; the new heredity and the old war one against another. SA. 111

Sin is not an act, but an hereditary disposition. Sin must be cleansed, and the revelation of Redemption is that God through Jesus Christ has power to cleanse us from the heredity of sin. The curious thing is that we are blind to the *fact* of sin, and deal only with the effects of sin. SA. 116

The revelation is not that Jesus Christ took on Him our fleshly sins—a man stands or falls by his own silly weaknesses—but that He took on Him *the heredity of sin*. SA. 120

. . . the marvel of the Redemption—that Jesus Christ can give me a new heredity, the unsullied heredity of the Holy Spirit, and if it is there, says Jesus, it will work out in actual history. SSM. 27

The great marvel of the salvation of Jesus is that He alters heredity. SSM. 34

HOLINESS

To the majority of men, holiness is all in the clouds, but take this message, "Holiness, without which no man shall see the Lord," and drive it home on every line until there is no refuge from the terrific application. Holy not only in my religious aspirations, but holy in my soul life, in my imagination and thinking; holy in every detail of my bodily life. AUG. 21

Never say God's holiness does not mean what it does mean. It means every part of the life under the scrutiny of God, knowing that the grace of God is sufficient for every detail. The temptation comes along the line of compromise, 'Don't be so unbendingly holy; so fiercely pure and uprightly chaste.' Never tolerate by sympathy with yourself or with others any practice that is not in keeping with a holy God. AUG. 60

Holiness is the agreement between a man's disposition and the law of God, as expressed in the life of Jesus. BE. 15

Holiness is militant, Satan is continually pressing and ardent, but holiness maintains itself. It is morality on fire and transfigured into the likeness of God. Holiness is not only what God gives me, but what I manifest that God has given me. I manifest this coruscating holiness by my reaction against sin, the world, and the devil. Wherever God's saints are in the world they are protected by a wall of fire which they do not see, but Satan does. "That wicked one toucheth him not." Satan has to ask and plead for permission; as to whether God grants him permission is to do with the sovereignty of God and is not in our domain to understand. BP. 27

The holiness of God is absolute, not progressive; that is, it knows no development by antagonism. BSG. 10

The characteristic of the holiness of Almighty God is that it is absolute, it is impossible to antagonize or strain it. The characteristic of the holiness of Jesus is that it manifested itself by means of antagonism, it was a holiness that could be tested. BSG. 36

There is only one type of humanity, and only one type of holiness, the holiness that was manifested in the life of the Lord Jesus, and it is that holiness which He gives to us. It is not that we are put in a place where we can begin to be like Him: we are put in a place where we *are* like Him. BSG. 58

The only holiness there is is the holiness derived through faith, and faith is the instrument the Holy Spirit uses to organize us into Christ. But do not let us be vague here. Holiness, like sin, is a disposition, not a series of acts. A man can *act* holily, but he has not a holy *disposition*. CHI. 81

A saint has had imparted to him the disposition of holiness, therefore holiness must be the characteristic of the life here and now. CHI. 81

The strenuous effort of the saint is not to produce holiness, but to express in actual circumstances the disposition of the Son of God which is imparted to him by the Holy Ghost. DI. 21

It is quite true to say 'I can't live a holy life'; but you can decide to let Jesus make you holy. 'I can't do away with my past'; but you can decide to let Jesus do away with it. That is the issue to push. DI. 58

The Spirit of God must have a deep indignation at the preaching of holiness that is not the holiness of Jesus. The holiness of Jesus is the most humble thing on earth. GW. 21

The characteristic of the holiness which is the outcome of the indwelling of God is a blazing truthfulness with regard to God's word, and an amazing tenderness in personal dealing. GW. 74

We do not evolve into holiness, it is a gift—we evolve *in* it, attainment after attainment, becoming sons and daughters of God, brothers and sisters of the Lord Jesus. GW. 130

'I beseech you . . . to present your bodies a living sacrifice holy, acceptable to God.' Practical holiness is the only holiness of any value in this world, and the only kind God will endorse. GW. 143

Goodness and purity ought never to attract attention to themselves, they ought simply to be magnets to draw to Jesus Christ. If my holiness is not drawing towards Him, it is not holiness of the right order, but an influence that will awaken inordinate affection and lead souls away into side-eddies. A beautiful saint may be a hindrance if he does not present Jesus Christ but only what Christ has done for him. He will leave the impression—"What a fine character that man is!" MUH. 85

Continually restate to yourself what the purpose of your life is. The destined end of man is not happiness, nor health, but holiness. Nowadays we have far too many affinities, we are dissipated with them; right, good, noble affinities which will yet have their fulfilment, but in the meantime God has to atrophy them. The one thing that matters is whether a man will accept the God Who will make him holy. At all costs a man must be rightly related to God. MUH. 245

If by your preaching you convince me that I am unholy, I resent your preaching. The preaching of the gospel awakens an intense resentment because it must reveal that I am unholy; but it also awakens an intense craving. God has one destined end for mankind, viz., holiness. MUH. 245

Holiness means unsullied walking with the feet, unsullied talking with the tongue, unsullied thinking with the mind—every detail of the life under the scrutiny of God. Holiness is not only what God gives me, but what I manifest that God has given me. MUH. 245

If we are born again of the Spirit of God, our one desire is a hunger and thirst after nothing less than holiness, the holiness of Jesus, and He will satisfy it. OBH. 22

No individual can develop a holy life with God without benefiting all other saints. OBH. 42

If I am set on my own holiness, I become a traitor to Jesus. PH. 165

Wherever Jesus comes He reveals that man is away from God by reason of sin, and he is terrified at His presence. That is why men will put anything in the place of Jesus Christ, anything rather than let God come near in His startling purity, because immediately God comes near, conscience records that God is holy and nothing unholy can live with Him, consequently His presence hurts the sinner. "If I had not come and spoken unto them, they had not had sin: but now they have no cloke for their sin." PS. 62

God is holy, therefore nothing that does not partake of His holiness can abide in His presence, and that means pain. PS. 63

Holiness, or spiritual harmony, is a perfect balance between our disposition and all the law of God. PS. 79

Holiness is untouched by panic. PS. 80

"The Son of Man came eating and drinking." One of the most staggering things in the New Testament is just this commonplace aspect. The curious difference between Jesus Christ's idea of holiness and that of other religions lies here. The one says holiness is not compatible with ordinary food and married life, but Jesus Christ represents a character lived straight down in the ordinary amalgam of human life, and His claim is that the character He manifested is possible for any man, if he will come in by the door provided for him. SA. 33

When once the holiness of God is manifested in human lives and in preaching (and the two go together), these two things happen: a great number durst not join themselves, and multitudes are added to the Lord. Never think that the blessing and benediction of God on the outside crowd is all. It is a mere fringe. Men and women are blessed, their bodies are healed, devils are turned out; but the point is that multitudes of those who believe are added to the Lord. WG. 105

HOLY SPIRIT

The great thing that the Holy Spirit reveals is that the supernatural power of God is ours through Jesus Christ, and if we will receive the Holy Spirit He will teach us how to think as well as how to live. BE. 97

The Holy Ghost is seeking to awaken men out of lethargy; He is pleading, yearning, blessing, pouring benedictions on men, convicting and drawing them nearer, for one purpose only, that they may receive Him so that He may make them holy men and women exhibiting the life of Jesus Christ. BE. 99

The Holy Spirit is not a substitute for Jesus, the Holy Spirit is all that Jesus was, and all that Jesus did, made real in personal experience now. BE. 99

Mind the Holy Spirit, mind His light, mind His convictions, mind His guidance, and slowly and surely the sensual personality will be turned into a spiritual personality. BP. 50

The thought is unspeakably full of glory, that God the Holy Ghost can come into my heart and fill it so full that the life of God will manifest itself all through this body which used to manifest exactly the opposite. If I am willing and determined to keep in the light and obey the Spirit, then the characteristics of the indwelling Christ will manifest themselves. BP. 146

By right of His Death and Resurrection and Ascension Our Lord can impart Holy Spirit to any and every man. BSG. 25

The gift of God to every fallen son of Adam is the gift of the Holy Spirit, that is, the essential power and nature of God coming into a man and lifting him to a totally new kingdom; and that power can be had for the asking—"If ye then, being evil, know how to give good gifts unto your children; how much more shall your heavenly Father give the Holy Spirit *to them that ask Him!*" BSG. 76

The great Lover of God is the Holy Spirit, and when we receive the Holy Spirit we find we have a God whom we can know and whom we can love with all our heart because we see "the light of the knowledge of the glory of God in the face of Jesus Christ." CHI. 77

Let our Lord be allowed to give the Holy Spirit to a man, deliver him from sin, and put His own love within him, and that man will love Him personally, passionately and devotedly. It is not an earning or a working for, but a gift and a receiving. CHI. 90

It is not what we feel, or what we know, but ever what we *receive* from God— and a fool can receive a gift. "If ye then, being evil, know how to give good gifts unto your children, how much more shall your heavenly Father give the Holy Spirit to them that ask Him?" It is so simple that everyone who is not simple misses it. DI. 20

We continually want to substitute our transactions with God for the great mystic powerful work of the Holy Spirit. "The wind bloweth where it listeth, and thou hearest the voice thereof, but knowest not whence it cometh and whither it goeth: *so is every one that is born of the Spirit.*" DI. 20

We "become partakers of the divine nature" by receiving the Holy Ghost who sheds abroad the love of God in our hearts, and the oneness is manifested in a life of abandon and obedience—both unconscious. DI. 22

When the Spirit of God gets hold of me, He takes the foundation of the fictitious out of me and leaves nothing but an aching cavern for God to fill. "Blessed are the poor in spirit." HG. 120

The first descent of the Holy Spirit was upon the Son of Man—that is, the whole human race represented in one Person, and that Person the historic Jesus Christ who was God Incarnate. HGM. 9

The second mighty descent of the Holy Spirit was on the Day of Pentecost, when the power of God came in Person. HGM. 10

As soon as Jesus Christ was glorified, the personal Holy Spirit descended, and in the decrees of God the fulness of time was reached when the Son of Man, on whom the Holy Spirit had descended as a dove, ascended to the right hand of the Father and sent forth the mighty Holy Spirit. HGM. 10

It is one thing to believe that the Holy Spirit is given individually, but another thing to receive the revelation that He is here. HGM. 10

All that Jesus Christ came to do is made experimentally ours by the Holy Spirit; He does *in* us what Jesus did *for* us. HGM. 11

The Holy Spirit regenerates my personal spirit, that is, I receive a quickening life which puts the 'beyond' within, and immediately the 'beyond' has come within it rises up to the 'above,' and I enter the domain where Jesus lives. HG. 12

The Holy Spirit is God Himself working to make the Redemption efficacious in human lives. No wonder men leap for joy when they get saved in the New Testament way! HGM. 13

The descent of the Holy Ghost can never be experimental, it is historical. The reception of the Holy Ghost into our hearts is experimental. HGM. 20

If the Holy Spirit is allowed to dwell in the human spirit He has energised, He will express the unutterable. Think what that means. It means being quickened by the incoming of the Holy Spirit Who comes in to dwell supremely, and the amazing revelation is that He intercedes in us, for us, with a tenderness exactly in accordance with the Mind of God. IYA. 103

Ask God on the authority of Jesus to give you the Holy Spirit, and He will do so; but you will never ask until you have struck the bottom board of your need. LG. 117

We must distinguish between the working of our own suspicions and the checking of the Spirit of God who works as quietly and silently as a breeze. LG. 138

The Holy Spirit does not become our spirit; He invades our spirit and lifts our personality into a right relationship with God, and that means we can begin now to work out what God has worked in. MFL. 44

The Holy Spirit enables us to fulfil all the commands of God, and we are without excuse for not fulfilling them. Absolute almighty ability is packed into our spirit, and to say 'can't,' if we have received the Holy Spirit, is unconscious blasphemy. MFL. 44

The Holy Spirit cannot be located as a Guest in a house, He invades everything. MUH. 102

"The love of God"—not the power to love God, but *the love of God*—"is shed abroad in our hearts by the Holy Ghost which is given unto us." The Holy Ghost is the gift of the ascended Christ. OBH. 57

"Grieve not the Holy Spirit." He does not come with a voice of thunder, but with a voice so gentle that it is easy to ignore it. OBH. 68

When the Holy Spirit comes into a man 'his beauty is consumed away,' the perfectly ordered completeness of his whole nature is broken up; then the Holy Spirit, brooding over the chaos that is produced, brings a word of God, and as that word is received and obeyed a new life is formed. OPG. 2

Holy Spirit is essential Deity, and He energises our spirit and presences us with Deity as our Lord was presenced. Holy Spirit never becomes our spirit, He quickens our spirit, and instantly we begin to express a new soul. PR. 14

If the man will obey the Holy Spirit, the new balance of holiness will be set up, the balance of his disposition with the law of God. Then he must obey God's will in his body, and this will mean crucifying the flesh with its affections and lusts. PR. 15

The Holy Spirit is the One Who makes experimentally real *in* us what Jesus Christ did *for* us. The Holy Spirit is the Deity in proceeding power Who applies the Atonement to our experience. PR. 112

Watch spiritual hardness, if ever you have the tiniest trace of it, haul up everything else till you get back your softness to the Spirit of God. RTR. 18

Just as the disposition of sin entered into the human race by one man, so the Holy Spirit entered the race by another Man, and Redemption means that I can be delivered from the heredity of sin, and through Jesus Christ can receive an unsullied heredity, viz; the Holy Spirit. RTR. 34

The Holy Spirit will take my spirit, soul and body and bring them back into communion with God, and lead me into identification with the death of Jesus Christ, until I know experimentally that my old disposition, my right to myself, is crucified with Him, and my human nature is now free to obey the commands of God. SA. 122

We do not need the Holy Spirit to reveal that immorality is wrong, but we do need the Holy Spirit to reveal that the complacency of the natural life has Satan at its basis. SHL. 40

The great mystic work of the Holy Spirit is in the dim regions of our personality where we cannot go. SHL. 49

HOLY SPIRIT, BAPTISM OF

The baptism of the Holy Ghost means the extinction of life-fires that are not of God, and everything becomes instinct with the life of God. DI. 24

The baptism with the Holy Ghost and with fire is Jesus Christ's own peculiar right; He is the true Baptizer. 'I indeed baptize you with water,' said John, 'but He shall baptize you with the Holy Ghost, and with fire'—a strange and amazing and supernatural baptism. GW. 22

Oh, the patience, the gentleness, the longing of the Lord Jesus after lives, and yet men are turning this way and that, and even saints who once knew Him are turning aside, their eyes are fixed on other things, on the blessings that come from the baptism with the Holy Ghost and have forgotten the Baptizer Himself. GW. 23

As soon as you receive the Holy Spirit He begins to awaken in you the tremendous 'want,' overwhelming, all-absorbing, passionate in its impelling rush, to be baptized with the Holy Ghost and with fire. GW. 24

. . . the baptism with the Holy Ghost is not an experience apart from Christ, it is the evidence that He has ascended. It is not the baptism with the Holy Ghost that changes men, it is the power of the ascended Christ coming into men's lives by the Holy Ghost that changes them. HGM. 22

The baptism of the Holy Ghost is the complete uniting of the quickened believer with Christ Himself. HGM. 26

The Holy Ghost is transparent honesty. When we pray, 'Oh, Lord, baptize me with the Holy Ghost whatever it means,' God will give us a glimpse of our self-interest and self-seeking until we are willing for everything to go and there is nothing left but Himself. As long as there is self-interest and self-seeking, something has to go. HGM. 30

The baptism with the Holy Ghost is the great sovereign work of the personal Holy Ghost; entire sanctification is our personal experience of it. HGM. 30

HOME

The description the Bible gives of home is that it is a place of discipline. Naturally we do not like what God makes; we prefer our friends to our God-made relations. We are undressed morally in our home life and are apt to be meaner there than anywhere else. HG. 10

HONESTY

If a man is honest because it pays him to be, he ceases to be honest. SHH. 91

Honesty ceases to be the best policy if I am honest for a reason. SHH. 119

Until the Son of God is formed in us we are not sincere, not even honest, but when His life comes into us, He makes us honest with ourselves and generous and kind towards others. SSM. 39

HONOUR

The discovery of whose honour I stand for is a clear revelation of who my god is. If it is my own honour that is at stake, my self is my god. The honour in the life of a saint is the honour of Jesus. When I am met by exacting and meanness, I do not say, That hurts me; I do not know it does, because I am taken up with the pain of the Holy Ghost over the hurt to Jesus. GW. 42

Never compromise with anything that would detract from the honour of the Lord. Remember that the honour of Jesus is at stake in your bodily life and rouse yourself up to act accordingly. MFL. 124

In the life of a disciple it is the honour of Jesus Christ that is at stake, not our own honour. SHH. 83

Stake everything on the honour of Jesus Christ, and you will find you have struck bedrock. SHH. 92

HOPE

To give 'a reason concerning the hope that is in you' is not at all the same thing as convincing by reasonable argument why that hope is in us. The work of the Spirit of God in us transcends reason, but never contradicts it, and when a Christian says 'the reason I am so-and-so is because I have received the Holy Spirit,' or, 'I have received from God something which has made this possible,' it does not contradict reason, it transcends it, and is an answer concern-ing the hope that is in you. The line we are continually apt to be caught by is that of argumentative reasoning out why we are what we are; we can never do that, but we can always say why the hope is in us. GW. 103

To give an answer concerning the hope that is in us is not the same thing as con-vincing by reasonable argument why that hope is in us. A line we are contin-ually apt to be caught by is that of argu-mentatively reasoning out why we are what we are; we cannot argue that out. There is not a saint amongst us who can give explicit reasonings concerning the hope that is in us, but we can always give this reason: we have received the Holy Spirit, and He has witnessed that the truths of Jesus are the truths for us. When we give that answer, anyone who hears it and refuses to try the same way of getting at the truth is condemned. IWP. 72

There is no such thing as dull despair anywhere in the Bible, there is tragedy of the most appalling order, but an equally amazing hopefulness—always a door deeper down than hell which opens into heaven. OPG. 55

HOSPITALITY

. . . we are to be given to hospitality. The point is that we are to be "given to hospi-tality" from God's standpoint; not be-cause other people deserve it, but because God commands it. BP. 171

Lack of hospitality and disbelief in holi-ness go together. God's Home is so sa-cred that He gave His only begotten Son to make it hospitable to us. RTR. 51

HUMAN AND DIVINE

Human nature is the home where the Divine manifests itself. BE. 51

No man is constituted to live a pure Divine life on earth; he is constituted to live a human life on earth presenced with Divinity. BE. 52

Human nature likes to read about the heroic and the intense: it takes the Divine nature to be interested in grass and sparrows and trees, because they are so unutterably commonplace, and also because God happens to have made them. God's order is the human; the devil's is the spectacular. The object of the crisis is that we may live the human life in perfect relation to God. NKW. 131

Sin has come in and made a hiatus between human and Divine love, between human virtues and God's nature, and what we see now in human nature is only the remnant and refraction of the Divine. PH. 26

In theoretic conception the human and the Divine are one; in actual human life sin has made them two. Jesus Christ makes them one again by the efficacy of the Atonement. Hence the distinction is not merely theological, but experimental. PH. 26

A religious fanatic says: "I will work from the Divine standpoint and ignore the human." You cannot do it; God Himself could not do it. He had to take upon Himself "the likeness of sinful flesh." There must be the right alloy. You cannot use pure gold as coin, it is too soft to be serviceable, and the pure gold of the Divine is no good in human affairs; there must be the alloy mixed with it, and the alloy is not sin. SA. 59

I may have the most beautiful sentiments in prayer and visions in preaching, but unless I have learned how God can mix the human and the Divine and make them a flesh and blood epistle of His grace, I have missed the point of Jesus Christ's revelation. SA. 60

Remember that we have to live a Christian life in these bodies, to get the right alloy which will produce the thing Jesus Christ stood for. The Incarnation reveals the amalgam of the Divine and the human, the right alloy, i.e., that which makes the Divine serviceable for current use. SA. 74

The Incarnation means the right alloy. For God to be of any use to human beings He must become incarnate; that means dust and Deity mixed in one. If you have merely an abstraction, the vision without the dust of the actual, you will never make the vision real. SA. 81

HUMANISM

The great phase at present is the sophistic conception that a man is a law unto himself. BFB. 88

Honeycombing all our Christian teaching to-day is the idea that the instinct in us is God and that as we allow the deepest instinct in us expression, we reveal ourselves as more or less God, and that the Being in whom this instinct had its greatest expression was the Lord Jesus Christ; therefore He stands in the modern movements and to everyone who follows that line of thinking, as the best expression of God. BE. 103

According to modern thinking, man is a great being in the making; his attainments are looked on as a wonderful promise of what he is going to be; we are obsessed with the evolutionary idea. Jesus Christ talks about a revolution— "Ye must be born again." CHI. 19

HUMANITY

If you want to know what the human race is to be like on the basis of the Redemption, you will find it mirrored in Jesus Christ—a perfect oneness between God and man, no gap; in the meantime there is a gap, and the universe is wild, not tame. BFB. 98

We are over-satiated with sympathisers with men, and with that mystic-sounding shibboleth, 'Humanity.' CD. VOL. 1, 31

There is engrained in the depths of human nature a dislike of the general ruck of mankind, in spite of all our modern jargon about "loving Humanity." We have a disparaging way of talking about the common crowd: the common crowd is made up of innumerable editions of you and me. CHI. 78

Ask the Holy Spirit to enable your mind to brood for one moment on the value of the "nobody" to Jesus. The people who make up the common crowd are nobodies to me, but it is astonishing to find that it is the nobodies that Jesus Christ came to save. The terms we use for men in the sense of their social position are nothing to Him. There is no room in Christianity as Jesus Christ taught it for philanthropic or social patronage. Jesus Christ never patronised anyone, He came right straight down to where men live in order that the supreme gift He came to give might be theirs. CHI. 78

If the indwelling of God cannot be manifested in human flesh, then the Incarnation and the Atonement are of no avail. NKW. 132

The enthusiasm of humanity for itself in its present state simply means irrevocable disaster ultimately. Nowadays people talk about the whole human race being in the making, that our natural virtues are promises of what we are going to be; they take no account at all of sin. We have to remember that an enthusiasm for humanity which ignores the Bible is sure to end in disaster; enthusiasm for the community of saints means that God can take hold of the muddle and can re-make men, not simply in accordance with the Master man before the fall, but "conformed to the image of His Son." PS. 70

It is quite possible for the human mind to blot God out of its thinking entirely, and to work along the line of the elements which are the same in every man, and to band the whole of the human race into a solid atheistic community. The only reason this has not been done up to the present is that the human race has been too much divided, but we shall find that these divisions are gradually resolving themselves. PS. 71

HUMAN NATURE

It was God who made human nature, not the devil; sin came into human nature and cut it off from the Divine, and Jesus Christ brings the pure Divine and the pure human together. BE. 52

It is not human nature that needs altering, it is man's spirit that needs to be brought back into right relationship with God, and before that can be done the disposition of sin has to be dealt with. BSG. 76

Never allow horror at crime to blind you to the fact that it is human nature like your own that committed it. CHI. 71

Jesus Christ never expected from human nature what it was not designed to give; consequently He was never bitter or cynical. HGM. 112

Human nature as God made it was not sinful, and it was human nature as God made it that Our Lord took on Him. OBH. 129

Love, more than any other experience in life, reveals the shallowness and the profundity, the hypocrisy and the nobility, of human nature. OPG. 43

. . . the presence of the life of the Son of God in us does not alter our human nature; God does remove the disposition of sin, but He demands of us that our human nature 'puts on the new man,' and no longer fashions itself according to its former natural desires. OPG. 47

Nothing has ever been done by human nature that any member of the human family may not be trapped into doing; the only safeguard is to keep in the light as God is in the light. OPG. 48

It is not being reconciled to the fact of sin that produces all the disasters in life. We talk about noble human nature, self-sacrifice and platonic friendship—all unmitigated nonsense. PH. 190

Jesus Christ never trusted human nature, but He was never cynical, He trusted absolutely what He could do for human nature. PH. 193

Sin dwells in human nature, but the Bible makes it very clear that it is an abnormal thing, it has no right there, it does not belong to human nature as God designed it. Sin has come into human nature and perverted and twisted it. PR. 16

People have the idea that because there is good in human nature (and, thank

God, there is a lot of good in human nature) that therefore the Spirit of God is in every man naturally, meaning that the Spirit of God in us will become the Christ in us if we let Him have His way. Take that view if you like, but never say it is the view of the New Testament. It certainly is not our Lord's view. PR. 30

Human nature is earthly, it is sordid, but it is not bad. SA. 59

The thing in human nature that is bad is the result of a wrong relationship set up between the man God created and the being God created who became the devil, and the wrong relationship whereby a man becomes absolute "boss" over himself is called sin. SA. 60

HUMILIATION/HUMILITY

If you are without something that is a humiliation to you, I question whether you have ever come into a personal relationship with Jesus Christ. LG. 56

We have the idea that we are meant to work for God along the heroic line; we are meant to do un-heroic work for God in the martyr spirit. The sphere of humiliation is always the place of more satisfaction to Jesus Christ, and it is in our power to refuse to be humiliated, to say, 'No, thank you, I much prefer to be on the mountaintop with God.' LG. 58

The way we continually talk about our own inability is an insult to the Creator. The deploring of our own incompetence is a slander against God for having overlooked us. Get into the habit of examining in the sight of God the things that sound humble before men, and you will be amazed at how staggeringly impertinent they are. MUH. 335

HUSBAND AND WIFE

Paul's counsel in dealing with marriage has been misrepresented—"Wives, submit yourselves unto your own husbands," because we have taken the word "submit" to mean the obedience due from a slave to his master. It is not the obedience of an inferior to a superior, but the obedience of the equality of love. In the New Testament the word "obey" is used to express the relationship of equals. SHH. 109

"For the husband is the head of the wife, even as Christ is the head of the church." If Christ is the Head of the husband, he is easily the head of the wife, not by effort, but because of the nature of the essentially feminine. But if Jesus Christ is not the Head of the husband, the husband is not the head of the wife.

Our Lord always touches the most sacred human relationships, and He says—You must be right with Me first before those relationships can be right, and if they hinder your getting right with Me, then you must hate them. SHH. 110

HYPOCRISY

Jesus taught His disciples to be hypocrites, "but thou, when thou fastest, . . . wash thy face," i.e. never allow anyone to imagine you are putting yourself through discipline. SSM. 61

A hypocrite is one who plays two parts consciously for his own ends. When we find fault with other people we may be quite sincere, and yet Jesus says in reality we are frauds. SSM. 81

I

IDEAS

It is not true to say that God gives us our ideas, that notion is the starting-point of all heresies. God never gave anyone their ideas, God makes a man uses his ideas in order to convey His mind; otherwise responsibility is destroyed. BSG. 20

When we are young we think things are simpler than they are; we have an idea for every domain. A man says he is a materialist, or an agnostic, or a Christian, meaning he has only one main idea, but very few will run that idea for all it is worth, yet this is the only way to discover whether it will work, and the same thing is true in the idea of the Christian religion that God is Love. LG. 21

IDENTIFICATION

It is the life of the Spirit made manifest in the flesh, and that is always the test of identification with Christ, not prayer meetings and times of devotion. If I have been identified with the Cross of Christ it must show through my finger-tips. BE. 91

Just as a man may become identified with Jesus Christ so he can be identified with the devil. Just as a man can be born again into the kingdom where Jesus Christ lives and moves and has His being and can become identified with Him in entire sanctification, so he can be born again, so to speak, into the devil's kingdom and be entirely consecrated to the devil. BP. 92

Jesus Christ took on the sin of the world by being identified with it, and we take on His righteousness by being identified with it. BSG. 52

When a man follows up by obedience the performing of the new creation in him, he enters into identification with Christ. Identification is not experienceable; it is infinitely more fundamental than experience. We enter into identification by the door of obedience, but the oneness is a revelation. 'Every spirit which confesseth that Jesus Christ is come in the flesh is of God'—*confess*, that is, say with every corpuscle of your blood that Christ is come in your flesh and is being manifested. GW. 66

We all have that in us which will connect us with the spirit of antichrist if we do not go through identification with Jesus in His death so that the life we now live proves that 'old things are passed away; behold, all things are become new.' GW. 66

Right at the threshold of His manhood our Lord took upon Him His vocation, which was to bear away the sin of the world—by *identification*, not by sympathy. MFL. 105

Jesus Christ does not give us power to put the "old man" to death in ourselves: *"our old man was crucified with Him"*; we can be identified with His death and know that this is true. We are not merely put into a state of innocence before God; by identification with Our

145

Lord's death we are delivered from sin in every bit of its power and every bit of its presence. OBH. 17

IMAGINATION

The imagination of a saint too often is vague and intractable. We have to learn to bring every thought and imagination into captivity to the obedience of Christ. An undisciplined imagination will destroy reliable judgment more quickly even than sin. Mental and spiritual insubordination is the mark of to-day. Jesus Christ submitted His intelligence to His Father. MFL. 125

Imagination is the greatest gift God has given us and it ought to be devoted entirely to Him. If you have been bringing every thought into captivity to the obedience of Christ, it will be one of the greatest assets to faith when the time of trial comes, because your faith and the Spirit of God will work together. Learn to associate ideas worthy of God with all that happens in Nature—the sunrises and the sunsets, the sun and the stars, the changing seasons, and your imagination will never be at the mercy of your impulses, but will always be at the service of God. MUH. 42

IMITATION

Imitation, doing what other people do, is an unmitigated curse. AUG. 34

When the child imitates his own mother he can do it with success, because the inherent nature of the child is like the mother; and when a Christian tries to imitate Jesus Christ he can do it easily because the Spirit of Jesus is in him. GW. 67

Imitation is the great stumbling-block to sanctification. Be yourself first, then

go to your own funeral, and let God forever after be All in all. IWP. 71

It is not that God patches up my natural virtues, but that I learn by obedience to make room for Jesus Christ to exhibit His disposition in me. It is impossible to imitate the disposition of Jesus. LG. 116

The Spirit of God lifts the natural reaction to imitation into another domain and by God's grace we begin to imitate Our Lord and shew forth His praises. MFL. 71

It is natural to be like the one we live with most; then if we spend most of our time with Jesus Christ, we shall begin to be like Him, by the way we are built naturally and by the Spirit God puts in. MFL. 71

We are not put into the place where we can imitate Jesus; the baptism of the Holy Ghost puts us into the very life of Jesus. OBH. 18

You cannot imitate reliance on God. OPG. 63

IMPULSIVENESS

There is abroad to-day a vague, fanatical movement which bases everything on spiritual impulse—'God gave me an impulse to do this, and that,' and there are the strangest outcomes to such impulses. BE. 107

Impulse is not choice; impulse is very similar to instinct in an animal. It is the characteristic of immaturity and ought not to characterize men and women. In spiritual matters take it as a safe guide never to be guided by impulse; always take time and curb your impulse, bring it back and see what form a choice based on that particular impulse would take. BP. 107

It is difficult to get yourself under control to do work you are not used to, the time spent seems wasted at first, but get at it again. The thing that hinders control is impulse. DI. 67

You can never work by impulse, you can only work by steady patient plod. It is the odd five minutes that tells. DI. 68

We have no business to go on impulses spiritually, we have to form 'the mind which was also in Christ Jesus.' People say their impulses are their guide—'I feel impelled to do this, or that'—that may be sufficient indication that they should not do it. DI. 69

'*Set* your affection on things above,' i.e., gather in your stray impulses and fix them. The spiritual life is not impulsive; we are impulsive when we are not spiritual. In every experience the safeguard is the Lord Himself, and He was not impulsive. The one thing Jesus always checked was impulse. Impulse has to be trained and turned into intuition by discipline. GW. 105

Watch Jesus Christ, the first thing He checked in the training of the twelve was impulse. Impulse may be all right morally and physically, but it is never right spiritually. IWP. 88

Wherever spiritual impulse has been allowed to have its way it has led the soul astray. We must check all impulses by this test—Does this glorify Jesus, or does it only glorify ourselves? IWP. 88

When once the will is roused it always has a definite end in view, an end in the nature of unity. Always distinguish between will and impulse. An impulse has

no end in view and must be curbed, not obeyed. MFL. 29

It is natural for a child to be impulsive; but it is a disgraceful thing for a man or woman to be guided by impulse. To be a creature of impulse is the ruin of mental life. The one thing our Lord checked and disciplined in the disciples was impulse; the determining factor was to be their relationship to Himself. MFL. 94

Natural impulse in a saint leads to perdition every time unless it is brought into obedience to the destiny of God, then it is turned into inspiration. It is not that impulse is wrong, but it will lead to wrong unless it is brought into obedience to the spiritual destiny of the life, and this can only be done by devotion to the One Who founds our destiny for us, Our Lord Himself. Beware of trying to forestall God's programme by your own impulse. NKW. 48

Beware of the inspiration that springs from impulse, because impulse enthrones self-lordship as God. My impulses can never be disciplined by anyone saving myself, not even by God. If my impulses are domineered over by somebody else, that one will find sooner or later that he or she has sat on a safety valve—always a risky thing to do. Unless I discipline my impulses they will ruin me, no matter how generous they may be. OPG. 49

Most of us develop our Christianity along the line of our temperament, not along the line of God. To try and develop Christianity along the line of impulse is an impertinence when viewed alongside the strong Son of God. Some of us are like grasshoppers spiritually. Impulse is a natural trait in natural life, but in spiritual things Our Lord absolutely checks it because it always hinders. SSY. 66

INCARNATION

Almighty God is nothing but a mental abstraction unless He becomes concrete and actual, because an ideal has no power unless it can be realized. The doctrine of the Incarnation is that God did become actual, He manifested Himself on the plane of human flesh, and 'Jesus Christ' is the name not only for God and Man in one, but the name of the personal Saviour who makes the way back for every man to get into a personal relationship with God. BFB. 90

In the Incarnation God proves Himself worthy in the sphere in which we live, and this is the sphere of the revelation of the Self-giving of God. BFB. 98

The great message of the Incarnation is that there the Divine and the human became one, and Jesus Christ's claim is that He can manifest His own life in any man if he will co-operate with Him. BE. 54

The Incarnation was not for the Self-realization of God, but for the purpose of removing sin and reinstating humanity into communion with God. BSG. 14

According to the Bible, the Son of God became incarnate in order to bear away the sin of the human race. Before a man can take on him the sin of a family, he must be a member of it; and Jesus Christ took on Him the form of the human family that was cursed with sin, and in that human form He lived a spotlessly holy life, and by means of His death He can introduce the shamed members of the human family into the life He lived. Our Lord made human solidarity His own: He represents the vilest sinner out of hell and the purest saint out of heaven. He stands as the one great Representative of the human race, atoning for its sin. It beggars language to describe what He did—He went into identification with the depths of damnation that the human race might be delivered. BSG. 51

In the Incarnation Jesus Christ came down to the lowest rung possible, He came on to the plane where Adam was originally, and He lived on that plane in order to show what God's normal man was like. And then He did what no man could ever do—He made the way for man to get back to the position he had lost. By the sheer might of the Atonement we can be reinstated in God's favour—that is the marvel. BSG. 77

To those who seek after wisdom the preaching of Christ crucified is foolishness; but when a man knows that his life is twisted, that the mainspring is wrong, he is in the state of heart and mind to understand why it was necessary for God to become Incarnate. MFL. 104

The whole meaning of the Incarnation is the Cross. Beware of separating *God manifest in the flesh* from *the Son becoming sin*. The Incarnation was for the purpose of Redemption. God became incarnate for the purpose of putting away sin; not for the purpose of Self-realization. The Cross is the centre of Time and of Eternity, the answer to the enigmas of both. MUH. 97

Just as our Lord came into human history from the outside, so He must come into us from the outside. PR. 29

He came down to the lowest reach of creation in order to bring back the whole human race to God, and in order to do this He must take upon Him, as representative Man, the whole massed sin of the race. That is why He is called "the Lamb of God." PR. 52

Beware of separating *God manifest in the flesh* from *the Son becoming sin*. In other words, never separate the doctrine of the Incarnation and the doctrine of Redemption. The Incarnation was for purposes of Redemption. The New Testament reveals that God became Incarnate only for the purpose of putting away sin. God did not become Incarnate for the purpose of Self-revelation. PR. 130

The Bible reveals that the sin which muddles men and society is ultimately going to appear in an incarnation called the man of sin, or the Antichrist. PS. 70

Jesus Christ is God incarnate coming into human flesh from the outside, His life is the Highest and the Holiest entering in at the lowliest door. RTR. 90

In the Incarnation we see the right amalgam—pure Deity and the pure human mixed. SHH. 98

INDEPENDENCE

The counterfeit of freedom is independence. When the Spirit of God deals with sin, it is independence that He touches, that is why the preaching of the Gospel awakens resentment as well as craving. BE. 25

Independence must be blasted right out of a Christian, there must be only liberty, which is a very different thing. BE. 25

There is nothing dearer to the heart of the natural man than independence, and as long as I live in the outskirts of my prideful independence Jesus Christ is nothing to me. BE. 27

Independence of one another is natural; independence of God is sin. When natural independence of one another is wedded with independence of God it becomes sin, and sin isolates and destroys, and ultimately damns the life. BE. 27

When natural independence merges into independence of God it becomes sin; and sin isolates and destroys and ultimately damns the personal life. Jesus Christ lays His axe at the root of independence. There is nothing dearer to the heart of the natural man than independence. Wherever there is authority, I go against it in order to show I am independent; I insist on my right to myself, my right to an independent opinion. That spirit does not fit in with Jesus Christ at all. SHL. 83

Independence and pride are esteemed by the natural man, but Jesus says, 'that which is highly esteemed among men is abomination in the sight of God.' SHL. 84

Independence must be blasted right out of a saint. SHL. 87

INDIVIDUALITY

Individuality is the husk of the personal life, it is all 'elbows'; it separates and isolates. The husk of individuality is God's created natural covering for the protection of the personal life, but unless individuality gets transfigured it becomes objectionable, egotistical and conceited, interested only in its own independence. BE. 27

It is the continual assertion of individuality that hinders our spiritual development more than anything else; individuality must go in order that personality may emerge and be brought into fellowship with God. BE. 27

Individuality is natural, but when individuality is indwelt by sin it destroys personal communion and isolates individuals, like so many crystals, and all possibility of fellowship is destroyed. BE. 27

The characteristics of individuality are independence and self-assertiveness. BE. 27

Positive individuality in any form is not only anti-Christian, but anti-human, because it instantly says, 'I care for neither God nor man, I live for myself.' BE. 28

Individuality ignores Jesus Christ; when He speaks our individual concerns make too much noise for us to hear His voice. HGM. 51

Jesus Christ deals always with our personal relationship to Him; He totally disregards individuality; it does not come into His calculations and He has no consideration for it, because individuality is simply the husk, personality is the kernel. HGM. 51

Individuality is the husk of the personal life, it cannot merge; personality always merges. HGM. 76

Individuality must go in order that the personal life may be brought out into fellowship with God. LG. 131

We are designed with a great capacity for God; and sin and our individuality are the things that keep us from getting at God. God delivers us from sin: we have to deliver ourselves from individuality, i.e., to present our natural life to God and sacrifice it until it is transformed into a spiritual life by obedience. MUH. 323

The dilemmas of our personal life with God are few if we obey and many if we are wilful. Spiritually the dilemma arises from the disinclination for discipline; every time I refuse to discipline my natural self, I become less and less of a person and more and more of an independent, impertinent individual. Individuality is the characteristic of the natural man; personality is the characteristic of the spiritual man. NKW. 101

Our Lord never taught individualism; He taught the value of the individual, a very different thing. OBH. 28

Individuality, impulse, and innocence are the husk of personal life. Individuality, if it goes beyond a certain point, becomes pig-headedness, determined independence. I have to be prepared to give up my independent right to myself in order that my personality may emerge. OPG. 68

As a spiritual disciple I have to lose my individuality for ever. Individuality is self-assertive and independent, it is all elbows. It is natural for a child to be strongly marked by individuality, but it is a despicable thing for a man or woman to be hide-bound by individual peculiarities. It means that the personality has never been transfigured, never been filled with the Holy Ghost, never come to the source of spiritual Reality. PH. 133

Our Lord can only be defined in terms of personality, never in terms of individuality. "I and my Father are one," and our Lord's conception of human personality is that it can be merged and made one with God without losing its identity. If we are going to be disciples we have to break the bands of individuality which cabin and confine, and launch out in abandon to Jesus Christ. PH. 133

The characteristics of the natural man, apart from sin, are independence and individuality. Individuality is the strong and emphatic and somewhat ugly husk that guards the personal life. PR. 16

Individuality is a right characteristic in a child, but in a man or woman it is not only objectionable but dangerous, because it means independence of God as well as of other people, and independence of God is of the very nature of sin. PR. 16

The only way we can get rid of the pride of individuality and become one with Jesus Christ is by being born from above. PR. 16

Personality is of the nature of light, it can be merged; individuality is like a lamp which cannot merge. There may be many lamps, but only one light. Individuality cannot mix; it is all "elbows," it separates and isolates; it is the thing that characterizes us naturally, in our elementary condition we are all individual. Individuality is the shell, as it were, holding something more valuable than itself—the kernel, which is personality. The shell of individuality is God's created natural coating for the protection of the personal life. It preserves the personality, and is the characteristic of the child; but if I stick to my individuality and mistake it for the personal life, I shall remain isolated, a disintegrating force ending in destruction. Individuality counterfeits personality as lust counterfeits love. God designed human nature for Himself; individuality debases human nature for itself. SA. 101

The natural life and individuality are practically one and the same. Individuality is the characteristic of a child, it is the natural husk of personality and it is there by God's creation to preserve the personal life; but if individuality does not become transfigured by the grace of God, it becomes objectionable, egotisti-

cal and conceited, interested only in its own independence. SHL. 83

INFLUENCE

The people who influence us most are not those who buttonhole us and talk to us, but those who live their lives like the stars in heaven and the lilies in the field, perfectly simply and unaffectedly. Those are the lives that mould us. MUH. 139

The lives that have been of most blessing to you are those who were unconscious of it. MUH. 244

The line of attraction is always an indication of the goal of the attracted; if you attract by personal impressiveness, the attracted will get no further than you. Our Lord said—'*I*, if *I* be lifted up, will draw all men unto Me.' NKW. 24

Which are the men who influence us most? The men who 'buttonhole' us, or the men who live their lives as the stars in the heaven and the lily of the field, perfectly simple and unaffected? These are the lives that mould us, our mothers and wives and friends who are of that order, and that is the order the Holy Ghost produces. SSM. 71

INNOCENCE

There is a difference between innocence and purity. Innocence is the true condition of a child; purity is the characteristic of men and women. Innocence has always to be shielded; purity is something that has been tested and tried and has triumphed; something that has character at the back of it, that can overcome, and has overcome. BP. 127

The innocence of Jesus was not the innocence of a babe born into our order of things, it was the innocence of Adam as God created him, the innocence of an untried possibility of holiness. Innocence is never safe, it is simply full of possibility. BSG. 10

Innocence is not purity, innocence is right for a child, but criminal for a man or woman. Men and women have no business to be innocent, they ought to be virtuous and pure. Character must be attained. OPG. 68

INSIGHT

We do not get insight by struggling, but by going to God in prayer. BFB. 76

The insight that relates us to God arises from purity of heart, not from clearness of intellect. All the education under heaven will never give a man insight into Jesus Christ's teaching, only one thing will, and that is a pure heart, i.e., intentions that go along the right line. MFL. 23

Insight into the instruction of Jesus depends upon our intention to obey what we know to be the will of God. If we have some doctrine or some end of our own to serve, we shall always find difficulty. MFL. 24

There are statements of Jesus which mean nothing to us just now because we have not been brought into the place where we need to understand them. When we are brought there, the Holy Spirit will bring back a particular word, and as we intend to obey He gives us the insight into it. MFL. 24

INSPIRATION

Inspiration won't come irrespective of study, but only because of it. Don't trust to inspiration, use your own 'axe.' Work! Think! DI. 67

It requires the inspiration of God to go through drudgery with the light of God upon it. Some people do a certain thing and the way in which they do it hallows that thing forever afterwards. It may be the most commonplace thing, but after we have seen them do it, it becomes different. When the Lord does a thing through us, He always transfigures it. MUH. 50

The proof that we are rightly related to God is that we do our best whether we feel inspired or not. MUH. 116

The great dominating note is not first the needs of men, but the command of Jesus Christ, consequently the real source of inspiration is always behind, never in front. To-day the tendency is to put the inspiration in front; the great ideal is to sweep everything in front of us and bring it all out in accordance with our conception of success. In the New Testament the inspiration is behind, viz., the Lord Jesus Christ Himself. We are called to be true to *Him*, to be faithful to *Him*, to carry out *His* enterprises. SSY. 74

INSTINCT

Whenever you stand in the presence of Jesus Christ, as He is portrayed in the Scriptures and made real to you by the Holy Spirit, the instincts of your heart will always be inspired: *let them lead*. MFL. 15

Animals are guided by instinct; human beings are not. SHH. 25

INTELLECT

The intellect works with the greatest intensity when it works continuously; the more you do, the more you can do. We must work hard to keep in trim for God.

Clean off the rust and keep bright by use. AUG. 37

The doctrines of the New Testament as applied to personal life are moral doctrines, that is, they are understood by a pure heart, not by the intellect. AUG. 45

The basis of things is not rational. Reason and intellect are our guides among things as they are, but they cannot explain things as they are. BFB. 97

The basis of things is tragic, and intellect makes a man shut his eyes to this fact and become a superior person. One of the great crimes of intellectual philosophy is that it destroys a man as a human being and turns him into a supercilious spectator; he cuts himself off from relationship with human stuff as it is and becomes a statue. BFB. 97

Instead of a fallen man's intelligence being able to lift up his body, it does exactly the opposite; a fallen man's intelligence severs his intellectual life more and more from his bodily life and produces inner hypocrisy. BP. 48

Notice the difference in the characteristics of the man who makes the head the centre and the man who makes the heart the centre. The man who makes the head the centre becomes an intellectual being, he does not estimate things at all as the Bible does. Sin is a mere defect to him, something to be overlooked and grown out of, and the one thing he despises is enthusiasm. Take the Apostle Paul, or any of the New Testament saints, the characteristic of this life is enthusiasm; the heart is first, not second. This is the antipodes of modern intellect life. BP. 103

A Christian accepts all he knows about God on the authority of Jesus Christ; he can find out nothing about God by his own unaided intellect. DI. 12

Note two things about your intelligence: first, when your intelligence feels numb, quit at once, and play or sleep; for the time being the brain must recuperate; second, when you feel a fidget of associated ideas, take yourself sternly in hand and say, 'You shall study, so it's no use whining.' DI. 69

Every new domain into which your personal life is introduced necessitates a new form of responsible intelligence. DI. 80

Intellectual obstinacy produces the sealed mind—"Jesus said unto them, If ye were blind, ye would have no sin: but now ye say, We see: your sin remaineth." DI. 81

If you teach anything out of an idle intellect, you will have to answer to God for it. DI. 82

We command what we can explain, and if we bring our explanation into the spiritual domain we are in danger of explaining Jesus away—"and every spirit which annulleth Jesus is not of God." We have to be intelligently more than intelligent, intellectually more than intellectual, that is, we have to use all our wits in order not to worship our wits but be humble enough to worship God. DI. 83

My reason and my intellect are the finest instruments I have, but they are not 'me,' I am much more than my intellect and my reason. If I am going to get at Reality I must have my conscience at work as well as my intellect and reason, otherwise I will ignore the fact of sin, ignore all the moral perplexities, ignore the fact that God became Incarnate. Intellect is meant to be the handmaid of God, not the dictator of God. GW. 16

The only way I can begin to understand the Son of God is by receiving His Spirit through regeneration; then when I am regenerated it is my duty to think about the Son of God, that is, I must see that I put my intellect at the disposal of the Holy Spirit, who will 'reveal the Son of God in me.' GW. 19

An intellectualist never pushes an issue of will. Our Lord uses the word 'believe' in a moral sense, not in an intellectual sense. 'Commit yourself to Me.' We are to believe in a Person, not to believe for something. LG. 119

The tyranny of intellect is that we see everything in the light of one principle, and when there is a gap, as there is in the moral development of man, the intellect has to ignore it and say these things are mere upsets. The Bible supplies the facts for the gap which the intellect will not accept. The intellect simply works on a process of logic along one line. MFL. 51

If we try to answer the problems of this world by intellect or scientific methods we shall go mad, or else deny that the problems exist. Never get into the ostrich-like attitude of Christian Science, and say that there is no such thing as death or sin or pain. Jesus Christ makes us open our eyes and look at these things. God is the only Being Who can stand the slander that arises because the devil and pain and sin are in the world. Stand true to the life hid with Christ in God and to the facts you have to face. You will have no answer intellectually, but your faith in God will be so unshakably firm that others will begin to see there is an answer they have never guessed. "I am the Way, the Truth, and the Life." PH. 74

Mere intellectual training turns a man into a psychological ostrich; his head is all right, but in actual life he is left floundering. PH. 220

Intellectual curiosity will not take us one inch inside moral problems, but immediately we obey, in the tiniest matter, instantly we see. PH. 220

We learn spiritual truth by atmosphere not by intellectual reasoning; God's spirit alters the atmosphere of our ways of looking at things and things begin to be possible which never were possible before. PH. 236

Intellectual thinking and reasoning never yet got a man to Reality, because these are instruments of life, and not the life itself. Our only organ for getting at Reality is conscience, and the Holy Spirit always deals with conscience first. Intellect and emotions come in afterwards as the instruments of human expression. PR. 77

As long as we are intellectualists and forget that we are men, our intellect tells us that God and man ought to be one, that there should be no gap between. Exactly so! But they are *not* one, and there *is* a gap, and a tragedy. SA. 40

Our intellect tells us that the universe ought to be the "garment of God." It ought to be, but it is not. We may hold any number of deistic and monistic theories, and theories about being one with God, but every man knows he is not God. Jesus Christ says we can only receive the at-one-ment with God on His basis, viz.: "Except a man be born again, he cannot see the kingdom of God." SA. 41

All our darkness comes because we will try to get into the thing head first. We must be born into the kingdom of God, Jesus says, before we can begin to think about it. SA. 112

INTENTION

Jesus Christ demands of His disciples that they live in conformity to the right standard in intention. We say, 'Though I didn't do well, I meant well'; then it is absolutely certain you did not mean well. BE. 21

The righteous man is the one whose inner intention is clearly revealed in his outer intention, there is no duplicity, no internal hypocrisy. A man's outer intention is easily discernible by other people; his inner intention needs to be continually examined. BE. 22

The marvel of the grace of God is that it can alter the mainspring of our make-up; then when that is altered we must foster in ourselves those intentions which spring from the Spirit of Jesus and make our nervous system carry them out. BE. 22

Beware of praying about an intention—*act*. To pray about what we know we should do is to piously push the whole thing overboard and think no more about it. Every intention must be acted out *now*, not presently, otherwise it will be stamped out. MFL. 21

When the intention of an honest soul is grasped by the Spirit of God he will know whether the teaching Jesus gives is of God or not. MFL. 22

Intentions are born of listening to others. Whenever we obey an intention, insight into either good or bad is sure to follow. If our intention is in agreement with God and we act on it, we get insight into Who God is. The discernment of right and wrong intentions depends on how we think. There is a spasmodic type of life which comes from never really thinking about things, it is at the mercy of every stray intention. MFL. 22

If you are sufficiently strong-minded you can generate any number of intentions in people and make them think anything you like; if they are not in the habit of thinking for themselves you can always sway them. MFL. 22

INTERCESSION, PRAYER OF

The place for the comforter is not that of one who preaches, but of the comrade who says nothing, but prays to God about the matter. BFB. 33

An abiding way of maintaining our relation to Reality is intercession. Intercession means that I strive earnestly to have my human soul moved by the attitude of my Lord to the particular person I am praying for. That is where our work lies, and we shirk it by becoming active workers; we do the things that can be tabulated and scheduled, and we won't do the one thing that has no snares. CHI. 32

Intercession keeps the relationship to God completely open. You cannot intercede if you do not believe in the Reality of Redemption, you will turn intercession into futile sympathy with human beings which only increases their submissive content to being out of touch with God. CHI. 32

Intercession means getting the mind of Christ about the one for whom we pray, that is what is meant by "filling up that which is behind of the afflictions of Christ"; and that is why there are so few intercessors. CHI. 32

Be careful not to enmesh yourself in more difficulties than God has engineered for you to know; if you know too much, more than God has engineered, you cannot pray, the condition of the people is so crushing that you can't get through to Reality. CHI. 32

It is not that my prayers are so important, that is not the point; God has so made it that by means of intercession certain types of blessing come upon men. DI. 39

We must steadfastly work out repentance in intercessory prayer. DI. 41

When God puts a weight on you for intercession for souls don't shirk it by talking to them. It is much easier to talk to them than to talk to God about them—much easier to talk to them than to take it before God and let the weight crush the life out of you until gradually and patiently God lifts the life out of the mire. That is where very few of us go. GW. 21

The knowledge of where people are wrong is a hindrance to prayer, not an assistance. 'I want to tell you of the difficulties so that you may pray intelligently.' The more you know the less intelligently you pray because you forget to believe that God can alter the difficulties. GW. 21

How many of us have ever entered into this Ministry of the Interior where we become identified with Our Lord and with the Holy Spirit in intercession? It is a threefold intercession: at the Throne of God, Jesus Christ; within the saint, the Holy Ghost; outside the saint, common-sense circumstances and common-sense people, and as these are brought before God in prayer the Holy Spirit gets a chance to make intercession according to the will of God. That is the meaning of personal sanctification, and that is why the barriers of personal testimony must be broken away and effaced by the realization of why we are sanctified—not to be fussy workers for God, but to be His servants, and this is the work, vicarious intercession. HGM. 127

How are we going to know when a man has sinned a sin unto death and when he has not? Only through intercession. If we make our own discernment the judge, we are wrong. We base it all on an abstract truth divorced from God, we pin our faith on what God has done and not on the God Who did it, and when the case begins to go wrong again, we do not intercede, we begin to scold God. We get fanatical, we upset the court of heaven by saying, 'I must do this thing.' That is not intercession, that is rushing in where angels fear to tread. It is fanatical frenzy, storming the throne of God and refusing to see His character while sticking true to our assertions of what He said He would do. Beware of making God run in the mould of His own precedent, that means, because He did a certain thing once, He is sure to do it again, which is so much of a truth that it becomes an imperceptible error when we subtly leave God Himself out of it. IYA. 84

In the matter of intercession, when we pray for another the Spirit of God works in the unconscious domain of that one's being about which we know nothing, and about which the one we pray for knows nothing, and after a while the conscious life of the one prayed for begins to shows signs of softening and unrest, of enquiry and a desire to know something. It seems stupid to think that if we pray all that will happen, but remember to Whom we pray; we pray to a

Being Who understands the unconscious depths of a man's personality, and He has told us to pray. MFL. 20

Intercession leaves you neither time nor inclination to pray for your own "sad sweet self." The thought of yourself is not kept out, because it is not there to keep out; you are completely and entirely identified with God's interests in other lives. MUH. 124

The real business of your life as a saved soul is intercessory prayer. Wherever God puts you in circumstances, pray immediately, pray that His Atonement may be realized in other lives as it has been in yours. Pray for your friends *now*; pray for those with whom you come in contact *now*. MUH. 172

The Spirit of God needs the nature of the believer as a shrine in which to offer His intercession. MUH. 313

Intercession is the one thing that has no snares, because it keeps our relationship with God completely open. MUH. 348

The passionate note of intercession is born in the secret place before God. PH. 88

Jesus Christ is asking God to save Him *out of* the hour, not *from* it. All through, that is the inner attitude of Jesus Christ, He received Himself in the fires of sorrow; it was never 'Do not let the sorrow come.' That is the opposite of what we do, we pray, 'Oh, Lord, don't let this or that happen to me'; consequently all kinds of damaging and blasphemous things are said about answers to prayer. PH. 191

I think sometimes we will be covered with shame when we meet the Lord Jesus and think how blind and ignorant

we were when He brought people around us to pray for, or gave us opportunities of warning, and instead of praying we tried to find out what was wrong. We have no business to try and find out what is wrong, our business is to pray, so that when the awakening comes Jesus Christ will be the first they meet. PS. 35

When we pray we give God a chance to work in the unconscious realm of the lives of those for whom we pray. When we come into the secret place it is the Holy Ghost's passion for souls that is at work, not our passion, and He can work through us as He likes. SSM. 59

INTERPRETATION

Strenuous mental effort to interpret the word of God will fag us out physically, whereas strenuous mental effort that lets the word of God talk to us will re-create us. We prefer the spiritual interpretation to the exegetical because it does not need any work. AUG. 42

INTROSPECTION

Because introspection cannot profoundly satisfy, it does not follow that introspection is wrong; it is right, because it is the only way in which we will discover our need of God. It is the introspective power that is made alert by conviction of sin. BE. 29

Introspection without God leads to insanity. We do not know the springs of our thinking, we do not know by what we are influenced, we do not know all the scenery psychically that Jesus Christ looked at. BP. 156

INTUITION

Never take it for granted because you have been used by God to a soul that

God will always speak through you, He won't. At any second you may blunt your spiritual intuition, it is known only to God and yourself. Keep the intuitive secret life clear and right with God at all costs.   DI. 84

Perception in the natural world is called intuition—I know I know, although I do not know how I know.   IWP. 13

Whenever the Spirit of God works in our conscious life it is like an intuition—I don't know how I know, but I know. The Holy Spirit witnesses only to His own nature, not to our reason. Jesus said "My sheep hear My voice," not because it is argued to them, but because they have His Spirit.   MFL. 23

Guard your intuition as the gift of God. You cannot judge virtue by its obverse; you can only judge virtue by intuition.   NKW. 141

Intuition in the natural world means that we see or discern at sight, there is no reasoning in connection with it, we see at once. When the Spirit of God is in us He gives us intuitive discernment, we know exactly what He wants; then the point is, are we going through identification with our Lord in order that that intuitive light may become the discipline of our lives? It is this practical aspect that has been ignored.   PH. 159

When we are beginning to be spiritual by means of the reception of the Holy Spirit, we get moments of intuitive light.   PH. 160

ISOLATION

Never reveal to anyone the profound depths of your isolation; when the life is going on profoundly with God, conceal it. 'Appear not unto men to fast.'   NKW. 119

ISRAEL

God created the people known as Israel for one purpose, to be the servant of Jehovah until through them every nation came to know Who Jehovah was. The nation created for the service of Jehovah failed to fulfil God's predestination for it; then God called out a remnant, and the remnant failed; then out of the remnant came One Who succeeded, the One Whom we know as the Lord Jesus Christ. The Saviour of the world came of this nation. He is called 'the Servant of God' because He expresses exactly the creative purpose of God for the historic people of God. Through that one Man the purpose of God for the individual, for the chosen nation, and for the whole world, is to be fulfilled. It is through Him that we are made 'a royal priesthood.'   SSY. 101

The essential pride of Israel and Judah (and of the Pharisees in Our Lord's day) was that God was obliged to select them because of their superiority to other nations. God did not *select* them: God *created* them for one purpose, to be His bondslaves.   SSY. 103

Israel is still in the shadow of God's hand, in spite of all her wickedness. God's purposes are always fulfilled, no matter how wide a compass He may permit to be taken first.   SSY. 108

J

JESUS, TEACHING OF

Be careful not to be caught up in the clap-trap of to-day which says, 'I believe in the teachings of Jesus, but I don't see any need for the Atonement.' Men talk pleasant, patronizing things about Jesus Christ's teaching while they ignore His Cross. By all means let us study Christ's teaching, we do not think nearly enough along New Testament lines, we are swamped by pagan standards, and as Christians we ought to allow Jesus Christ's principles to work out in our brains as well as in our lives; but the teaching of Jesus apart from His Atonement simply adds an ideal that leads to despair. BE. 9

Jesus Christ did not come to tell men they ought to be holy—there is an 'ought' in every man that tells him that, and whenever he sees a holy character he may bluster and excuse himself as he likes, but he knows that is what he ought to be: He came to put us in the place where we can be holy, that is, He came to *make* us what He teaches we should be, that is the difference. BE. 10

The words Jesus spoke were the exact garment of His Person, they exactly revealed Him, because He spoke out of actualities all the time. 'I spake openly in the world, and in secret have I said nothing.' GW. 17

If Jesus Christ had said to us, 'All you need to do is to be as holy as you can, overcome sin as far as you can, and I will overlook the rest,' no intelligent man under heaven would accept such a salvation. GW. 24

What Jesus says *is* hard, it is only easy when it comes to those who really are His disciples. Beware of allowing anything to soften a hard word of Jesus. GW. 78

It is a terrible thing to see how we keep Jesus Christ waiting. We serve God, but there is a drawback, and it is that drawback which Jesus gets at by His talk when once we come to Him as this man did. We twist His words and debate about their meaning, we discuss His teachings and expound His Gospel, and all the time we leave Him absolutely alone because at the centre of our heart there is the gnawing grip of one of His hard sayings that keeps us sorrowful, and He waits till we come and lay it all down. All the time in between has been utterly wasted as far as Jesus Christ is concerned, no matter how active we have been, or how much we have been a blessing to others, because none of it has sprung from devotion to Him but from devotion to an idea. GW. 78

"Think not that I am come to destroy the law, or the prophets: I am come not to destroy, but to fulfil." That is why it is so absurd to put our Lord as a Teacher first, He is not first a Teacher, He is a Saviour first. He did not come to give us a new code of morals: He came to enable us to keep a moral code we had not been able to fulfil. HG. 57

159

Jesus says that men are capable of missing the supreme good and His point of view is not acceptable to us because we do not believe we are capable of missing it. We are far removed from Jesus Christ's point of view to-day, we take the natural rationalistic line, and His teaching is no good whatever unless we believe the main gist of His gospel, viz., that we have to have something planted into us by supernatural grace. Jesus Christ's point of view is that a man may miss the chief good; we like to believe we will end all right somehow, but Jesus says we won't. If my feet are going in one direction, I cannot advance one step in the opposite direction unless I turn right round. HG. 63

The majority of us are apologetic about the teachings of Jesus, we are much too easily cowed by modern good taste. The modern mind is the infallible god to the majority of us. HG. 74

If we would have the blunt courage of ordinary human beings and face the teachings of Jesus, we would have to come to one of two conclusions—either the conclusion His contemporaries came to, that He was devil-possessed, or else to the conclusion the disciples came to, that He is God Incarnate. HG. 75

In interpreting our Lord's teaching, watch carefully who He is talking to; the parable of the prodigal son was a stinging lash to the Pharisees. We need to be reminded of the presentation of Jesus in the New Testament for the Being pictured to us nowadays would not perturb anybody; but He aroused His whole nation to rage. Read the records of His ministry and see how much blazing indignation there is in it. For thirty years Jesus did nothing, then for three years He stormed every time He went down to Jerusalem. Josephus says He tore through the Temple courts like a madman. We hear nothing about that Jesus Christ to-day. The meek and mild Being pictured to-day makes us lose altogether the meaning of the Cross. We have to find out why Jesus was beside Himself with rage and indignation at the Pharisees and not with those given over to carnal sins. Which state of society is going to stand a ripping and tearing Being like Jesus Christ Who drags to the ground the highest respected pillars of its civilized society, and shows that their respectability and religiosity is built on a much more abominable pride than the harlot's or the publican's? The latter are disgusting and coarse, but these men have the very pride of the devil in their hearts. HG. 78

The best and most spiritual people to-day turn Jesus Christ's teaching out of court. They say He could never have meant what He said, and, we have to use common sense. HG. 82

The teachings of Jesus have not made so much difference to the world as the teachings of Socrates and Plato, but to those who are born from above they make all the difference. HG. 96

The New Testament is the posthumous writing of Jesus Christ; He departed, and the Holy Spirit used these men as His pens to expound His teaching. HGM. 11

The summing up of the life of faith is the teaching of Jesus in the Sermon on the Mount—*Be carefully careless about everything saving your relationship to God.* HGM. 145

Jesus Christ always taught vaguely; in the beginning of our Christian life we think He teaches definitely, and we get hold of trite definitions until we find the marvellous life of God is not there at all. HGM. 144

Our Lord's statements seem so simple and gentle that we swallow them and say, 'Yes, I accept Jesus as a Teacher,' then His words seem to slip out of our minds; they have not, they have gone into the subconscious mind, and when we come across something in our circumstances, up comes one of those words and we hear it for the first time and it makes us reel with amazement. "He that hath ears to hear, let him hear." What have we ears for? IWP. 119

The teaching of Jesus only begins to apply to us when we have received the disposition that ruled Him. LG. 126

Our Lord taught His Lordship to His disciples, and said that after He had ascended He would send forth the Holy Spirit, Who would be the Disposer of affairs, both individual and international. We have not made Jesus Christ Lord, we have not given up the right to ourselves to Him, consequently we continually muddle our affairs by our own intuitions and desires for our own ends. LG. 127

To know that the teaching of Jesus is of God means that it must be obeyed. It may be difficult to begin with, but the difficulty will become a joy. MFL. 22

Studying our Lord's teaching will not profit us unless we intend to obey what we know is the immediate present duty. MFL. 23

Jesus says we shall know, i.e., discern, whether His teaching is of God or not when we do what we know to be His will. We discern according to our disposition. MFL. 25

Distempers of mind make all the difference in the discernment of Jesus Christ's teaching. MFL. 25

Our Lord's teaching is God-breathed. MFL. 25

Beware of tampering with the springs of your life when it comes to the teaching of Jesus. MFL. 26

At the bar of common sense Jesus Christ's statements may seem mad; but bring them to the bar of faith, and you begin to find with awestruck spirit that they are the words of God. MUH. 151

. . . messages of Jesus Christ are for the will and the conscience, not for the head. MUH. 183

. . . if Jesus Christ was merely a Teacher, He adds to the burdens of human nature, for He erects an ideal that human nature can never attain. He tantalises us by statements that poor human nature can never fit itself for. PH. 4

If all Jesus Christ came to do was to put before us an ideal we cannot attain, we are happier without knowing it. But Jesus Christ did not come primarily to teach: He came to put within us His own disposition, viz., Holy Spirit, whereby we can live a totally new life. PH. 61

The revelation of the New Testament is not that Jesus Christ came to teach primarily but that He came to redeem, to make us what He teaches we should be. PR. 25

Whenever Jesus Christ brought His teaching to a focus it was on two points, viz., Marriage and Money. In ordaining sex God took the bigger risk and made either the most gigantic blunder or the most sublime thing. Sex has to be controlled, so have money and food. By what? By the highest. SA. 73

If Jesus Christ is only a Teacher, then all He can do is to tantalize us, to erect a standard we cannot attain to; but when we are born again of the Spirit of God, we know that He did not come only to teach us, *He came to make us what He teaches we should be.* SA. 85

"If any man will do His will, he shall know of the teaching, whether it be of God or whether I speak from Myself." Intellectually, curiosity is the thing; morally, obedience is what is needed. SHH. 88

Beware of placing our Lord as Teacher first instead of Saviour. That tendency is prevalent to-day, and it is a dangerous tendency. We must know Him first as Saviour before His teaching can have any meaning for us, or before it can have any meaning other than that of an ideal which leads to despair. SSM. 12

Fancy coming to men and women with defective lives and defiled hearts and wrong mainsprings, and telling them to be pure in heart! What is the use of giving us an ideal we cannot possibly attain? We are happier without it. If Jesus is a Teacher only, then all He can do is to tantalise us by erecting a standard we cannot come anywhere near. But if by being born again from above we know Him first as Saviour, we know that He did not come to teach us only: *He came to make us what He teaches we should be.* SSM. 12

The teaching of Jesus Christ comes with astonishing discomfort to begin with, because it is out of all proportion to our natural way of looking at things; but Jesus puts in a new sense of proportion, and slowly we form our way of walking and our conversation on the line of His precepts. Remember that our Lord's teaching applies only to those who are His disciples. SSM. 15

The whole point of our Lord's teaching is, 'Obey Me, and you will find you have a wealth of power within.' SSM. 33

Our Lord teaches a complete reversal of all our practical sensible reasonings. SSM. 67

The summing up of Our Lord's teaching is that it is impossible to carry it out unless He has done a supernatural work in us. SSY. 63

We have to face ourselves with the teaching of Jesus, and see that we do not wilt it away. The demands Our Lord makes on His disciples are to be measured by His own character. The Sermon on the Mount is the statement of the working out in actuality of the disposition of Jesus Christ in the life of any man. SSY. 64

JOY

All degrees of joy reside in the heart. BP. 115

It cost Jesus the Cross, but He despised the shame of it because of the joy that was set before Him. He had the task of taking the worst piece of broken earthenware and making him into a son of God. If Jesus cannot do that, then He has not succeeded in what He came to do. The badness does not hinder Him, and the goodness does not assist Him. HGM. 48

God can take any man and put the miracle of His joy into him, and enable him to manifest it in the actual details of his life. HGM. 49

The first element in the life of faith is joy, which means the perfect fulfilment of that for which we were created. Joy is not happiness; there is no mention in the Bible of happiness for a Christian, but there is plenty said about joy—". . . that they might have My joy fulfilled in themselves," said Jesus. HGM. 144

When a man or woman realizes what God does work in them through Jesus Christ, they become almost lunatic with joy in the eyes of the world. It is this truth we are trying to state, viz., the realization of the wonderful salvation of God. IWP. 66

The joy of the Lord Jesus Christ lay in doing exactly what He came to do. He did not come to save men first of all, He came to do His Father's will. The saving of men was the natural outcome of this, but Our Lord's one great obedience was not to the needs of men but to the will of His Father. LG. 63

The joy of anything, from a blade of grass upwards, is to fulfil its created purpose. ". . . that we should be to the praise of His glory." LG. 63

The way God's life manifests itself in joy is in a peace which has no desire for praise. When a man delivers a message which he knows is the message of God, the witness to the fulfilment of the created purpose is given instantly, the peace of God settles down, and the man cares for neither praise nor blame from anyone. That is the joy of the life of God; it is uncrushable life, and there is never life without joy. LG. 65

Many will confide to you their secret sorrows, but the last mark of intimacy is to confide secret joys. Have we ever let God tell us any of His joys, or are we telling God our secrets so continually that

we leave no room for Him to talk to us? MUH. 155

It is an insult to use the word happiness in connection with Jesus Christ. The joy of Jesus was the absolute self-surrender and self-sacrifice of Himself to His Father, the joy of doing that which the Father sent Him to do. "I delight to do Thy will." Jesus prayed that our joy might go on fulfilling itself until it was the same joy as His. MUH. 244

This earth is like a sick chamber, and when God sends His angels here He has to say—'Now be quiet; they are so sick with sin that they cannot understand your hilarity.' Whenever the veil is lifted there is laughter and joy. These are the characteristics that belong to God and God's order of things; sombreness and gloom, oppression and depression, are the characteristics of all that does not belong to God. NKW. 70

Every bit of knowledge that we have of God fills us with ineffable joy. Remember what Jesus said to His disciples— "That My joy might be in you." What was the joy of Jesus? That He understood the Father. OBH. 43

It is a crime to allow external physical misery to make us sulky with God. There *are* desolating experiences . . . , and he says, "Then will I go . . . unto God my exceeding joy,"—not 'with joy,' but unto God *Who is my joy*. No calamity can touch that wealth. OBH. 87

The one thing that Jesus Christ does for a man is to make him radiant, not artificially radiant. There is nothing more irritating than the counsel, 'keep smiling'; that is a counterfeit, a radiance that soon fizzles out. PH. 198

It is a tremendous thing to know that God reigns and rules and rejoices, and that His joy is our strength.   PH. 238

The joy that Jesus exhibited in His life was in knowing that every power of His nature was in harmony with His Father's nature, therefore He did with delight what God designed Him for as Son of Man. Anything that exactly fulfils the purpose of its creation experiences joy, and . . . our joy is that we fulfil the purpose of God in our lives by being saints.   PR. 132

Thank God, the joy of the Lord is an actual experience now, and it goes beyond any conscious experience, because the joy of the Lord takes us into the consciousness of God, and the honour at stake in our body is the honour of God.
PR. 136

Undaunted radiance is not built on anything passing, but on the love of God that nothing can alter. The experiences of life, terrible or monotonous, are impotent to touch "the love of God which is in Christ Jesus our Lord."   RTR. 32

The Bible talks plentifully about joy, but it nowhere talks about a "happy Christian." Happiness depends on what happens; joy does not. Remember, Jesus Christ had joy, and He prays "that they might have My joy fulfilled in themselves."   RTR. 47

The thing that really sustains is not that we feel happy in God, but that God's joy is our energy, and that when we get out of this "shell" we shall find an explanation that will justify our faith in Him.
SHH. 23

Solomon rattles the bottom board out of every piece of deception. The only true joy in life, he says, is based on a personal

relationship to God. You cannot find joy in being like animals, or in art, or aestheticism, in ruling or being ruled—the whole thing is passed in survey in a most ruthless examination by a man whose wisdom is profounder than the profoundest and has never been excelled, and in summing it all up he says that joy is only found in any of these things when a man is rightly related to God.   SHH. 78

The joy of Jesus Christ was in the absolute self-surrender and self-sacrifice of Himself to His Father, the joy of doing what the Father sent Him to do—'I delight to do Thy will,' and that is the joy He prays may be in His disciples.   SSY. 98

One of the consolations of the way is the fathomless joy of the Holy Ghost manifesting itself in us as it did in the Son of God in the days of His flesh.   SSY. 98

This is the age of the gospel of cheerfulness. We are told to ignore sin, ignore the gloomy people, and yet more than half the human race is gloomy. Sum up your own circle of acquaintants, and then draw your inference. Go over the list, and before long you will have come across one who is gloomy, he has a 'sick' view of things, and you cannot alter that one. How are you going to get that oppression taken off? Tell him to take so many weeks' holiday by the sea? Take iron pills and tonics? No! Living in the peace and joy of God's forgiveness and favour is the only thing that will brighten up and bring cheerfulness to such an one.   WG. 64

The Scriptures are full of admonitions to rejoice, to praise God, to sing aloud for joy; but only when one has a cause to rejoice, to praise, and to sing aloud, can these things truly be done from the heart. In the physical realm the average sick man does not take a very bright view of life, and with the sick in soul true brightness and cheer are an impossibility. Until the soul is cured there is always an underlying dread and fear which steals away the gladness and "joy unspeakable and full of glory" which God wishes to be the portion of all His children. WG. 64

JUDGING

There is a difference between retaliation and retribution. The basis of life is retribution—"For with what judgement ye judge, ye shall be judged, and with what measure ye mete, it shall be measured to you again." This statement of our Lord's is not a haphazard guess, it is an eternal law and it works from God's throne right down. HGM. 104

It takes God a long time to get us out of the way of thinking that unless everyone sees as we do, they must be wrong. MUH. 127

There is no getting away from the penetration of Jesus. If I see the mote in your eye, it means I have a beam in my own. Every wrong thing that I see in you, God locates in me. Every time I judge, I condemn myself. Stop having a measuring rod for other people. MUH. 169

Don't glory in men; don't think of men more highly than you ought to think. We always know what the other man should be, especially if he is a Christian. We are all lynx-eyed in seeing what other people ought to be. We erect terrific standards, and then criticise men for not reaching them. SHH. 133

The counsel of Jesus is to abstain from judging. This sounds strange at first because the characteristic of the Holy Spirit in a Christian is to reveal the things that are wrong, but the strangeness is only on the surface. SSM. 77

"Judge not, that ye be not judged." If we let that maxim of our Lord's sink into our hearts we will find how it hauls us up. "Judge not"—why, we are always at it! The average Christian is the most penetratingly critical individual, there is nothing of the likeness of Jesus Christ about him. A critical temper is a contradiction to all our Lord's teaching. Jesus says of criticism, 'Apply it to yourself, never to anyone else.' "Why dost thou judge thy brother? . . . for we shall all stand before the judgment seat of Christ." SSM. 78

The first thing the Holy Spirit does is to give us a spring-cleaning, and there is no possibility of pride being left in a man after that. I never met a man I could despair of after having discerned all that lies in me apart from the grace of God. SSM. 78

Jesus says regarding judging, *'Don't*; be uncritical in your temper, because in the spiritual domain you can accomplish nothing by criticism.' One of the severest lessons to learn is to leave the cases we do not understand to God. SSM. 78

The measure you mete is measured to you again. . . . If you have been shrewd in finding out the defects of others, that will be exactly the measure meted out to you, people will judge you in the same way. SSM. 79

We cannot get away from the penetration of Jesus Christ. If I see the mote in my brother's eye, it is because I have a beam in my own. It is a most homecoming statement. If I have let God remove the beam from my own outlook by His mighty grace, I will carry with me the implicit sunlight confidence that what God has done for me He can easily do for you, because you have only a splinter, I had a log of wood! This is the confidence God's salvation gives us, we are so amazed at the way God has altered us that we can despair of no one; 'I know God can undertake for you, you are only a little wrong, I was wrong to the remotest depths of my mind; I was a mean, prejudiced, self-interested, self-seeking person and God has altered me, therefore I can never despair of you, or of anyone'   SSM. 81

JUDGMENT

The judgments of God leave scars, and the scars remain until I humbly and joyfully recognize that the judgments are deserved and that God is justified in them.   CHI. 70

The man who knows God has no right to estimate other men according to his common-sense judgment, he has to bring in revelation facts which will make him a great deal more lenient in his judgment. To have a little bit only of God's point of view makes us immensely bitter in our judgment.   DI. 47

Never say, 'That truth is applicable to So-and-so,' it puts you in a false position. To know that the truth is applicable to another life is a sacred trust from God to you, you must never say anything about it. Restraint in these matters is the way to maintain communion with God.   DI. 84

You cannot judge a man by his head, but only by his character.   HG. 68

The modern Christian laughs at the idea of a final judgment. That shows how far we can stray away if we imbibe the idea that the modern mind is infallible and not our Lord. To His mind at least the finality of moral decision is reached in this life. There is no aspect of our Lord's mind that the modern mind detests so fundamentally as this one. It does not suit us in any shape or form.   HG. 73

Jesus did not stand as a prophet and utter judgments; wherever He went the unerring directness of His presence located men. We are judged too by children, we often feel ashamed in their presence; they are much more our judges than we theirs, their simplicity and attitude to things illustrates our Lord's judgments.   HGM. 42

If we judge ourselves by one another we do not feel condemned . . . ; but immediately Jesus Christ is in the background—His life, His language, His looks, His labours, we feel judged instantly. "It is for judgment that I have come into the world."   HGM. 43

We are apt to think the judgments of Jesus are wrong, but when they come straight home in our personal lives we judge in the same way. At first we are certain that our common-sense is wise, that we see and understand; when Jesus comes He makes that seeing blind.   HGM. 45

Before we received the Holy Spirit we used to have very clear and emphatic judgments, now in certain matters we have not even ordinary common-sense judgment, we seem altogether impoverished. The way Jesus judges makes us know we are blind. We decide what is the most sensible common-sense thing to do, then Jesus comes instantly with His judgment and confuses everything, and in the end He brings out something that proves to be the perfect wisdom of God. The judgments of Jesus are always

unexpected; unexpected in every way.
HGM. 45

Our Lord is unceasingly deliberate, the beginning and the end of His judgment is the same; He will not pass a hasty judgment on us. When He comes He will judge us straightaway, and we shall accept His judgment. HGM. 45

We pronounce judgments, not by our character or our goodness, but by the intolerant ban of finality in our views, which awakens resentment and has none of the Spirit of Jesus in it. Jesus never judged like that. It was His presence, His inherent holiness that judged. Whenever we see Him we are judged instantly. HGM. 46

The revelation of Jesus comes in the way He walks on our deeps; He tells us to do something which in the light of our own discernment sounds ridiculous, but immediately we do it, we experience the judgment of Jesus. The judgment is not in what He says, it is Himself. HGM. 91

Life serves back in the coin you pay. You are paid back what you give, not necessarily by the same person; and this holds with regard to good as well as evil. If you have been generous, you will meet generosity again through someone else; if you have been shrewd in finding out the defects of others, that is the way people will judge you. Jesus Christ never allows retaliation, but He says that the basis of life is retribution. HGM. 104

God's condemnations as well as His promises are conditional; as long as we remain with the wrong disposition unremoved, every truth of God will harden us and ripen us for judgment. HGM. 109

Do not judge by ordinary reasoning, or weighing up by carnal suspicion, but

keep in the light. By keeping in the light we judge even angels. It is done by following God's life in judgment. LG. 67

God never gives us reliable judgment; He gives us a disposition which leads to a perfect judgment if we will work out that disposition. MFL. 125

We have to learn to see things from Jesus Christ's standpoint. Our judgment is warped in every particular in which we do not allow it to be illuminated by Jesus Christ. MFL. 125

In the teachings of Jesus Christ the element of judgment is always brought out, it is the sign of God's love. Never sympathize with a soul who finds it difficult to get to God, God is not to blame. It is not for us to find out the reason why it is difficult, but so to present the truth of God that the Spirit of God will show what is wrong. The great sterling test in preaching is that it brings everyone to judgment. The Spirit of God locates each one to himself. MUH. 126

The pronouncement of coming doom is a combining of judgment and deliverance. When God's limit is reached He destroys the unsaveable and liberates the saveable; consequently judgment days are the great mercy of God because they separate between good and evil, between right and wrong. OPG. 19

Most of us suspend judgment about ourselves, we find reasons for not accusing ourselves entirely, consequently when we find anything so definite and intense as the Bible revelation we are apt to say it exaggerates, until we are smitten with the knowledge of what we are like in God's sight. OPG. 54

There are times when the Heavenly Father will look as if He were an unjust

Judge, but remember, Jesus says, He is not. PH. 97

We cannot judge ourselves by ourselves or by anyone else, there is always one fact more in everyone's life that we do not know. We cannot put men into types, we are never at the balance of one another's heredity; therefore the judgment cannot lie with us. SHH. 37

Solomon says that God's judgment is right and true and that a man can rest his heart there. SHH. 37

It is a great thing to notice the things we cannot answer just now, and to waive our judgment about them. Because you cannot explain a thing, don't say there is nothing in it. SHH. 37

It is a great education to try and put yourself into the circumstances of others before passing judgment on them. SHH. 113

Which of us would dare stand before God and say, 'My God, judge me as I have judged my fellow-men'? We have judged our fellow-men as sinners; if God had judged us like that we would be in hell. God judges us through the marvellous Atonement of Jesus Christ. SSM. 80

JUSTICE

Always remain true to facts and to the intuitive certainty that God must be just, and do not try to justify Him too quickly. The juggling trick tries to justify God for allowing sin and war. Sin and war are absolutely unjustifiable, and yet the instinct of every Christian is—'I know that in the end God will justify Himself.' Meantime you can only justify Him by a venture of faith which cannot be logically demonstrated. BFB. 50

Justice means rightness with God; nothing is just until it is adjusted to God. MFL. 87

To look for justice from other people is a sign of deflection from devotion to Jesus Christ. Never look for justice, but never cease to give it. MFL. 88

In the Sermon on the Mount our Lord teaches us not to look for justice, but never to cease to give it. That is not common sense, it is either madness or Christianity. PH. 66

To look for justice is to educate myself not in the practice of Divine living, but in my 'divine' right to myself. PH. 67

One of the great stirring truths of the Bible is that the man who looks for justice from others is a fool. In moral and spiritual life if a man has a sense of injustice, he ceases to be of value to his fellow men. SHH. 35

Never waste your time looking for justice; if you do you will soon put yourself in bandages and give way to self-pity. Our business is to see that no one suffers from our injustice. SHH. 35

Never look for justice but never cease to give it. If you do look for justice, you will become bitter and cease to be a disciple of Jesus Christ. SHH. 135

JUSTIFICATION

By justification God anticipates that we are holy in His sight, and if we will obey the Holy Spirit we will prove in our actual life that God is justified in justifying us. CHI. 58

The wisdom of God is shown in that Jesus Christ was made unto us righteousness. That means that God can justly justify the unjust and remain righteous. HG. 108

In the Cross of Calvary Our Lord is revealed as the Just One making men just before God. God never justifies men outside Christ. No man can stand for one second on any right or justice of his own; but as he abides in Christ, Jesus Christ is made righteousness unto him. HG. 108

The justification of every sinner is by faith and by faith alone, and when a man walks in that faith, his justification appears in his flesh and justifies God. NKW. 46

We may be consciously free of sin, but we are not justified on that account; we may be walking in the light of our conscience, but we are not justified on that account either; we are only justified in the sight of God through the Atonement at work in our inner life. SHL. 52

The great thing is not the teaching of Jesus, but what He came to do for the human race, viz., to make the way back to God. BE. 67

If Jesus Christ came to teach a man to be what he never can be, would He had never come! He is the greatest tantalizer of mankind if all He came to do was to tell us to be pure in heart, to be so holy that when God scrutinizes us He can see nothing to censure. But what He came to do was to make it possible for any man to receive the disposition that ruled Him, viz., the Holy Spirit. BE. 94

... if all Jesus came to do was to tell me I must have an unsullied career, when my past has been blasted by sin and wickedness on my own part, then He but tantalizes me. If He is simply a teacher, He only increases our capacity for misery, for He sets up standards that stagger us.

But the teaching of Jesus Christ is not an ideal, it is the statement of the life we will live when we are readjusted to God by the Atonement. The type of life Jesus lived, the type of character He expressed, is possible for us by His death, and only by His death, because by means of His death we receive the life to which His teaching applies. BE. 119

The majority of us do not accept Jesus Christ's statements. Immediately we look at them, their intensity and profundity make us shrink. BP. 137

Our Lord is not the great Teacher of the world, He is the Saviour of the world and the Teacher of those who believe in Him, which is a radically different matter. His teaching is of no use saving to agonise mankind with its unattainable ideals until men are made anew through the Cross. Unless I am born from above the only result of the teachings of Jesus is to produce despair. People say that Jesus Christ came to teach us to be good; He never did! All the teaching in the world about a man having a pure heart won't make it pure. Our Lord's teaching has no power in it unless I possess His nature. CHI. 36

Our Lord never teaches first by principles, but by personal relationship to Himself. CHI. 59

We reverse the teaching of Jesus, we don't seek first the Kingdom of God, we seek every other thing first, and the result accords with what Jesus said, the word He puts in is choked and becomes unfruitful. CHI. 109

The teaching of Jesus is not first; what *is* first is that He came to give us a totally new heredity, and the Sermon on the Mount describes the way that heredity will work out. DI. 71

If you have never been brought close enough to Jesus to realize that He teaches things that grossly offend you as a natural man, I question whether you have ever seen Him.   DI. 73

Immediately you get out of touch with God, you are in a hell of chaos. That is always in the background of the teaching of Jesus. That is why the teaching of Jesus produces such consternation in the natural man.   DI. 73

The scrutiny we give other people should be for ourselves. You will never be able to cast out the mote in your brother's eye unless you have had a beam removed, or to be removed, from your own eye.   DI. 74

It is perilously possible to do one of two things—bind burdens on people you have no intention of helping them lift, or placidly to explain away the full purport of our Lord's teaching.   DI. 74

Divorced from supernatural new birth the teaching of Jesus has no application to me, it only results in despair.   DI. 74

Our Lord's teaching about the maimed life and the mature life has not been sufficiently recognized. You can never be mature unless you have been fanatical. DI. 74

K

KINDNESS

Am I as spontaneously kind to God as I used to be, or am I only expecting God to be kind to me? Am I full of the little things that cheer His heart over me, or am I whimpering because things are going hardly with me? There is no joy in the soul that has forgotten what God prizes. It is a great thing to think that Jesus Christ has need of me—"Give Me to drink." How much kindness have I shown Him this past week? Have I been kind to His reputation in my life? MUH. 21

KINGDOM

The prevailing characteristics of the Kingdom Jesus represents are moral characteristics. There must be an alteration in me before I can be in the Kingdom, or the Kingdom can be in me, and that can only be by means of an inner crisis, viz., regeneration. There must be something outside me which will alter me on the inside. GW. 53

The central meaning of the Kingdom is my personal relationship to my Lord. GW. 54

The only entrance into the Kingdom is the Cross; then when we are born again by means of the Cross and are in the Kingdom of God, we have to live out its laws. it is not that we take the precepts of the Sermon on the Mount and try to live them out literally, but that as we abide in Christ we live out its precepts unconsciously. Being in the Kingdom, we are fit now to live out its laws, and we obey Jesus Christ's commands because of our love for Him. GW. 55

Too often the Kingdom is thought of as something to which Jesus is not at all necessary. He does not stand in relation to it where the New Testament places Him, viz., as King. It is not natural to us to think of Jesus as King; in the New Testament it is the most natural view. We are much more inclined to think of Him in a sentimental way as Saviour and sympathizing Friend; in the New Testament there is something much more vigorous. He is Saviour in order that He might be King. GW. 55

'You can have no notion of My kingdom from the kingdoms of this world.' It is the duty of any upright man to oppose wrong, but Jesus Christ did not come to enable us to do that. He came to put within us a new spirit, to make us members of His Kingdom while we are in this world—not *against* the world, and not *of* it, but *in* the world, exhibiting an otherworldly spirit. GW. 56

The kingdom of God in this dispensation is the rule of God discerned by individuals alone. 'Unless you are born from above,' Jesus says, 'you will never see the rule of God.' It is not seen by the intellect. The rule of God which individual saints see and recognize is 'without observation' in this dispensation. There is another dispensation coming when the whole world will see it as individuals have seen it. HG. 51

Whenever Jesus talked about His kingdom the disciples misinterpreted what He said to mean a material kingdom to be established on this earth; but Jesus said, "My kingdom is not of this world: if My kingdom were of this world, then would My servants fight, that I should not be delivered to the Jews." IYA. 23

At the basis of Our Lord's Kingdom is this unaffected loveliness of the commonplace. The thing in which I am blessed is my poverty. If I know I have no strength of will, no nobility of disposition, then, says Jesus, 'Blessed are you,' because it is through that poverty that I enter into the Kingdom of Heaven. LG. 37

I cannot enter the Kingdom of Heaven as a good man or woman; I can only enter the Kingdom of Heaven as a complete pauper. LG. 37

We can never earn our place in the Kingdom of God by doing anything. Immediately we obey the instinct born in us of God's Spirit we are fitted into the Kingdom of God. MFL. 16

"Fear not, little flock; for it is your Father's good pleasure to give you the kingdom," a tiny insignificant crowd in every age. PS. 75

"The kingdom of God cometh not with observation: . . . for, behold, the kingdom of God is within you." Men are called on to live out His teaching in an age that will not recognise Him, and that spells limitation and very often persecution. SSM. 19

KNOWLEDGE

The characteristic of being born again is that we know Who Jesus is. The secret of the Christian is that he knows the absolute Deity of the Lord Jesus Christ. When we are saved by God's grace our minds are opened by the incoming of the Holy Spirit and we understand the Scriptures. HG. 97

We only know God's thought and the expression of it in Jesus Christ, and we only know the meaning of 'God and man one' in Jesus Christ. HGM. 96

It is a great boon to know there are deep things to know. The curse of the majority of spiritual Christians is that they are too cocksure and certain there is nothing more to know than they know. That is spiritual insanity. IWP. 76

The depths of personality are hidden from our sight; we do not know anything beyond the threshold of consciousness, God is the only One Who knows. When we try to go beyond our conscious life into the depths of our personality, we do not know where we are, our only refuge is the 139th Psalm—"Search me, O God, and know my heart." MFW. 28

It is a dangerous thing to refuse to go on knowing. MUH. 160

When you know you should do a thing, and do it, immediately you know more. MUH. 160

When the Spirit of God has opened your mind by His incoming and you are determining to know more, you will find that external circumstances and internal knowledge go together, and by obedience you begin to fulfil your spiritual destiny. The counterfeit of obedience is the state of mind in which you work up occasions to sacrifice yourself, ardour is mistaken for the discernment built on knowledge. OBH. 119

If we are ever going to know the Father and the Son, we must have their nature, and we are not born with it. PR. 28

Modern teaching implies that we must be grossly experienced before we are of any use in the world. That is not true. Jesus Christ knew good and evil by the life which was in Him, and God intended that man's knowledge of evil should come in the same way as to our Lord, viz., through the rigorous integrity of obedience to God. SHL. 62

The great characteristic of our Lord's life was that of 'golden ignorance'; there were things He did not know and that He refused to know. SHL. 66

When we are born again we have to obey the Spirit of God, and as we draw on the life of Jesus and learn to assimilate and carry out what He speaks to us, we shall grow in ignorance of certain things and be alive and alert only to what is God's will for us. SHL. 69

L

LAMB

The Lamb is not only the supreme Sacrifice for man's sin, He is the Searcher of hearts, searching to the inmost recesses of mind and motive. It is not a curious searching, not an uncanny searching, but the deep wholesome searching the Holy Spirit gives in order to convict men of their sin and need of a Saviour; then when they come to the Cross, and through it accept deliverance from sin, Jesus Christ becomes the Sovereign of their lives, they love Him personally and passionately beyond all other loves of earth. CHI. 120

We know what the wrath of a lion is like—but *the wrath of the Lamb!*—it is beyond our conception. All one can say about it is that the wrath of God is the terrible obverse side of the love of God. CHI. 121

Do we "follow the Lamb whithersoever He goeth"? He will take us through the strange dark things—we must follow Him "whithersoever He goeth." "For the Lamb which is in the midst of the throne shall feed them, and shall lead them unto living fountains of waters; and God shall wipe away all tears from their eyes." RTR. 85

It is possible to take any phase of Our Lord's life, the healing phase, the teaching phase, the saving and sanctifying phase, but there is nothing limitless about any of these. But take this: 'the Lamb of God, which taketh away the sin of the world!' That is limitless. SSY. 143

The significance of the sermon on Christ the Lamb of God is limitless because He is the Lamb *of God*, not of man. 'Behold the Lamb of God, which taketh away the sin of the world!' SSY. 145

LAW

. . . there *is* a law in the natural world so there *is* a law in the spiritual world, i.e., a way of explaining things, but the law is not the same in both worlds. BFB. 35

Laws are effects, not causes. BFB. 96

We only realize the moral law when it comes with an IF, that means, I have the power not to obey it. BE. 12

Man has to fulfil God's laws in his physical life, in his mental and moral life, in his social and spiritual life, and to offend in one point is to be guilty of all. BE. 15

The law of gravitation is the explanation given by scientific men of certain observed facts, and to say that Jesus Christ "broke the law of gravitation" when He walked on the sea, and when He ascended, is a misstatement. He brought in a new series of facts for which the law of gravitation, so-called, could not account. BP. 55

. . . as there is a law in the natural world whereby we reason and think and argue about natural things, so there is a law in the spiritual world; but the law which runs through the natural world is not the same as in the spiritual world. BP. 210

Our lawlessness can be detected in relation to the words, "Come unto Me." DI. 27

We transgress a law of God and expect an experience akin to death, but exactly the opposite happens, we feel enlarged, more broad-minded, more tolerant of evil, but we are more powerless; knowledge which comes from eating of the tree of the knowledge of good and evil, instead of instigating to action, paralyses. OPG. 7

LAZINESS

The discipline of our mind is the one domain God has put in our keeping. It is impossible to be of any use to God if we are lazy. God won't cure laziness, we have to cure it. DI. 67

More danger arises from physical laziness (which is called 'brain fag') than from almost any other thing. DI. 67

The demand for inspiration is the measure of our laziness. Do the things that don't come by inspiration. DI. 67

"The great defect in all branches of Christian work is laziness." The only cure for laziness is to be filled with the life of God to such an overwhelming extent that He can spend you to the last cell of your body, to the last drop of your blood, for His own glory. WG. 91

God grant we may learn how to be instant in season and out of season, always at it, night and day, whether we feel like it or not. When you come to read deeper down between the lines in the Bible, you will find running all through it the awful curse on laziness and spiritual sloth. WG. 99

God grant we may be roused up in the spiritual domain to put energy and vim into our work and never say, 'I can't'; 'I have no time.' Of course you have not, no man worthy of the name ought to have time to give to God, he has to take it from other things until he knows how God values time. Take heed to yourself, and never allow anything to produce laziness and sloth. WG. 99

LEADERSHIP

When once the Face of the Lord Jesus Christ has broken through, all ecstasies and experiences dwindle in His presence, and the one dominant Leadership becomes more and more clear. We have seen Jesus as we never saw Him before, and the impulsion in us by the grace of God is that we must follow in His steps. IWP. 106

One of the outstanding miracles of God's grace is to make us able to take any kind of leadership at all without losing spiritual power. There is no more searching test in the whole of Christian life than that. LG. 91

LEGALISM

A bird flies persistently and easily because the air is its domain and its world. A legal Christian is one who is trying to live in a rarer world than is natural to him. Our Lord said 'If the Son shall make you free, ye shall be free indeed,' i.e., free from the inside, born from above, lifted into another world where there is no strenuous effort to live in a world not natural to us, but where we can soar continually higher and higher because we are in the natural domain of spiritual life. GW. 67

LIFE

No amount of sacrifice on the part of man can put the basis of human life right: God has undertaken the responsibility for this, and He does it on redemptive lines. BFB. 28

The basis of things is tragic; therefore God must find the way out, or there is no way out. BFB. 60

... we cannot explain life, yet it is a very commonplace fact that we are alive. We cannot explain love; we cannot explain death; we cannot explain sin; yet these are all everyday facts. The world of Nature is a confusion; there is nothing clear about it; it is a confusing, wild chaos. Immediately we receive the Spirit of God, He energizes our spirits not only for practical living but for practical thinking, and we begin to 'discern the arm of the Lord,' i.e., to see God's order in and through all the chaos. BP. 230

We are here for one purpose: "to fill up that which is lacking of the afflictions of Christ"—spoilt for this age, alive to nothing but Jesus Christ's point of view. CHI. 72

The deepest clamour of a man's nature once he is awake is to know the "whence" and "whither" of life— "Whence came I?" "Why am I here?" "Where am I going?" In all ages men have tried to pry into the secrets of the future, astrologers, necromancers, spiritualists, or whatever name you may call them by, have all tried to open the Book, but without success, because it is a sealed Book. "I wept much," says John, "because no one was found worthy to open the book, or to look thereon." CHI. 118

'Except you are crucified with Christ until all that is left is the life of Christ in your flesh and blood, *you have no life in you.*' 'Except your self-love is flooded away by the inrush of the love of Jesus so that you feel your blood move through you in tender charity as it moved through Him, *you have no life in you.*' 'Except your flesh becomes the temple of His holiness, and you abide in Christ and He in you, *you have no life in you.*' GW. 118

Our Lord bases everything on life as it is, and life is implicit. For instance, you cannot explicitly state what love is, but love is the implicit thing that makes life worth living. You cannot explicitly state what sin is, but sin is the implicit thing that curses life. You cannot explicitly state what death is, all the scientific jargon in the world cannot define death; death is the implicit thing which destroys life as we know it. A child is a good illustration of the implicit, you cannot imagine a child without emotion, always logical, reasonable and well-balanced, he would not be a child but a prig. HG. 33

If I am in living personal relationship to Jesus the things that make the common affairs of life become conveyors of the real presence of God. HGM. 36

When a man sees life as it really is there are only two alternatives—the Cross of Jesus Christ as something to accept, or suicide. HGM. 59

It is only when we get full of dread about life apart from God that we leave ourselves in His hands. IWP. 37

Jesus said, "Ye have not (this) life in yourselves." What life? The life He had. Men have moral life, physical life and in-

tellectual life apart from Jesus Christ.
IWP. 115

Immediately we have life imparted to us by the Holy Spirit, we realize that it is the very life that was in Jesus that is born into us; we are loosened from the old bondage and find that we can fulfil all the expectations of the life which has been imparted to us. It is a strenuous life of obedience to God, and God has given us bodies through which to work out the life, and circumstances to react against in order to prove its reality. MFL. 21

The life of sanctification, of service, and of sacrifice, is the threefold working out in our bodies of the life of Jesus until the supernatural life is the only life. These are truths that cannot be *learned*; they can only be habitually *lived*. MFL. 110

Get into the habit of saying, "Speak, Lord," and life will become a romance.
MUH. 30

His Cross is the door by which every member of the human race can enter into the life of God; by His Resurrection He has the right to give eternal life to any man, and by His Ascension Our Lord enters heaven and keeps the door open for humanity. MUH. 138

The shallow amenities of life, eating and drinking, walking and talking, are all ordained by God . . . . We are so abominably serious, so desperately interested in our own characters, that we refuse to behave like Christians in the shallow concerns of life. MUH. 327

One individual life may be of priceless value to God's purposes, and yours may be that life. MUH. 335

My actual life is given me by God, and I can live in it either as an atheist or as a worshipper. NKW. 40

In personal life despise these two things—dumps and hurry; they are worse than the devil, and are both excessively culpable. Dumps is an absolute slur against God—I won't look up, I have done all I could but it is all up, and I am in despair. Hurry is the same mood expressed in an opposite way—I have no time to pray, no time to look to God or to consider anything, I must do the thing. Perspiration is mistaken for inspiration. Consequently I drive my miserable little wagon in a rut instead of hitching it to a star and pulling according to God's plan. NKW. 45

The Holy Spirit destroys our personal private life and turns it into a thoroughfare for God. NKW. 65

The only supernatural life ever lived on earth was the life of our Lord, and He was at home with God anywhere. Wherever we are not at home with God, there is a quality to be added. We have to let God press through us in that particular until we gain Him, and life becomes the simple life of a child in which the vital concern is putting God first. OBH. 65

Self-interest, self-sympathy, self-pity—anything and everything that does not arise from a determination to accept my life entirely from Him will lead to a dissipation of my life. PR. 57

The life of Jesus is the life we have to live here, not hereafter. There is no chance to live this kind of life hereafter, we have to live it here. PR. 80

The way into the life of Jesus is not by imitation of Him, but by identification with His Cross. That is the meaning of being born from above: we enter into His life by its entering into us. PR. 80

To say that reason is the basis of human life is absurd, but to say that the basis of human life is tragedy and that the main purpose of it as far as Jesus Christ is concerned, is holiness, is much nearer the point of view given in the Bible. SA. 32

The summing up of all practical life is that the basis of things is tragic. Sum up your life as it actually is, and, unless you look at actual things from a religious or a temperamental or an intellectual standpoint, everything is to be said for this philosophy: Eat, drink, and be merry, for to-morrow we die. SHH. 5

Unless a man can get into a relationship with the God Whom the Bible reveals, life is not worth living. SHH. 44

Jesus Christ can make the weakest man into a Divine dreadnought, fearing nothing. He can plant within him the life that was in Himself, the life Time cannot touch. SHL. 28

LIFE AND DEATH

Whenever Jesus speaks about life He is referring to the life which is in Himself, and it is this life which He imparts by means of His death. BSG. 76

"Be thou faithful unto death, and I will give thee a crown of life." The crown of life means I shall see that my Lord has got the victory after all, even in me.
HG. 17

If when you are sanctified you turn for one second to the natural life, the sentence of death is there. Never take your guidance from the natural life, but learn to sacrifice the natural to the will of God. HGM. 139

God showed to man that compliance with His dictates would ever mean eternal bliss and joy unspeakable and life and knowledge for evermore, but that ceasing to comply would mean loss of life with God and eternal death. LG. 11

If we do not put to death the things in us that are not of God, they will put to death the things that are of God. There is never any alternative, some thing must die in us—either sin or the life of God. PR. 101

Life is a far greater danger than death. SHL. 26

Jesus Christ has destroyed the dominion of death, and He can make us fit to face every problem of life, more than conqueror all along the line. SHL. 27

LIFE ETERNAL

All we know about eternal life, about hell and damnation, the Bible alone tells us. BP. 95

Whenever Our Lord speaks of "life" He means *eternal* life, and He says, "Ye have not (this) life in yourselves." Men have natural life and intellectual life apart from Jesus Christ. HG. 110

The life which Jesus Christ exhibited was eternal life, and He says—anyone who believes in Me, i.e., commits himself to Me, has that life. To commit myself to Jesus means there is nothing that is not committed. HG. 110

The upward look towards God of eternal life is an indication of the inherent nature of the life; that is, it is not attained by effort. Natural characteristics, natural virtues and natural attainments have nothing to do with the life itself. HG. 111

Our Lord's life is the exhibition of eternal life in time. Eternal life in the Christian is based on redemptive certainty; he is not working to redeem men; he is a fellow worker with God among men because they are redeemed.   HG. 111

Jesus did not say that eternal life was satisfaction, but something infinitely grander: "This is life eternal, that they might know Thee."   MFL. 30

Eternal Life has nothing to do with Time, it is the life which Jesus lived when He was down here. The only source of Life is the Lord Jesus Christ.   MUH. 103

"As He is, so are we." The sanctified life is a life that bears a strong family likeness to Jesus Christ, a life that exhibits His virtues, His patience, His love, His holiness. Slowly and surely we learn the great secret of eternal life, which is to know God.   OBH. 43

By His Death and Resurrection our Lord has the right to give eternal life to every man; by His Ascension He enters Heaven and keeps the door open for humanity.   PH. 37

Jesus Christ came to give us eternal life, a life in which there is neither time nor space, which cannot be marked with suffering or death; it is the life Jesus lived.   PH. 76

Jesus Christ is the normal man, and in His relationship to God, to the devil, to sin and to man we see the expression in human nature of what He calls 'eternal life.'   PR. 13

Eternal life is the gift of the Lord Jesus Christ. "He that believeth on Me hath everlasting life, i.e., the life He manifested in His human flesh when He was here, and says Jesus, 'Ye have not (that) life in yourselves.'" His life is not ours

by natural birth, and it can only be given to us by means of His Cross. Our Lord's Cross is the gateway into His life; His Resurrection means that He has power now to convey that life to us.   PR. 111

The only thing that makes eternal life actual is the entrance of the Holy Spirit by commitment to Jesus Christ.   PR. 112

Eternal life is not a present given to me by God, it is Himself. "The gift *of* God," not *from* God.   PR. 114

LIGHT

If Jesus Christ had not come with His light, and the Holy Ghost had not come with His light, men had not known anything about sin.   BP. 155

. . . nothing is cleaner or grander or sweeter than light. Light cannot be soiled; a sunbeam may shine into the dirtiest puddle, but it is never soiled. A sheet of white paper can be soiled, so can almost any white substance, but you cannot soil light.   BP. 173

A searchlight illuminates only what it does and no more; but let daylight come, and you find there are a thousand and one things the searchlight had not revealed. Whenever you get the light of God on salvation it acts like a searchlight, everything you read in the Bible teaches salvation and you say, 'Why, it is as simple as can be!' The same with sanctification, and the Second Coming. When you come to the place where God is the dominant light you find facts you never realised before, facts which no one is sufficient to explain saving the Lord Jesus Christ.   BSG. 62

We have to get into the white light of Jesus Christ where He is easily first, not our experience of Him first, but Jesus

Christ Himself first, and our experience the evidence that we have seen Him. BSG. 62

The trouble with most of us is that we will walk only in the light of our conviction of what the light is. IWP. 82

"Ye are the light of the world." We have the idea that we are going to shine in heaven, but we are to shine down here, "in the midst of a crooked and perverse nation." We are to shine as lights in the world in the squalid places, and it cannot be done by putting on a brazen smile, the light must be there all the time. LG. 45

It is better never to have seen the light, better never to wish to be what you are not than to have the desire awakened and never to have resolved it into action. MFL. 14

There is another thing about the possession of light in Jesus Christ: my possession of light is quite different from yours. Each of us has a particular possession of light that no one else can have, and if we refuse to take our possession, everyone else will suffer. OBH. 42

There is a possession of light that the Spirit distributes to each one according to the perfect wisdom of God. It is Satan, not God, who makes a man say everyone must be just as he is. As we participate in the light and the Son of God is manifested in us in our particular setting, there will be marvellous blessing to all the people round about. OBH. 42

What we have in the kingdom of light, we give. That is always the characteristic. If we try to picture to others the glory of communion with God without being in close contact with God our-

selves, we will paralyse the imagination of those we talk to. OBH. 44

As we are made partakers of the inheritance of the saints in light, we begin to understand that there is no division into sacred and secular, it is all one great glorious life with God as the Son of God is manifested in our mortal flesh. OBH. 45

God is Light, and He lifts us up in Himself, no matter who we are, and poises us as surely as He established the stars, in the very light that He is in. He makes us meet to be partakers of that wonderful inheritance, and slowly and surely the marvel of the life of the Son of God is manifested in our mortal flesh. OBH. 46

We have to walk in the light "as He is in the light," keep continually coming to the light, don't keep anything covered up. If we are filled with the life of Jesus we must walk circumspectly, keep the interest in life going, have nothing folded up. PH. 198

I am not judged by the light I have, but by the light I have refused to accept. SA. 49

Light is the description of clear, beautiful, moral character from God's standpoint, and if we walk in the light, "the blood of Jesus Christ cleanses us from all sin;" God Almighty can find nothing to censure. SA. 52

"Ye are the light of the world." Light cannot be soiled; you may try to grasp a beam of light with the sootiest hand, but you leave no mark on the light. A sunbeam may shine into the filthiest hovel in the slums of a city, but it cannot be soiled. A merely moral man, or an innocent man, may be soiled in spite of his integrity, but the man who is made pure by the Holy Ghost cannot be soiled, he is as light. SSM. 20

LIGHT AND DARKNESS

There is darkness which comes from excess of light as well as darkness which is caused by sin. There are times when it is dark with inarticulateness; there is no speech, no understanding, no guide, because you are in the centre of the light. HGM. 53

As long as you are in the dark you do not know what God is doing; immediately you get into the light, you discover it. HGM. 53

In actual life we must be always in the light, and we cease to be in the light when we want to explain why we did a thing. The significant thing about Our Lord is that He never explained anything; He let mistakes correct themselves because He always lived in the light. There is so much in us that is folded and twisted, but the sign that we are following God is that we keep in the light. 'I have been saved and sanctified, therefore I am all right'—that brings darkness at once. LG. 66

If the Spirit of God detects anything in you that is wrong, He does not ask you to put it right; He asks you to accept the light, and He will put it right. A child of the light confesses instantly and stands bared before God; a child of the darkness says—"Oh, I can explain that away." When once the light breaks and the conviction of wrong comes, be a child of the light, and confess, and God will deal with what is wrong; if you vindicate yourself, you prove yourself to be a child of the darkness. MUH. 83

If you do not obey the light, it will turn into darkness. MUH. 240

To walk in the light means that everything that is of the darkness drives me closer into the centre of the light. MUH. 361

If we have entered into the heavenly places in Christ Jesus, the light has shone, and, this is the marvellous thing, as we begin to do what we know the Lord would have us do, we find He does not enable *us* to do it, He simply puts through us all His power and the thing is done in His way. Thank God for everyone who has seen the light, who has understood how the Lord Jesus Christ clears away the darkness and brings the light by showing His own characteristics through us. OBH. 40

One step in the right direction in obedience to the light, and the manifestation of the Son of God in your mortal flesh is as certain as that God is on His throne. When once God's light has come to us through Jesus Christ, we must never hang back, but obey; and we shall not walk in darkness, but will have the light of life. OBH. 43

"What I tell you in the darkness . . ." Let it be understood that the darkness our Lord speaks of is not darkness caused by sin or disobedience, but rather darkness caused from excess of light. PH. 10

The light always reveals and guides, and men dislike it, and prefer darkness when their deeds are evil. SSM. 20

The light produces hell where before there was peace; it produces pain where before there was death. God's method in the pathway of light is destructive before it is constructive. SSY. 151

LOCK AND KEY

Everything a man takes to be the key to a problem is apt to turn out another lock. For instance, the theory of evolution was supposed to be the key to the problem of the universe, but instead it has turned out a lock.   BFB. 99

... the atomic theory was thought to be the key; then it was discovered that the atom itself was composed of electrons, and each electron was found to be a universe of its own, and that theory too becomes a lock and not a key.   BFB. 99

Everything that man attempts as a simplification of life, other than a personal relationship to God, turns out to be a lock, and we should be alert to recognize when a thing turns from a key to a lock.   BFB. 99

LOGIC

There are people who can silence you with their logic while all the time you know, although you cannot prove it, that they are wrong. This is because the basis of things is not logical, but tragic. Logic and reasoning are only methods of dealing with things as they are; they give no explanation of things as they are.   BFB. 22

Logic and reason are always on the hunt for definition, and anything that cannot be defined is apt to be defied.   BFB. 34

If you are a logician you may often gain your point in a debate and yet feel yourself in the wrong. You get the best of it in disputing with some people because their minds are not clever, but when you get away from your flush of triumph you feel you have missed the point altogether; you have won on debate, but not on fact.   BFB. 35

You cannot get at the basis of things by disputing. Our Lord Himself comes off second best every time in a logical argument, and yet you know that He has in reality come off 'more than conqueror.'   BFB. 35

A logical position is satisfying to intellect, but it can never be true to life. Logic is simply the method man's intellect follows in making things definable to himself, but you can't define what is greater than yourself.   DI. 83

Life is never a process of logic, life is the most illogical thing we know. The facts of life are illogical, they cannot be traced easily. Intellect is secondary, not primary. An intellectualist never pushes an issue of will.   MFL. 51

The findings of higher criticism may be logically proved, but the biggest facts in life are not logical. If they were, we should be able to calculate our ends and make sure of things on rational logical lines. Logical truth is merely the explanation of facts which common sense has gathered.   PR. 21

In spiritual matters logical processes do not count. Curiosity does not count, nor argument, nor reasoning; these are of no avail for spiritual discernment.   PR. 22

Logic and reasoning are methods of expounding Reality, but we do not get at Reality by our intellect. Reality is only got at by our conscience.   PR. 22

Things cannot be worked out on a logical line, there is always something incalculable.   SHH. 124

LOSTNESS

Jesus Christ's thought about man is that he is lost, and that He is the only One who can find him. "For the Son of Man came to seek and to save that which was lost."   CHI. 97

. . . from Jesus Christ's point of view all men are lost, but we have so narrowed and so specialised the term 'lost' that we have missed its evangelical meaning; we have made it mean that only the people who are down and out in sin are lost. WG. 30

The healthy-minded tendency is very strong to-day. It is the explanation of Unitarianism in its shallower aspect; the explanation of the New Thought movement and the Mind Cure movement, of Christian Science; it is the explanation of how people can be quite happy, quite moral, quite upright, without having anything to do with the Lord Jesus Christ. Our Lord describes these people in terms of the once-born, as 'lost.' The problem for us as workers is, how are we to get these irreligious people who are quite happy and healthy-minded, to the place where they want Jesus? WG. 31

LOVE

We have defined love, in its highest sense, as being the sovereign preference of my person for another person. BP. 134

Love in the Bible is ONE; it is unique, and the human element is but one aspect of it. It is a love so mighty, so absorbing, so intense that all the mind is emancipated and entranced by God; all the heart is transfigured by the same devotion; all the soul in its living, working, waking, sleeping moments is indwelt and surrounded and enwheeled in the rest of this love. CD. VOL. 2, 154

Most of us love other people for what they are to us instead of for what God wants them to be. CHI. 69

You don't love a person with your heart and leave the rest of your nature out,

you love with your whole being, from the crown of the head to the sole of the foot. GW. 9

The Bible makes no distinction between Divine love and human love, it speaks only of 'love.' The majority of us have an impersonal, ethereal, vague abstraction we call love to God; Jesus says I must love God with all my heart and soul and mind and strength, then my love for my fellow men will be relative to that centre. GW. 39

Fundamentally it is impossible to *love* a human being wrongly—it is possible to have an affection for a human being as a sop to my personal conceit: it is never possible to love a human being *rightly* if I love from the centre of self-interest. The love which springs from self-conceit or self-interest ends in being cruel because it demands an infinite satisfaction from another human being which it will never get. The love which has God as its centre makes no demands. Why our Lord appears to be the enemy of natural love is because we do not understand that He deals with fundamentals always. GW. 40

'Love is of God'; it never came from the devil and never can go to the devil. When I am rightly related to God, the more I love the more blessing does He pour out on other lives. The reward of love is the capacity to pour out more love all the time, 'hoping for nothing again.' That is the essential nature of perfect love. GW. 41

The true import of love is the surrender of my self, I go out of myself in order to live in and for God. To be indwelt by the Spirit of Jesus means I am willing to quit my own abode from the self-interested standpoint and live only in and for God. It is not the surrender to a conqueror, but the surrender of love, a sovereign preference for God. GW. 41

When you are sentimentally interested in a person you are conscious of it; when you are in love with a person you are not conscious of it because the love is deeper than consciousness and is only revealed in a crisis. When you love God you become identified with His interests in other people, and He will bring around you those He is interested in— the sinners, the mean, the ungrateful, and you will soon know by your attitude to them whether you love God. GW. 41

Love springs spontaneously, that is, it is not premeditated; but love does not develop like that. Both naturally and spiritually love requires careful developing; love won't stay if it is not sedulously cultivated. If I am not careful to keep the atmosphere of my love right by cultivation, it will turn to lust—'I must have this thing for myself.' HGM. 134

No love of the natural heart is safe unless the human heart has been satisfied by God first. HGM. 134

The one characteristic of love is that it thinks of nothing for itself, it is absorbed in God. IWP. 21

Love produces such pain (apart from a knowledge of God) that it makes the sensitive soul wonder if it is worth while to love. IWP. 25

Love is the sovereign preference of my person for another person, and when the Holy Spirit is in a man, that other Person is Jesus. The only Lover of the Lord Jesus Christ is the Holy Ghost. LG. 122

If human love does not carry a man beyond himself, it is not love. If love is always discreet, always wise, always sensible and calculating, never carried beyond itself, it is not love at all. It may be affection, it may be warmth of feeling, but it has not the true nature of love in it. MUH. 52

We cannot love to order, and yet His word stands—"If any come to Me, and *hate not* his father, and mother, and wife, and children, and brethren, and sisters, yea, and his own life also," (i.e., a hatred of every loyalty that would divide the heart from loyalty to Jesus)" he cannot be My disciple." OBH. 57

Love means deliberate self-limitation; we deliberately identify ourselves with the interests of our Lord in everything. OBH. 59

God does not give us power to love as He loves; the love of God, the very nature of God, possesses us, and He loves through us. OBH. 100

An unemotional love is inconceivable. Love for the good must involve displeasure and grief for the evil. OPG. 16

Love is not blind; love sees a great deal more than the actual, it sees the ideal in the actual, consequently the actual is transfigured by the ideal. OPG. 45

"Love never faileth!" What a wonderful phrase that is! but what a still more wonderful thing the reality of that love must be; greater than prophecy—that vast forth-telling of the mind and purpose of God; greater than the practical faith that can remove mountains; greater than philanthropic self-sacrifice; greater than the extraordinary gifts of emotions and ecstasies and all eloquence; and it is *this* love that is shed abroad in our hearts by the Holy Ghost which is given unto us. PH. 24

This is the characteristic of the Divine love: not that God lays down His life for His friends, but that He lays down His life for His enemies. That is not human love. It does not mean that no human being has ever laid down his life for his enemies, but it does mean that no human being ever did so without having received the Divine nature through the Redemption of our Lord. PH. 25

The highest Christian love is not devotion to a work or to a cause, but to Jesus Christ. PH. 28

Jesus has loved me to the end of all my meanness and selfishness and sin; now, He says, show that same love to others. PH. 81

It is the most ordinary business to fall in love; it is the most extraordinary business to abide there. The same thing with regard to the love of our Lord. The Holy Ghost gives us the great power to love Jesus Christ. That is not a rare experience at all; the rare experience is to get into the conception of loving Him in such a way that the whole heart and mind and soul are taken up with Him. PH. 109

Love is not blind. Love has insight, it sees the things that are not seen. We are told that when we are in love with a person we do not see his defects: the truth is that we see what others do not see, we see him in the ideal, in the real relationship. PH. 155

Love is not measured by what it gets, but by what it costs, and our relationship to Jesus Christ can never be on the line of, 'Why shouldn't I do this?' Our Lord simply says, 'If any man will be My disciple, those are the conditions.' PR. 93

Unless we are willing to give up good things for Jesus Christ, we have no realisation of Whom He is. 'But really I cannot give up things that are quite legitimate!' Then never mention the word love again in connection with Jesus Christ if you cannot give up the best you have for Him. This is the essential nature of love in the natural life, otherwise it is a farce to call it love, it is not love, but lust; and when we come to our relationship with Jesus Christ, this is the love He demands of us. PR. 103

We have to love where we cannot respect and where we must not respect, and this can only be done on the basis of God's love for us. "This is My commandment, that you love one another, as I have loved you." RTR. 56

'Love . . . taketh not account of evil'; it does not ignore the fact that there is evil, but it does not take it into calculation. SHL. 93

"This is My commandment, That ye love one another; as I have loved you." It is not done once and for all, it is a continual stedfast growing habit of the life. SSM. 86

Love never professes; love confesses. SSY. 159

'Things are not happening in the way I expected they would, therefore I am going to give it all up.' To talk like that is a sure sign that we are not possessed by love for Him, but only by love for ourselves. SSY. 170

LOYALTY

Intercessory prayer is the test of our loyalty. GW. 61

In a crisis we are always in danger of standing true to something that is acclaimed by this world rather than standing absolutely loyal to God. HG. 11

Loyalty is not to be to loving God, or to the love of God, but to Jesus Christ's redemption of us. LG. 69

Many of us are loyal to our notions of Jesus Christ, but how many of us are loyal to Him? Loyalty to Jesus means I have to step out where I do not see anything; loyalty to my notions means that I clear the ground first by my intelligence. Faith is not intelligent understanding, faith is deliberate commitment to a Person where I see no way. MUH. 88

It is easier to be a fanatic than a faithful soul, because there is something amazingly humbling, particularly to our religious conceit, in being loyal to God. MUH. 319

Loyalty to Jesus Christ is the thing that we "stick at" to-day. We will be loyal to work, to service, to anything, but do not ask us to be loyal to Jesus Christ. Many Christians are intensely impatient of talking about loyalty to Jesus. Our Lord is dethroned more emphatically by Christian workers than by the world. God is made a machine for blessing men, and Jesus Christ is made a Worker among workers.

The idea is not that we do work for God, but that we are so loyal to Him that He can do His work through us—"I reckon on you for extreme service, with no complaining on your part and no explanation on Mine." God wants to use us as He used His own Son. MUH. 353

We are apt to mistake the sense of the heroic for being heroes. It is one thing to go through a crisis grandly, but a different thing to go through every day glorifying God when there is no witness, no

limelight, and no one paying the remotest attention to you. If we don't want medieval haloes, we want something that will make people say—What a wonderful man of prayer he is! What a pious, devoted woman she is! If anyone says that of you, you have not been loyal to God. NKW. 130

Our Lord has no illusions about men, and He knows that every relationship in life that is not based on loyalty to Him will end in disaster. PH. 52

The discipline of Divine loyalty is not that I am true to a doctrine, but so true to Jesus that other people are nourished in the knowledge of Him. PH. 67

Whenever you meet with difficulties, whether they are intellectual or circumstantial or physical, remain loyal to God. Don't compromise. If you do, everyone around you will suffer from your faithlessness, because you are disloyal to Jesus Christ and His way of looking at things. PH. 76

Remain loyal to God and to His saints in private and in public, and you will find that not only are you continually with God, but that God is counting on you. PH. 76

When Jesus calls, there is the ordeal of conflicting loyalties. Probably the most intense discipline we have to go through is that of learning loyalty to God by the path of what looks like disloyalty to our friends. SSY. 51

Learn to estimate the disproportion in your loyalties. A man will put his Lord to open shame before he will be disloyal to a friend. But when any soul learns how to lay down his life for his Friend, Jesus Christ, other people promptly become shadows until they become realities in Him. SSY. 52

The sense of loyalty to father or mother or friends may easily slander Jesus because it implies that He does not understand our duty to them. If Jesus had been loyal to His earthly mother, He would have been a traitor to His Father's purpose. SSY. 52

We put sensitive loyalty to relationships in place of loyalty to Jesus; every other love is put first, and He has to take the last place. We will readily give up sin and worldliness, but God calls us to give up the very closest, noblest and most right tie we have, if it enters into competition with His call. SSY. 52

There is no test to equal the test of remaining loyal to Jesus Christ's character when the ungodly man is in the ascendant. We are apt to become cynical, and a cynical view is always a distorted view, a view arising out of pique because some personal object is being thwarted.
SSY. 162

Loyalty to the call of Our Lord means not merely that we keep the letter of His command, but that we keep in contact with His nature, i.e., His Name. SSY. 162

Our loyalty is not to stand by the letter of what Jesus says, but to keep our soul continually open to the nature of the Lord Jesus Christ. SSY. 163

LUCIFER

Who were these 'sons of God'? They were not men; they were unquestionably angels and archangels, and the indirect inference is that God had put that former world under the charge of an archangel, Lucifer. BP. 2

God gave the rule of this universe to Lucifer, who opposed himself to God's authority and rule. In falling, he dragged everything down with him, and consequently called forth on this earth a tremendous judgment which resulted in chaos—"and the earth was without form and void." BP. 2

LUST

Our natural life is a fury of desire for the things we can see. That is the meaning of lust—I must have it at once, a fury of desire without any regard for the consequences. HGM. 111

When the disposition of sin rules in my body it takes my organs and uses them for lust. Lust means, I will satisfy myself; whether I satisfy myself on a high or a low level makes no difference, the principle is the same. BE. 68

Lust in its highest and lowest form simply means I seek for a creature to give me what God alone can give, and I become cruel and vindictive and jealous and spiteful to the one from whom I demand what God alone can give. IWP. 90

Lust is—I must have it at once. Love can wait. Lust makes me impulsively impatient, I want to take short cuts, and do things right off. Love can wait endlessly. If I have ever seen God and been touched by Him and the Spirit of God has entered into me, I am willing to wait for Him; I wait in the certainty that He will come. PH. 170

Lust is used in other ways in the Bible than merely of immorality, it is the spirit of 'I must have it at once,' no matter what it is. Temptation yielded to is lust deified. PS. 56

Lust applies not only to the bestial side of things; lust means literally—"I must have it at once, and I don't care what the consequences are." It may be a low, animal lust, or it may be a mental lust, or a moral or spiritual lust; but it is a characteristic that does not belong to the life hid with Christ in God. Love is the opposite; love can wait endlessly. SHH. 74

Remember, lust can be spiritual. Lust disputes the throne of God in us—'I have set my mind to this, or that, and I must have it at once.' SHL. 68

The nature of any dominating lust is that it keeps us from arriving at a knowledge of ourselves. For instance, a covetous man will believe he is very generous. SHL. 81

If ever a man is going to stand where lust never strikes him, it can only be because Jesus has altered his disposition; it is impossible unless Jesus Christ can do what He says He can. A disciple has to be free from the degradation of lust, and the marvel of the Redemption is that Jesus can free him from it. Jesus Christ's claim is that He can do for a man what he cannot do for himself. Jesus does not alter our human nature, it does not need altering: He alters the mainspring. SSM. 34

M

MAMMON

Never compromise with the spirit of mammon. It is easy to associate mammon only with sordid things; mammon is the system of civilised life which organises itself without any consideration of God. MFL. 116

Men who have worshipped mammon have the mark of the beast in thought and grasp, and when the realization of where they are comes, they 'faint for fear.' SHL. 91

"Ye cannot serve God and mammon." A man of the world says we can; with a little subtlety and wisdom and compromise (it is called diplomacy, or tact), we can serve both. The devil's temptation to our Lord to fall down and worship him, i.e., to compromise, is repeated over and over again in Christian experience. SSM. 64

Never compromise with the spirit of mammon. When you are right with God, you become contemptible in the eyes of the world. SSM. 65

MAN

Man was the climax of the six days' work; in God's plan the whole of the six days' work of creation was for man. The tendency nowadays is to put the six days' work of creation above man. Some people are far more concerned about dogs and cats than about human beings. BP. 7

The majority of us are shockingly ignorant about ourselves simply because we will not allow the Spirit of God to reveal the enormous dangers that lie hidden in the centre of our spirit. Jesus Christ taught that dangers never come from outside, but from within. If we will accept Jesus Christ's verdict and receive the Spirit of God, we need never know in conscious life that what He says about the human heart is true, because He will re-relate the heart from within. BP. 141

There are possibilities below the threshold of our lives which no one but God knows. BP. 153

A certain type of mind gets impatient when one talks about the incalculable element in man, and says it is nonsense to talk of man being a spiritual personality, man is nothing more than an animal. That outlook is prevalent to-day, it is called 'healthy-mindedness'; it is rather blatant ignorance. MFL. 42

Immediately man begins to examine himself, he finds he is inscrutable; there are possibilities below the threshold of his life which no one knows but God. MFL. 43

"A double minded man," i.e., a discreet man, diplomatic and wise—"is unstable in all his ways." The man who does not put God first in his calculations is always double minded. 'If I do,' 'Supposing,' and 'But'—these are all in the vocabulary of the double minded man. OBH. 53

Every one of us has the possibility of every type of meanness any human being has ever exhibited; not to believe this is to live in a fool's paradise. OPG. 57

The disposition of sin, i.e., my claim to my right to myself, entered into the human race by one man, and the Holy Spirit entered into the human race by another Man, so that "where sin abounded, grace did much more abound." PR. 57

The tendency nowadays is to take the management of the universe out of God's hands, while at the same time neglecting our business, viz., the government of our own universe within. PS. 68

Jesus Christ stands as the type of man, and the only type of man, who can come near to God. PS. 73

Common sense says, what a wonderful being man is in the making! The New Testament says, what a magnificent ruin of what man was once! SA. 105

The best of men are but the best of men. SHH. 101

The natural man is not in distress, he is not conscious of conviction of sin, or of any disharmony, he is quite contented and at peace. SHL. 40

We are far too big for ourselves, infinitely too big. The majority of us try to put ourselves in a bandbox, but we cannot cabin and confine our lives. SHL. 52

MAN AND WOMAN

A full-orbed bad man or woman (bad in God's sight) is a wonderful being to look at; and a full-orbed man or woman who is right with God is also a wonderful being to look at. The rest of us are simply beings in the making. There is a tremendous fascination about a completely 'bad' man; there is nothing more desirable from the standpoint of this world than a thoroughly well-trained 'bad' man or woman, but they are the opponents of Jesus Christ, they hate Him with every power of the soul; I mean the Jesus Christ of the New Testament. BP. 80

It is significant to note that both Adam and Abraham receive the severe judgment of God; they heeded the voice of their wives and they had no business to. The full force of God's judgment comes on the man, not on the woman. NKW. 49

The emphasis put on the nobility of man is largely a matter of fiction. Men and women are men and women, and it is absurd to pretend they are either better or worse than they are. Most of us begin by demanding perfect justice and nobility and generosity from other people, then we see their defects and become bitter and cynical. PH. 186

The relationship of man and woman has been totally misrepresented. The revelation in the Bible is not that it is a question of the one being unequal to the other but of the two being one. "In the day that God created man, in the likeness of God made He him; male and female created He them and blessed them, and called their name Adam, in the day when they were created." SHH. 106

In human life as it is there is something perfidious in the perpetual relationship of man and woman. SHH. 109

MARTYRDOM

Our attitude in this dispensation manifests itself in a humility that cannot sting us into action on our own account.

That is the thing that maddens the prince of this world. When the prince of this world and his minions scandalize Jesus Christ and misrepresent Him, the weakest saint becomes a giant, he is ready to go to martyrdom any time and anywhere all the world over for the Lord Jesus Christ. We hear it said that the spirit of martyrdom has died out; the spirit of martyrdom is here. BP. 188

God is trying to educate us in inner martyrdom and we won't have it, we get tired of being educated spiritually. HGM. 112

In the history of the Church inner martyrdom and external martyrdom have rarely gone together. We are familiar with external martyrdom, but inner martyrdom is infinitely more vital. PR. 63

If we are to be in fellowship with Him we must deliberately go through the annihilation, not of glory, but of our former right to ourselves in every shape and form. Until this inner martyrdom is gone through, temptation will always take us unawares. PR. 63

Beware of saying that Jesus Christ was a martyr. Nowadays He is frequently looked upon as a martyr, His life is acknowledged to be very beautiful, but the Atonement and the Cross are not being given their rightful place, and the Bible is being robbed of its magnitude and virility. PR. 99

If Jesus Christ was a martyr, our salvation is a myth. PS. 18

The Son of God. . . . He was immaculate, without blemish, yet He was crucified. This rules out once and forever the conception that Jesus died the death of a martyr; He died a death no martyr could touch. He died the death not of a good man but of a bad man, with the vicarious pain of Almighty God in His heart. PS. 19

Being a martyr does not necessarily involve being a witness, but being a witness will involve martyrdom. SSY. 96

MASTERSHIP

When Jesus Christ came He was easily Master of the life in the air and earth and sky, and in Him we see the order God originally intended for man. BFB. 98

The oft-repeated modern phrase 'self-mastery' is misleading; profoundly speaking, a man can never master what he does not understand, therefore the only master of a man is not man himself, or another man, but God. BE. 29

No man was ever created to be his own master, or the master of other men; there is only one Master of men, and that is Jesus Christ. BE. 52

It does not awaken antipathy in a man when you tell him God will forgive him his sins because of what Jesus did on the Cross, but it does awaken antipathy when you tell him he has to give up his right to himself. Nothing is so much resented as the idea that I am not to be my own master. CHI. 18

Discard any emotion or call to work which cannot find itself at home in the absolute mastery of Jesus Christ. DI. 10

To say "Master, say on" as a mere homage of the lips, while we are quietly determined to go on just as we have always done, is false and damaging, and this is bound to be the result in the most sincere soul among us unless we allow the Holy Spirit to continually renew our

minds by concentration on The Truth.
HGM. 122

To believe in Jesus means retiring and letting God take the mastership inside. That is all God asks of us. IWP. 65

If our idea is that we are being mastered, it is a proof that we have no master; if that is our attitude to Jesus, we are far away from the relationship He wants. He wants us in the relationship in which He is easily Master without our conscious knowledge of it, all we know is that we are His to obey. HUM. 266

Jesus Christ's consciousness being what it is, viz., that He is Master, if I am rightly related to God and walking in the light, no matter what happens to me, it is His look-out, not mine. I have simply to abandon to Him and smilingly wash my hands of the consequences. He will engineer my circumstances, He will dump me down where He chooses, He will give me money or give me none, as He likes; all I have to do is to keep my soul carefully in the conception of Him as Master. PH. 112

The mastership of a man who does not defy the ordinances of God is that of worth-ship, he is worthy; whereas men who are mastered by those given to defying the law of God come to an appalling condition. SHH. 139

Am I willing to sell myself to Jesus, to become simply His bondslave, in order that He may see of the travail of His soul and be satisfied? SSY. 23

Have you ever realized Who the Lord is in your life? The call to service is not the outcome of an experience of salvation and sanctification, there must be the recognition of Jesus Christ as Lord and Master as well as Saviour. 'Who say ye that I am?' SSY. 56

The only word by which to describe mastership in experience is *love*—'If ye love me, ye will keep my commandments.' SSY. 87

The Master dominates, not domineers over, His disciples. His is the domination of holy love. If once, for one moment, we see the Lord, we may fall and slip away, but we shall never rest until we find Him again. SSY. 157

A great point in spiritual nobility has been reached when we can really say, 'I am not my own.' It is only the noble nature that can be mastered—an unpalatable truth if we are spiritually stiff-necked and stubborn, refusing to be mastered. SSY. 166

MATTER

The way we see things depends on our nerves, but what the thing is in itself that makes us see things in a particular way we do not know; that is, we do not know what matter is. BP. 226

The Bible says the world of matter was created by God; the way we interpret it will depend on what spirit we have. BP. 226

"In the beginning" God created things out of nothing; matter did not exist before God created it. It was God Who created it, out of nothing; not out of Himself. BP. 226

MATURITY

Spiritual maturity is not reached by the passing of the years, but by obedience to the will of God. BSG. 15

". . . and Jesus Himself began to be about thirty years of age." That is the time in human life when man reaches maturity and all his powers are perfected; the time when he is spared no requirement of his manhood. Up to that time, life is full of promise, after that it is a matter of testing and attainment. After the baptism of Jesus and the descent of the Holy Ghost upon Him, God, as it were, took His sheltering hand off Him and let the devil do his worst. PS. 57

When we become mature in godliness God trusts His own honour to us by placing us where the world, the flesh, and the devil may try us, knowing that "greater is He that is in you, than he that is in the world." SSM. 66

MEDITATION

Meditation is an intense spiritual activity, it means bringing every bit of the mind into harness and concentrating its powers; it includes both deliberation and reflection. Deliberation means being able to weigh well what we think, conscious all the time that we are deliberating and meditating. BP. 112

Meditation means getting to the middle of a thing, pinning yourself down to a certain thing and concentratedly brooding upon it. The majority of us attend only to the 'muddle' of things, consequently we get spiritual indigestion, the counterpart of physical indigestion, a desperately gloomy state of affairs. MFL. 64

MEMORY

A truth may be of no use to us just now, but when the circumstances arise in which that truth is needed, the Holy Spirit will bring it back to our remembrance. MFL. 52

If we have been storing our minds with the word of God, we are never taken unawares in new circumstances because the Holy Spirit brings back these things to our remembrance and we know what we should do; but the Holy Spirit cannot bring back to our minds what we have never troubled to put there. MFL. 54

MIND

Scolding is characteristic of the mind which is in a corner and does not see the way out; it falls back therefore to its own entrenched position. BFB. 54

I explain the world outside me by thinking; then if I can explain the world outside me by my mind, there must have been a Mind that made it. That is logical, simple and clear; consequently atheism is what the Bible calls it, the belief of a fool. BP. 226

. . . when Jesus was led away to be crucified, they "come unto a place called Golgotha, that is to say, a place of a skull," and that is where Jesus Christ is always crucified; that is where He is put to shame to-day, viz., in the heads of men who won't bring their thinking into line with the Spirit of God. BP. 232

When we receive the Spirit of God, we are lifted into a totally new realm, and if we will bring our minds into harmony with what the Spirit of God reveals, begin to discipline ourselves and bring every thought into captivity, we shall not only begin to discern God's order in the Bible, but our eyes will be opened and the secrets of the world will be understood and grasped. BP. 235

The particular forms of nature, i.e., rocks and trees, animals and men, are all the outcome of the breathing of the Spirit of God. There is a true law of correspondence between the things which we see and the Mind that is behind them. When we have in us the Mind behind the things we see, we begin to understand how these things manifest that Mind, but if we have not that Mind we shall never understand them. BP. 247

Mental stodge is the result of one of three forms of over-feeding—too much dinner, too much reading, or too much meetings. DI. 69

Before the mind has begun to grapple with problems it is easy to talk; when the mind has begun to grapple with problems it is a humiliating thing to talk. DI. 83

There must be two centres to our mental life as workers: the first is personal faith in Jesus Christ; the second, personal reliance on the human reason that God made. Most of us think from one centre only, the centre of human reason, consequently all that Jesus Christ stands for beyond the reach of human reason is ignored. GW. 108

The thing to heed is not so much damage to our faith in God as damage to our temper of mind. HG. 20

The temper of mind if it is not right with God is tremendous in its effects, it is the enemy that penetrates right into the soul and distracts us from God. There are certain tempers of mind we never dare indulge in; if we do, we find that they distract us from God, and until we get back into the quiet mood before God our faith in Him is *nil*, and our confidence in human ingenuity the thing that rules. HG. 20

The only mind that understands the things of God is the child mind; our Lord continually mentioned this sim-

plicity. . . . It is the simplicity of God, not of an imbecile, a fundamental simplicity of relationship. MFL. 66

If we are saved and sanctified by God's grace, it is unadulterated mental laziness on our part not to rouse ourselves up to think. It is not a question of the opportunities of learning, but of the determination to be continually renewed in the spirit of our mind. MFL. 85

Our minds are apt to be all abroad, like an octopus with its tentacles out to catch everything that comes along— newspaper garbage, spiritualistic garbage, advertisement garbage, we let them all come and make a dumping ground of our heads, and then sigh and mourn and say we cannot think right thoughts. MFL. 86

Glean your thinking; don't allow your mind to be a harbourage for every kind of vagabond sentiment; resolutely get into the way of disciplining your impulses and stray thinking. The law of attention controls the mind and keeps it from shifting hither and thither. MFL. 96

. . . "the carnal mind is enmity against God"; he does not say it is 'at enmity,' it *is* enmity against God. MFL. 117

Every mind has two storeys, the conscious and the unconscious. Most of what we hear passes out of our conscious mind into our unconscious mind and we think we have forgotten it, but we have not, we never forget anything; we cannot always recall it when we want to, but that is a different matter. We forget nothing; it is there, although not in the conscious mind, and when certain circumstances arise, suddenly the thing we thought we had forgotten is there to our amazement right enough. This is exactly what Jesus said the Holy

Ghost would do, "He shall . . . bring all things to your remembrance, whatsoever I have said unto you." PR. 41

The Holy Spirit is forming the unconscious mind all the time, and as we 'mop up' His teaching—simply take it in, not try to estimate it as we would a mathematical study—we shall find God is putting in the right soil for His life to grow in. Our one concern is to keep in the right atmosphere. PR. 41

The dissolving of the Person of Jesus by analysis is prevalent because men refuse to know Him after the Spirit, they will only know Him after the reasoning of their own minds. PR. 76

If a man lets his garden alone, it pretty soon ceases to be a garden; and if a saint lets his mind alone, it will soon become a garbage patch for Satan's scarecrows. PS. 31

A wrong temper of mind is the most blameworthy thing there is. It is not only what we say but what we think that tells. SSY. 46

We receive the Spirit of Christ as a gift, but we do not receive His mind, we have to construct that, and this is done in the same way that we construct the natural mind, viz., by the way our disposition reacts when we come in contact with external things. Mind, or soul, is the way the personal spirit expresses itself in the body. We have to lose our own way of thinking and form Jesus Christ's way. SSY. 93

MIRACLE

Why should it be thought more of a miracle for God to transform me into the image of His Son than for me to be alive now? How is it that I am alive now? How

is it that the material wood of this table and the fleshly material of my hand are different? If we can explain the one, we can explain the other; God Who has made the one made the other. The point we are emphasizing is that we have to remember that at any moment God may turn a man's calculations upside down concerning what He will do and what He will not do. BP. 257

. . . our Lord turned water into wine, but the same thing is done every year all over the world in process of time: water is sucked up through the stem of the vine and turned into grapes. Why should it be considered more of a miracle when it is done suddenly by the same Being Who does it gradually? When Jesus Christ raised a man from the dead, He simply did suddenly what we all believe implicitly He is going to do by and by. BP. 258

When God is educating us along the line of turning the natural into the spiritual, we are apt to become fanatical. Because by God's grace things have been done which are miraculous, we become devoted to the miracle and forget God, then when difficulties come we say it is the antagonism of the devil. MFL. 69

In the Christian faith the basis of human life is Redemption, and on that basis God can perform His miracles in any man. SA. 18

Things that were called miracles a hundred years ago are not thought of as miracles to-day because men have come to a fuller knowledge. SHL. 32

The miracle of the creation of Redemption in our soul is that we suddenly feel an insatiable desire for salvation. Our Lord said, 'No man can come to Me, except the Father which hath sent Me

195

draw him,' and that is the way He draws him. SHL. 46

MISSIONARY

Everyone who is born from above wants to be a missionary, it is the very nature of the Spirit they receive, viz., the Spirit of Jesus, and the Spirit of Jesus is expressed in John iii. 16, "God so loved the world . . ." HGM. 29

Beware how you treat the messengers of God because there is only one aim in the true messengers of God, and that is unflinching loyalty to the Lordship of Jesus Christ, and we shall have to account to God for our heedfulness of them or our heedlessness. HGM. 131

The secret of the missionary is—I am His, and He is carrying out His enterprises through me. Be entirely His. MUH. 248

The purpose for which the missionary is created is that he may be God's servant, one in whom God is glorified. When once we realize that through the salvation of Jesus Christ we are made perfectly fit for God, we shall understand why Jesus Christ is so ruthless in His demands. MUH. 265

The aim of the missionary is to do God's will, not to be useful, not to win the heathen; he *is* useful and he *does* win the heathen, but that is not his aim. His aim is to do the will of his Lord. MUH. 267

A missionary is one who is wedded to the charter of his Lord and Master, he has not to proclaim his own point of view, but to proclaim the Lamb of God. It is easier to belong to a coterie which tells what Jesus Christ has done for me, easier to become a devotee to Divine healing, or to a special type of sanctifica-

tion, or to the baptism of the Holy Ghost. MUH. 289

The missionary message is the limitless significance of Jesus Christ as the propitiation for our sins, and a missionary is one who is soaked in that revelation. MUH. 289

A missionary is one sent by Jesus Christ as He was sent by God. The great dominant note is not the needs of men, but the command of Jesus. MUH. 300

The greatest need of the missionary is to be ready to face Jesus Christ at any and every turn, and it is not easy to be ready to do that, whatever our experience of sanctification may be. The great battle all along is not so much against sin, as against being so absorbed in work that we are not ready to face Jesus Christ. The one great need is not to face our beliefs and our creeds, or the question whether we are of any use or not, but to face our Lord. This attitude of being ready to face Him means more and more disentanglement from so-called religious work, and more and more intense spiritual reality in so-called secular work. SSY. 34

The one dominating purpose and passion at the heart of the missionary is his own personal relationship to Jesus Christ. A missionary is a construction made through the Atonement by the God Who made the universe. It is not a sentiment, it is true, that God spoils a man or woman for any other use in the world saving for one thing only, to win souls to Jesus and to disciple them in His Name. SSY. 80

The missionary is one whom Jesus Christ has taken aside from the multitude, and, having put His fingers into his ears and touched his tongue, has sent him straight forth from hearing his Master, with his own tongue loosened and his speech plain, to speak 'all the words of this life.' SSY. 91

The creative purpose of God for the missionary is to make him His servant, one in whom He is glorified. When once we realize this, all our self-conscious limitations will be extinguished in the extraordinary blaze of what the Redemption means. We have to see that we keep the windows of our soul open to God's creative purpose for us, and not confuse that purpose with our own intentions. Every time we do so, God has to crush our intentions and push them on one side, however it may hurt, because they are on the wrong line. We must beware lest we forget God's purpose for our life. SSY. 105

The only reason for a Christian to go out to the mission field is that his own life is hid with Christ in God, and the compulsion of the providence of God outside, working with the imperative call of His Spirit inside, has wedded itself to the command of Jesus—'Go ye therefore, and make disciples of all the nations.' SSY. 121

The Sermon on the Mount is the perpetual standard of measurement for those at work for God, and yet the statements of Jesus Christ are continually being watered down, and even contradicted by many to-day. There is not the slightest use in going to the foreign field to work for God if we are not true to His ideal at home. We should be a disgrace to Him there. SSY. 122

Unless the missionary is based on a right relationship to God, he will fizzle out in the passing of the years and become a negligible quantity from God's standpoint. The men and women who stand absolutely true to God's ideal are the ones who are telling for God. God has staked His honour on the work of Jesus Christ in the souls of those whom He has saved, and sanctified, and sent. SSY. 124

Jesus Christ alone is the key to the missionary. SSY. 133

The type for the missionary is God's own Son, and He did not go about button-holing men. SSY. 137

A missionary is one sent by Jesus Christ as the Father sent Him. Our Lord's first obedience was not to the needs of men, but to the will of His Father, and the first great duty of the Christian is not to the needs of his fellow men, but to the will of his Lord. SSY. 153

Jesus Christ is not first a Teacher, He is first a Saviour; and the thing that tells in the long run in the missionary's life is not successful understanding of His teaching, but the realization in his own personal life of the meaning of the Cross. SSY. 154

There is only One Who saves men, and that is God. The missionary is there to proclaim the marvel of that salvation, and what he proclaims becomes a sacrament in himself, he is made the incarnation of what he preaches. SSY. 154

To demand a declaration of love beyond comparison is to risk losing all. A missionary must be dominated by this love beyond compare to the Lord Jesus Christ, otherwise he will be simply the servant of a denomination or a cause, or a seeker for relief from a crushing sorrow in work. Many go into Christian work not for the sake of His Name, but in order to find surcease from their own sorrow; because of unrequited love; or because of a bereavement or a disappointment. Such workers are not dominated by the Master, and they are likely to strew the mission field with failure and sighs, and to discourage those who work with them. There is only one thing stronger than any of these things, and that is love. SSY. 159

A missionary is not sent by Jesus Christ to do medical work, educational work, industrial work; all that is part of the ordinary duty of life, and a missionary ought to be so equipped that he does these things naturally. But Jesus Christ never sends His disciples to do these things; He sends His disciples to *teach*, to *'make disciples of all the nations.'* SSY. 163

'God could never expect me to give up my magnificent prospects and devote my life to the missionary cause.' But He happens to have done so. The battle is yours. He says no more, but He waits. SSY. 164

We are out for one thing only, for Jesus Christ's enterprises. That is the inner secret of the missionary—I know that I am His, and that He is carrying on His enterprises through me; I am His possession and He can do as He likes with me. SSY. 166

Where he is placed is a matter of indifference to the missionary; if he maintains his contact with God, out of him will flow rivers of living water. We have the idea that we engineer missionary enterprise; but it is the genius of the Holy Spirit that makes us 'go.' God does not do anything *with* us, only *through* us; consequently the one thing God estimates in His servants is the work of the Holy Spirit. SSY. 167

MISSIONS

The missionary message is not patriotic, it is irrespective of nations and of individuals, it is for the whole world. MUH. 289

The key to the missionary problem is in the hand of God, and that key is prayer not work, that is, not work as the word is popularly understood to-day because that may mean the evasion of concentration on God. The key to the missionary problem is not the key of common sense, nor the medical key, nor the key of civilization or education or even evangelization. The key is prayer. "Pray ye therefore the Lord of the harvest." MUH. 290

Personal attachment to the Lord Jesus and His point of view is the one thing that must not be overlooked. In missionary enterprise the great danger is that God's call is effaced by the needs of the people until human sympathy absolutely overwhelms the meaning of being sent by Jesus. The needs are so enormous, the conditions so perplexing, that every power of mind falters and fails. We forget that the one great reason underneath all missionary enterprise is not first the elevation of the people, nor the education of the people, nor their needs; but first and foremost the command of Jesus Christ—"Go ye therefore, and teach all nations." MUH. 300

There is no 'foreign field' to our Lord. PR. 32

The first purpose of missionary enterprise is evangelistic, and the evangel is that of personal sanctification. SSY. 118

The key to the missionary problem is in the hand of God, not of man, and according to Our Lord, the key is prayer, not work, as that word is popularly understood, because work may mean evading spiritual concentration. Our Lord says— '*Pray* ye therefore. . . .'

We are not speaking of the lock which the key has to open, viz., the problems of missionary enterprise, but of the *key* to those problems. That key is put into our hands by Jesus Christ, and it is not a common-sense key. It is not a medical key, nor a civilizing key, nor an educational key, not even an evangelical key; the key is prayer. SSY. 125

To-day a number of hysterical and sentimental things are apt to gather round the missionary appeal. The need of the heathen is made the basis of the appeal instead of the authority of Jesus Christ. The need is made the call. It may be good up to a certain point, but it is not the line for the disciples of Jesus Christ. SSY. 137

The key to the missionary message, whether the missionary is a doctor, a teacher, an industrial worker, or a nurse—the key is the remissionary purpose of Our Lord Jesus Christ's death. SSY. 142

The key to the missionary message is not man's views or predilections regarding Redemption, but the revelation given by Our Lord Himself concerning His life and death, 'the Son of man came . . . to give his life a ransom for many.' SSY. 144

Sin against Christ the Lamb of God is world-wide, the propitiation of Christ is world-wide, and the missionary's message is world-wide; it is a message not of condemnation, but of remission. 'That repentance and remission of sins should be preached in his name unto all the nations.' SSY. 145

To-day many are interested in the foreign field because of a passionate interest in something other than the Lord Jesus and His command—'Go ye therefore and make disciples.' All this organization ought to mean that we can go ahead as never before; but if once the dethronement of Jesus creeps in, the finest organization will but perfect the lock which cannot open of itself. SSY. 150

To elevate the heathen, to lift up the down-trodden and oppressed, is magnificent, but it is not the reason for missionary enterprise. The teaching of the New Testament is that we ought to be doing all these things to the best of our ability, but missionary enterprise is another thing. A missionary is one who is fitted with the key to the missionary lock while he pursues the ordinary callings of life. SSY. 154

There is no more wholesome training for the foreign field than doing our duty in the home field. The foreign field is apt to have a glamour over it because it is away somewhere else. There is an inspiration and a sense of the heroic about going to the foreign field—until we get there, and find that the most terrible things we ever touched at home were clean and vigorous compared to the corruption that has to be faced there. SSY. 155

MONEY

If we can save and do justly with money, we are absolutely certain we are right in the sight of God. HG. 67

One of the most besmirching impurities lies in money matters. LG. 72

No man can stand in front of Jesus Christ and say, 'I want to make money.' MFL. 11

"The love of money is a root of all kinds of evil." Money is a test, another thing which proves a man's religion. SHH. 99

MOODS

The false mood creeps in when you have the idea that you are to be 'a written epistle'—of course you are! but you have not to know it. DI. 77

It is a great moment when we realize that we have the power to trample on certain moods. MFL. 63

The first things a Christian is emancipated from is the tyranny of moods and the tyranny of feeling that he is not understood. MFL. 63

There are certain things we must not pray about—moods, for instance. Moods never go by praying, moods go by kicking. A mood nearly always has its seat in the physical condition, not in the moral. It is a continual effort not to listen to the moods which arise from a physical condition, never submit to them for a second. We have to take ourselves by the scruff of the neck and shake ourselves, and we will find that we can do what we said we could not. The curse with most of us is that we *won't*. The Christian life is one of incarnate spiritual pluck. MUH. 141

If we imagine we have to put on our Sunday moods before we come near to God, we will never come near Him. We must come as we are. MUH. 187

Spiritual moods are as sensitive and delicate as the awakenings of early love; the most exquisite thing in the human soul is that early mood of the soul when it first falls in love with the Lord. PH. 21

MORALITY/IMMORALITY

We are staggered at immorality, but Jesus faced those things in the most amazingly calm way. When He was roused to a state of passionate indignation it was by people who were never guilty of such things. What Our Lord continually faced was the disposition behind either the morality or the immorality. BSG. 12

The transactions which tell in my life for God are moral decisions, not mental ones. I may think through everything there is in Christian doctrine and yet remain exactly the same; but I never make a moral decision and remain the same, and it is the moral decisions to which the Holy Spirit is always leading us on the basis of the Redemption. CHI. 62

'Morality is altogether based on utilitarian standards'—it is not; a man's conscience will come in every time when he doesn't want it to. DI. 26

When Jesus Christ faced men with all the forces of evil in them and men who were clean living, and moral, and upright, He did not pay any attention to the moral degradation of the one or to the moral attainment of the other; He was looking at something we do not see, viz., at the disposition in both, not at the immorality or the morality, but at the disposition—my claim to my right to myself, self-realization, and He said: "If you would be My disciple, that must go." SA. 104

Immorality has its seat in every one of us, not in some of us. If a man is not holy, he is immoral, no matter how good he may seem. Immorality is at the basis of the whole thing; if it does not show itself outwardly, it will show itself before God. AUG. 45

Personal love for men will make you call immorality a weakness, and holiness a mere aspiration; personal love for the Lord will make you call immorality devilish, and holiness the only thing that can stand in the light of God. AUG. 46

The most valuable instruction in moral life never comes from people who consciously instruct us, for we are not taught morally as we are intellectually. BFB. 44

. . . every bit of moral wrong is counted by God. BE. 8

Beware of being cute enough to detect immorality only in a moral pigstye, learn to detect it in your own spiritual imaginations. BE. 15

The tendency to repose physically is a right law of our physical nature; morally and spiritually it is a tendency towards immorality and unspirituality. PS. 47

MORAL LAW

The problem in practical experience is not to know what is right, but to do it. My natural spirit may know a great many things, but I never can be what I know I ought to be until I receive the Life which has life in itself, viz., the Holy Spirit. That is the practical working of the Redemption. DI. 26

Why are men not worse than they are? The reason is the existence of the moral law of God which restrains men in spite of the impulse towards wrong, consequently you find remnants of the strivings of the moral law where you least expect it because the moral law is independent entirely of the opposition to it on the part of individual men. DI. 26

When God's law is presented beware of the proud self-confidence which says, 'This is good enough for me, I don't intend to soar any higher.' DI. 27

In dealing with the question of disease both moral and physical, we must deal with it in the light of the Redemption. If you want to know how far wrong the world has got you learn it, not in a hospital, but at the Cross. We learn by what it cost God to redeem the world how criminally out of moral order the universe has got. DI. 27

Very few of us know what *love of God* is, we know what *love of moral good* is, and the curious thing is that that leads us away from God more quickly than does a terror of moral evil; 'the good is ever the enemy of the best.' DI. 27

Beware of giving way to spiritual ecstasies, it disconnects you from the great ordinances of God and shakes the very basis of sane morality God has made. DI. 28

Second thoughts on moral matters are always deflections. DI. 28

It is only when a moral act is performed and light thrown on realities that we understand the relationship between our human lives and the Cross of Christ. DI. 28

MOTIVE

. . . "made unto us . . . righteousness." That is the doctrine of the Atonement—that we are made undeserving of censure in God's sight, so that God looking down into the motives of our heart can see nothing to blame. BE. 121

"That ye may be blameless"—if ever we are to be blameless, undeserving of censure in the sight of God who sees down to the motive of our motives, it must be by the supernatural power of God. The meaning of the Cross is just that—I can not only have the marvellous work of God's grace done in my heart, but can have the proof of it in my life. CHI. 105

It cannot be too often emphasized that our Lord never asks us to do other than all that good upright men do, but He does ask that we do just those same things from an entirely different motive. DI. 72

Our feet carry us in secret and they carry us in public; they carry us into shops and into streets, into houses and into churches; God says, 'You profane My holy Name, not because of the places you went into, but by the way you went into them.' GW. 74

In times of peace 'honesty may be the best policy,' but if we work on the idea that it is better physically and prosperously to be good, that is the wrong motive; the right motive is devotion to God, remaining absolutely true to God, no matter what it costs. HG. 31

It is impossible for the natural man once born, to have a single motive. We know when the love of God has been shed abroad in our hearts because of this miracle of a single motive. The moral discipline of spiritual will is that I re-relate myself all through according to this motive. PH. 162

No man knows the springs of his motives or of his will; when we begin to examine ourselves we come to the threshold of the unconscious and cannot go any further. The Psalmist realized this when he prayed, 'Search me, O God; explore me to the beginning of my motives.' SHL. 53

I may never be angry in deed, but Jesus Christ demands the impossibility of anger in disposition. The motive of my motives, the spring of my dreams, must be so right that right deeds will follow naturally. SSM. 28

MYSTERY

By the word mystery we mean something known only to the initiated, therefore if we are going to understand the gospel mystery of Sanctification and fully experience it, we must belong to the initiated, that is, we must be born from above by the Spirit of God. OBH. 11

The sense of mystery must always be, for mystery means being guided by obedience to Someone Who knows more than I do. PH. 10

MYSTICISM

All false mysticism arises from the fact that teachers insist on an inner experience, which by the simple process of introspection ultimately kills itself.
CD. VOL. 2, 95

Every sanctified soul is a mystic, but he does not live in that region only, he is soul and body as well as spirit, and what is true in the mystical sphere is true in the moral sphere. Soul is man's spirit becoming rational in the body, explaining itself. IYA. 73

Man is not only mystical and moral, but material; never say because you have a body you cannot progress. IYA. 74

N

NATURAL/SUPERNATURAL

God does not tell us to leave the natural life entirely alone; the natural life has to be turned into the spiritual, and it is because we do not realise this that we become whining people spiritually where we would have scorned to whine naturally. MFL. 73

Remain true to God, although it means the sword going through the natural, and you will be brought into a supernaturally clear agreement with God. NKW. 23

My natural life must be in subordination and under the absolute control of the spiritual. The natural must be turned into the spiritual by obedience, whatever sword has to go through its heart. The natural life must be 'spiked' for the glory of God. The characteristic of the natural life is the independent passion for free dominion over itself. Immediately the natural life fights to get away, it comes into opposition. NKW. 50

If we do not resolutely cast out the natural, the supernatural can never become natural in us. NKW. 104

Beware of blaspheming the Creator by calling the natural sinful. The natural is not sinful, but un-moral and unspiritual. It is the home of all the vagrant vices and virtues, and must be disciplined with the utmost severity until it learns its true position in the providence of God. NKW. 105

God is not with my natural life as long as I pamper it and pander to it, but when I put it out in the desert, resolutely cast it out and keep it under, then God is with it and He opens up wells and oases, and fulfils His promise for it. It must be stern discipline, rigorous severity to the last degree on my part, then God will be with the natural life and bring it to its full purpose. NKW. 106

We have the idea that the body, individuality, and the natural life are altogether of the devil; they are not, they are of God, designed by God, and it is in the human body and in the natural order of things that we have to exhibit our worship of God. The danger is to mistake the natural for the spiritual, and instead of worshipping God in my natural life to make my natural life God. NKW. 108

God is always at work on the principle of lifting up the natural and making it and the spiritual one, and very few of us will go through with it. We will cling to the natural when God wants to put a sword through it. If you go through the transfiguration of the natural, you will receive it back on a new plane altogether. God wants to make eternally our own what we only possessed intermittently. NKW. 128

The natural has to be denied, not because it is bad and wrong, but because it has nothing to do with our life of faith in God until it is turned into the spiritual by obedience. It is the attitude of the maimed life, which so few of us understand. NKW. 149

By "old things" Paul does not mean sin and the "old man" only, he means everything that was our life as natural men before we were re-created in spirit by Christ. That means a great deal more than some of us mean. The "old things" means not only things that are wrong, any fool will give up wrong things if he can, but things that are right.   OBH. 28

Our Lord lived a natural life as we do, it was not a sin for Him to eat, but it would have been a sin for Him to eat during those forty days in the wilderness, because during that time His Father's will for Him was otherwise, and He sacrificed His natural life to the will of God. That is the way the "old things" pass away.   OBH. 28

Beware of the hesitation of the natural against being turned into the spiritual— 'I do not mind being a saint if I can remain natural and be a saint entirely on my own initiative; if I can instruct God in regard to my temperament, my affinities, and my upbringing.' If we have a religious strut about us, some prejudice, some particular refinement, some possession of natural heredity, it is like putting a piece of new cloth into an old garment. All has to go. "If any man be in Christ . . . , old things are passed away."
OBH. 98

These two things, dust and Divinity, make up man. That he is made of the dust of the ground is man's glory, not his shame—it is only his shame in so far as he is a sinner, because in it he is to manifest the image of God. We are apt to think because we are "of the earth, earthy," that this is our humiliation, but it is not so; it is the very thing God's word makes most of.   OPG. 4

If I maintain my right to my natural self I will begin to degenerate and get out of

God's purpose. What happens in my personal life when I am born from above is that the Son of God is born in me, then comes in this law of the sacrifice of the natural to the spiritual, and the possibility of degeneration. If I refuse to sacrifice the natural, the God-life in me is killed.
OPG. 47

We have to nourish the life of the Son of God in us, and we do it by obedience, that is, by bringing our natural life into accordance with His life and transforming it into a spiritual life.   PR. 39

The natural is not sinful, but the natural is not spiritual.   PR. 74

One of the principles of our Lord's teaching which we are slow to grasp is that the only basis of the spiritual is the sacrifice of the natural.   SSM. 36

The natural life is not sinful, the disposition that rules the natural life is sinful, and when God alters that disposition, we have to turn the natural life into the spiritual by a steady process of obedience to God, and it takes spiritual concentration on God to do it.   SSM. 63

Human nature unaided by God can do the heroic business; human pride unaided by God can do the self-sacrificing; but it takes the supernatural power of God to keep us as saints in the drab commonplace days.   SSY. 161

NATURE

The sublimities of Nature cannot be explained on the line of reason, but only on the line of the a-logical, that which goes beyond and underneath the logical.   BFB. 79

We talk about laws and findings, we give scientific explanations of thunder and of a sunset, and come to the conclusion that there is no unexplained sublimity in Nature at all. The wildness of Nature has to be recognized, there are forces in the earth and air and sea which baffle attempts at explanation or of control; all we can do is to give a direction for thought along certain lines. BFB. 79

Neither logic nor science can explain the sublimities of Nature. Supposing a scientist with a diseased olfactory nerve says that there is no perfume in a rose, and to prove his statement he dissects the rose and tabulates every part, and then says, 'Where is the perfume? It is a fiction; I have demonstrated that there is none.' There is always one fact more that science cannot explain, and the best thing to do is not to deny it in order to preserve your sanity, but to say, as Job did, 'No, the one fact more which you cannot explain means that God must step in just there, or there is no explanation to be had.' BFB. 79

There is evidence that God is in the facts of Nature, but also evidence that He is other than Nature. We may make a working definition of the laws of Nature, 'but, remember,' says God, 'behind those laws I come.' BFB. 96

The poet talks about God being revealed in Nature, but the poet does not remember that there is sin in the world: he sees clearly what God's idea is for man, but he forgets that we belong to a fallen race, consequently his poetry is only a vision, it cannot be worked out on Mother Earth. BSG. 64

The Bible explanation is that Nature is in a disorganized condition, that it is out of gear with God's purposes, and will only become organized when God and man are one. GW. 135

God is responsible for the established order of nature, so if God created Nature and we have not the Spirit of God, we shall never interpret the order of Nature as God does. LG. 25

When Our Lord described the spiritual life, He always took His illustrations from His Father's handiwork, never from man's work. We take our illustrations from motor-cars, or aeroplanes, or electric light, or something go-ahead and self-advertising. We illustrate by means of things which compel our attention; Jesus mentions things we are not compelled to look at, things which we would pass by. How many of us notice sparrows and daisies and grass? They are so plentiful that we ignore them, yet it is these things Jesus tells us to consider. LG. 40

We do not get at God through Nature, as the poets say, we get at Nature through God when once we are rightly related to Him, and Nature becomes a sacrament of His Presence. MFL. 62

Our Lord did not point out wonderful sights to His disciples all the time; He pointed out things that were apparently insignificant—lilies, and grass, and sparrows. God does not deal with the things that interest us naturally and compel our attention; He deals with things which we have to will to observe. The illustrations Jesus Christ used were all taken from His Father's handiwork because they express exactly how the life of God will develop in us. MFL. 67

God's appeal to the stars is not to furnish proof for a doubting mind, but to provide nourishment for a faltering faith. Nature to the saint is a sacrament of God, not merely a series of facts; not symbols and signs, but the real evidence of the coming of God as a sacrament to His faithful children. NKW. 45

NEED

"We have to bring an Absolute Christ to the needs of men, not to their conditions." So many preach the human aspect of Christ, His sympathy for the bereaved and the suffering and sin-stained, and men listen whilst Christ is brought down to their conditions; but a preacher has to bring the Gospel of God to men's needs, and to do this he has to uncover their need and men resent this—'I don't want to accept the verdict on myself that Jesus Christ brings; I don't believe I am so sinful as He reveals.' AUG. 48

If we are ever free from the sense of need, it is not because the Holy Ghost has satisfied us, but because we have been satisfied with as much as we have. "A man's reach should exceed his grasp." IYA. 60

The bedrock in Jesus Christ's Kingdom is not sincerity, not deciding for Christ, not a determination to serve Him, but a complete and entire recognition that we cannot begin to do it; then, says Jesus, 'Blessed are you.' Jesus Christ can do wonderful things for the man who enters into His Kingdom through the moral frontier of need. LG. 110

God loves the man who needs Him.
OPG. 38

The first obedience of Jesus was to the will of His Father, not to the needs of men. Then our first accepted vocation is not to help men, but to obey God, and when we accept that vocation we enter into relationship with the despised and the neglected. PR. 55

So long as our wits and human solutions are on the throne, to satisfy the needs of men is ostensibly the grandest thing to do. Every temptation of Satan will certainly seem right to us unless we have the Spirit of God. Fellowship with our Lord is the only way to detect them as being wrong. PR. 65

Our Lord in His agony was devoted to God's purpose. The supreme obedience of Jesus was never to the needs of men, but always to the will of His Father. The Church goes astray whenever she makes the need the call. The need is never the call; the need is the opportunity; the call is the call of God. PR. 95

The need is never the call; God's redemption is the call, the need is the opportunity. RTR. 70

You have no right to say, because you realize a need "I must go"; if you are sanctified you cannot go unless you are sent. RTR. 70

The need can never be the call for missionary enterprise. The need is the opportunity. The call is the commission of Jesus Christ and relationship to His Person. 'All power is given unto *me . . . go ye therefore.'* SSY. 161

NEW BIRTH

God does something infinitely grander than give a man a new start: He remakes him from the inside. We have the power, because we have received it, to transform the natural into the spiritual even as Jesus did, because the life generated into us is His own life. BSG. 11

Our new birth is the birth of the Son of God into our human nature, and our human nature has to be transfigured by the indwelling life of the Son of God. We have the power now to sacrifice the life of nature to the will of God, keeping our minds dependent on Jesus Christ as He was dependent on God. To-day the characteristic is spiritual insubordination; we will not bring "every thought into captivity to the obedience of Christ." BSG. 11

In the New Testament new birth is always spoken of in terms of sanctification, not of salvation; to be saved means that a man receives the gift of eternal life, which is "the gift *of God*"; sanctification means that his spirit becomes the birthplace of the Son of God. CHI. 20

If we cannot be made all over again on the inside and indwelt by the Spirit of God, and made according to the teaching of the Sermon on the Mount, then fling your New Testament away, for it will put before you an ideal you cannot reach. HG. 61

The conception of new birth in the New Testament is not of something that springs out of us, what modern psychology calls 'a subliminal uprush,' but of something that comes into us. HGM. 13

Some teachers make new birth a simple and natural thing, they say it is necessary, but a necessity along the line of natural development. When Jesus Christ talks about it He implies that the need to be born again is an indication of something radically wrong—"Marvel not that I said unto thee. Ye must be born again." It is a crisis. HGM. 54

After you have entered into life, come and fulfil the conditions of that life. We are so desperately wise, we continually make out that Jesus did not mean what He said and we spiritualize His meaning into thin air. IWP. 117

Being born again of the Spirit is an unmistakable work of God, as mysterious as the wind, as surprising as God Himself. We do not know where it begins, it is hidden away in the depths of our personal life. Being born again from above is a perennial, perpetual and eternal beginning; a freshness all the time in thinking and in talking and in living, the continual surprise of the life of God. MUH. 20

When we are born again of God and are indwelt by the Spirit of God, He expresses for us the unutterable. MUH. 313

God does not discard the old and create something entirely new; He creates something in the old until the old and the new are made one. NKW. 59

The phrase "born from above" as our Lord used it does not mean being saved from hell or from sin, but that I am born into the realm in which He lives. PH. 151

The 'natural' has not life in itself, therefore we must be born from above. PR. 14

To be born from above means that we are lifted into heavenly places in our personal spirit by the Holy Spirit Who comes into us, He quickens us all through. PR. 14

To be born from above means more than conversion. It means that Christ is formed in us, and the Christ in us must be exactly like the Christ outside us. PR. 18

The modern tendency is to talk of birth from beneath, not of birth from above, of something rising up out of our unconscious life into our conscious life, not of something coming into us from above. This preaching has so permeated people's views to-day that many who name the Name of Christ and are supposed to be preaching His Gospel are at the same time undermining the very foundations of their own faith. PR. 30

To-day people are dethroning Jesus Christ and belittling the need of salvation by making new birth to mean nothing more than a rising up from beneath. The conception of new birth in the New Testament is of something that enters into us, not of something that springs out of us. PR. 30

One great characteristic of new birth is that we come to Jesus not only because of what we have heard about Him, but because of what we see He is to us now. PR. 31

Another characteristic of new birth is that Jesus Christ is easily first . . . If we are born from above and Jesus Christ is Lord and Master, we will go direct as a homing pigeon to Him. PR. 32

Another evidence of new birth is that we see the rule of God. We no longer see the haphazard of chance or fate, but by the experience of new birth we are enabled to see the rule of God everywhere. PR. 33

The characteristic of new birth is that we deliberately obey all that God reveals through His Spirit. We yield ourselves so completely to God that Christ is formed in us. When He is formed in us, the characteristics of His life in our mortal flesh are that we see Jesus for ourselves; we see the rule of God; and we quit sinning—all by the wonder of His supernatural new birth in us, and that is how it works all through. PR. 35

The new birth is illustrated by the supernatural advent of our Lord, not by the birth of a child into the world. Just as our Lord came into history from the outside, so He comes into our human nature from the outside. Our new birth is the birth of the Son of God into our old human nature, and our human nature has to be transfigured by the indwelling life of the Son of God. PR. 37

The formation of the Son of God in us and our putting on of the new man must go together. We are brooded over by the Holy Ghost, and that which is formed in us is the Holy Son of God. PR. 50

The putting on of the new man means that we must not allow our natural life to dictate to the Son of God, but see to it that we give Him ample chance to dominate every bit of us. He has delivered us from sin, now we must see that He dominates our natural life also, until the life of Jesus is manifested in our mortal flesh. PR. 51

When you are identified with Jesus Christ you become a new creation in the same surroundings. SA. 30

The meaning of new birth is receiving His nature. SSY. 162

O

OBEDIENCE/DISOBEDIENCE

God will have us discern what He is doing, but it takes time because we are so slow to obey, and only as we obey do we perceive morally and spiritually. BFB. 52

If the 'Oughts' of the Old Testament were difficult to obey, Our Lord's teaching is unfathomably more difficult. BE. 8

Our Lord's first requirement is a personal relationship to Himself, and then obedience to His principles. BE. 10

The truth laid down abides, that certain types of moral disobedience produce sicknesses which physical remedies cannot touch; obedience is the only cure. For instance nothing can touch the sicknesses produced by tampering with spiritualism; there is only one cure—yielding to the Lord Jesus Christ. BP. 90

The one word ringing out over our mental life is 'Obey! Obey!' Those of you who know what obedience means in the moral realm, bring it into the intellectual realm. BP. 236

The beginnings of God's life in a man or woman are directly across the will of nature, because nature has to be transformed in your particular bodily life and mine into a spiritual life by obedience. Obedience to the Spirit of God means a maimed life, maimed in a hundred and one ways, and in the closest relationships of all. CD. VOL: 1, 146

The gathering in of God's salvation around a man means that he is checked at first by the merest zephyr touch, there is nothing so gentle as the check of the Holy Spirit; if he obeys, emancipation is at once, if he does not obey, the zephyr touch will turn into a destructive blow from which there is no escape. CHI. 74

How long it takes for all the powers in a Christian to be at one depends on one thing only, viz., obedience. DI. 31

It is not a question of being willing to go straight through, but of *going* straight through. Not a question of saying, 'Lord, I will do it,' but of *doing* it. There must be the reckless committal of everything to Him with no regard for the consequences. GW. 79

God does not destroy our personal power to disobey Him; if He did, we would become mechanical and useless. No power outside, from the devil downward, can take us out of God's hand; so long as we remain faithful, we are as eternally secure as God Himself. HG. 29

God never insists on our obedience; human authority does. Our Lord does not give us rules and regulations; He makes very clear what the standard is, and if the relation of my spirit to Him is that of love, I will do all He wants me to do without the slightest hesitation. If I begin to object it is because I love someone else in competition with Him, viz., myself. HGM. 148

"I am crucified with Christ; nevertheless I live; yet not I, but Christ liveth in me." These words mean the breaking of my independence and surrendering to the supremacy of the Lord Jesus. No one can do this for me, I must do it myself. There is no possibility of debate when once I am there. It is not that we have to do work for God, we have to be so loyal to Jesus Christ that He does His work through us. We learn His truth by obeying it. HGM. 148

There are hidden perils in our life with God whenever we disobey Him. If we are not obeying God physically we experience a craving for drugs, not only physical drugs out of a bottle, but drugs in certain types of meetings and certain types of company—anything that keeps away the realization that the habits of the bodily life are not in accordance with what is God's will. If in the providence of God, obedience to God takes me into contact with people and surroundings that are wrong and bad, I may be perfectly certain that God will guard me; but if I go there out of curiosity, God does not guard me, and the tendency is to 'drug' it over—'I went with a good idea to try and find out about these things.' Well, you plainly had no business to go, and you know you had no business to go because the Spirit of God is absolutely honest. The whole thing starts from disobedience on a little point. We wanted to utilize God's grace for our own purposes, to use God's gifts for our own reasoning out of things in a particular way. IWP. 38

Always act according to the wish that is born in you by the Spirit of God. Take the initiative to obey, never wobble spiritually. MFL. 16

If a man is hesitating between obeying and not obeying God, the tiniest thing contrary to obedience is quite sufficient to swing the pendulum right away from the discernment of Jesus Christ and of God. MFL. 25

"Consider the lilies of the field"—they grow where they are put. Many of us refuse to grow where we are put, consequently we take root nowhere. Jesus says that if we obey the life God has given us, He will look after all the other things. MUH. 26

The questions that matter in life are remarkably few, and they are all answered by the words—"Come unto Me." Not—Do this, or don't do that: but—"Come unto Me." MUH. 163

Jesus Christ is laying down this principle—Do what you know you must do, now, and do it quickly; if you do not, the inevitable process will begin to work and you will have to pay to the last farthing in pain and agony and distress. God's laws are unalterable; there is no escape from them. The teaching of Jesus goes straight to the way we are made up. MUH. 182

Spiritual muddle is only made plain by obedience. Immediately we obey, we discern. MUH. 258

You cannot think a spiritual muddle clear, you have to obey it clear. In intellectual matters you can think things out, but in spiritual matters you will think yourself into cotton wool. If there is something upon which God has put His pressure, obey in that matter, bring your imagination into captivity to the obedience of Christ with regard to it and everything will become as clear as daylight. MUH. 258

In the Bible obedience is based on the relationship of equals, that of a son with

his father. Our Lord was not God's servant, He was His Son. *"Though He were a Son,* yet learned He obedience . . ."
MUH. 266

Our Lord never enforces obedience; He does not take means to make me do what He wants. At certain times I wish God would master me and make me do the thing, but He will not; in other moods I wish He would leave me alone, but He does not. MUH. 266

To have a master and to be mastered is not the same thing. To have a master means that there is one who knows me better than I know myself, one who is closer than a friend, one who fathoms the remotest abyss of my heart and satisfies it, one who has brought me into the secure sense that he has met and solved every perplexity and problem of my mind. To have a master is this and nothing less—"One is your Master, even Christ." MUH. 266

Jesus does not mention the other person, He says—*you* go. There is no question of your rights. The stamp of the saint is that he can waive his own rights and obey the Lord Jesus. MUH. 270

"I suppose I shall understand these things some day!" You can understand them now. It is not study that does it, but obedience. The tiniest fragment of obedience, and heaven opens and the profoundest truths of God are yours straight away. God will never reveal more truth about Himself until you have obeyed what you know already. Beware of becoming "wise and prudent." MUH. 284

All God's revelations are sealed until they are opened to us by obedience. You will never get them open by philosophy or thinking. Immediately you obey, a

flash of light comes. Let God's truth work in you by soaking in it, not by worrying into it. The only way you can get to know is to stop trying to find out and by being born again. Obey God in the thing He shows you, and instantly the next thing is opened up. One reads tomes on the work of the Holy Spirit, when one five minutes of drastic obedience would make things as clear as a sunbeam. MUH. 284

In spiritual relationship we do not grow step by step; we are either there or we are not. God does not cleanse us more and more from sin, but when we are in the light, walking in the light, we *are* cleansed from all sin. It is a question of obedience, and instantly the relationship is perfected. Turn away for one second out of obedience, and darkness and death are at work at once. MUH. 284

If I obey Jesus Christ, the Redemption of God will rush through me to other lives, because behind the deed of obedience is the Reality of Almighty God. MUH. 307

Jesus Christ will not help me to obey Him, I must obey Him; and when I do obey Him, I fulfil my spiritual destiny. MUH. 307

Our Lord never insists upon obedience; He tells us very emphatically what we ought to do, but He never takes means to make us do it. MUH. 307

We have nothing to do with the afterwards of obedience. NKW. 14

Obedience is impossible to us naturally, even when we do obey, we do it with a pout in our moral underlip, and with the determination to scale up high enough and then 'boss my boss.' In the spiritual domain there is no pout to be removed because the nature of God has come into me. The nature of God is exhibited in the life of Our Lord, and the great characteristic of His life is obedience. NKW. 126

When the love of God is shed abroad in my heart by the Holy Ghost, I am possessed by the nature of God, and I show by my obedience that I love Him. NKW. 126

There is no possibility of questioning on my part when God speaks, if He is speaking to His own nature in me; prompt obedience is the only result. NKW. 127

If we look at obedience apart from the presupposition of the Atonement, it makes it seem absurd. Obedience means that we bank everything on the Atonement, and the supernatural grace of God is a delight. We cannot do anything pleasing to God unless there is this deliberate building on the presupposition of the Atonement. OBH. 113

Beware of obeying anyone else's obedience to God because it means you are shirking responsibility yourself. OPG. 36

If once I have been indwelt by the Holy Spirit, He will always discern that I have done the fundamentally wrong thing when I disobey Jesus Christ. Let me disobey Him, and I am the most miserable wretch out of hell. PH. 109

The first obedience of our Lord was not to the needs of men but to the will of His Father; and our first obedience is to Jesus Christ, not to the poor and the despised and afflicted. My sympathy with them is the proof that I have a loving sympathy greater than them all, viz., sympathy with my Lord. PH. 141

Our obedience to Jesus Christ is going to cost other people a great deal, and if we refuse to go on because of the cost to them, or because of the stab and the jeer, we may find that we have prevented the call of God coming to other lives; whereas if we will go through with God, all these natural relationships will be given to our credit spiritually in the final wind-up. PR. 17

Woe be to you if you hanker for a second after the thing about which God has said 'No' to you. If you do, you will put to death the life of God in you. PR. 54

We can never get into touch with God by our own effort; but we must maintain touch with God by our own effort. Jesus Christ can take anyone, no matter who he is, and presence him with His wonderful Divine salvation. The nature of God is shed abroad in our hearts by the Holy Ghost, but we have to maintain contact with His nature by obedience. PR. 123

"Why don't You tell us plainly who You are?" Jesus Christ could not, because He could only be discerned through moral obedience. SA. 58

'I would like to obey God, but don't ask me to take a step in the dark.' We enthrone common-sense as almighty God and treat Jesus Christ as a spiritual appendage to it. Jesus Christ hits desperately hard at every one of the institutions we bank all our faith on naturally. SSM. 73

If we could not disobey God, our obedience would not be worth anything. SSM. 104

Beware of the inclination to dictate to God as to what you will allow to happen if you obey Him. SSY. 53

The Son of God is the Highest of all, yet the characteristic of His life was obedience. SSY. 166

OBSTINACY

The element in you which makes you say 'I shan't' to God is something less profound than your will, it is perversity, or obstinacy, which are never in agreement with God. Obstinacy is a remnant of the disposition of sin, and it fights against that which a man's will and conscience indicate to be right. If we persist in being perverse and obstinate, we shall ultimately get to the place where the emotions of will and conscience are stultified. OBH. 129

We are apt to confound the strong-minded man with the obstinate man. An obstinate man refuses to be reasoned with; his arguement is—'I have said it and I will stick to it.' Spiritually the strong-minded man is one who has learned to construct his reasoning on the basis of the Redemption, he faces every issue of life in the light of the Lord Jesus. PH. 132

The one thing that keeps us from coming to Jesus Christ is obstinacy; we will do anything rather than come. It is not God's will that a man should be smashed before he is saved, it is the man's obstinacy that does it. There is no need to go through the agonies and distress that so many do go through, it is because men will not *come.* PR. 23

God narrows our "shant's" to one explosive point. I don't need to go that way, but God will have to bring me there if I persist in the little disobediences which no one knows but myself, because it is engendering in me a spirit God cannot allow. RTR. 9

The one great enemy of discipleship is obstinacy, spiritual obstinacy. We deify independence and wilfulness and call them by the wrong name. RTR. 12

A stubborn man is always a "small potato." SHH. 89

OFFENDING

Offence means going contrary to someone's private opinion, and it is sometimes our moral duty to give offence. BP. 203

'And they were offended at Him.' The Jews were offended at Jesus because they looked for a warrior king in their coming Messiah, and the carelessness of Jesus over temporal positions and honour did not commend itself to them. The Pharisees were offended at Him because His teaching showed up the hollow emptiness of their profession. His own disciples were offended at Him—'All ye shall be offended in Me this night'—they all forsook Him and fled, one betrayed Him, and another denied Him. GW. 118

The faithful few, who are an offence to our great organizations, are the disguised citizens of the Kingdom of God, their step is strong with coming triumph, they walk, a mighty concourse of the redeemed; angels are their servants, the Almighty is set for their defence; Jesus Himself walks with them day by day, a constant Friend. GW. 119

We get much more concerned about not offending other people than about offending Our Lord. Our Lord often offended people, but He never put a stumbling-block in anyone's way. LG. 46

OLD AGE

. . . a description of Old Age in its frailty. The keepers of the house (arms) and the strong men (legs) are weak and trembling; the grinders cease (teeth) and the windows are darkened (eyesight dimmed), the doors shut (ears are deaf), the grinding low (slow and tedious mastication), the easily startled nerves, and the loss of voice, the inability to climb, and the fear of highway traffic; the whitened hair like the almond tree in blossom, when any work seems a burden, and the failing natural desire, all portray the old man nearing the end of his earthly journey. SHH. 151

ONENESS

If my inward man is possessed and strengthened by the Spirit it means not only am I in union with Christ, but I am identical with Christ. Our Lord was not one with His Father by a union: the Father and the Son were identical. '*I and My Father are one,*' said Jesus. The Apostle Paul mentions this identical oneness when he says, 'I live; and yet no longer I, but Christ liveth in me.' What sounds mystical and unpractical to anyone not born again is a glorious reality to the saint. GW. 64

The remarkable thing about our Lord is that He never explained anything to anybody. Nothing ever distracted Him out of His oneness with God, and He prays "that they may be one, *even as We are one.*" HG. 22

The Christianity of the New Testament is not individual, it is personal, we are merged into God without losing our identity—"that they may be one, even as We are one." HGM. 76

"I and my Father are one." It was a oneness not of union, but of identity. It was impossible to distinguish between the Father and the Son, and the same is to be true of the saint and the Saviour: "that

they may be one, even as We are one." MFL. 112

Nothing was hidden from Jesus, all was faced with fearless courage because of His oneness with the Father. MFL. 113

His Resurrection Deity means that He can take us into union with God, and the way into that relationship of oneness is by the Cross and the Resurrection. PR. 115

When I receive the Holy Spirit, I receive not a possible oneness with Jesus Christ, but a real intense oneness with Him. SHL. 86

When the Spirit of Jesus comes into me He comes into my personal spirit and makes me incandescent with God. The individual peculiarisms are seen no longer but only the manifestation of oneness with God. One person can merge with another person without losing his identity; but an individual remains definitely segregated from every other individual. SHL. 87

'That they may be even as we are one.' Are we as close to Jesus Christ as that? God will not leave us alone until we are. There is one prayer that God must answer, and that is the prayer of Jesus. SSY. 99

OPPOSITION

The basis of physical, mental, moral and spiritual life is antagonism. Physical life is maintained according to the power of fight in the corpuscles of the blood. If I have sufficient vital force within to overcome the forces without, I produce the balance of health. The same is true of mental life. If I want to maintain a clear, vigorous mental life, I have to fight, and in this way I produce the balance of thought. Morally it is the same. Virtue is the result of fight; I am only virtuous according to the moral stability I have within. If I have sufficient moral fighting capacity, I produce the moral balance of virtue. We make virtue out of necessity, but no one is virtuous who is good because he cannot help it. Virtue is the outcome of conflict. And spiritually it is the same. NKW. 36

'In the world ye shall have tribulation'; i.e., everything that is not spiritual makes for my undoing; 'but be of good cheer; I have overcome the world.' When once this is understood it is a perfect delight to meet opposition, and as we learn to score off the things that come against us, we produce the balance of holiness. NKW. 36

ORGANIZATION

Civilized organizations were never more deadly opposed to the teaching of Jesus than in the present age. DI. 73

Whenever an organization begins to be conscious of itself, its spiritual power goes because it is living for its own propaganda. Movements which were started by the Spirit of God have crystallized into something God has had to blight because the golden rule for spiritual work has been departed from. DI. 73

"I am not come to destroy, but to fulfil." Our Lord was not *anti* anything; He put into existing institutions a ruling principle which if obeyed would reconstruct them. DI. 73

OTHERS

Each one of us is an isolated person with God, and He will put us through experiences that are not meant for us at all,

but meant to make us fit stuff to feed others. AUG. 25

If my love is first of all for God, I shall take no account of the base ingratitude of others, because the mainspring of my service to my fellow-men is love to God. BP. 181

We make the mistake of imagining that service for others springs from love of others; the fundamental fact is that supreme love for our Lord alone gives us the motive power of service to any extent for others—"ourselves your servants for Jesus' sake." That means I have to identify myself with God's interests in other people, and God is interested in some extraordinary people, viz., in you and in me, and He is just as interested in the person you dislike as He is in you. CHI. 90

One of the cruellest experiences is the disappointment over what we find in other lives. The last thing we learn is not to glory in men. HGM. 112

No human being can ever give satisfaction, and when I demand it and do not get it I become cruel and spiteful. HGM. 113

Never look for other people to be holy; it is a cruel thing to do, it distorts your view of yourself and of others. MFL. 90

We must keep in unbroken touch with God by faith, and see that we give other souls the same freedom and liberty that God gives us. MFL. 123

When once a man has been 'undressed' by the Holy Ghost, he will never be able to despair of anyone else. PH. 54

The direction of Divine living is that I identify myself with God's interests in other people, and He is interested in some funny people, viz., you and me! PH. 66

We see the humour of our Heavenly Father in the way He brings around us the type of people who are to us what we have been to Him; now He will watch how we behave to them. PH. 66

I have to learn to identify myself with God's interests in other people, and God's interests are never my selfish interests, but always His interests. PH. 81

The benefit of my life to others is in proportion to whether I am making this struggle for the self God designed me to be, and my worth to God is in proportion to my getting into co-relation with Him, getting His point of view about everything. PH. 81

God is interested in some strange people; He is interested in the man whom I am inclined to despise. PH. 133

No one on earth is more mean than I am, no one more capable of doing wrong, and yet we are always more afraid of the other fellow than of ourselves. PH. 224

The evidence that we are in love with God is that we identify ourselves with His interests in others, and other people are the exact expression of what we ourselves are; that is the humiliating thing! PR. 107

Jesus Christ came down to a most miserably insignificant people in order to redeem them. When He has lifted us into relationship with Himself, He expects us to identify ourselves with His interests in others. PR. 107

A self indwelt by Jesus becomes like Him. "Walk in love, even as Christ also loved you." Jesus has loved me to the end of all my meanness and selfishness and sin; now, He says, show that same love to others. RTR. 40

Never let anything deter you from spending for other souls every ounce of spiritual energy God gives you. SSY. 24

The apostolic office is not based on faith, but on love. The two working lines for carrying out Jesus Christ's command are, first, the sovereign preference of our person for the Person of Jesus Christ; and second, the willing and deliberate identification of our interests with Jesus Christ's interests in other people. SSY. 160

Not only is the life of the missionary sacred to God, but the lives of others are sacred also, and when one tries to pry into another's concerns, he will receive the rebuke of Our Lord—'What is that to thee? *follow thou me.*' SSY. 165

OVERCOMING

When we are born again the Holy Spirit brings to us the realization of what Jesus Christ has done, and the great emancipating point of personal experience is not that we have power to overcome, but that He has overcome; then the Holy Spirit instructs us all along the line how we can successfully battle against the encroachments of Satan. GW. 102

"To him that overcometh . . ." Life is given as we overcome—overcome the tendency to indolence, above all the tendency not to do what we know we should, and instantly we get a revelation. HGM. 72

When we are born into the kingdom of God we realise that we are not fighting against flesh and blood, but against spiritual enemies, "against spiritual wickedness in high places." The Book of The Revelation is based on the reaction to overcome. "To him that overcometh . . ." You cannot overcome if there is nothing to overcome. MFL. 73

The remarkable thing about spiritual initiative is that the life comes after we do the "bucking up." God does not give us overcoming life; He gives us life *as we overcome.* MUH. 47

If you struggle and overcome, you will see that the other man gets a chance to fight his own moral battle too. PH. 80

P

PASSION

We are much more concerned over the passion for souls than the passion for Christ. The passion for Christ is the counterpart of His passion for God. LG. 64

'Passion' is a wonderful word, it is all that we mean by passive suffering and magnificent patience, and spiritually, all that is meant by human passion is lifted to the white, intense, welding heat of enthusiasm for Jesus Christ. PH. 30

There is only one Lover of the Lord Jesus and that is the Holy Ghost; when we receive the Holy Ghost He turns us into passionate human lovers of Jesus Christ. PH. 31

PAST/PRESENT/FUTURE

This Age is the last of the ordered ages which condition man's life on this earth, and the New Testament writers look on to the time when creation's thraldom ends in deliverance and in the manifestation of the sons of God. BE. 36

It is to those 'in whom is no guile,' to 'babes,' to 'little children,' that the revelation comes. God never guides presently, He always guides now. No wonder Jesus said, 'Let not your heart be troubled'"! GW. 27

When we take thought for the morrow, it becomes the dominating calculation of our life. Our Lord is not saying, 'Take no anxious thought,' but, 'Don't make

to-morrow the ruling factor in to-day's work.' Most of us do. To-day is lived without the power God means us to have because taking thought for the morrow is the dominating calculation, not Jesus Christ. Jesus Christ is not telling us to be careless, but to be carefully careless about everything saving one thing, seeking first the Kingdom of God and His righteousness. Many of us have no time for God and His Kingdom, we are so busy seeking other things. GW. 81

There is no other time than *now* with God, no past and no future. GW. 105

The great characteristic of God is not that He says He will pay no more attention to what we have done, but that He forgives us, and in forgiving He is able to deal with our past, with our present and our future. HGM. 105

There is a tendency in us all to mourn over something—to say that the past was a great deal better than the present, or that the future will be better; the worst time we ever lived in is the present—forgetting that we never lived in any other time! SHH. 85

PATIENCE

"The word of My patience" is a striking phrase. It cannot be the patience of pessimism because that was not the characteristic of the patience of our Lord; neither is it the patience of exhaustion, for "He shall not fail nor be discouraged." It is surely the patience of love, the patience of joyfulness, which knows that God reigns and rules and rejoices, and that His joy is our strength. CD. VOL. 2, 155

The patience of the saints may be illustrated by the figure of a bow and arrow in the hands of God. He sees the target and takes aim, He strains the bow, not to breaking-point, however severe the strain may seem to the saint, but to just that point whence the arrow will fly with surest, swiftest speed to the bull's-eye. CD. VOL. 2, 155

The patience of the saints, like the patience of our Lord, puts the sovereignty of God over all the saint's career, and because the love of God is shed abroad in our hearts by the Holy Ghost, we choose by our free will what God predestinates, for the mind of God, the mind of the Holy Spirit, and the mind of the saint are all held together by a oneness of personal passionate devotion. CD. VOL. 2, 156

God is amazingly patient. HGM. 30

Patience is not the same as endurance because the heart of endurance is frequently stoical, whereas the heart of patience is a blazing love that sees intuitively and waits God's time in perfect confidence. OPG. 23

It is impossible to be patient and proud because pride weakens into lust, and lust is essentially impatient. OPG. 23

Beware of egging God on; possess your soul in patience. OPG. 34

It takes a long time to realise what Jesus is after, and the person you need most patience with is yourself. PH. 102

Jesus says we are to keep the word of His patience. There are so many things in this life that it seems much better to be impatient about. The best illustration is that of an archer, he pulls the string further and further away from his bow with the arrow fixed, then, when it is adjusted, with his eye on the mark he lets fly. The Christian's life is like that. God is the archer; He takes the saint like a bow which He stretches, and we get to a certain point and say 'I can't stand any more, I can't stand this test of patience any longer,' but God goes on stretching. He is not aiming at our mark, but at His own, and the patience of the saints is that we hold on until He lets the arrow fly straight to His goal. PH. 149

Beware of the thing of which you say—"O that doesn't matter much." The fact that it does not matter to you may mean that it matters a very great deal to God. Nothing is a light matter with a child of God. How much longer are some of us going to keep God trying to teach us one thing? He never loses patience. RTR. 69

PATRIOTISM

Had our Lord been a patriot, He would have been a traitor to His country in submitting to the Roman dominance; He ought to have led an insurrection—'This dominance is wrong, We must break it.' Instead of that, He bowed His head to it. He submitted to the providential order of tyranny knowing that through it God was working out His purposes. HG. 11

It is a matter of indifference to the Spirit of God where we are, and it ought to be equally indifferent to us. As saints, we are cursed, not blessed, by patriotism. NKW. 135

The Holy Ghost sheds abroad the love of God in our hearts, and the love of God is worldwide; there is no patriotism in the

missionary message. This does not mean that patriots do not become missionaries, but it does mean that the missonary message is not patriotic. The missionary message is irrespective of all race conditions, it is for the whole world. 'God so loved *the world. . . .'*
SSY. 144

PEACE

The path of peace for us is to hand ourselves over to God and ask Him to search us, not what we think we are, or what other people think we are, or what we persuade ourselves we are or would like to be, but 'Search *me* out, O God, explore *me* as I really am in Thy sight.'
BP. 158

The new creation is not something you can hold in your hand and say, 'What a wonderful thing God has done for me'; the one indelible sign of the new creation is *'My peace.'* It is never safe to trust in manifestations and experiences; where the miracle of the new creation touches the shores of our individual lives it is always on the line of 'My peace I give unto you.' That is the meaning of, *'And all things are of God, who hath reconciled us to Himself by Jesus Christ.'* GW. 66

The Redemption at work in my actual life means the nature of God garrisoning me round; it is *the God of peace* Who sanctifies wholly; the security is almighty. The gift of the peace of Christ on the inside; the garrison of God on the outside, then I have to see that I allow the peace of God to regulate all that I do, that is where my responsibility comes in—"and let the peace of Christ rule," i.e., arbitrate, "in your hearts," and life will be full of praise all the time. HG. 113

Jesus is the 'Prince of Peace' because only in Him can men have God's goodwill and peace on earth. Thank God, through that beloved Son the great peace of God may come to every heart and to every nation under heaven, but it can come in no other way. None of us can ever have good-will towards God if we won't listen to His Son. HGM. 9

Whenever you obey God, His seal is always that of peace, the witness of an unfathomable peace, which is not natural, but the peace of Jesus. Whenever peace does not come, tarry till it does or find out the reason why it does not.
MUH. 349

Thousands of people are happy without God in this world. If I was happy and moral till Jesus came, why did He come? Because that kind of happiness and peace is on a wrong level; Jesus Christ came to send a sword through every peace that is not based on a personal relationship to Himself. MUH. 354

In all the rush of life, in working for our living, in all conditions of bodily life, wherever God engineers our circumstances—"My peace"; the imperturbable, inviolable peace of Jesus imparted to us in every detail of our lives. "Your life is hid with Christ in God." Have we allowed the wonder of it to enwrap us round and soak us through until we begin to realise the ample room there is to grow there? "The secret place of the Most High," absolutely secure and safe. OBH. 34

. . .when we are born again from above, quickened and raised up by God, we find it is possible to consider the lilies because we have not only the peace of God, but the very peace that characterised Jesus Christ; we are seated in heavenly places in Christ Jesus, absolutely safe, the mind imperturbably ensphered in Christ. OBH. 35

The Son of God had pre-intimations of what was to happen, and as we walk with the mind stayed where God places it by sanctification, in that way steadfastly keeping our garments white, we will find that nothing strikes us with surprise or with panic. God never allows it to; He keeps us in perfect peace while He whispers His secrets and reveals His counsels. OBH. 37

"My help cometh from the Lord Who made heaven and earth." He will take you up, He will re-make you, He will make your soul young and will restore to you the years that the cankerworm hath eaten, and place you higher than the loftiest mountain peak, safe in the arms of the Lord Himself, secure from all alarms, and with an imperturbable peace that the world cannot take away.
PH. 5

The New Testament does not say that the angels prophesied peace: they proclaimed peace—"on earth peace among men in whom He is well pleased," i.e., peace to men of goodwill towards God.
PH. 59

The coming of Jesus Christ is not a peaceful thing, it is a disturbing thing, because it means the destruction of every peace that is not based on a personal relationship to Himself. PH. 61

The peace that Jesus gives is never engineered by circumstances on the outside; it is a peace based on a personal relationship that holds all through. "In the world ye shall have tribulation: . . . in Me . . . peace." PH. 63

When God is revealed as Love, as Holy, and as Near, it is man's conscience that

alarms him from his sleep of death; it makes hell for a man instead of a life of peace. "Think not that I am come to send peace on earth: I came not to send peace, but a sword." PS. 62

In our own spiritual experience some terror comes down the road to meet us and our hearts are seized with a tremendous fear; then we hear our own name called, and the voice of Jesus saying, "It is I, be not afraid," and the peace of God which passeth all understanding takes possession of our hearts. RTR. 54

If you allow anything to hide the face of Jesus Christ from you, you are either disturbed or you have a false security. "My peace I give unto you" is a peace which comes from looking into His face and realizing His undisturbedness. RTR. 74

Thank God, we are coming to the end of the shallow presentation of Christianity that makes out that Jesus Christ came only to give us peace. SHL. 41

Thousands of people are happy without God in this world, but that kind of happiness and peace is on a wrong level. Jesus Christ came to send a sword through every peace that is not based on a personal relationship to Himself. He came to put us right with God that His own peace might reign. SHL. 41

'Think not that I am come to send peace on the earth: I came not to send peace, but a sword.' The old order and the old peace must go, and we cannot get back peace on the old level. Immediately Jesus Christ comes in that peace is gone, and instead there is the sword of conviction. SHL. 43

If once we have allowed Jesus Christ to upset the equilibrium, holiness is the

inevitable result, or no peace for ever.
SHL. 43

Before the Spirit of God can bring peace of mind He has to clear out the rubbish, and before He can do that He has to give us an idea of what rubbish there is.
SHL. 45

'Oh, the peace my Saviour gives!' That peace is the deepest thing a human personality can know, it is almighty.   SHL. 45

The peace Jesus refers to here is not the peace of a conscience at rest, but the peace that characterized His own life. 'My peace I give unto you.' His peace is a direct gift through the personal presence of the Holy Ghost.   SSY. 99

PERCEPTION

The only way to maintain perception is to keep in contact with God's purpose as well as with His Person. I have to place myself in relation to facts—facts in nature and facts in grace. If I refuse to do this my perception will be wrong, no matter how right my disposition may be; but the two working together will produce a life perfectly in accordance with the life of the Son of God when He walked this earth.   HG. 115

The characteristic of the man without the Spirit of God is that he has no power of perception, he cannot perceive God's working behind ordinary occurrences.
IWP. 13

The profound nature of each one of us is created by God, but our perception of God depends entirely upon our own determined effort to understand what we come in contact with, and that perception is always coloured by the ruling disposition.   MFL. 50

PERFECTION

Perfect life does not mean perfection. Perfection means perfect attainment in everything. Perfect life means the perfect adjustment of all our relationships to God, nothing out of joint, everything rightly related; then we can begin to live the perfect life, that is, we can begin to attain.   BP. 141

When a man says he is sanctified the charge is often made, and there is no reply to it, 'Remember, you are not perfect.' A saint is required to be perfect towards God. "*Walk before Me,* and be thou perfect"; the standard of judgment is not man's standard, but God's.   HG. 42

In every profession under heaven the great ambition of the natural heart is to be perfect.   IWP. 52

"If thou wilt be perfect . . ."—'If you want to be perfect, perfect as I am, perfect as your Father in Heaven is'—then come the conditions. Do we really want to be perfect? Beware of mental quibbling over the word 'perfect.' Perfection does not mean the full maturity and consummation of a man's powers, but perfect fitness for doing the will of God.   IWP. 117

Supposing Jesus Christ can perfectly adjust me to God, put me so perfectly right that I shall be on the footing where I can do the will of God, do I really want Him to do it? Do I want God at all costs to make me perfect? A great deal depends on what is the real deep desire of our hearts.   IWP. 117

God always ignores the present perfection for the ultimate perfection. He is not concerned about making you blessed and happy just now; He is working out His ultimate perfection all the time—"that they may be one even as We are." MUH. 118

'Walk before Me, and be thou perfect,' not faultless, but blameless, undeserving of censure in the eyes of God. NKW. 129

Christian perfection is not, and never can be, human perfection. Christian perfection is the perfection of a relationship to God which shows itself in the total irrelevancy of human life. NKW. 148

Bitterness and cynicism are born of broken gods; bitterness is an indication that somewhere in my life I have belittled the true God and made a god of human perfection. NKW. 150

PERSECUTION

Our designation of 'Christian' is of Divine appointment, whether it comes from the versatile wit of Antioch, or from the reverent respect of the Gentile; to live worthily of the name of Christian is to suffer persecution. CD. VOL. 1, 68

After Pentecost there was the sword and great persecution and they were all scattered abroad, but nothing could stop them preaching the word. There was a hilarious shout all through these men's lives because of the mighty baptism of the Holy Ghost and fire. There was running then! No power on earth or heaven above or hell beneath could stop the tremendous strength of the child-life of the Holy Ghost in them. IYA. 45

God's Book reveals all through that holiness will bring persecution from those who are not holy. PS. 80

Persecution is not only met with at the threshold, it increases as we go on in the Christian life. A man may get through persecution from his own crowd, but when it comes to persecution from principalities and powers, that is a domain he knows nothing about. SHL. 15

Persecution is the thing that tests our Christianity, and it always comes in our own setting; the crowd outside never bothers us. SHL. 16

To have brickbats and rotten eggs flung at you is not persecution, it simply makes you feel good and does you no harm at all. But when your own crowd cut you dead and systematically vex you, then says Jesus, 'count it all joy.' 'Leap for joy when men shall hate you, and when they shall separate you from their company, and reproach you, and cast out your name as evil *for the Son of man's sake*'—not for the sake of some crotchety notion of our own. SHL. 16

Persecution is systematic vexation, it does not leave you alone, it is something that throngs you; but to be boycotted means to be left alone, destitute of the comrades you used to have—'they think it strange that ye run not with them to the same excess of riot, speaking evil of you.' But they don't know that you carry a wonderful kingdom within, a kingdom full of light and peace and joy no matter how destitute and alone you may be on the outside. That is the wonderful work of the Lord in a man's soul. 'Rejoice in that day, and leap for joy.' SHL. 21

When you begin to deport yourself amongst men as a saint, they will leave you absolutely alone, you will be reviled and persecuted. No man can stand that unless he is in love with Jesus Christ; he cannot do it for a conviction or a creed, but he can do it for a Being Whom he loves. Devotion to a Person is the only thing that tells; devotion to death to a Person, not devotion to a creed or a doctrine. SSM. 17

Very few of us walk up to the light we get unless someone else will go with us. For instance, if we notice how often Jesus Christ talks about being persecuted and cast out for His Name's sake, we shall soon see how far we have fallen away from His ideal. Even the most spiritual among us have little of the genius of the Holy Ghost in our lives. We accept the ordinary common-sense ways of doing things without ever examining them in the light of God. When we do begin to re-relate our lives in accordance with God's ideal, we shall encounter the scorn, or the amazement, or the ridicule, or pity of the crowd we belong to. SSY. 123

PERSONALITY

The majority of us are not personalities as yet, we are beginning to be, and our value to God in His Kingdom depends on the development and growth of our personality. AUG. 18

Personality, not individuality, is the great Christian doctrine, but we misunderstand the teaching of Our Lord when we confound the natural with the spiritual, and individuality with sin. BE. 27

Personality is the characteristic of the spiritual man as individuality is the characteristic of the natural man. BE. 31

When Jesus Christ emancipates the personality, individuality is not destroyed, it is transfigured, and the transfiguring, incalculable element is love, personal passionate devotion to Himself, and to others for His sake. BE. 31

When the Holy Spirit emancipates my personality no attention is paid to my individuality, to my temperament or prejudices; He brings me into oneness with God entirely when once I am will-

ing to waive my right to myself and let Him have His way. No man gets there without a crisis, a crisis of a terrific nature in which he goes to the death of something. BE. 87

When our personality is sanctified, it is not God's Spirit that is sanctified, it is our spirit. BP. 14

Jesus Christ was a spiritual Personality; the Holy Spirit filled His spirit and kept His soul and body in perfect harmony with God. BP. 49

Individuality, then, is a smaller term than personality. BP. 151

Our Lord can never be defined in terms of individuality, but only in terms of personality. "I and My Father are one." Every bit of the personality of Jesus, conscious and unconscious, fulfilled the purpose of God. BSG. 54

The part of our personality of which we are conscious is the tiniest bit; underneath are the deep realms of unconscious life known only to God. BSG. 54

Jesus Christ is not a Being with a dual personality, He is a unique Personality with two manifestations: Son of God and Son of Man. He gives clear indication of how He lived a holy life, of how He thought and spoke, and He also gives clear expositions of God. Those expositions were given in a human body like ours, and the New Testament reveals how it is possible for us to live the same kind of life that Jesus lived through the marvel of the Atonement because the disposition which ruled Him is ruling us. BSG. 60

Unless I have received the Holy Spirit my personality is dead to all God has to say, I have no affinity with anything God wants, I am my own god; but through the Atonement I can receive the Holy Spirit who imparts to me the life of Jesus and I am lifted into the domain where He is, and by obedience I can be led to the place of identification with His death. BSG. 75

If a man attracts by his personality, then his appeal must come along the line of the particular work he wishes to do; but stand identified with the personality of your Lord, like John the Baptist, and the appeal is for *His* work to be done. The danger is to glory in men—"What a wonderful personality!" CHI. 94

Nothing in connection with our personality is so disastrously enervating as disillusionment about ourselves. We much prefer our own idea of ourselves to the stern realization of what we really are. Paul warns, "Let no man think of himself more highly than he ought to think." DI. 29

The one perfect Personality is our Lord. IWP. 16

Anything that partakes of the nature of swamping our personality out of our control is never of God. IWP. 88

We are designed with a great capacity for God, and the nature of personality is that it always wants more and more. MFL. 54

Personality is that peculiar, incalculable thing that is meant when we speak of ourselves as distinct from everyone else. Our personality is always too big for us to grasp. An island in the sea may be but the top of a great mountain. Personality is like an island, we know nothing about the great depths underneath, consequently we cannot estimate ourselves. We begin by thinking that we can, but

we come to realize that there is only one Being Who understands us, and that is our Creator. MUH. 347

Personality is the characteristic of the spiritual man as individuality is the characteristic of the natural man. Our Lord can never be defined in terms of individuality and independence, but only in terms of personality, "I and My Father are one." Personality merges, and you only reach your real identity when you are merged with another person. MUH. 347

Our Lord can never be defined in terms of individuality or independence, but only in terms of personality. He was the antipodes of the individual; there was nothing independent or wilful or self-assertive about Him. Jesus Christ emancipates the personality; the individuality is transfigured in the mastership of God's purpose in Christ Jesus, and the transfiguring element is love; personal, passionate devotion to Himself, and to others. SA. 102

My personality, as far as I am conscious of it, and a great deal more than I am conscious of, is the shrine of the Holy Ghost. SHL. 77

PHARISAISM

The nature of Pharisaism is that it must stand on tiptoe and be superior. The man who does not want to face the foundation of things becomes tremendously stern and keen on principles and on moral reforms. BFB. 72

A Pharisee shuts you up, not by loud shouting, but by the unanswerable logic he presents; he is bound to principles, not to a relationship. BFB. 72

There is a great amount of Pharisaism abroad to-day, and it is based on 'devotee-ness' to principles. BFB. 72

This is always the dodge of a Pharisee, whether he is a demagogue or a religious man, he must make a moral issue somewhere. If he can rouse up a passion for a neglected principle, it is exactly what he wants, but there is no reality in it. BFB. 73

Many of the religious phases of to-day do not touch reality, but only the Pharisaic insistence on a certain form of sound doctrine, and the man who is up against things finds nothing but chaff. BFB. 73

In the religious life of the Pharisee, prayer becomes a rite, a ceremony. BFB. 75

The conspicuous point of view in which the Pharisees always figure in the Gospels is as incapable of repentance. HG. 79

"I am not come to call the righteous, but sinners to repentance." Remember, that kind of statement hits the Pharisees to the very core of their being. HG. 79

It was the ruthless way He went straight to the very root of Pharisaism that enraged them until they became the devil incarnate and crucified the Son of God. HG. 79

PHILOSOPHY

No man can get at God as Jesus Christ presents Him by philosophy. The philosopher has vision, so has the poet, but neither of them has any memory; the preacher of the Gospel has vision and memory; he realizes there is a gap between God and man, and knows that the only way that gap can be bridged is by Jesus Christ making the Divine and the human one. BE. 54

We are not called on to preach a philosophy of thought, which is the tendency nowadays—but to preach "Jesus Christ, and Him crucified," because that preaching enables God to create His miracles in human lives. BE. 54

The greatest philosophy ever produced does not come within a thousand leagues of the fathomless profundity of our Lord's statements, e.g., "Learn of Me; for I am meek and lowly in heart." HG. 60

Beware of philosophies. It is much more satisfactory to listen to a philosopher than to a proclaimer of the Gospel, because the latter talks with the gibes and the cuts of God, and they go straight to that in man which hates the revelation of the gap there is between man and God. PR. 121

PIETY

The piety which is not built on a personal relationship to Jesus Christ is simply religious egotism, and the scunner that most of us have against 'pi' people is wholesomely right. A 'pi' person is simply overweeningly conceited religiously; he substitutes prayer and consecration for devotion to Jesus—'I am going to give so much time to prayer, so much time to Bible study, and by doing these things I shall produce the type of life which will please God.' BSG. 70

Piety always pretends to be going through what it is not. NKW. 123

'Pi' people try to produce the life of God by sheer imitation; they pretend to be sweet when really they are bitter. OPG. 29

PITY

Beware lest human pity pervert the meaning of Calvary so that you have more compassion for a soul than for the Saviour. DI. 89

Self-pity is Satanic; but pity for God is the betrayal of your affections. NKW. 44

POSSESSIONS

The religion of Jesus Christ is a religion of personal relationship to God and has nothing to do with possessions. Professional Christianity is a religion of possessions that are devoted to God. The disciple realizes that his life does not consist in the abundance of things he possesses, because what we possess often possesses us—we are possessed by possessions. BSG. 47

According to Jesus Christ a man's life does not consist in the abundance of the things he possesses—not only in the way of goods and chattels, but in the way of a good name, a virtuous character; these things are a man's inheritance, but not his *life*. GW. 29

The rich young ruler had deliberately to be destitute, deliberately to distribute, deliberately to discern where his treasure was, and devote himself to Jesus Christ. The principle underlying it is that I must detach myself from everything I possess. GW. 78

A sense of property is a hindrance to spiritual growth, that is why so many of us know nothing about communion with Jesus Christ. HGM. 111

Anything we possess as our own, as a possession of our own personality, is the very essence and principle of sin at work. IWP. 22

"If thou wilt be perfect, go and sell that thou hast, and give to the poor." The words mean a voluntary abandoning of property and riches, and a deliberate devoted attachment to Jesus Christ. IWP. 118

To the rich young ruler Jesus said, 'Loosen yourself from your property because that is the thing that is holding you.' The principle is one of fundamental death to possessions while being obliged to use them. "Sell that thou hast . . ."—reduce yourself till nothing remains but your consciousness of yourself, and then cast that consciousness at the feet of Christ. That is the bedrock of intense spiritual Christianity. IWP. 118

Jesus did not claim any of the rich young ruler's possessions; He did not say, 'Consecrate them to Me'; He did not say, 'Sell that thou hast, and give it to My service'; He said, 'Sell that thou hast, and give to the poor, and for you, you come and follow Me, and you shall have treasure in heaven.' IWP. 120

One of the most subtle errors is that God wants our possessions; they are not any use to Him. God does not want our possessions, He wants us. IWP. 120

A dominant ownership, such as the ownership of the Lord means that we own everything He owns. "The meek shall inherit the earth." MFL. 75

Whatever we possess for ourselves is of the nature of sin. The fuss and distress of owning anything is the last remnant of the disposition of sin; whatever we own as Christians apart from Jesus Christ is a chance for the devil. MFL. 115

To be detached from our possessions is the greatest evidence that we are beginning to form the mind of Christ. MFL. 116

Neither fear of hell nor hope of heaven has anything to do with our personal relationship to Jesus Christ, it is a life hid with Christ in God, stripped of all possessions saving the knowledge of Him. The great lodestar of the life is Jesus Himself, not anything He does for us. MFL. 116

When Jesus Christ came He possessed nothing; the only symbol for our Lord is the symbol of poverty and this is true of the saint—'having nothing, and yet possessing all things.' NKW. 33

When we partake in an earthly inheritance it becomes a particular possession of our own that no one else can have, and not only so but by taking it we may impoverish someone else. The marvellous thing about the inheritance of the saints in light is that when we take our part of the inheritance, everyone else is blessed in the taking; but if we refuse to be partakers of the inheritance of the saints in light, we rob others of its glory and its wonder. OBH. 41

There comes a time when the only way to save what is of enormous value to a life is to cast away all its possessions. "Thy life will I give unto thee for a prey"—you will have nothing else, but you will escape with your life. There is a time when a man may have to lose everything he has got in order to save himself. SHH. 27

One of the greatest dangers of Satan when he comes as an angel of light is that he tries to persuade the saint of God that he must let go the possession of what God wants him to have and take a possession belonging to someone else. OBH. 42

No sense of property or possession can go along with an abiding detachment. In civilised life it is the building up of possessions that is the snare—This is *my* house, *my* land; these are *my* books, and *my* things—imagine when they are touched! I am consumed with distress. Over and over again Jesus Christ drives this point home—Remember, don't have your heart in your possessions, let them come and go. SHH. 63

. . . whatever possessions you have will consume the nobility of the life in an appalling way. SHH. 63

. . . every now and again Satan gets permission from God to play havoc with all our material possessions. 'For a man's life consisteth not in the abundance of the things which he possesseth.' SHL. 20

'Sell that thou hast,' strip yourself of every possession, disengage yourself from all things until you are a naked soul; be a man merely and then give your manhood to God. Reduce yourself until nothing remains but your consciousness at the feet of Jesus Christ. SSY. 59

Our Lord told the rich young ruler to loosen himself from his property because that was the thing that was holding him. The principle is one of fundamental death to possessions while being careful to use them aright. SSY. 59

POSSIBLE/IMPOSSIBLE

Potential means existing in possibility, not in reality. By regeneration in its twofold phase of salvation and sanctification we are potentially able to perform all the will of God. That does not mean we are doing it, it means that we can do it if we will because God has empowered us. IWP. 105

God will do the absolutely impossible. MUH. 60

When it begins to dawn in my conscious life what God's purpose is, there is the laughter of the possibility of the impossible. The impossible is exactly what God does. NKW. 65

When once we strike the 'Everlasting Yes,' there is something positive all through our life. So many of us never get beyond the 'Everlasting No,' there is a nebulous 'knockoutedness' about us. PH. 186

For anyone to leave unattained anything Our Lord has revealed as possible for him, is the beginning of Satan's chance over that soul. PS. 51

The glibness and ease with which men proclaim the great standards of Jesus Christ and then sweep them away by saying, 'God forbid I should say I am there,' makes one tremble, because such a statement implies, Jesus Christ cannot bring me there, it is an ideal to which I cannot attain. When we come to the New Testament there is the quiet and grandly-easy certainty that we *can* attain. All God's commands are enablings. PS. 52

Because a thing is impossible in a man's present moral imperfection it does not mean he is exonerated from it. God's law has nothing to do with possibility or impossibility. RTR. 74

POVERTY

Because God gives the almighty gift of salvation from sin to paupers; He gives the Holy Spirit to paupers. BE. 11

Immediately we begin to have fellowship with Jesus we have to live the life of faith at all costs; it may be bitter to begin with, but afterwards it is ineffably and indescribably sweet—willing poverty for God, a determined going outside myself and every earthly thing. IWP. 58

We have to get to the place about which Jesus talked to the rich young ruler where we are so absolutely empty and poor that we have nothing, and God knows we have nothing, then He can do through us what He likes. Would that we would quickly get rid of all we have, give it away till there is nothing left, then there is a chance for God to pour through in rivers for other people. IWP. 79

The knowledge of our own poverty brings us to the moral frontier where Jesus Christ works. LG. 111

POWER

"Power from on high"—the words have a fascinating sound in the ears of men; but this power is not a magical power, not the power to work miracles; it is the power that transforms character, that sanctifies faculties. "But ye shall receive power, when the Holy Ghost is come upon you;" said Jesus to the disciples, and they did—the power that made them like their Lord. HGM. 22

There is only one 'power from on high,' a holy power that transfigures morality. Never yield to a power unless you know its character. LG. 121

Our Lord never drew power from Himself, He drew it always from without Himself, that is, from His Father. "The Son can do nothing of Himself, but what He seeth the Father do." MFL. 112

If you are rightly devoted to the Lord Jesus, you have reached the sublime height where no one ever thinks of noticing you, all that is noticed is that the power of God comes through you all the time.   MUH. 321

The whole almighty power of God is on our behalf, and when we realise this, life becomes the implicit life of the child. No wonder Jesus said—"Let not your heart be troubled"!   PR. 116

As Son of Man Jesus Christ deliberately limited omnipotence, omnipresence, and omniscience in Himself; now they are His in absolute full power. As Deity, they were always His; now as Son of Man they are His in absolute full power.   PR. 124

At the throne of God, Jesus Christ has all power as Son of Man. That means He can do anything for any human being in keeping with His own character.   PR. 124

While we are on this earth, living in alien territory, it is a marvellous emancipation to know that we are raised above it all through Jesus Christ, and that we have power over all the power of the enemy in and through Him.   PS. 75

The Bible characters fell on their strong points, never on their weak ones. "Kept by the power of God"—that is the only safeguard.   RTR. 47

Before we were saved we had not the power to obey, but now He has planted in us on the ground of Redemption the heredity of the Son of God, we have the power to obey, and consequently the power to disobey.   SSM. 104

PRACTISING

If we do not go on practising day by day and week by week, working out what God has worked in, when a crisis comes God's grace is there right enough, but

our nature is not. Our nature has not been brought into line by practice and consequently does not stand by us, and down we go and then we blame God. We must bring our bodily life into line by practice day by day, hour by hour, moment by moment, then when the crisis comes we shall find not only God's grace but our own nature will stand by us, and the crisis will pass without any disaster at all, but exactly the opposite will happen, the soul will be built up into a stronger attitude towards God.   BP. 62

The grace of God never fails us, but we often fail the grace of God because we do not practise. If we do not practise when there is no need, we shall never do it when there is a need.   MFL. 81

If we are practising godliness, i.e., practising in our life day by day and week by week, working out what God works in, then we shall find when the crisis comes that our nature will stand by us, because we have disciplined and trained our nature to work out what God works in. We make what we practise second nature, and in the crisis as well as in the details of life we find that not only does God's grace stand by us, but also our own nature, we have made it an ally. If we have not been practising in the daily round, it is not God's grace that fails when the crisis comes, but our nature that deserts us, and we fail.   OBH. 131

If we refuse to practise, it is not God's grace that fails when a crisis comes, but our own nature. When the crisis comes, we ask God to help us, but He cannot if we have not made our nature an ally. The practising is ours, not God's.   PR. 26

If we will obey the Spirit of God and practise through our physical life all that God has put in our hearts by His Spirit, then when the crisis comes we shall find that we have not only God's grace to stand by us but our own nature also, and the crisis is passed without any disaster, but exactly the opposite happens, the soul is built up into a stronger attitude towards God. PR. 27

Practise means continually doing that which no one sees or knows but ourselves. Habit is the result of practice, by continually doing a thing it becomes second nature. SSM. 37

We have to learn to form habits according to the dictates of the Spirit of God. The power and the practice must go together. When we fail it is because we have not practised, we have not brought the mechanical part of our nature into line. If we keep practising, what we practise becomes our second nature, and in a crisis we will find that not only does God's grace stand by us, but our own nature also. The practising is ours not God's and the crisis reveals whether or not we have been practising. SSM. 38

PRAISE

Everything that God has created is like an orchestra praising Him. AUG. 10

Praising God is the ultimate end and aim of all we go through. "Whoso offereth praise glorifieth Me." AUG. 10

PRAYER

Don't say 'I will endure it till I can get away and pray'; draw now, it is the most practical thing on earth. AUG. 125

The biggest thing you can do for those who are suffering is not to talk platitudes, not to ask questions, but to get into contact with God, and the "greater works" will be done by prayer. BFB. 34

The man who prays ceases to be a fool, while the man who refuses to pray nourishes a blind life within his own brain and he will find no way out that road. BFB. 82

The life of God in us is manifested by spiritual concentration, not by pious self-consciousness; pious self-consciousness produces the worship of prayer, which is anti-Christian. CD. VOL. 2, 8

It is absurd to imagine anyone trying to think how they will live before they are born, yet it is this absurdity which the intellect tries to perform in connection with prayer. If the dominion of intellectual explanation is the characteristic of a naturally cultured life, dominion by obedience is the characteristic of the spiritually disciplined life. Intellectual expression in life is the effect of a naturally educated life, but is not the cause of the life; and the Christian experience of prayer is not its own cause, but the effect of the life of God in me. CD. VOL. 2, 10

Prayer is the instrument of the life of worship, it is not worship itself. CD. VOL. 2, 10

Intellect and prayer are united in the saint in the consciousness of Christ which we share, consequently the consciousness of self-realization is a perversion and a snare. Our spiritual certainty in prayer is God's Divine certainty, not a side eddy of sanctimoniousness. CD. VOL. 2, 10

Do it now, *"enter into thy closet"* and remember, it is a place selected to pray in, not to make little addresses in, or for any other purpose than to pray in, never forget that. CD. VOL. 2, 33

The real reason for prayer is intimacy of relation with our Father. CD. VOL. 2, 36

In all the temptations that contend in our hearts, and amidst the things that meet us in the providence of God which seem to involve a contradiction of His Fatherhood, the secret place convinces us that He is our Father and that He is righteousness and love, and we remain not only unshaken but we receive our reward with an intimacy that is unspeakable and full of glory. CD. VOL. 2, 38

The Holy Spirit has special prayers in every individual saint which bring him or her at times under the powerful searching of God to find out what is the mind of the Spirit. This searching of the heart is bewildering at first because we are tortured by our unsyllabled lack of utterance, but we are soon comforted by the realization that God is searching our hearts not for the convicting of sin, but to find out what is the mind of the Spirit. CD. VOL. 2, 54

Our Lord says that God the Father will give the Holy Spirit much more readily than we would give good gifts to our children, and the Holy Spirit not only brings us into the zone of God's influence but into intimate relationship with Him personally, so that by the slow discipline of prayer the choices of our free will become the pre-ordinations of His Almighty order. CD. VOL. 2, 48

Spiritual certainty in prayer is God's certainty, not a side-eddy of sanctimoniousness. DI. 40

The very powers of darkness are paralysed by prayer. No wonder Satan tries to keep our minds fussy in active work till we cannot think to pray. DI. 40

The lost sight of God inevitably follows spiritual teaching that has not a corresponding balance of private prayer. DI. 42

What happens when a saint prays is that the Paraclete's almighty power is brought to bear on the one for whom he is praying. DI. 42

The seeking by prayer is determined by the circumstances we are in and by the life we habitually live; we have to concentrate on the ordinary obvious things we are in all the time. HGM. 73

We cannot talk to God unless we walk with Him when we are not talking. HGM. 73

Any soul who has not that solitary place alone with God is in supreme peril spiritually. HGM. 115

Some of us seem to have the idea that we are away in a howling wilderness and we must cry and agonize before we can get God's ear. Turn to the New Testament and see what Jesus says—"Father, I thank Thee that Thou hast heard Me. And I knew that Thou hearest Me always." HGM. 125

One of the first lessons learnt in the Ministry of the Interior is to talk things out before God in soliloquy—tell Him what you know He knows in order that you may get to know it as He does. HGM. 127

The knowledge of where people are wrong is a hindrance to prayer, not an assistance. HGM. 128

We hear it said that a man will suffer in his life if he does not pray; I question it. Prayer is an interruption to personal ambition, and no man who is busy has time to pray. What will suffer is the life of God in him, which is nourished not by food but by prayer. IYA. 9

Jesus Christ does not pay any attention to the gift of 'religious gab,' and His words—"But when ye pray, use not vain repetitions, as the heathen do: for they think that they shall be heard for their much speaking," refer not to the mere repetition and form of words, but to the fact that it is never our earnestness that brings us into touch with God, but our Lord Jesus Christ's vitalizing death. IYA. 12

When a man is at his wits' end, it is not a cowardly thing to pray, it is the only way to get in touch with Reality. As long as we are self-sufficient and complacent, we don't need to ask God for anything, we don't want Him; it is only when we know we are powerless that we are prepared to listen to Jesus Christ and to do what He says. IYA. 13

Beware of placing the emphasis on what prayer costs us; it cost God everything to make it possible for us to pray. IYA. 22

Prayer imparts the power to walk and not faint, and the lasting remembrance of our lives is of the Lord, not of us. IYA. 28

Prayer is easy to us because of what it cost God to enable us to pray. It is the Redemption of God, the agony of our Lord, that has made our salvation so easy and prayer so simple. When we put the emphasis on the line of prayer being a cost to us, we are wrong. The cost to us is nothing, it is a supreme and superb privilege marked by supernatural ease because of what it cost God. IYA. 30

There is a difference in the prayers of the Old and New Testament. In the Old Testament the prophet bases his prayer on the character of God, and appeals to God's great mercies. In the New Testament, prayer is based on a relationship with God through Jesus Christ: "When ye pray, say, Our Father." IYA. 38

A great many people do not pray because they do not feel any sense of need. The sign that the Holy Ghost is in us is that we realise, not that we are full, but that we are empty, there is a sense of absolute need. IYA. 60

"Pray without ceasing." Keep the child-like habit of continually ejaculating in your heart to God, recognise and rely on the Holy Ghost all the time. IYA. 63

The only one who prays in the Holy Ghost is the child, the child-spirit in us, the gay spirit of utter confidence in God. IYA. 64

Prayer is usually considered to be devotional and more or less unpractical in ordinary life. Our Lord in His teaching always made prayer, not preparation for work, but *the* work. IYA. 92

We pray on the great fundamental basis of Redemption, and our prayers are made efficacious by the wonderful presence of the personal Holy Ghost in the world. IYA. 93

Prayer is not only the work and the way fruit abides, but prayer is the battle. "Put on the whole armour of God, . . . Stand therefore, . . ." and then pray. IYA. 95

The key to all our work for God is in that one word we are apt to despise—"Pray." And prayer is 'labourer' work. IYA. 96

"Pray ye therefore." Prayer is labour, not agony, but labour on the ground of our Lord's Redemption in simple confidence in Him. IYA. 97

When I realise that I cannot approach God, that I cannot see as God sees, that I am choked up with things my eyes see and my flesh wants, and the empty spaces round my heart want, then Jesus says, 'If you, being evil,'—you know that is your infirmity—'if you ask God for the Holy Spirit, He will give Him to you.' That is, God will be merged into me, and I can begin to think about real prayer, relying on what God has planted in me for prayer. Otherwise we could never get near Him, the crush of our infirmities would paralyse the words on our lips. We can only pray acceptably in the Spirit, that is, by the Holy Spirit in us, all the rest is being 'cumbered about.' IYA. 102

We can only keep ourselves in the love of God by building up ourselves on our most holy faith and by Holy Ghost-praying, and by nothing else. If we try to fight God's battles with our own weapons, in our own moral resisting power, we shall fail, and fail miserably; but if we use the spiritual weapons of implicitly trusting in God and maintaining a simple relationship to Jesus Christ by praying in the Holy Ghost, we shall never fail. LG. 17

If God were human, how sick to the heart and weary He would be of the constant requests we make for our salvation, for our sanctification. We tax His energies from morning till night for things for ourselves—something for *me* to be delivered from! When we touch the bedrock of the reality of the Gospel of God, we shall never bother God any further with little personal plaints. MUH. 32

The reason many of us leave off praying and become hard towards God is because we have only a sentimental interest in prayer. It sounds right to say that we pray; we read books on prayer which tell us that prayer is beneficial, that our minds are quieted and our souls uplifted when we pray; but Isaiah implies that God is amazed at such thoughts of prayer. MUH. 90

We make prayer the preparation for work, it is never that in the Bible. Prayer is the exercise of drawing on the grace of God. Don't say—I will endure this until I can get away and pray. Pray *now*; draw on the grace of God in the moment of need. MUH. 178

God always hears the prayers of His Son, and if the Son of God is formed in me the Father will always hear my prayers. MUH. 222

Jesus did not say—Dream about thy Father in secret, but *pray* to thy Father in secret. Prayer is an effort of will. After we have entered our secret place and have shut the door, the most difficult thing to do is to pray; we cannot get our minds into working order, and the first thing that conflicts is wandering thoughts. MUH. 236

We must have a selected place for prayer and when we get there the plague of flies begins—This must be done, and that. "Shut thy door." A secret silence means to shut the door deliberately on emotions and remember God. God is in secret, and He sees us from the secret place; He does not see us as other people see us, or as we see ourselves. MUH. 236

When we live in the secret place it becomes impossible for us to doubt God, we become more sure of Him than of anything else. Your Father, Jesus says, is in secret and nowhere else. Enter the secret place, and right in the centre of the common round you find God there all the time. MUH. 236

Get into the habit of dealing with God about everything. Unless in the first waking moment of the day you learn to fling the door wide back and let God in, you will work on a wrong level all day; but swing the door wide open and pray to your Father in secret, and every public thing will be stamped with the presence of God. MUH. 236

It is no use praying unless we are living as children of God. Then, Jesus says— "Everyone that asketh receiveth." MUH. 237

Give Jesus Christ a chance, give Him elbow room, and no man will ever do this unless he is at his wits' end. When a man is at his wits' end it is not a cowardly thing to pray, it is the only way he can get into touch with Reality. MUH. 241

Prayer is not simply getting things from God, that is a most initial form of prayer; prayer is getting into perfect communion with God. If the Son of God is formed in us by regeneration, He will press forward in front of our common sense and change our attitude to the things about which we pray. MUH. 260

Naturally, prayer is not practical, it is absurd; we have to realize that prayer is stupid from the ordinary common-sense point of view. MUH. 290

Prayer does not fit us for the greater works; prayer *is* the greater work. We think of prayer as a common-sense exercise of our higher powers in order to prepare us for God's work. In the teaching of Jesus Christ prayer is the working of the miracle of Redemption in me which produces the miracle of Redemption in others by the power of God. MUH. 291

Prayer is the battle; it is a matter of indifference where you are. Whichever way God engineers circumstances, the duty is to pray. MUH. 291

If you ask me to pray for you and I am not complete in Christ, I may pray but it avails nothing; but if I am complete in Christ my prayer prevails all the time. MUH. 351

In the beginning of our spiritual life our prayers are not of faith but of fretfulness. But when you get into the inner place I defy you to go on praying for yourself, it never occurs to you to do so because you are brought into relationship with God Who makes your spirit partake of His own. Whenever Our Lord spoke of importunity in intercession it was never for ourselves but for others. When by imperceptible degrees we stop praying for ourselves, we are 'getting there.' NKW. 79

Prayer does not place God first; prayer is the evidence that our minds are fixed on God. We have to get our minds used to putting God first, it is conscious to begin with. The snare is putting common sense first. Jesus says—Reverse the order, put God first. OBH. 112

It is not part of the life of a natural man to pray. We hear it said that a man will suffer in his life if he does not pray; I question it. What will suffer is the life of the Son of God in him, which is nourished not by food but by prayer. OBH. 116

When we cling to God we learn to kneel for the first time. OPG. 64

Silent prayer is, in reality, concentration on God. You say—'But it is not easy to concentrate on God'; it is just because it is not easy that so few learn the secret of doing it. PH. 91

Prayer is an effort of will, and the great battle in prayer is the overcoming of mental wool-gathering. We put things down to the devil when we should put them down to our own inability to concentrate. "My soul, wait thou only upon God," i.e., 'pull yourself together and be silent unto God.' PH. 91

It is much easier to ask God to do our work for us than to do it ourselves—'Oh well, I will pray and ask God to clean this thing up for me.' God won't. We must do our own work. PH. 98

Prayer is always a temptation to bank on a miracle instead of a moral issue until we are disciplined. God will do more than we can do, but only in relationship to our spiritual growth. PH. 98

We are apt to think of prayer as an aesthetic religious exercise. PH. 224

Until we are born from above, prayer with us is honestly nothing more than a mere exercise; but in all our Lord's teaching and in His own personal life, as well as in the emphasis laid on prayer by the Holy Ghost after He had gone, prayer is regarded as *the* work. PR. 73

Prayer is not meant to develop us, but to develop the life of God in us after new birth. PR. 74

The prayers of some people are more efficacious than those of others, the reason being that they are under no delusion, they do not rely on their own earnestness, they rely absolutely on the supreme authority of the Lord Jesus Christ. PR. 126

In every place you are in, insist on taking the initiative for God. Every time you pray your horizon is altered, your disposition and relationship to things is altered, and you wonder why it is you don't pray more. RTR. 20

The very powers of darkness are paralysed by prayer. No wonder Satan tries to keep our minds fussy in active work 'till we cannot think to pray. RTR. 39

Prayer is not a question of altering things externally, but of working wonders in a man's disposition. When you pray, *things* remain the same, but *you* begin to be different. RTR. 43

The prayer Our Lord taught us is full of wisdom along this line, "Give us this day our daily bread." That does not mean that if we do not pray we shall not get it. The word "give" has the sense of "receiving." When we become children of God we receive our daily bread from Him, the basis of blessing lies there, otherwise we take it as an animal with no discernment of God. SHH. 64

Prayer based on the Redemption creates what could not be until the prayer is offered. The Spirit needs the nature of a believer as a shrine in which to offer His intercessions. SHL. 77

All our fuss and earnestness, all our gifts of prayer, are not of the slightest use to Jesus Christ, He pays no attention to them. If you have a gift of prayer, may God wither it up until you learn how to get your prayers inspired by God the Holy Ghost. SSM. 60

Prayer is the outcome of our apprehension of the nature of God, the means whereby we assimilate more and more of His mind, and the means whereby He unveils His purposes to us. SSY. 126

The reason we do not pray is that we do not own Jesus Christ as Master, we do not take our orders from Him. The key to the Master's orders is prayer, and where we are when we pray is a matter of absolute indifference. In whatever way God is engineering our circumstances, that is the duty—*pray*. SSY. 127

Wherever He has engineered your circumstances, pray, ejaculate to Him all the time. Impulsive prayer, the prayer that looks so futile, is the thing God heeds more than anything else. Jesus says—'If ye abide in me, and my words abide in you, ask *whatsoever ye will*, and it shall be done unto you.' SSY. 130

PRAYER ANSWERS

God is not meant to answer *our* prayers, He is answering the prayer of Jesus Christ in our lives; by our prayers we come to discern what God's mind is, and that is declared in John xvii. DI. 40

It is always a wonder when God answers prayer. We hear people say, 'We must not say it is wonderful that God answers prayer'; but it is wonderful. It is so wonderful that a great many people believe it impossible. Listen!—"Whatsoever ye shall ask in My name, that will I do." Isn't that wonderful? It is so wonderful that I do not suppose more than half of us really believe it. "Every one that asketh receiveth." Isn't that wonderful? It is so wonderful that many of us have never even asked God to give us the Holy Spirit because we don't believe He will. "If two of you shall agree on earth as touching any thing that they shall ask, it shall be done for them of My Father which is in heaven." Isn't that wonderful? It is tremendously wonderful. "The effectual ferevent prayer of a righteous man availeth much." Isn't that wonderful? IYA. 40

When through Jesus Christ we are rightly related to God, we learn to watch and wait, and wait wonderingly. 'I wonder how God will answer this prayer.' 'I wonder how God will answer the prayer the Holy Ghost is praying in me.' 'I wonder what glory God will bring to Himself out of the strange perplexities I am in.' 'I wonder what new turn His providence will take in manifesting Himself in my ways.' IYA. 42

To ask how we are to get our prayers answered is a different point of view from the New Testament. According to the New Testament, prayer is God's answer to our poverty, not a power we exercise to obtain an answer. We have the idea that prayer is only an exercise of our spiritual life. IYA. 100

Jesus never mentioned unanswered prayer, He had the boundless certainty that prayer is always answered. MUH. 147

The idea of prayer is not in order to get answers from God; prayer is perfect and complete oneness with God. MUH. 219

We are not here to prove God answers prayer; we are here to be living monuments of God's grace. MUH. 219

A child of God never prays to be conscious that God answers prayer, he is so restfully certain that God always does answer prayer. MUH. 233

Only a child gets prayer answered; a wise man does not. MUH. 291

Some prayers are so big, and God has such a surprising answer for us, that He keeps us waiting for the manifestation. PH. 76

God always answers the stumbling questions which arise out of personal problems. We bristle with interrogation points, but we don't wait for the answer because we do not intend to listen to it. RTR. 11

We have 'boldness to enter into the holiest *by the blood of Jesus,*' and in no other way. We take the crown off Redemption as the ground on which God answers prayer and put it on our own earnestness. SSY. 126

PREACHER

An orator moves men to do what they are indifferent about; a preacher of the Gospel has to move men to do what they are dead-set against doing, viz., giving up the right to themselves. AUG. 20

Of all the different kind of men one meets the preacher takes the longest to get at, for this very reason; you can get at a doctor or any professional man much more quickly than you can a professionally religious man. BFB. 59

By regeneration Jesus Christ can put into any man the disposition that will make him the living example of what he preaches. BFB. 108

There is no use condemning sensuality or worldly-mindedness and compromise in other people if there is the slightest inclination of these in our own soul. DI. 44

Don't be impatient with yourself, because the longer you are in satisfying yourself with an expression of the Truth the better will you satisfy God. DI. 45

If you are living a life of reckless trust in God the impression given to your congregation is that of the reserve power of God, while personal reserve leaves the impression that you are condescending to them. DI. 47

We should give instruction unconsciously; if you give instruction consciously in a dictatorial mood, you simply flatter your own spiritual conceit. DI. 47

Remember two things: be natural yourself, and let God be naturally Himself through you. Very few of us have got to the place of being worthily natural, any number of us are un-worthily natural, that is, we reveal the fact that we have never taken the trouble to discipline ourselves. DI. 48

Always come from God to men; never be so impertinent as to come from the presence of anyone else. DI. 48

It is by thinking with your pen in hand that you will get to the heart of your subject. DI. 50

Don't chisel your subject too much. Trust the reality of your nature and the reality of your subject. DI. 51

The discipline of your own powers is a very precious acquirement in the service of God; it delivers you from breathless uncertainty and possible hysterics. Learn to respect the findings of your own mind. DI. 51

Let the centre of your subject grip you, then you will express its heart unconsciously. DI. 52

In the New Testament it is never the personality of the preacher that counts, what counts is whether he knows how to direct those who come to him to Jesus. If a man preaches on the ground of his personality he is apt to be a detractor from Jesus. HGM. 141

If you are called to preach, preach; if you are called to teach, teach. Keep obedient to God on that line. The proof that you are on God's line is that other people never credit you with what comes through you. Jesus said, "Let your light so shine before men, that they may see your good works, and glorify your Father which is in heaven." Go on doing God's will, and you will be recreated while you do it. MFL. 128

If a teacher or preacher has not an evangelical experience himself, his preaching and teaching will degenerate into mere intellectual common sense. It may be smeared over with the teachings of Jesus and may sound beautiful, but there is no power in it to alter anything in us. PR. 25

It is an easy business to preach, an appallingly easy thing to tell other people what to do; it is another thing to have God's message turned into a boomerang—"You have been teaching these people that they should be full of peace and joy, but what about yourself? Are you full of peace and joy?" RTR. 85

The more facile the expression in words, the less likely is the truth to be carried out in life. There is a peril for the preacher that the listener has not, the peril of expressing a thing and letting the expression react in the exhaustion of never doing it. That is where fasting has to be exercised—fasting from eloquence, from fine literary finish, from all that natural culture makes us esteem, if it is going to lead us into a hirpling walk with God. "This kind can come forth by nothing, but by prayer and fasting." SSM. 100

When the message you have to deliver, brother preacher, strikes straight home, don't water it down just a little. Go straight for God if you come from Him. Neither for fear nor favour alter the mes-

sage. What happened to John the Baptist? He went straight back to God, minus his head. That was the result of his message. WG. 57

Be a walking, talking, living example of what you preach, in every silent moment of your life, known and unknown; bear the scrutiny of God, until you prove that you are indeed an example of what He can do, and then "make disciples of all the nations." WG. 88

PREACHING

There must be a sense of need before your message is of any use. AUG. 22

Remember, God calls us to *proclaim the Gospel.* AUG. 42

A man may know the plan of salvation, and preach like an archangel, and yet not be a Christian. BFB. 104

Preaching about the life of Jesus awakens an immense craving, but it leaves us with the luxury of sympathy with ourselves—'Oh well, I know that is very high and holy, but I was not born that way and God cannot expect that kind of life from me.' We like to hear about the life of Jesus, about His teaching and His works, about His sympathy and tenderness, but when we stand face to face with Him in the light of God and He convicts us of sin, we resent it. BSG. 13

Our message acts like a boomerang; it is dangerous if it does not. DI. 44

Jesus Christ never preached down to the level of His audience; He did not rely on human understanding, but on the interpreting power of the Holy Spirit in a human mind. HGM. 33

We are nowhere commissioned to preach salvation or sanctification; we are commissioned to lift up Jesus Christ. MUH. 32

Never water down the word of God, preach it in its undiluted sternness; there must be unflinching loyalty to the word of God; but when you come to personal dealing with your fellow men, remember who you are—not a special being made up in heaven, but a sinner saved by grace. MUH. 180

The preaching of to-day is apt to emphasize strength of will, beauty of character—the things that are easily noticed. The phrase we hear so often, Decide for Christ, is an emphasis on something Our Lord never trusted. He never asks us to decide for Him, but to yield to Him—a very different thing. MUH. 234

Concentrate on God's centre in your preaching, and though your crowd may apparently pay no attention, they can never be the same again. MUH. 331

We preach our own experiences and people are interested, but no sense of need is awakened by it. If once Jesus Christ is lifted up, the Spirit of God will create a conscious need of Him. Behind the preaching of the Gospel is the creative Redemption of God at work in the souls of men. It is never personal testimony that saves men. "The words that *I* speak unto you, they are spirit and they are life." MUH. 352

We are sent by God to lift up Jesus Christ, not to give wonderfully beautiful discourses. MUH. 355

Look at the standard of the preaching of to-day; sympathy with human beings is put first, not sympathy with God, and the truth of God is withheld. It must be withheld, it dare not be preached, because immediately the fullness of a personal salvation is preached—which means I must be right with God, must have a disposition which is in perfect harmony with God's laws and which will enable me to work them out, it produces conviction and resentment and upset. Jesus Christ taught His disciples never to keep back the truth of God for fear of persecution. PS. 81

Human sympathy and human emotions and human hypnotism in preaching are the signs of a spiritual hireling and a thief. Sow emotions, and the human heart will not get beyond you. SHL. 114

There are men and women at work for God who steal hearts from God, not intentionally, but because they do not preach the Word of God. SHL. 115

Paul puts out of court the idea that the preaching of the gospel is chosen as the choice of a profession is made. He says it is a necessity laid upon him. He was called to preach, even from his mother's womb, although for years he did not recognize it. Then suddenly the call awakened in him, and he realized that that was what God had been after all the time. SSY. 17

The characteristic of God's elective purpose in the finished condition of His servant is that of preaching. 'It pleased God by the foolishness of preaching to save them that believe.' SSY. 107

'Woe is unto me if I do not preach what Jesus Christ has done for me,' but—'Woe is unto me if I preach not the gospel.' SSY. 149

Thank God for the countless numbers of individuals who realize that the only

Reality is Redemption; that the only thing to preach is the Gospel; that the only service to be rendered is the sacramental service of identification with Our Lord's Death and Resurrection. SSY. 155

PRE-EXISTENCE

The false idea of pre-existence is that we existed as human beings before we came into this world; the true idea is pre-existence in the mind of God. It is not an easy subject to state, but it is one which is revealed in Scripture, viz., the pre-existence in the mind of God not only with regard to the great fact of the human race, but with regard to individual lives. Individual lives are the expression of a pre-existing idea in the mind of God; this is the true idea of pre-existence. BP. 84

There are racial memories which obtrude themselves into our consciousness whereby a person may be distinctly conscious of a form of life he never lived, it may be a form of life centuries past. The explanation of this does not lie in the fact that that particular individual lived centuries ago, but that his progenitors did, and there are traces in his nerve substance which by one of the incalculable tricks of individual experience may suddenly emerge into consciousness. BP. 85

We have in Genesis i. 26 a splendid example of true pre-existence. God deliberately said what was in His mind before He created man—"Let us make man in our image," after our likeness—the pre-existence of man in the mind of God. BP. 86

The Bible nowhere teaches that individuals existed in a world before they came

here; the only pre-existence is in the Divine mind. BP. 87

PREJUDICE

Not one of us is free from prejudices, and the way we reveal them most is by being full of objection to the prejudices of other people. BFB. 107

Remember, we only see along the line of our prejudice, and prejudice means ignorance; we are always prejudiced over what we know least about and we foreclose our judgement about it—'I have sealed the question, docketted it and put it into a pigeon-hole and I refuse to say anything more about it.' BSG. 61

Every point of view which I hold strongly makes me prejudiced and I can see nothing else but that point of view, there is a ban of finality about it which makes me intolerant of any other point of view. BSG. 62

Beware of prejudices being put in place of the sovereignty of Jesus Christ, prejudices of doctrine, of conviction or experience. IWP. 126

Prejudice means a foreclosed judgment without sufficiently weighing the evidence. When first we get right with God we are all prejudiced, ugly and distorted. When we come up against a prejudice we are stubborn and obstinate, and God leaves us alone; then the prejudice comes up again, and God waits, until at last we say 'I see,' and we learn how to be restored after our prejudices. MFL. 122

Our Lord is the only standard for prejudice, as He is the only standard for sin. Our Lord never worked from prejudice, never foreclosed His judgment without weighing the evidence. MFL. 123

Are we letting God restore us after prejudice, or are we tied up in compartments? 'I have always worshipped God in this way and I always intend to.' Be careful! 'I have always believed this and that, and I always shall.' Be careful! MFL. 123

It is part of moral and spiritual education to watch how God deals with prejudices. We imagine that God has a special interest in our prejudices, and we magnify our conceptions and prejudices and put them on the throne. We are quite sure that God will never deal with our prejudices as we know He must deal with other people's. 'God must deal very sternly with other people, but of course He knows that my prejudices are all right, they are from Him.' We have to learn—not a bit of it! OBH. 97

I have my personal life, my home life, my national life, my individual attitude to things, and it takes time for me to believe that the Almighty pays no regard to any of these; I come slowly into the idea that God ignores my prejudices, wipes them out absolutely. PH. 233

The majority of us are blind on certain lines, we see only in the light of our prejudices. A searchlight lights up only what it does and no more, but the daylight reveals a hundred and one facts that the searchlight had not taken into account. SA. 57

PRESENT

We do not trust in a Christ who died and rose again twenty centuries ago; He must be a present Reality, an efficacious power now. One of the great words of God in our spiritual calendar is NOW. It is not that we gradually get to God, or gradually get away from Him; we are either there now or we are not. HGM. 35

We may get into touch with God instanter if we will, not because of our merit, but simply on the ground of the Redemption; and if any man has got out of touch with God in the tiniest degree he can get back now, not presently; not by trying to recall things that will exonerate him for what he has done, but by an unconditional abandon to Jesus Christ, and he will realize the efficacious power of the resurrected Lord *now*. HGM. 35

Draw now, not presently. The one word in the spiritual vocabulary is *now*. LG. 96

God's command is—'Take *now* . . .' not presently. To go to the height God shows can never be done presently, it must be done now. NKW. 114

PRETENCE

You can't indulge in pious pretence when you come to the atmosphere of the Bible. If there is one thing the Spirit of God does it is to purge us from all sanctimonious humbug, there is no room for it. BE. 22

If you have known Me, says Jesus, and pretend to be abiding in Me and yet are not bringing forth fruit, either My Father will remove you, or if you persist in masquerading, men will gather you and burn you in the fire. PH. 229

We have to beware of pretence in ourselves. It is an easy business to appear to be what we are not. It is easy to talk and to preach, and to preach our actual life to damnation. It was realising this that made Paul say—"I keep under my body, . . . lest that by any means, when I have preached to others, I myself should be a castaway." SSM. 100

Pretending . . . is the first characteristic of the stupid soul. WG. 74

PRIDE

There is a subtle thing that goes by the name of unworthiness which is petulant pride with God. When we are shy with other people it is because we believe we are superior to the average person and we won't talk until they realise our importance. Prayerlessness with God is the same thing, we are shy with God not because we are unworthy, but because we think God has not given enough consideration to our case, we have some peculiar elements He must be pleased to consider. IYA. 87

Pride is the deification of self, and this to-day in some of us is not of the order of the Pharisee, but of the publican. To say "Oh, I'm no saint," is acceptable to human pride, but it is unconscious blasphemy against God. It literally means that you defy God to make you a saint, "I am much too weak and hopeless, I am outside the reach of the Atonement." Humility before men may be unconscious blasphemy before God. Why are you not a saint? It is either that you do not want to be a saint, or that you do not believe God can make you one. It would be all right, you say, if God saved you and took you straight to heaven. That is just what He will do! "We will come unto him, and make our abode with him." Make no conditions, let Jesus be everything, and He will take you home with Him not only for a day, but for ever. MUH. 164

Natural pride has to do with my standing before men, not before God—I shall not bow, I will make others bow to me. That is natural domination, and represents the antagonism of the natural life to the domination of the Holy Spirit. Wherever there is natural pride the Lord must inevitably be put to open shame. NKW. 53

If I enthrone natural pride or natural virtue, I am in total insubordination to God in just that particular and cannot be His son or daughter. NKW. 54

There is something in human pride that can stand big troubles, but we need the supernatural grace and power of God to stand by us in the little things. RTR. 57

PRIGGISHNESS

Beware of priggishness as you would of poison. BFB. 23

If you have the idea that your duty is to catch other people, it puts you on a superior platform at once and your whole attitude takes on the guise of a prig. This too often is the pose of the earnest religious person of to-day. BFB. 58

Always beware of the presentation of Redemption which produces a dangerous state of priggishness in moral life—that I can receive forgiveness and yet go on being bad; if I do, God is not justified in forgiving me. BE. 63

Priggishness is based on concern for my own whiteness, a pathetic whine—"I am afraid I am not faithful"; "I am afraid I shall never be what God wants me to be." Get into contact with Reality and what you feel no longer matters to you, the one terrific Reality is God. CHI. 32

It is easy to be priggish and profess, but it takes the indwelling of the Holy Spirit to so identify us with Jesus Christ that when we are put in a corner we confess Him, not denounce others. HGM. 30

A spiritual prig is one who has had an experience from God and has closed down on it, there is no further progress, no manifestation of the graces of the Spirit. The world pours contempt on that kind of Christian; they seem to have very little conscience, no judgment, and little will. MFL. 120

Sin destroys the power of knowing that we sin, and one of the dangerous outcomes of a mood that is not right with God is that it turns a man into a prig. PH. 229

PRINCIPLE

There are no infallible principles, only an infallible Person. DI. 72

Jesus says that the eternal principle of human life is that something must be sacrificed; if we won't sacrifice the natural life, we do the spiritual. Our Lord is not speaking of a punishment to be meted out, He is revealing what is God's eternal principle at the back of human life. IWP. 95

We may rage and fret, as men have done, against God's just principles, or we may submit and accept and go on; but Jesus reveals that these principles are as unalterable as God Himself. IWP. 95

PROBLEMS

The biggest benediction one man can find in another is not in his words, but that he implies: 'I do not know the answer to your problem, all I can say is that God alone must know; let us go to Him.' BFB. 33

If our problems can be solved by other men, they are not problems but simply muddles. BFB. 32

Watch the tendency to pathetic humbug in your approach to God. If we could see the floor of God's immediate presence, we would find it strewn with the 'toys' of God's children who have said—This is

broken, I can't play with it any more, please give me another present. Only one in a thousand sits down in the midst of it all and says—I will watch my Father mend this. God must not be treated as a hospital for our broken 'toys,' but as our Father. NKW. 77

The majority of us begin with the bigger problems outside and forget the one inside. A man has to learn the "plague of his own heart" before his own problems can be solved, then he will be free to help solve the problems outside. SA. 76

PROMISES

"All the promises of God in Him are yea, and in Him Amen." The "yea" must be born of obedience; when by the obedience of our lives we say "Amen" to a promise, then that promise is ours. MUH. 322

Never settle down in the middle of the dance of circumstances and say that you have been mistaken in your natural interpretation of God's promise to you because the immediate aftermath is devastation; say that God did give you the promise, and stick to it, and slowly God will bring you into the perfect, detailed fulfilment of that promise. NKW. 22

I claim the fulfillment of God's promises, and rightly, but that is only the human side; the Divine side is God's claim on me, which I recognize through the promises. RTR. 32

Never forget that our capacity in spiritual matters is measured by the promises of God. Is God able to fulfil His promises? Our answer depends on whether we have received the Holy Spirit. RTR. 90

PROPHET

A prophet is not a sanctified gipsy telling fortunes, but one who speaks as he is moved by the Holy Spirit within. CD. VOL. 2, 113

The prophets of God have always one burden when they deal with the judgments of God, and that is that they come not from the east, nor from the west, but are directly stamped as "from the Lord." CHI. 66

One essential difference between before Pentecost and after Pentecost is that from God's standpoint there are no great men after Pentecost. We make great men and women, God does not. No one is called now to be an isolated lonely prophet; the prophets are a figure of the whole Christian Church which is to be isolated collectively from the world. HGM. 27

The outstanding characteristic of the ancient people of God, of Our Lord Jesus Christ, and of the missionary, is the 'prophet,' or preaching, characteristic. SSY. 107

In the Old Testament the prophet's calling is placed above that of king and of priest. It is the lives of the prophets that prefigure the Lord Jesus Christ. The character of the prophet is essential to his work. SSY. 107

PROVIDENCE

The attitude of a Christian towards the providential order in which he is placed is to recognize that God is behind it for purposes of His own. BE. 35

Occasionally we have to revise our ways of looking at God's Providence. The usual way of looking at it is that God presents us with a cup to drink, which is strangely mixed. But there is another aspect which is just as true, perhaps more vitally true, viz., that we present God with a cup to drink, full of a very strange mixture indeed. God will never reverse the cup. He will drink it. Beware of the ingredient of self-will, which ought to have been dissolved by identification with the Death of Jesus, being there when you hand the cup of your life back to God. DI. 38

We have to accept God's purpose in the providential jumble of things, then He leads us in the paths of righteousness wherever we are placed, and continually restores our souls. GW. 45

There are no such things as 'calamities' or 'accidents' to God's children—'all things work together for good.' Sin and evil and the devil are not God's order; they are here by the direct permission of His providence. If we governed the universe we would clear them all out at once, but God does not work in that way. He did not work in that way with us— think how patient God has been with us! When the world, the flesh and the devil do their worst, it is for us to understand where our true life is to be lived, not in the outer courts, but 'hid with Christ in God.' Whatever happens, happens by God's permission. GW. 128

When we become 'amateur providences' and arrange times and meetings, we may cause certain things to happen, but we very rarely meet God in that way; we meet Him most effectively as we go on in the ordinary ways. HGM. 32

It is our wisdom to follow providence, but folly to force it. NKW. 143

You will always know whether you believe in God personally by your impertinent insistence on being an amateur providence for someone else. RTR. 17

God's providences come to you unawares and they produce flurry or faith. If they produce flurry there is no nourishment in God's Word. The tiniest touch of the wing of God's providential angel is enough to keep you from concentration on God, and the Bible is of no practical use. RTR. 18

It is difficult to realize that it is God who arranges circumstances for the whole mass of human beings; we come to find, however, that in the Providence of God there is, as it were, a surgical knife for each one of us individually, because God wants to get at the things that are wrong and bring us into a right relationship to Himself. SHL. 79

At first we trust our ignorance and call it innocence; we trust our innocence and call it purity, until God in His mercy surrounds us with providences which act as an alchemy transmuting things and showing us our real relation to ourselves. SHL. 79

PSYCHOLOGY

The basis of Christian Psychology is not a knowledge of man, but a knowledge of our Lord Jesus Christ. PR. 18

The point of the study of Christian Psychology is not only that we might understand salvation for ourselves, but that we might understand how to assist others. PR. 19

The basis of Christian Psychology is in Jesus Christ, not in Adam. Therefore, if we are to study the characteristics of the Christian soul, we must not look to Adam or to our own experience, but to Jesus Christ, the Foundation. PR. 28

Christian Psychology is the study of a supernatural life made natural in our human life by the Redemption. PR. 28

PUNISHMENT

The wrong things I do I shall be punished for and whipped for, no matter how I plead. For every wrong that I do, I shall be inexorably punished and shall have to suffer. BP. 157

To our Lord's mind the definiteness of the finality of punishment was as clear as could be, and nothing but lack of intelligence ever makes us say He did not put it in that way, and if those of us who take Him to be Lord and Master, take Him to mean what He says, where ought we to be in regard to these questions? HG. 74

The moral demand is for the punishment of sin. NKW. 78

When a man sins magnificently he is always punished monotonously, that is the ingenuity of punishment. PH. 238

PURITY

The detached life is the result of an intensely narrow moral purity, not of a narrow mind. The mental view of Jesus Christ was as big as God's view, consequently He went anywhere—to marriage feasts, into the social life of His time, because His morality was absolutely pure; and that is what God wants of us. AUG. 66

When we hear Jesus say "Blessed are the pure in heart," our answer, if we are awake is, 'My God, how am I going to be pure in heart? If ever I am to be blameless down to the deepest recesses of my intentions, You must do something mighty in me.' That is exactly what

Jesus Christ came to do. He did not come to *tell us* to be holy, but to *make* us holy, undeserving of censure in the sight of God. BE. 22

How are we going to be pure in heart? We shall have to go through the humiliation of knowing we are impure. If you want to know what a pure heart is, read the life of the Lord Jesus Christ as recorded in the New Testament. His is a pure heart, anything less is not. HG. 53

The purer we are through God's sovereign grace, the more terribly poignant is our sense of sin. It is perilous to say, 'I have nothing to do with sin now'; you are the only kind of person who can know what sin is. Men living in sin don't know anything about it. HG. 89

The natural life of a saint is neither pure nor impure; it is not pure necessarily because the heart is pure, it has to be made pure by the will of the person. IWP. 97

No man or woman ought to be innocent, a woman ought to be pure and a man ought to be virtuous. Innocence has to be transformed into purity through being brought into contact with things that are impure and overcoming them, thus establishing purity. PH. 80

Innocence has always to be shielded, purity is something that has been tested and tried and has triumphed, something that has character at the back of it, that can overcome, and has overcome. SA. 93

The most terrible verdict on the human soul is that it no longer believes in purity, and no man gets there without being himself to blame. SHL. 64

No man can make himself pure by obeying laws. SSM. 26

PURPOSE

God's purpose is to bring 'many *sons* to glory.' BFB. 14

God's ultimate purpose is that His Son might be manifested in my mortal flesh. MUH. 152

The whole human race was created to glorify God and enjoy Him for ever. Sin has switched the human race on to another tack, but it has not altered God's purpose in the tiniest degree; and when we are born again we are brought into the realization of God's great purpose for the human race, viz., I am created for God, He made me. This realization of the election of God is the most joyful realization on earth, and we have to learn to rely on the tremendous creative purpose of God. The first thing God will do with us is to "force through the channels of a single heart" the interests of the whole world. MUH. 265

There are times when we do know what God's purpose is; whether we will let the vision be turned into actual character depends upon us, not upon God. MUH. 278

It is a snare to imagine that God wants to make us perfect specimens of what He can do; God's purpose is to make us one with Himself. MUH. 337

When God gets me to realise that I am being taken up into *His* enterprises, then I get rest of soul, I am free for my twenty-four hours. Whenever I have an important fuss on, I have no room for God; I am not being taken by God, I have an aim and purpose of my own. PH. 179

To have a purpose of my own will destroy the simplicity and the gaiety of a child of God, and the leisureliness which enables me to help other people. When a man is taken up into the big compellings of God, God is responsible.   PH. 179

If I maintain communion with God and recognise that He is taking me up into His purposes, I will no longer try to find out what those purposes are.   PH. 182

When we accept God's purpose for us in Christ Jesus, we know that "*all things work together* for good."   SHH. 95

When the Holy Spirit enters into us He brings the marvellous revelation that God guards the unfathomable part of our personality; He goes to the springs of our personal life which we cannot touch, and prevents our being tampered with and bewitched out of God's purpose in Redemption.   SHL. 52

There is a purpose in every life that is in God's keeping of which we know little, but which He will fulfil if we let Him rightly relate us to Himself.   SHL. 52

How ever much of wrong or of the devil there may seem to be at work, if a man is called of God, every force will be made to tell for God's purpose in the end. God watches all these things when once a man agrees with His purpose for him, and He will bring not only the conscious life, but all the deeper regions of life which we cannot reach, into harmony with His purpose.   SSY. 16

As Son of Man, Jesus Christ mirrors what the human race is to be like on the basis of Redemption. Sin and the devil may do their worst, but God's purpose will only be made manifest all the more gloriously.   SSY. 107

It is the individual men and women living a life rooted and grounded in God, who are fulfilling God's purpose in the world.   SSY. 117

R

READING

Have a perfect machine ready for God to use. It is impossible to read too much, but always keep before you why you read. AUG. 36

Keep yourself full to the brim in reading; but remember that the first great Resource is the Holy Ghost Who lays at your disposal the Word of God. The thing to prepare is not the sermon, but the preacher. AUG. 37

REALITY

When a man gets to Reality he has to get there alone, there is no comradeship. BFB. 66

It takes the whole man—conscience, intellect, will and emotions, to discover God as Reality. BFB. 97

When Eternal Reality strikes, pose is no good, religious humbug is no good. BFB. 106

God is not an abstract truth; He is the Eternal Reality, and is discerned only by means of a personal relationship. BFB. 106

When one is found out by Eternal Reality the danger is to become defiant or despairing. When the friends were scourged by God they took the right attitude and did not get into despair. If the scourge of Eternal Reality comes, see that it leaves you face to face with God, not with yourself. BFB. 106

Unless God has become a concrete reality in Jesus Christ, He has no meaning for us at all. Jesus nowhere said, 'He that hath seen *man* hath seen the Father': He emphatically states that He is the only medium God has for revealing Himself. BE. 106

We can only get at Reality by means of our conscience which ultimately embraces both head and heart. There is always a practical proof when we do get at Reality, viz., actuality is made in accord with it. CHI. 30

Never look at actual things as if they were all; look at actual things in the light of the real, i.e., in the light of Jesus Christ. HGM. 84

It is quite possible to be a sincere person, to be in earnest in proclaiming the truth of God, and yet not have one iota of reality along with it. This does not mean that the sincere person is a hypocrite or a sham, but it does mean that he has never understood that God wants him to be *real*. HGM. 121

Custom in spiritual matters is apt to make us peculiarly dead to much that Jesus Christ has to say—our perfectly sincere mood blinds us to the terrible fact that we are utterly un-real. What about all our sincere talk of sanctification—are we *really* sanctified? our sincere talk about the Holy Spirit—are we *really* indwelt by the Spirit? our sincere talk about the Sermon on the Mount—are we *really* living out its teaching? HGM. 121

The strength of a *real* man or *real* woman cannot be estimated. HGM. 122

Reality is only possible where person comes in contact with person, all the rest is a shadow of reality. That is why Jesus said, '*I am the truth.*' MFL. 58

We have to learn to pay attention to reality; one soul attending to reality is an emancipation to hundreds more. We are impertinently inquisitive about everything saving that one thing. Through inattention to our own true capacity we live as in a dream, when all around us and in us are the eternal realities. MFL. 64

If we have been living in unrealities, we shall find ourselves faced with a great impatience when we do endeavour to face reality, and we are apt to behave like caged wild beasts. We have to take a grip of ourselves when we come to the true centre of things, and it means discipline *and discipline*, until we face nothing but realities. We have to exert a tremendous effort, and God is pleased to see us exert it. If you try and settle down before God in prayer when you are been dwelling in unrealities, you will recognize instantly the condition of things. MFL. 65

Reality is not human goodness, nor holiness, nor heaven, nor hell; but Redemption; and the need to perceive this is the most vital need of the Christian worker to-day. MUH. 31

Reality is not found in logic; Reality is a Person. '*I am the Truth.*' NKW. 36

I am brought into contact with actuality by my senses, and into contact with reality by my faith. The test in actual things is—Am I living a life of faith, or a life of common sense which denies faith? Faith does not make me *actually per-*

fect; faith makes me *perfectly actual.* NKW. 39

The Bible pays no attention to intellectual and emotional conceptions, but only to the actual manifestation of the ideal. A man may have remarkable conceptions, fine intellectual views, noble ideals and his actual life be beneath contempt, proving that all the high ideals and intellectual conceptions in the world have not the slightest power to bring the life into contact with Reality. OPG. 69

The Redemption of our Lord Jesus Christ is the great abiding Reality; to be spiritual disciples means that we have been brought into experimental contact with Redemptive Reality by the power of the grace of God. PH. 131

When we deal with the records of Christ we are dealing with fundamental realities, not with intellectual problems. Faith in God is the only way of coming in touch with the fundamental realities, and there is nothing logical about faith; it is of the nature of life. PR. 22

The basis of Reality is Redemption and not reason. Reason is the basis of the way we work on reality, it is an instrument. Thank God for logic and for reason, they are instruments for expressing our life, but life itself is not reasonable. Man's intellect has no power to lead him; his intellect makes him either a polished hypocrite or, in the case of a disciple of Jesus Christ, it becomes the bond slave of the right discernment of God's will. PR. 134

. . . in order to get at reality we have not only to use our heads, but our consciences. No man as yet has ever reached reality by his intellect. SA. 82

Redemption is the great Reality that is continually creating within us a longing for God. SHL. 46

What is nonsense rationally is Redemptive Reality. SSY. 165

REASON

The Bible reveals that the basis of things is not reasonable, but tragic. When a man is driven to the bottom board, he gets to the tragedy, not to the reason; he is alone with God, and if God does not see him through, despair is the only place for him. BFB. 62

No creed or school of thought or experience can monopolize the Spirit of God. The great snare of some aspects of presenting the Gospel is that everything is put in the head, everything must be rational and logical, no room is left for the great power of life which shows itself in surprising ways. BE. 72

Never try to pillory Incarnate Reason by your own petty intelligence. DI. 82

Reason is the faculty of mind by which man draws conclusions. Every man is always striving after a true expression of what he is. GW. 103

The great snare is to make reason work in the circle of our experience instead of in the circle of God. As long as we use the image of our own salvation, our experience, the image of our feelings, or answers to prayer, we shall never begin to understand what Paul meant when he said 'Christ liveth in me.' The exercise of man's essential reason is drawing on God as the Source of life. GW. 103

We can give a reason for what we know, but we cannot reason it out with the man who has not the same spirit. We can state that we are right with God because we have received His Spirit on the word of Jesus, but our reasonings are nonsense to the man who has not accepted the Holy Spirit. IWP. 14

The essence of reason in the saint—what is it? The Holy Ghost in me being obeyed, revealing the things of Jesus. IWP. 75

The Holy Spirit never swamps our personal spirit, He invades it and energizes it so that the light of God in our reason gives us the power and delight of forgetting earthly things. IWP. 76

The Atonement of our Lord never contradicts human reason, it contradicts the logic of human intellect that has never partaken of regeneration. MFL. 24

Rational commonsense talk does not deal with eternal things, and is an insult when we are dealing with the things that are not seen. We have to learn to live in the reality of the eternal things. PH. 156

Incarnate Reason is the Lord Jesus, and any man who exercises his reason in contradiction to Incarnate Reason is a fool. We must never take our Lord's words and interpret them by our own human reason; we must always interpret them by His life. PR. 131

The basis of things, according to the Bible, is tragic, and the way out is the way made by God in Redemption, not by intellect or by reason. SA. 15

A man reasons not only on what his senses bring him, but on what his conscience brings him; and immediately he is faced by the white light of Jesus Christ, his conscience recording exactly, his reason is startled and amazed. SA. 45

When I receive the Spirit of God, I am lifted not out of reason, but into touch with the infinite Reason of God. SA. 93

A rationalist is not simply one who uses his reason, but one who says there is nothing at the basis of life that cannot be solved by ordinary reason and enlightenment. The question of tragedy, of the gap between man and God, on which the Bible bases everything, has nothing to do with the philosophy of a rationalist. To him sin is not a positive thing, it is a mere defect; consequently the need for Redemption is emphatically ruled out. There is a tragedy and an agony at the basis of things that cannot be explained by reason; it must either be explained away, or faced in the way the Bible faces it. There is something wrong, and it can only be put right by Redemption. SHH. 68

Rationalism can never be the basis of things. Reason is my guide among things as they are, but reason cannot account for things being as they are. SHH. 106

The boldness of Rationalism is not in what it does, but in the way it criticises. Rationalism is a method of criticism, but when it comes to action the rationalist is amazingly timid. Nothing bold has ever been done in the name of rationalism. In all the big crises of life the rationalist is at a discount. He is great at writing books, at pointing out the futilities of religion, etc., but no rationalist has ever produced the heroism, the adventure, or the nobility that the people and the things he criticised have produced. The reasonable man is, after all, the timid man, when it comes to certain things he refuses to venture. SHH. 140

We can always find a hundred and one reasons for not obeying our Lord's commands, because we will trust our reasoning rather than His reason, and our reason does not take God into calculation. SSM. 46

REDEMPTION

The basis of things is not rational, common sense tells him it is not; the basis of things is tragic, and the Bible reveals that the only way out is through the Redemption. BFB. 17

Redemption must be seen to be God's 'bit,' not man's. A man cannot redeem himself. At present 'Redemption' is not in the vocabulary of the average earnest Christian man. When the traditional believer hears men talk as they are doing, he is apt to get scared and to squash the life out of what, behind its insufficient expression, is going to be a re-illumination of traditional truth. BFB. 56

The reason the experience of Redemption is so easy is because it cost God so much. If my religion slips easily into my life it is because someone else has paid the price for it. BFB. 74

There is a gap and a wildness in things and if God does not step in and adjust it, there is no hope; but God has stepped in by the Redemption, and our part is to trust confidently in Him. BFB. 83

Either the pessimist is right when he says we are autumn leaves driven by the blast of some ultimate power without mind, or else the way out is by the Redemption of Jesus Christ. BFB. 83

On the ground of the Redemption I am saved and God puts His Holy Spirit into me, then He expects me to react on the basis of that relationship. I can evade it by dumping my responsibility on to a Church, or a Book or a creed, forgetting what Jesus said—"Ye search the Scriptures, because ye think that in them ye have eternal life; and these are they which bear witness of Me; and ye will not come to Me, that ye may have life." BFB. 91

God has paid the price of redeeming a race that had become degenerate; He is not *going* to redeem it, He *has* redeemed it. BE. 65

The whole purpose of the Redemption is to give back to man the original source of life, and in a regenerated man this means "Christ formed in you." BE. 80

To any man who thinks, the basis of life is not reason, but Redemption. The miracle of the work of God is performed when he places himself on the "It is finished" side of the Cross. We take our salvation and our sanctification much too cheaply. We ought to rejoice when a man says he is saved, but remember what it cost God to make His grace a free gift. It cost agony we cannot begin to understand. BSG. 53

Redemption is the great outside fact of the Christian faith; it has to do not only with a man's experience of salvation, but with the basis of his thinking. The revelation of Redemption means that Jesus Christ came here in order that by means of His Death on the Cross He might put the whole human race on a redemptive basis, so making it possible for every man to get back into perfect communion with God. "I have finished the work which Thou gavest Me to do." What was finished? The redemption of the world. CHI. 8

Through the Redemption we have deliverance from the disposition of sin which is within us, and severance from the body of sin to which we are connected by our "old man"; that is, we are absolutely and completely delivered from sin both in disposition and domination. CHI. 10

Unless the universality of sin is recognized we will never understand the need for the Redemption. What the Redemption deals with is the sin of the whole human race, not primarily with the sins of individuals, but something far more fundamental, viz., the heredity of sin. CHI. 10

The meaning of Redemption is not simply the regeneration of individuals, but that the whole human race is rehabilitated, put back to where God designed it to be, consequently any member of the human race can have the heredity of the Son of God put into him, viz., Holy Spirit, by right of what Jesus did on the Cross. CHI. 15

If Jesus Christ is going to be in me, He must come into me from the outside; He must be "formed" in me. It is not a question of being saved from hell, the Redemption has to do with that; this is the Redemption at work in my conscious life. CHI. 20

Do I believe that everything that has been touched by the consequences of man's sin is going to be put absolutely right by God through the Redemption? DI. 56

Redemption is the Reality which alters inability into ability. DI. 57

The mighty Redemption of God is made actual in my experience by the living efficacy of the Holy Ghost. DI. 57

Beware of preaching a Redemption that is past; it *is* past, but it must be seen to be ever-present, and I can only make it an ever-present reality by becoming a new creation in Christ Jesus. GW. 18

Through the forces that are against him God is making a finer type of man than the first Adam, a man more worthy to be His son. That is the meaning of His marvellous Redemption. Everything that Satan and sin have marred is going to be reconstructed and readjusted. GW. 102

We can never expound the Redemption, but we must have strong unshaken faith in it so that we are not swept off our feet by actual things. That the devil and man are allowed to do as they like is a mere episode in the providence of God. Everything that has been touched by sin and the devil has been redeemed; we are to live in the world immovably banked in that faith. HG. 95

We must make a distinction in our minds between the revelation of Redemption and conscious participation in it. When we are born again we consciously enter into participation of the Redemption. We do not help God to redeem the world: we realize that God has redeemed it. Redemption is not dependent on our experience of it. The human race is redeemed; we have to be so faithful to God that through us may come the awakening of those who have not yet realized that they are redeemed. HG. 95

A sinner knows what the Redemption has wrought in him, but it is only long afterwards that he begins to grasp the revelation of how that Redemption was made particularly and in detail possible in him. It is one thing to be saved by God's grace, but another thing to have a clear revelation as to how God did it. HG. 95

We can do nothing for the redemption of the world; we have to do in the world

that which proves we believe it is redeemed; all our activities are based on that unshakable knowledge, therefore we are never distressed out of that sanctuary. God make us go a solitary way until we get there, but through one life that is there, comes all the force of the Redemption. HG. 104

Redemption partakes of God's character, therefore it is not fleeting; but we have the power and the privilege of exhibiting the Redemption in the fleeting moments of our actual life. This is the real meaning of being born from above. HG. 116

The effective working of Redemption in our experience makes us leap for joy in the midst of things in which other people see nothing but disastrous calamity. When the Redemption is effectually at work it always rises to its source, viz., God. HG. 120

The Redemption of Jesus Christ effectively at work in me puts me where He was, and where He is, and where we shall for ever be. It is the terrific lift by the sheer, unaided love of God into a precious oneness with Himself, if I will only let Him do it. It is not a magic-working necromantic thing, but the energy of His own life. HG. 121

The Redemption means that God has done His 'bit': men are not *going to be* redeemed, they *are* redeemed. "It is finished," said Jesus on the Cross. HGM. 64

Every man is redeemed, and the Holy Spirit is here to rouse us up to the fact that we are redeemed. Once that realization dawns, the sense of gratitude springs up in a man and he becomes of use to God in practical life. HGM. 64

If the Redemption cannot get hold of the worst and vilest, then Jesus Christ is a fraud. HGM. 65

The basis of human life is Redemption. There is nothing more certain in Time or Eternity than what Jesus Christ did on the Cross. He switched the whole of the human race back into right relationship to God, and any one of us can get into touch with God *now*, not presently. HGM. 105

The natural has to be sacrificed for a time, but we shall find the Redemption of Jesus works out *via* the natural in the end—"And I saw a new heaven *and a new earth.*" IWP. 101

It is a travesty to say that Jesus Christ travailed in Redemption to make *me* a saint. Jesus Christ travailed in Redemption to redeem the whole world, and place it unimpaired and rehabilitated before the throne of God. The fact that Redemption can be experienced by us is an illustration of the power of the reality of Redemption, but that is not the end of Redemption. MUH. 32

The marvel of the Redemptive Reality of God is that the worst and the vilest can never get to the bottom of His love. MUH. 34

A man cannot redeem himself; Redemption is God's "bit," it is absolutely finished and complete; its reference to individual men is a question of their individual action. MUH. 281

Just as the disposition of sin entered into the human race by one man, so the Holy Spirit entered the human race by another Man; and Redemption means that I can be delivered from the heredity of sin and through Jesus Christ can re-ceive an unsullied heredity, viz., the Holy Spirit. MUH. 280

The inner reality of Redemption is that it creates all the time. As the Redemption creates the life of God in us, so it creates the things belonging to that life. Nothing can satisfy the need but that which created the need. This is the meaning of Redemption—it creates and it satisfies. MUH. 352

God manifest in the flesh—that is what is made profoundly possible for you and me by the Redemption. MUH. 360

A man cannot save his own soul, or forgive his sins, or get hold of God in prayer, or sanctify himself; but Jesus reveals that God has done all this in Redemption. PH. 225

Redemption means that Jesus Christ can give us His own disposition, and all the standards He gives are based on that disposition—i.e., His teaching is for the life He puts in us. PR. 25

A saved soul is simply one who has partaken of the mighty efficacy of Redemption. A son or daughter of God is one who has not only partaken of Redemption, but has become of value to God in this order of things. PR. 50

Our Lord's object in becoming Deity Incarnate was to redeem mankind; and He did get through as Son of Man, which means that any and every man has freedom of access straight to God by right of the Cross of Jesus Christ. That is regeneration being made effectual in human lives, and the Holy Spirit is the One Who makes this marvellous Redemption actual in us. PR. 120

By the "dimensions of effective Redemption" understand the Redemption of

God expressing itself in individual experience; but beware of limiting the Redemption to our individual experience of it.   RTR. 71

According to the Bible, the basis of things is tragedy, and the way out is the way made by God in Redemption.   SA. 14

Redemption is not a man's bit.   SA. 16

The great fundamental revelation regarding the human race is that God has redeemed us; and Redemption enters into our lives when we are upset enough to see we need it.   SA. 17

Through the agonies in human life we do not make Redemption, but we see why it was necessary for God to make it.   SA. 17

It is in times of intense suffering that we begin to see the reason for Redemption, and realize that Redemption is worth what it cost the original Designer.   SA. 31

He did not go to heaven from the Mount of Transfiguration because He had Redemption to fulfil. He emptied Himself of His glory a second time, and came down into the world again to identify Himself with the sin of man.   SA. 47

REFUGE

In tribulation, misunderstanding, slander, in the midst of all these things, if our life is hid with Christ in God, He will keep us at ease. We rob ourselves of the marvellous revelation of this abiding companionship of God. "God is our refuge"—nothing can come through that shelter.   RTR. 92

When a man receives the Holy Spirit, his problems are not altered, but he has a Refuge from which he can deal with them; before, he was out in the world being battered, now the centre of his life is at rest and he can begin, bit by bit, to get things uncovered and rightly related.   BFB. 42

"The Lord is my rock," my encircling guard. Where did the Psalmist learn this truth? In the school of silent waiting upon God. The Rock of Ages is the great sheltering encirclement; we are watched over by the Mother-guardianship of God.   RTR. 66

". . . He only is my rock and my salvation." A rock conveys the idea of an encircling guard, as that of a mother watching her child who is learning to walk; should the child fall, he falls into the encircling love and watchfulness of the mother's care. "The Lord is my rock." my encircling guard.   RTR. 89

REGENERATION

If Redemption is confounded with regeneration, we get confused. In the majority of cases men have had an experience of regeneration, but they have not thought about what produced the experience, and when the great revelation fact of the Redemption is expounded there is misunderstanding.   CHI. 9

By regeneration we are put into perfect relationship to God, then we have the same human nature, working along the same lines, but with a different mainspring.   CHI. 107

In regeneration God works us into relation with Himself that by our bodily expression we may prove Whose we are.   IWP. 63

If we have experienced regeneration, we must not only talk about the experience, we must exercise it and work out what

God has worked in . . . We have to show it in our finger-tips, in our tongue, and in our bodily contact with other people, and as we obey God we find we have a wealth of power on the inside. PR. 26

RELATIONSHIPS

All that the one out of whom the rivers of living water are flowing is conscious of is belief in Jesus and maintaining a right relationship to Him; then day by day God is pouring the rivers of living water through you, and it is of His mercy He does not let you know it.
HGM. 18

. . . the first and foremost relationship in Christianity is the sovereign preference for Jesus Christ. BE. 68

The coming of Jesus Christ to the natural man means the destruction of all peace that is not based on a personal relationship to Himself. BE. 77

Man's relationship with God in the beginning was such that the consciousness of union with Him was a delight: as soon as sin entered that went and man become *self*-conscious: he realized he was no longer in union with God and tried to hide himself from His presence. BE. 89

Don't shut up any avenue of your nature, let God come into every avenue, every relationship, and you will find the nightmare curse of 'secular and sacred' will go. DI. 81

My relationship to Jesus is not on the ground of Christian evidences, that I can pass an examination on the doctrine of the Person of Christ, but suddenly by the great surprise of the indwelling Spirit of God I see who Jesus is, the Son

of the Living God, absolute Lord and Master. HGM. 38

The real enemy to the delight of intimacy with Jesus is not sin, but individual relationships. Distraction comes from intimacy with those who are not intimate with Jesus. HGM. 52

If I am rightly related to Jesus Christ, He says, 'Out of you will flow rivers of living water.' HGM. 76

We can only get rightly related to God through Jesus Christ. The coming of the Perfect means that we are made one with God by Jesus. Immediately we are rightly related to God, perfectly adjusted to Him, the Perfect life comes to us and through us. IWP. 16

The relationship to God must be recognised and lived up to from the crown of the head to the soles of the feet; nothing is unimportant in this relationship. MFL. 59

"Take no thought for your life. Be careful about one thing only," says our Lord, "—your relationship to Me." Common sense shouts loud and says: "That is absurd, I *must* consider how I am going to live, I *must* consider what I am going to eat and drink." Jesus says you must not. Beware of allowing the thought that this statement is made by One Who does not understand our particular circumstances. Jesus Christ knows our circumstances better than we do, and He says we must not think about these things so as to make them the one concern of our life. Whenever there is competition, be sure that you put your relationship to God first.
MUH. 27

Are you seeking great things for yourself? Not seeking to be a great one, but seeking great things from God for yourself. God wants you in a closer relationship to Himself than receiving His gifts, He wants you to get to know Him. A great thing is accidental, it comes and goes. God never gives us anything accidental. There is nothing easier than getting into a right relationship with God except when it is not God Whom you want but only what He gives. MUH. 118

Resting in the Lord does not depend on external circumstances at all, but on your relationship to God Himself. MUH. 186

The main thing about Christianity is not the work we do, but the relationship we maintain and the atmosphere produced by that relationship. That is all God asks us to look after, and it is the one thing that is being continually assailed. MUH. 217

Keep your relationship right with Him, then whatever circumstances you are in, and whoever you meet day by day, He is pouring rivers of living water through you, and it is of His mercy that He does not let you know it. MUH. 243

It is the will of God that human beings should get into moral relationship with Him, and His covenants are for this purpose. Why does not God save me? He has saved me, but I have not entered into relationship with Him. Why does not God do this and that? He has done it, the point is—Will I step into covenant relationship? All the great blessings of God are finished and complete, but they are not mine until I enter into relationship with Him on the basis of His covenant. MUH. 341

. . . the tendency to *do* instead of to devote one's self to God, is nearly always

the sign of a smudged purity of relationship to God. NKW. 82

If you are outside the crucible you will say that Jesus Christ is cruel, but when you are in the crucible you see that it is a personal relationship with Himself that He is after all the time. He is after the true gold, and the devil is after it too. NKW. 115

There is a difference between a perfect human life lived on earth and a personal life with God lived on earth; the former grasps that for which it reaches, the latter is grasped by that which it never can reach. The former chains us to earth by its very completeness; the latter causes us to fling ourselves unperplexed on God. The difference is not a question of sin, but the paradox of the incomplete perfection of a right relationship to God. NKW. 146

Beware of the storms of spiritual misgiving. The security of the saint's life is his relationship to Jesus and obedience to His Word. RTR. 10

You can never measure what God will do through you if you are rightly related to Jesus Christ. RTR. 36

There are three facts of our personal life that are restored by Jesus Christ to their pristine vigour. We get into real definite communion with God through Jesus Christ; we get to right relationship with our fellow-men and with the world outside; and we get into a right relationship with ourselves. We become Christ-centred instead of self-centred. SA. 40

If we make our life a muddle, it is to a large extent because we have not discerned the great underlying relationship to God. SHH. 25

The decrees of despair lie underneath everything a man does when once he rules out his relationship to God and takes rationalism as the basis of life ... unless a man is rightly related in confidence to God, everything he tries to do will end in despair.   SHH. 29

Our first concern is to be personally related to God.   SHH. 49

Jesus Christ taught that a man was to be carefully careless about everything saving his relationship to God. The great care of the life, Jesus says, is to make the relationship to God the one care. Most of us are careful about everything saving that.   SHH. 126

Get into the habit of having such a relationship to God that you do good without knowing you do it, then you will no longer trust your own impulse, or your own judgment, you will trust only the inspiration of the Spirit of God. The mainspring of your motives will be the Father's heart, not your own; the Father's understanding, not your own. When once you are rightly related to God, He will use you as a channel through which His disposition will flow.   SSM. 57

A single eye is essential to correct understanding. One idea runs all through our Lord's teaching—Right with God, first, second and third.   SSM. 63

Jesus does not say, 'Blessed is the man who does not think about anything'; that man is a fool; He says, 'Be carefully careless about everything saving one thing, viz., your relationship to God.' That means we have to be studiously careful that we are careless about how we stand to self-interest, to food, to clothes, for the one reason only, that we are set on minding our relationship to

God. Many people are careless about what they eat and drink, and they suffer for it; they are careless about what they put on, and they look as they have no right to look; they are careless over property, and God holds them responsible for it. Jesus is saying that the great care of the life is to put the relationship to God first and everything else second.   SSM. 67

"Take no thought for your life, . . ." Immediately we look at these words of our Lord, we find them the most revolutionary of statements. We argue in exactly the opposite way, even the most spiritual of us: 'I *must* live, I *must* make so much money, I *must* be clothed and fed.' That is how it begins; the great concern of the life is not God, but how we are going to fit ourselves to live. Jesus Christ says, 'Reverse the order, get rightly related to Me first, see that you maintain that as the great care of your life, and never put the concentration of your care on the other things.'   SSM. 68

... our Lord told the disciples not to rejoice because the devils were subject to them, but to rejoice because they were rightly related to Himself. We are brought back to the one point all the time—an unsullied relationship to Jesus Christ in every detail, private and public.   SSM. 106

In work for God it is not sufficient to be awake to the need, to be in earnest, to want to do something; it is necessary to prove from every standpoint, moral, intellectual and spiritual, that the only way to live is in personal relationship to God.   SSY. 116

RELEVANCE/IRRELEVANCE

The first thing faith in God does is to remove all thought of relevant perfection. Some lives may seem humanly perfect and yet not be relevant to God and His purpose. The effect such lives leave is not of a reach that exceeds its grasp, but of a completed little circle of their own. It takes a man completely severed from God to be perfect in that way.   NKW. 146

The outstanding characteristic in the life of a saint is its irrelevance, an irrelevance which is amazingly relevant to the purpose of God. If you become a devotee to a principle, you become a religious lunatic; you are no longer loyal to the life of Jesus, but loyal only to the logic of your convictions about Him. A fanatic dismisses all irrelevancy in life. We say that a lunatic is a man who has lost his reason; a lunatic is a man who has lost everything but his reason. A madman's explanation of things is always complete. The main thing is life, not logic. It is the irrelevant running all through life that makes it what it is worth.   NKW. 147

Much of our life is irrelevant to any and every mind saving God's mind. When you obey the call of God the first thing that strikes you is the irrelevancy of the things you have to do, and you are sure to be brought up full butt against the perfect human specimens. The net result of such lives does not leave you with the 'flavour' of God at all, it leaves you with the idea that God is totally unnecessary—by human effort and human devotion we can reach the standard God wants. Well, in a fallen world it cannot be done.   NKW. 148

RELIGION

The reason many of us refuse to think and discover the basis of true religion is because evangelical Christianity has been stated in such a flimsy way. We get at Truth through life and personality,

not by logic or scientific statements.   BFB. 101

If I have for my religious ideal a good social life lived among the societies of men, that is to be 'of' the world, no matter how religious it may be in terms.   BE. 34

Natural sinners are called "children of wrath," but when our Lord used the phrase, "children of the devil," He was referring to religious disbelievers, viz., those who had seen the light and refused to walk in it, they would not have it.   BP. 137

The great snare in religion without genuine spirituality is that people ape being good when they are absolutely mean.   IWP. 64

There is no value whatever in religious externals, the only thing that is of value is spiritual reality, and this is spiritual reality—that I allow God to work in me to will and to do of His good pleasure, and then work out what He has worked in, being carefully careless about everything saving my relationship to God.   IWP. 64

We have to live perfectly actual lives, not actually perfect lives. This fact makes all the difference between religious faith and religious farce . . .   NKW. 39

Reverence and solemnity are not the same. Solemnity is often nothing more than a religious dress on a worldly spirit. Solemnity which does not spring from reverence towards God is of no use whatever. The religious solemnity of the Pharisees was grossly offended at the social life of Our Lord. Our Lord paid the scantiest attention to all their solemnity; but one thing Our Lord was never

lacking in, and that was reverence.
OBH. 97

Unless the blessings of God can deal with our bodies and make them the temples of the Holy Ghost, then the religion of Jesus Christ is in the clouds.
PH. 130

The test of a man's religious life and character is not what he does in the exceptional moments of his life, but what he does in the ordinary times when he is not before the footlights, when there is nothing tremendous or exciting on.
PH. 231

Have you never met the person whose religious life is so exact that you are terrified to come near him? Never have an exercise of religion which blots God clean out. RTR. 78

The religion of Jesus Christ means that a man is delivered from sin into something which makes him forget all about himself. SA. 84

The trick of pseudo-evangelism is that it drives a man into concentrated interest in himself. The curse of much modern religion is that it makes us desperately interested in ourselves, overweeningly concerned about our own whiteness.
SA. 84

Beware of a religion which makes you neglect the basis of your ordinary life. If you can be a beast, you can also be a son of God. "The Son of man came eating and drinking, . . ." "Have ye here any meat? . . . And He took it, and did eat before them." SHH. 18

. . . a man may suddenly in the rashness of reaction pretend he is religious; but there is nothing in it. The characteristic of true religion is recollectedness; pull

yourself together, stop wool-gathering, and remember that you are in the presence of God. SHH. 53

It is not enough to say that because my religious beliefs do for me, therefore they are satisfactory. If everyone were well brought up and had a good heredity, any number of intellectual forms of belief would do. The test of a man's religion is not that it does for him, but that it does for the worst man he knows.
SHH. 87

REPENTANCE

The bedrock of Christianity is repentance. BFB. 103

The reality of the heredity of Jesus Christ comes into us through regeneration, and if ever we are to exhibit a family likeness to Him it must be because we have entered into repentance and have received something from God.
BFB. 104

Repentance does not spring out of the human heart, it springs from a ground outside the human heart, viz., the ground of the Redemption. CHI. 28

One of the great marks that the blessings of God are being rightly used is that they lead us to repentance. '. . . not knowing that the goodness of God leadeth thee to repentance?' Repentance in the New Testament sense means just the difference between a sanctified and an unsanctified soul. The only repentant man in the New Testament sense is the holy man, one who is rightly related to God by the Atonement of Jesus and has become a written epistle, 'known and read of all men.' GW. 51

Jesus Christ is not an individual Who died twenty centuries ago; He is God and mankind centred in His Cross. The Cross is the revelation of the deepest depth in Almighty God. What should be the reaction of that in my life? Holiness, rugged, fierce holiness in every detail of the life. That is the meaning of New Testament repentance. HG. 102

Repentance is needed not only for individual sins, but for social sins. HGM. 109

Scriptural repentance leads to positive salvation and sanctification; the only truly repentant man is the holy man.
HGM. 118

Repentance does not bring a sense of sin, but a sense of unutterable unworthiness. MUH. 235

It is not repentance that saves me, repentance is the sign that I realize what God has done in Christ Jesus. The danger is to put the emphasis on the effect instead of on the cause. It is my obedience that puts me right with God, my consecration. Never! I am put right with God because prior to all, Christ died. When I turn to God and by belief accept what God reveals I can accept, instantly the stupendous Atonement of Jesus Christ rushes me into a right relationship with God; and by the supernatural miracle of God's grace I stand justified, not because I am sorry for my sin, not because I have repented, but because of what Jesus has done. The Spirit of God brings it with a breaking, all-over light, and I know, though I do not know how, that I am saved. MUH. 302

The entrance into the Kingdom is through the panging pains of repentance crashing into a man's respectable goodness; then the Holy Ghost, Who produces these agonies, begins the formation of the Son of God in the life. The new life will manifest itself in conscious repentance and unconscious holiness, never the other way about.
MUH. 342

Remorse is never repentance, remorse is the rebellion of man's own pride which will not agree with God's judgment on sin but accuses God because He has made His laws too stern and holy.
OPG. 10

"And it repented the Lord . . ." God does not repent like a man, He repents like God, that is, without change of plan or purpose. "God is not a man, that He should lie; neither the son of man, that He should repent: hath He said, and shall He not do it?" OPG. 16

There is a difference between a man altering his life, and repenting. A man may have lived a bad life and suddenly stop being bad, not because he has repented, but because he is like an exhausted volcano; the fact that he has become good is no sign that he is a Christian. SA. 121

Strictly speaking, repentance is a gift of God; no man can repent when he chooses. A man can be remorseful when he chooses, but remorse is something less than repentance. When God handles the wrong in a man it makes him turn to God and his life becomes a sacrament of experimental repentance.
SA. 121

The prodigal son had his self-love wounded; he was full of shame and indignation because he had sunk to such a level. There was remorse, but no repentance yet, no thought of his father.

'I will arise and go to my father, and will say unto him, Father I have sinned against heaven and in thy sight and am no more worthy to be called thy son: And he arose and came to his father.'

That is repentance. The surgery of Providence had done its work, he was no longer deluded about himself. A repentant soul is never allowed to remain long without being gripped by the love of God. SHL. 82

RESENTMENT

There is something in every man that resents the interference of God. Before a man can be saved, the central citadel of his being has to be stormed and taken possession of by the Holy Spirit. AUG. 38

Note the thing which makes you say, 'I don't believe it,' it will prove where you are spiritually. What I resent reveals who governs me. DI. 32

RESPONSIBILITY

The one word to be written indelibly on each one of us is 'God's.' There is no responsibility in the life that is there, it is full of speechless child-like delight in God. Whenever a worker breaks down it is because he has taken responsibility upon himself which was never God's will for him to take. 'Think of the responsibility it will be for you!' There is no responsibility whatever, saving that of refusing to take the responsibility. The responsibility that would rest on you if you took it would crush you to the dust; but when you know God you take no responsibility upon yourself, you are as free as a child, and the life is one of concentration on God. AUG. 68

As soon as a man becomes responsibly intelligent, he comes to the conclusion that there must be responsible intelligence not less than his own behind everything there is, and God holds every man responsible for knowing that. BP. 239

When by God's grace we enter into the amazing liberty of salvation and sanctification, then comes the responsibility of walking in the light, and as we keep in the light we are able to identify ourselves with Jesus Christ's victory in such a way that it is manifested in us; but this depends on our keeping in the light. GW. 102

What we call responsibility our Lord never had, and what He called responsibility men are without. Men do not care a bit for Jesus Christ's notion of their lives, and Jesus does not care for our notions. HG. 71

It is a responsibility for us to continually realize the Eternal Fact of the Atonement. OBH. 121

God holds us responsible for two things in connection with the lives He brings around us in the apparent haphazard of His providence, viz., insistent waiting on God for them, and inspired instruction and warning from God to them. OPG. 65

The thing that astonishes us when we get through to God is the way God holds us responsible for other lives. OPG. 65

The Redemption of the human race does not necessarily mean the salvation of every individual. Redemption is of universal application, but human responsibility is not done away with. Jesus Christ states emphatically that there are possibilities of eternal damnation for the man who positively neglects or positively rejects His Redemption. PR. 79

"Until Christ be formed in you"—that brings me to the margin of my responsibility. Am I allowing Him to manifest Himself, or am I saying: "I shall not submit to that." Then the blow will fall on the Son of God. RTR. 12

God holds us responsible for what we won't look at. We are nowhere judged by the light we have, but by the light we have refused. RTR. 49

God did not create sin; but He took the responsibility for it; and that He did so is proved in the Cross of Jesus Christ. SA. 46

God, on the ground of Redemption, has undertaken the responsibility for sin and for the removal of it, and Jesus Christ claims that He can plant in any of us His own heredity, which will re-make us into the new order of humanity. SA. 119

If things were fore-ordained, there would be no sense of responsibility at all. A false spirituality makes us look to God to perform a miracle instead of doing our duty. We have to see that we do our duty in faith in God. Jesus Christ undertakes to do everything a man cannot do, but not what a man can do. SHH. 18

REST

Resting in the Lord does not depend upon external circumstances, but on the relationship of the life of God in me to God Himself. GW. 80

We are told to "rest in the Lord," not to rust. We talk of resting in the Lord but it is often only a pious expression; in the Bible, resting in the Lord is the patience of godly confidence. PH. 93

The rest which is the outcome of entire sanctification is not the rest of stagnation, but the rest of the reality of union with God. PS. 48

"I will give you rest"—not a reasonable explanation, but the staying power of knowing that I am unperplexed. RTR. 48

RESURRECTION

Our Lord died and was buried and He rose again, and this is the declaration of the Resurrection in all its incredibleness. Any question that arises in connection with the Resurrection arises in the minds of those who do not accept the necessity of being born from above. PR. 110

Our Lord rose to an absolutely new life, to a life He did not live before He was Incarnate, He rose to a life that had never been before. There had been resurrections before the resurrection of Jesus Christ, but they were all resuscitations to the same kind of life as heretofore. Jesus Christ rose to a totally new life, and to a totally different relationship to men and women. PR. 113

The resurrection of Jesus Christ grants Him the right to give His own destiny to any human being—viz., to make us the sons and daughters of God. His Resurrection means that we are raised to His risen life, not to our old life. PR. 114

The Resurrection of Jesus Christ has given Him the right, the authority, to impart the life of God to us, and our experimental life must be constructed on the basis of His life. PR. 115

REVELATION

No one knows anything about the Father unless he accepts the revelation made of Him by Jesus Christ. BP. 34

God never reveals Himself in the same way to everyone, and yet the testimony of each one who has had a revelation of

God is the same, viz., that God is love.
GW. 145

Whenever God reveals Himself to a man he instantly finds the limitation of human language and reasoning—'It is impossible! Yet it shall be!' GW. 146

Our Lord Jesus Christ is the Revelation complete; the Bible is the revelation come down to the shores of our life in words. The grace of God can never alter; Redemption can never alter; and the evidence that we are experiencing the grace of God in Redemption is that it is manifestly working out in us in actual ways. HG. 96

We have to face ourselves with the revelation of the Redemption, mirrored and concentrated in the Cross of Jesus Christ as it is presented in the New Testament, before we get the shallow, pious nonsense shaken out of our religious beliefs. HG. 99

The great fundamental revelation regarding the human race is that God has redeemed us. HGM. 63

The Redemption is a revelation, not something we get at by thinking, and unless we grant that Redemption is the basis of human life we will come up against problems for which we can find no way out. I can no more redeem my own soul and put myself right with God than I can get myself upstairs by hanging on to my shoestrings—it is an impossibility; but right at the basis of human life is the Redemption. HGM. 64

When anything begins to get vague, bring yourself up against the revelation of Jesus Christ, He is a Fact, and He is the Pattern of what we ought to be as Christians. IWP. 86

God cannot reveal Himself to anyone; the revelations of God are determined by the condition of individual character; God takes up the man who is worthy to be the recipient of a revelation. NKW. 77

If Jesus Christ is not revealed to us it is because we have views of our own, and we want to bend everything to those views. In order to realise Christ we must come to Him. That is, we must learn to trust Someone other than ourselves, and to do this we must deliberately efface ourselves. PR. 87

Revelation is that upon which we must nourish our faith; experience is that which encourages us that our faith is on the right track. The need to connect revelation and experience must never be overlooked. PR. 87

If you had lived in His day and someone had pointed Him out and said to you, "That carpenter is God manifest in the flesh," you would have thought him mad. The New Testament is either unmitigated blether or it conveys a revelation. SA. 33

REVIVAL

If there is to be another revival, it will be through the readjustment of those of us on the inside who call ourselves Christians. RTR. 76

If revival does not bring forth fruits meet for repentance it will end in riot and ultimately in ruin. SHL. 22

REWARD

Reward is the ultimate delight of knowing that God has fulfilled His purpose in my life; it is not a question of resting in satisfaction, but the delight of being in perfect conscious agreement with God. HGM. 144

"If I am good, I shall be blessed." The logic of mathematics does not amount to anything in the spiritual realm. SHH. 96

If you go on the mathematical or the rational line, you will come across something you cannot calculate, something that can only be described as an act of God. You cannot say that because a man is good and has been well brought up and behaves well that he will reach success and prosperity; you will find that bad men who overreach and tyrannise come to prosperity while good men do not. SHH. 124

RICHES

Beware of being rich spiritually on earth, only be rich spiritually in heaven. Jesus said to the rich young ruler, 'If you will strip yourself and have no riches here, you will lay up for yourself treasure in heaven.' IWP. 58

Thank God if you are going through a drying-up experience! And beware of pumping up the dregs with the mud at the bottom of the well when all the Almighty power and grace of God is at your disposal. We have superabounding supplies, the unsearchable riches of Jesus Christ; and yet some of us talk as if our Heavenly Father had cut us off with a shilling! OBH. 89

It is easy for me to talk about what I could do with a thousand pounds if I had it; the test is what I do with the 2½d I have got. It may be hard for a rich man to enter into the kingdom of heaven, but it is just as hard for a poor man to seek first the kingdom of God. RTR. 59

The right thing to do with riches is to enjoy your portion, and remember that what you lay by is a danger and a snare. SHH. 67

RIDICULE

Sarcasm is the weapon of a weak, spiteful nature, its literal meaning is to tear the flesh from the bone. The antipodes of sarcasm is irony—conveying your meaning by saying the opposite; irony is frequently used by the prophets. HG. 10

You can ridicule anyone, even Jesus Christ. SHH. 83

There are books and teachers that tell us that when God is at work in our lives, it will be manifested in ostensible ways of blessing. Jesus says that the ostensible way in which it will work out is the way of ridicule. SSY. 123

RIGHT AND WRONG

God's 'ought's' never alter; we never grow out of them. Our difficulty is that we find in ourselves this attitude—'I ought to do this, but I won't'; 'I ought to do that, but I don't want to.' That puts out of court the idea that if you teach men what is right they will do it—they won't; what is needed is a power which will enable a man to do what he knows is right. BE. 8

It is possible to do right in the wrong spirit. BP. 90

It is never right to do wrong in order that right may come, although it may seem justifiable from every standard saving one. In the long run you can never produce right by doing wrong, yet we will always try to do it unless we believe what the Bible says. If I tell a lie in order to bring about the right, I prove to my own conviction that I do not believe the One at the back of the universe is truthful. OPG. 28

Judge everything in the light of Jesus Christ, who is The Truth, and you will never do the wrong thing however right it looks. OPG. 28

If once we lose sight of the personal relationship to God, right and wrong become relative, not absolute. 'Make allowances.' Never! We can only learn by the life hid with Christ in God with what a fierce purity we must confront the horror of the world. PH. 75

If you stand true to the purity of Christ, you will have to meet problems connected with the margins of your bodily life, and if you turn for one second in public or in secret from walking in the light as God is in the light, you will lose the distinction between absolute right and wrong and make the word 'affinity' an excuse to further orders. PH. 75

State definitely to yourself the things that are confused; note the things that are not clear black and white. There are no problems at all over right and wrong. Human life is not made up of right and wrong, but of things which are not quite clear—'I do not know what God would have me do in this matter.' Stand off in faith that what Jesus said is true— *everyone that asks receives,* and in the meantime do the duty that lies nearest, waiting and watching. PH. 97

No man can do wrong in his heart and see right afterwards. If I am going to approach the holy ground, I must get into the right frame of mind—the excellency of a broken heart. SA. 13

RIGHTEOUSNESS

Righteousness—conformity to a right standard, where no one but God sees us. That is where very few of us are Christians. BE. 21

"Except your righteousness shall exceed"—not be different from but *'exceed,'* that is, we have to be all they are and infinitely more! We have to be right in our external behaviour, but we have to be as right, and 'righter,' in our internal behaviour. We have to be right in our words and actions, but we have to be as right in our thoughts and feelings. We have to be right according to the conventions of the society of godly people, but we have also to be right in conscience towards God. HG. 59

Jesus says we have got to say 'Thank you' for our salvation, and the 'Thank you' is that our righteousness is to exceed the righteousness of the most moral man on earth. HG. 60

No one is ever united with Jesus Christ until he is willing to relinquish not sin only, but his whole way of looking at things. To be born from above of the Spirit of God means that we must let go before we lay hold, and in the first stages it is the relinquishing of all pretence. What Our Lord wants us to present to Him is not goodness, nor honesty, nor endeavour, but real solid sin; that is all He can take from us. And what does He give in exchange for our sin? Real solid righteousness. But we must relinquish all pretence of being anything, all claim of being worthy of God's consideration. MUH. 68

It is God's long-suffering patience ultimately coming to the conclusion that He must let the full destruction of His righteousness have its way. OPG. 19

We must be right ourselves before we can help others to be right. PH. 79

We cannot exceed the righteousness of the most moral man we know on the line of what he *does*, but only on the line of what he *is*. SSM. 23

RIGHTS

Every right brings with it an obligation. Legally, a man can do what he likes with his own; morally, he is under obligation to use it for the general good; spiritually, he is bound to devote it to God. BE. 23

Think of the miserable little 'struts' we exhibit—'I must insist on my rights.' Then take them! But if you are a saint, you have a glorious opportunity of following the example of Jesus and being strong enough to decline to exercise your rights. BSG. 33

As surely as we begin our life of faith with God, fascinating, luxurious and rich prospects will open to us, which are ours by right, but if we are living the life of faith we will exercise the right to waive our rights and give them away, letting God choose for us. It is the discipline of transforming the natural into the spiritual by obedience to God's voice. NKW. 32

In the life of faith God allows us to get into a place of testing where the consideration of our own welfare would be the right and proper thing if we were not living the life of faith; but if we are living the life of faith, we will heartily waive our own rights in favour of those whose right it is not, and leave God to choose for us. Whenever we make 'right' our guidance, we blunt our spiritual insight. NKW. 32

We have the perfect right not to insist on our rights, it is the privilege of a Christian to waive his rights; but we do not always recognize that we must insist on those associated with us getting their rights. If they prefer to take the line of faith that we take, that is their responsibility, but we are not exonerated from seeing that they get their rights. NKW. 42

The only right a Christian has is the right to give up his rights. This is the tender grace which is usually looked upon as an exhibition of lack of gumption. OPG. 29

You will find nothing more searching than what the New Testament has to say with regard to the miserable, petty line of insisting on my rights. The Holy Ghost gives me power to forgo my rights. RTR. 15

Who can be defrauded better than a Christian? Yet we take our standards from the world and insist on our rights. RTR. 27

The stamp of the saint is that he can waive his own rights and obey the Lord Jesus. SSY. 46

S

SABBATH/SUNDAY

In every family, and in every Christian community, keeping the Sabbath day holy is a chance for ostensibly declaring to the world that we recognise that God is the Head. PH. 239

SACRAMENT

'Sacrament' means the real Presence of God coming through the common elements. A great point in the sacramental teaching of the New Testament is that God brings His real Presence through the common elements of friendship, and air, and sea, and sky. Very few of us see it. It is only when we develop in spiritual devotion to Jesus Christ that we begin to detect Him in our friendships, in our ordinary eating and drinking. The ecclesiastical doctrine of the sacraments with too many of us confines it to a particular thing, and we do not scent that it is a symbol of all life that is "hid with Christ in God." PH. 170

Jesus Christ teaches that He can come to us through anything, and the great sign of a Christian man is that he finds God in ordinary ways and days, and partakes of the sacrament of His Presence here. PH. 170

'Sacramented' means that the elements of the natural life are presenced by Divinity as they are broken in God's service providentially. We have to be entirely adjusted into Jesus before He can make us a sacrament. SSY. 165

SACRED AND SECULAR

Most of us are spiritually inefficient because we cannot do certain things and remain spiritual. We can be spiritual in prayer meetings, in congenial spiritual society, in what is known as Christian work, but we cannot be spiritual in drudgery. We are all capable of being spiritual sluggards; if we live a sequestered life and continually don't do what we ought to do, we can develop a spiritual life, but in actual things we are easily knocked out. We are trying to develop a life that is sanctified and holy but it is spiritually inefficient—it cannot wash feet, it cannot do secular things without being tainted. PH. 172

Spiritual means *real*, and the only type of spiritual life is the life of our Lord Himself; there was no sacred and secular in His life, it was all real. Jesus Christ did secular things and was God Incarnate in doing them. PH. 172

Experience must be worked out into expression; the expression is a strong family likeness to Jesus, and its mark is found in the secular life, not in the sequestered life. PH. 173

Don't shut up any avenue of your nature, let God come into every avenue, every relationship, and you will find the nightmare curse of "secular and sacred" will go. RTR. 39

SACRIFICE

Self-sacrifice may be a disease; we are not to sacrifice for our own sake, or for the sake of anyone else, but for God's sake. BE. 48

It is easy to be thrilled by the sacrifices men make: it takes the Spirit of Almighty God to get us even interested in the cost of our redemption to God. BE. 60

We do not often put together the words 'sacrifice' and 'praise.' Sacrifice means giving the best we have, and it embraces an element of cost. Our own flesh and blood relationships have to be the scene of the sacrifice of praise on our part, whether it is accepted or not. That is where the *sacrifice* of praise comes in. BP. 170

If I give up to God because I want the hundredfold more, I never see God. CHI. 86

The only sacrifice acceptable to God is "a broken and a contrite heart," not a moral upright life built on pride. When I stand on the basis of penitence, God's salvation is manifested immediately. DI. 32

'Behold, to obey is better than sacrifice.' Self-sacrifice may be simply a disease of the nerves, a morbid self-consciousness which is the obverse of intense selfishness. Our Lord never confounds selfishness and self. Whenever I make self-sacrifice the aim and end of my life, I become a traitor to Jesus; instead of placing Him as my lodestar I place Him as an example, One who helps me to sacrifice myself. I am not saved to sacrifice; I am saved to fulfil my destiny in Christ. It is much easier to sacrifice myself, to efface myself, than to do God's will in His way. Self-sacrifice is always eager to do things and then say, 'That is God's will.' There was no trace in our Lord's life of self-sacrifice being the idea—'For their sakes I sanctify Myself.' These words give the key to the saint's life; I have deliberately to give God my self, my self which He has sanctified, that He might use me as His hands and His feet. GW. 42

The real burnt offering God requires is 'a living sacrifice,' the giving back to God the best He has given me that it might be His and mine for ever. GW. 65

He deliberately laid down His life without any possibility of deliverance. There was no compulsion, it was a sacrifice made with a free mind; nor was there anything of the impulsive about it, He laid down His life with a clear knowledge of what He was doing. Jesus understood what was coming, it was not a foreboding, but a certainty; not a catastrophe which might happen, but an ordained certainty in the decrees of God, and He knew it. GW. 113

There is no room for the pathetic in our Lord's attitude; it is we who take the pathetic view and look at His sacrifice from a point of view the Spirit of God never once uses. The Spirit of God never bewitches men with the strange pathos of the sacrifice of Jesus: the Spirit of God keeps us at the passion of the sacrifice of Jesus. The great passion at the back of His heart and mind in all Jesus did was devotion to His Father. GW. 113

When we are identified with Jesus Christ the Spirit of God would have us sacrifice ourselves for Him, point for point, as He did for His Father. We pray and wait, and need urging, and want the thrilling vision; but Jesus wants us to narrow and limit ourselves to one thing—clearly and intelligently knowing what we are doing, we deliberately lay down our lives for Him as He laid down His life for us in the purpose of God. GW. 114

When we come to the Cross we do not go through it and out the other side; we abide in the life to which the Cross is the gateway, and the characteristic of the life is that of deep profound sacrifice to God. HG. 99

The natural life in a sanctified man or woman is neither moral nor immoral, it is the gift God has given the saint to sacrifice on the altar of love to God. IWP. 55

Jesus sacrificed His natural life and made it spiritual by obeying His Father's voice, and we have any number of glorious opportunities of proving how much we love God by the delighted way we go to sacrifice for Him. IWP. 82

Jesus Christ laid down His holy life for His Father's purposes, then if we are God's children we have to lay down our lives for His sake, not for the sake of a truth, not for the sake of devotion to a doctrine, but for Jesus Christ's sake—the personal relationship all through. IWP. 85

Every morning we wake, and every moment of the day, we have this glorious privilege of sacrificing our holy selves to and for Jesus Christ. IWP. 85

Sacrifice in its essence is the exuberant passionate love-gift of the best I have to the one I love best. MFL. 108

We seem to think that God wants us to give up things! God nowhere tells us to give up things for the sake of giving them up. He tells us to give them up for the sake of the only thing worth having—viz., life with Himself. MUH. 8

The only way we can offer a spiritual sacrifice to God is to do what He tells us to do, discipline what He tells us to discipline. NKW. 105

To give God my life for death is of no value; what is of value is to let Him have all my powers that have been saved and sanctified, so that as Jesus sacrificed His life for His Father, I can sacrifice my life for Him. 'Present your bodies a *living* sacrifice.' NKW. 125

'To obey is better than sacrifice.' It is a great deal better to fulfil the purpose of God in your life by discerning His will than it is to perform great acts of self-sacrifice. OBH. 119

Sacrifice for love is never conscious; sacrifice for duty always has margins of distress. OPG. 45

When once the Holy Spirit has come in, the thought of sacrifice never occurs to a saint because sacrifice is the love passion of the Holy Ghost. PH. 166

When we have been delivered from sin, the characteristics of our natural life have to be sacrificed, not murdered, not denied in the sense of being ignored, but sacrificed, that is, transformed into agreement with the heavenly by obedience. PR. 16

The idea of sacrifice is giving back to God the best we have in order that He may make it His and ours for ever. PR. 102

SADDUCEE

The Sadducee is the type of person who in all ages destroys the treasure of the spirit; he is a common-sense individual. HG. 80

It is not the brutal sceptic who is the Sadducee, he does not destroy anybody's shrines, it is the religious man or woman with particularly bright conceptions of their own, but who are far more concerned with the visible success of this world than with anything else. You go to them with some insurgent doubt in your mind, and they smile at you, and say, 'Oh, don't exercise your mind on those things, it is absurd.' That is the Sadducee who has done more to deface in modern life what Jesus Christ began to do than all the blackguardism and drunkenness in our modern civilization. The subtle destruction of all that stands for the invisible is what is represented by the Sadducee. HG. 81

SAINT

There was never a saint yet who did not have to start with a maimed life. BE. 49

Men of the world hate a thoughtful saint. They can ridicule a living saint who does not think, but a thinking saint—I mean of course, one who lives rightly as well—is the annoyance, because the thinking saint has formed the Mind of Christ and re-echoes it. Let us from this time forth determine to bring into captivity every thought to the obedience of Christ. BE. 124

You may put a saint in tribulation, amid an onslaught of principalities and powers, in peril, pestilence or under the sword, you may put a saint anywhere you like, and he is 'more than conqueror' every time. Why? Because his heart being filled with the love of God, he has the power to perceive and understand that behind all these things is God making them 'work together for good.' BP. 111

A sheet of white paper can be soiled, a sunbeam cannot be soiled, and God keeps His saints like light. Oh, the power of full-orbed righteousness! Thank God for the sanity of His salva-

tion! He takes hold of our hearts *and* our heads! BP. 112

Once let God's honour be slandered, and instantly there is something else to deal with in your 'meek' saint. BP. 114

As saints, we should smart and suffer keenly whenever we see pride and covetousness and self-realization, because these are the things that go against the honour of God. BP. 185

You cannot appeal to a saint on the line of self-interest; you can only appeal to him on the line of the interests of Jesus Christ. The feeblest, weakest saint becomes a holy terror immediately Jesus Christ is scandalized. BP. 205

The work of Jesus is the creation of saints; He can take the worst, the most misshapen material, and make a saint. BSG. 55

The strenuous effort of the saint is not to produce holiness, but to express in every circumstance the life of Jesus which is imparted to him by the Holy Ghost. GW. 68

We are all possible saints or possible devils. HGM. 40

No one can be with a superior person without having a feeling of envy and jealousy unless he is a saint; the saint knows no jealousy or envy because the life of the Lord Jesus is being manifested in him. HGM. 133

Never say, if you are a thoughtful saint, 'Since I have been sanctified I have done what I liked.' If you have, you are immoral in that degree. If it were true, it would be true of the holiest Being Who ever lived, but it is said of Him that

"even Christ pleased not Himself."
IWP. 98

We must be able to mount up with wings as eagles, but we must know also how to come down. It is the coming down and the living down that is the power of the saint. LG. 58

Saints have to become absolutely loyal to the disposition of Jesus Christ in their lives. LG. 69

The sanctified saint has to alter the horizon of other people's lives, and he does it by showing that they can be lifted on to a higher plane by the grace of God, viz., into the heavenly places in Christ Jesus. LG. 86

The weakest saint can experience the power of the Deity of the Son of God if once he is willing to "let go." Any strand of our own energy will blur the life of Jesus. We have to keep letting go, and slowly and surely the great full life of God will invade us in every part, and men will take knowledge of us that we have been with Jesus. MUH. 103

The initiative of the saint is not towards self-realization, but towards knowing Jesus Christ. The spiritual saint never believes circumstances to be haphazard, or thinks of his life as secular and sacred; he sees everything he is dumped down in as the means of securing the knowledge of Jesus Christ. MUH. 193

A saint is never consciously a saint; a saint is consciously dependent on God. MUH. 320

The saint is to be consistent to the Divine life within him, not logically consistent to a principle. A fanatic is concerned not about God but about

proving his own little fanatical ideas. It is a danger peculiar to us all. NKW. 144

God wants to do with the saints what His Son prayed He would do—make them one with Himself. NKW. 149

'Oh, I'm no saint.' To talk like that is acceptable to human pride, but it is unconscious blasphemy against God. It literally means I defy God to make me a saint. OBH. 103

A saint must measure his life by self-expenditure, that is, by what God pours through him. PH. 138

The characteristic of the life of a saint is essential elemental simplicity. PS. 42

The individual saint cannot be perfected apart from others. "He gave some to be apostles . . .," for what purpose? To show how clever they were, what gifts they had? No, "for the perfecting of the saints." PS. 44

. . . apostles, prophets, evangelists, pastors and teachers, are all meant for one thing by God, viz., "for the perfecting of the saints, . . . unto the building up of the body of Christ." No saint can ever be perfected in isolation or in any other way than God has laid down. There are very few who are willing to apprehend that for which they were apprehended, they thank God for salvation and sanctification and then stagnate, consequently the perfecting of the saints is hindered. PS. 44

We lose saintliness whenever we take our eyes for one second off the Source of our life, the Lord Jesus Christ. PS. 52

. . . after the work of sanctification, when the life of the saint really begins, God lifts His hand off us and lets the world do its worst, for He is assured that "He that is in him is greater than he that is against him." PS. 60

. . . the life of God within the saint produces agony every now and again, because God won't leave us alone, He won't say, 'Now that will do.' He will keep at us, blazing and burning us, He is a 'consuming fire.' PS. 66

Around the saints is the great power of God which keeps watch and ward over them so that 'that wicked one toucheth them not.' PS. 75

A saint is one in whom the life of Jesus Christ is formed. SHL. 89

You will find the things God uses, not to develop you, but to develop the manifestation of God in you, are just the things we are apt to ignore—successful worldliness, other people, trials of our faith—these are the things that either make a saint un-saintly, or give God the chance to exhibit Himself. SHL. 97

Not only does God waste His saints according to the judgments of men, He seems to bruise them most mercilessly. You say, 'But it could never be God's will to bruise me': if it pleased the Lord to bruise His own Son, why should He not bruise you? SHL. 121

The saint is meant to satisfy the heart of Jesus first, and then be used to feed His saints. '. . . and ye shall be My witnesses'; 'a perfect delight to Me wherever I place you.' The saints who satisfy the heart of Jesus make other saints strong and mature for God. SHL. 122

A saint is made by God, 'He made me.' Then do not tell God He is a bungling workman. We do that whenever we say 'I

can't.' To say 'I can't' literally means we are too strong in ourselves to depend on God. 'I can't pray in public; I can't talk in the open air.' Substitute 'I won't,' and it will be nearer the truth. The thing that makes us say 'I can't' is that we forget that we must rely entirely on the creative purpose of God and on this characteristic of perfect finish for God. SSY. 108

God sows His saints in the places that are most useless according to the judgment of the world; He puts them where He likes. Where God is being glorified is where He puts His saints, and we are no judge of where that is. SSY. 131

SALVATION

As Christian workers we must never forget that salvation is God's thought, not man's; therefore it is an unfathomable abyss. AUG. 58

Salvation is not an experience; experience is only a gateway by which salvation comes into our conscious lives. We have to preach the great thought of God behind the experience. AUG. 58

If we are Christians we have to live according to the teaching of the Sermon on the Mount; and the marvel of Jesus Christ's salvation is that He puts us in the place where we can fulfil all the old law and a great deal more. BE. 9

"Now is the day of salvation," and to *do it now* is the 'thank you' of our acceptance of that salvation. BE. 59

Most of us take our salvation much too cheaply. BFB. 26

The measure of the salvation of Jesus is not that it does for the best man we know, but that it does for the worst and most sin-stained. BSG. 14

The last possible reach of faith is the cry of a sinner who begins to realize that God can save him. Immediately he cries out to God he will find the marvel of Jesus Christ's salvation wrought out in his personal experience. BSG. 50

Salvation is an immense marvel to me—I, a sinner, can be made into a saint; but it is only possible because of what Jesus Christ did. BSG. 53

The meaning of salvation in experience is that we are enabled to manifest in our mortal flesh the family likeness that Jesus had to God. BSG. 58

When I want to translate all God's redemptive work into the consciousness of being saved, I become a pious humbug. God does not save me in order that I may feel saved, but to take me up into His redemptive purpose. CHI. 37

We are apt to make salvation mean the saving of our skin. The death of our body, the sudden breaking-up of the house of life, may be the salvation of our soul. HG. 31

Jesus Christ's salvation deals not only with the outcast and downtrodden, it deals with clean-living, upright, sterling men and women, and immediately you present the Gospel as Jesus presents it, it is this class you clash with. HGM. 13

It is possible to be grossly selfish in absorbing the salvation of Jesus, to enjoy all its benedictions, and never follow Him one step. IWP. 57

The Bible never refers to degrees of salvation, but there are degrees of it in actual experience. The spiritual privileges and opportunities of all disciples are equal; it has nothing to do with education or natural ability. "One is your Master, even Christ." IWP. 110

Salvation is sudden, but the working out of salvation in our life is never sudden. It is moment by moment, here a little and there a little. The Holy Spirit educates us down to the scruple. MFL. 46

Salvation is not merely deliverance from sin, nor the experience of personal holiness; the salvation of God is deliverance out of self entirely into union with Himself. My experimental knowledge of salvation will be along the line of deliverance from sin and of personal holiness; but salvation means that the Spirit of God has brought me into touch with God's personality, and I am thrilled with something infinitely greater than myself, I am caught up into the abandonment of God. MUH. 73

The salvation of God does not stand on human logic, it stands on the sacrificial Death of Jesus. We can be born again because of the Atonement of Our Lord. Sinful men and women can be changed into new creatures, not by their repentance or their belief, but by the marvellous work of God in Christ Jesus which is prior to all experience. The impregnable safety of justification and sanctification is God Himself. We have not to work out these things ourselves; they have been worked out by the Atonement. The supernatural becomes natural by the miracle of God; there is the realization of what Jesus Christ has already done—"It is finished." MUH. 302

There is a difference between conscious and unconscious salvation. To be consciously saved means that we become of immense practical value to God in this order of things. NKW. 19

Salvation will never be actual until you physically commit yourself to it. NKW. 71

When I am saved by God's almighty grace I realize that I am delivered completely from what He has condemned—and *that* is salvation; I don't palliate it any longer, but agree with God's verdict on it on the Cross. At the back of all the condemnation of God put 'Calvary.' OPG. 16

Salvation to be experimental in me is always a judgment inasmuch as it is concerned with some kind of separation. 'The Cross condemns men to salvation.' OPG. 20

It is God who is the Architect of salvation, therefore salvation is not a common-sense design; what we have to do is to get inside that salvation. If I put my faith in any erection of my own, my vows and decisions, my consecration, I am building something for myself; I must co-operate with God in His plan of salvation. OPG. 20

God does not ask us to believe that men can be saved; we cannot pull men out of hell by believing that we can pull them out. When we see a man in hell, every attitude of our souls and minds are paralysed; we cannot believe he can be saved. God does not ask us to believe that he can be saved; He asks us whether we will believe that Jesus believes He can save him. PH. 32

Have patience with yourself, and remember that this is salvation not for the hereafter, but for here and now. PH. 67

The cure for triviality spiritually is a new note of greatness born of the realisation of what it cost Jesus Christ to produce His salvation in us. PH. 87

The test of Jesus Christ's salvation is that it produces Christ-likeness, a life of absolute simplicity before God. Let us be what will satisfy His heart. PH. 90

Our salvation comes to us so easily because it cost God so much. PH. 129

The Christian worker is apt to say—'Oh, well, I have been saved by God's grace and that is sufficient.' It may be sufficient for you, but if you are going to be "a workman that needeth not to be ashamed," you must do more than 'be saved,' you must take the trouble to find out what the Bible says about that salvation. PR. 19

There is no respect of persons with God for salvation, but there are degrees of position hereafter. PR. 89

There is no 'if' in connection with salvation, only in connection with discipleship. PR. 93

Unless our salvation works out through our finger tips and everywhere else, there is nothing to it, it is religious humbug. PR. 101

The centre of salvation is the Cross of Jesus Christ, and why it is so easy to obtain salvation is because it cost God so much; and why it is so difficult to experience salvation is because human conceit will not accept, nor believe, nor have anything to do with unmerited salvation. PR. 107

We have not to experience God saving the world; it is a revelation that God has saved the world through Christ, and we can enter into the experience of His salvation through the Cross. PR. 107

Salvation means the incoming into human nature of the great characteristics that belong to God, and there is no salvation that is not supernatural. PR. 121

Salvation is always supernatural. The Holy Ghost brings me into union with God by dealing with that which broke the union. It is dangerous to preach a persuasive gospel, to try and persuade men to believe in Jesus Christ with the idea that if they do, He will develop them along the natural line. Jesus Christ said, 'I did not come to send peace, but a sword'; there is something to be destroyed first. PR. 122

So many go into raptures over God's supernatural salvation, over the wonderful fact that God saves us by His sovereign grace (and we cannot do that too much), but they forget that now He expects us to get ourselves into trim to obey Him. We have to live in this mortal flesh as sons and daughters of God; we have to bring out to our finger tips the life that is hid with Christ in God, and we can do it because our ascended Lord has all power. PR. 123

We may not only be supernaturally saved, we may be supernaturally sanctified. PR. 128

If sin is a radical twist with a supernatural originator, salvation is a radical readjustment with a supernatural Originator. To present salvation as less than that is deplorable. PS. 15

. . . salvation is as radical as sin, and if God has not radically altered your heredity, thank God you may know He can by the power of Jesus Christ's Atonement. PS. 16

Salvation is the biggest, gladdest word in the world; it cannot mean pretence in any shape or form, therefore suppression is no element of the word, neither is

counteraction. Salvation is God's grace to sinful men, and it takes a lifetime to say the word properly. Most of us restrict the meaning of salvation, we use it to mean New Birth only, or something limited. PS. 24

Thank God, salvation does not mean that God turns us into milksops; God's salvation makes us for the first time into men and women. PS. 29

Thank God for His safeguarding, for His salvation which keeps us, waking and sleeping, conscious and unconscious, in danger and out of it. RTR. 55

"Enter ye in at the strait gate . . ." If a man tries to enter into salvation in any other way than Jesus Christ's way, he will find it a broad way, but the end is distress. SSM. 93

We take our salvation and our sanctification too cheaply, without realising that Jesus Christ went through the deep waters of uttermost damnation that we might have it. WG. 102

SANCTIFICATION

May God save us from the selfish meanness of a sanctified life which says, 'I am saved and sanctified, look what a wonderful specimen I am.' If we are saved and sanctified we have lost sight of ourselves absolutely, self is effaced, it is not there. BSG. 27

Our Lord does not teach a consecrated anaema, i.e., the destruction of personality: He teaches a very positive *death for ever to my right to myself*—a positive destruction of the disposition of sin and a positive placing in, in Entire Sanctification, of the Holy Spirit, a pronounced identity that bears a strong family likeness to Jesus. CD. VOL. 2, 98

The moment in which a man enters into the experience of supreme sanctification is the crisis that marks his evangelical perfection; all alien things that retarded and deformed him have been removed. Then begins his life as a Master Christian, and there is no other kind of Christian on this road. In this supreme sanctification he develops and attains height after height. CD. VOL. 2, 106

"Jesus Christ is made unto us sanctification," that is, *He* is the holy nature which we receive. CHI. 22

The process of sanctification begins at the moment of birth from above and is consummated on the unconditional surrender of my right to myself to Jesus Christ. CHI. 81

The time that elapses between new birth and entire sanctification depends entirely on the individual. CHI. 81

Individual sanctification is one thing; collective sanctification is another; when Paul talks about 'attaining unto the measure of the stature of the fulness of Christ,' he is not talking of individual saints, but of all the saints. It is the sanctification of God's people together that is required. When we isolate ourselves we hinder instead of further that end. Very few of us have got beyond the need for the searching which God gave these people. We are all too set on our own sanctification, forgetting that we are to be broken bread and poured-out wine for the lifting up of others who are not there yet. Individual sanctification has a world-wide benefit so long as the sanctified soul remains right with God. The sanctified soul keeps right with God by placing God's methods first, and God's methods are foolish to everyone who is not sanctified. GW. 75

Numbers of people say, 'I have asked God to sanctify me and He has not done it.' Of course He has not! Do we find one word in the Bible which tells us to pray, 'Lord, sanctify me'? What we do read is that God sanctifies what we give. IWP. 17

The more people there are who enter into sanctification through Jesus Christ, the more is Satan's dominance ruined. IWP. 28

Sanctification may take a few moments of realized transaction, but all the rest of the life goes to prove what that transaction means. IWP. 85

Sanctification is not our idea of what we want God to do for us, sanctification is what God does for us, and He has to get us into the right relationship, the right attitude of mind and heart, where at any cost we let Him do it. IYA. 69

People say, 'I don't understand this doctrine of sanctification.' Well, get into the experience first. You only get home by going there. You may think about getting there, but you will never get there till you go. IYA. 69

The great mighty power of the God of peace is slipped into the soul under the call for supreme sanctification. Some of us are far too turbulent in spirit to experience even the first glimpse of what sanctification means. IYA. 71

Obedience to the supremacy of the Lord Jesus is the only legitimate outcome of sanctification. Thank God, He wants us to be human, not spooks! NKW. 133

The majority of us have never allowed our minds to dwell as they should on these great massive truths; consequently sanctification has been made to mean a second dose of conversion. Sanctification can only be named in the presence of God, it is stamped by a likeness to Christ. IYA. 71

Sanctification must never be made synonymous with purification; Jesus Christ had no need of purification, and yet He used the word 'sanctify.' In the words, "I sanctify Myself," Jesus gives the key to the saint's life. MFL. 107

We take the term sanctification much too lightly. Are we prepared for what sanctification will cost? It will cost an intense narrowing of all our interests on earth, and an immense broadening of all our interests in God. Sanctification means intense concentration on God's point of view. MUH. 39

We talk as if it were the most precarious thing to live the sanctified life; it is the most secure thing, because it has Almighty God in and behind it. The most precarious thing is to try and live without God. If we are born again it is the easiest thing to live in right relationship to God and the most difficult thing to go wrong, if only we will heed God's warnings and keep in the light. MUH. 359

Sanctification means that I become a child of God, consequently my common-sense decisions are God's will unless He gives the check of His Spirit. I decide things in perfect fellowship with God, knowing that if my decisions are wrong, He will check. When He checks, I must stop at once. It is the inner check of the Spirit that prevents common sense being our god. NKW. 142

The great mighty work of God's grace in sanctification is a Divine work. OBH. 30

The meaning of sanctification is that the Son of God is formed in us; then our human nature has to be transfigured by His indwelling life, and this is where our action comes in. We have to put on the new man in accordance with the life of the Son of God in us. If we refuse to be sanctified, there is no possibility of the Son of God being manifested in us, because we have prevented our lives being turned into a Bethlehem; we have not allowed the Spirit of God to bring forth the Son of God in us. OBH. 73

Sanctification means being identified with Jesus until all the springs of our being are in Him. PH. 225

To say after sanctification, 'Now I can do what I like,' is a perilously dangerous statement. If it were true, it would never have been recorded that "even Christ pleased not Himself." PS. 50

If our experience of sanctification ends in pious sentiment, the reason is that it has never dawned on us that we must deliberately set our sanctified selves apart for God's use as Jesus did. SSY. 95

The first thing God does with us after sanctification is to 'force through the channels of a single heart' the interests of the whole world by introducing into us the nature of the Holy Ghost. The nature of the Holy Ghost is the nature of the Son of God; the nature of the Son of God is the nature of Almighty God, and the nature of the Almighty God is focused in John iii. 16. SSY. 102

SATAN

Satan thwarted God's purpose, and then laughed his devilish laugh against God, but the Bible says that God will laugh last. "The Lord shall laugh at him: for He seeth that His day is coming." BP. 16

Satanic anarchy is conscious and determined opposition to God. Wherever

God's rule is made known, Satan will put himself alongside and oppose it. Satan's sin is at the summit of all sins; man's sin is at the foundation of all sins, and there is all the difference in the world between them. BP. 24

When Satan rules, men's souls are in peace, they are not troubled or upset like other men, but quite happy and peaceful. BP. 28

Satan . . . is as subtle as God is good, and he tries to counterfeit everything God does, and if he cannot counterfeit it, he will limit it. Do not be ignorant of his devices! BP. 101

Every temptation of Satan is perfectly wise. The wisest, shrewdest, subtlest things are said by Satan, and they are accepted by everybody as the acme of human philosophy; but when the Spirit of God is at work in a man, instantly the hollow mockery at the heart of what Satan is trying to do, is seen. When we understand the inwardness of the temptation we see how Satan's strategy is turned into confusion by the Spirit of God. BSG. 30

Health and happiness is what is wanted to-day and Jesus Christ is simply exploited. We who name the Name of Christ, are we beginning to discern what Satan is after? He is trying to fatigue out of us what God has put in, viz., the possibility of being of value to God. Our only safety is to watch Our Lord and Saviour. BSG. 31

Satan did not tempt Jesus to sin, as we think of sin; he knew better. The one thing Satan aims at is that we put ourselves as master instead of God. BSG. 31

Jesus Christ deals with Satan as the manifestation of something for which

man is held responsible. Man is nowhere held responsible for the devil. DI. 75

When we say a thing is 'Satanic' we mean something abominable according to our standards: the Bible means something remarkably subtle and wise. Satanic temptations are not bestial, those temptations have to do with a man's own stupidity and wrongdoing. DI. 75

The Holy Ghost is the only One who can detect the temptations of Satan, neither our common sense nor our human wisdom can detect them as temptations. DI. 75

If Satan in his malice and cunning can slander God to His own children, he will do it because that is his whole aim. GW. 98

Satan is not removed now from the presence of the saints, but the saint is still kept in the world where the evil one rules, consequently the saint is continually being badgered by the evil one. Jesus prayed, not that we should be taken out of the world, but that we should be "kept from the evil one." IWP. 28

When a man has received the Holy Spirit, the watching of Satan is keen, his whole desire is to split up the personality. IWP. 39

God does not deal with Satan direct, man must deal with Satan because man is responsible for his introduction. That is why God became Incarnate. Put it in any other way—why God could banish Satan in two seconds; but it is man who, through the Redemption, is to overcome Satan, and much more than overcome him, he is to do that which will exhibit the perfect fulfilment of this prophecy.

Jesus Christ, the last Adam, took on Him our human form, and it is through His seed in that human form that Satan is to be overcome. OPG. 9

Satan is to be overcome and conquered by human beings. That is why God became Incarnate. It is in the Incarnation that Satan is overcome. PR. 62

Satan tried to put Jesus Christ on the way to becoming King of the world and Saviour of men in a way other than that pre-determined by God. PR. 63

For a thing to be Satanic does not mean that it is abominable and immoral. The satanically managed man is moral, upright, proud, and individual; he is absolutely self-governed and has no need of God. PR. 105

The disposition of self-realisation is the manifestation in us of the devil as Satan, and when we come to the Cross we leave Satan outside, Satan cannot take one step inside the Cross. PR. 105

The onslaught of Satan in Gethsemane was that Jesus Christ would never get through His agony as Son of Man. As Son of God, Satan could not prevent His getting through, but his challenge was that he would prevent Jesus Christ bringing one soul through with Him—and Satan was hopelessly defeated. PR. 111

It is the presence of the saints that upsets the calculations of Satan; and it is the presence of Jesus that involves not only Satan but humanity in all kinds of distractions. PS. 72

Everything that Satan and sin have marred, God holds in an unimpaired state for every son of man who will

come to Him by the way back which Jesus Christ has made. RTR. 37

There is a difference between the Devil and Satan. The Bible holds man responsible for the introduction of Satan. Adam started a communication with another of God's creations, and the result was Satan. Jesus Christ calls the self-realization point of view, "Satan," anti-Christ. SA. 86

The prince of this world and Satan are synonymous terms. Satan is the manifestation of the devil for which man is held responsible, that is, Satan is the result of a communication between man and the devil. PR. 104

Our Lord revealed that the public power of Satan would be greater in the days in which we live than ever before. 'For there shall arise false Christs, and false prophets, and shall shew great signs and wonders; so as to lead astray, if possible, even the elect.' SHL. 33

When Satan rules the hearts of natural men under the inspiration of the devil, they are not troubled, they are at peace, entrenched in clean worldliness, and before God can rule a man's kingdom He must first overthrow this false rule. SHL. 42

The one thing the prince of this world will guard against is the incoming of Jesus Christ, the 'stronger than he,' because 'he taketh from him his whole armour wherein he trusted.' SHL. 43

One of the most cunning travesties of Satan is to say that he is the instigator of drunkenness and external sins. Man himself is responsible for doing wrong things, and he does wrong things because of the wrong disposition that is in him. The true blame for sin lies in the wrong disposition, and the cunning of our nature makes us blame Satan when we should blame ourselves. SHL. 43

When men go into external sins Satan is probably as much upset as the Holy Ghost, but for a different reason. Satan knows perfectly well that when men go into external sin and upset their lives, they will want another Ruler, a Saviour, a Deliverer; but as long as he can keep them in peace and unity and harmony apart from God he will do so. SHL. 44

. . . the two things that disintegrate Satan's kingdom—breaking out into acts of sin, and conviction by the Spirit of God. This is the solution of a number of moral problems. SHL. 44

SATISFACTION

The claim of the salvation of Jesus Christ is that the Spirit of God can satisfy the last aching abyss of the human soul, not only hereafter, but here and now. Satisfaction does not mean stagnation; satisfaction is the knowledge that we have gained the right type of life for our souls. BP. 87

Every man who knows what his soul is capable of, knows its possibilities and terrors, but knows also the salvation of God, will bear equal testimony with the written Word of God that Jesus Christ can satisfy the living soul. BP. 88

Satisfaction and the demand for satisfaction is a God-given principle in human nature, but it must be satisfaction in the highest. 'Blessed are they which do hunger and thirst after righteousness: for they shall be filled.' SHL. 39

SAVIOUR

The emphasis to-day is being put on the fact that we have to save men; we have

not. We have to exalt the Saviour Who saves men, and then make disciples in His Name. BSG. 28

". . . and thou shalt call His name JESUS: for it is He that shall save His people from their sins." The character of the Name is that Jesus Christ is Saviour, and the evidence that I belong to Him is that I am delivered from sin; if I am not, I have a name to live, but am dead. HGM. 97

Think of the invincible, unconquerable, unwearying patience of Jesus—*"Come unto Me."* The attitude of coming is that you fling yourself entirely on Him, and that is salvation, because *He* is salvation. Stake your all on God, and never be impertinent enough to tell Him that that is what you are doing. *Come,* if you are weary and heavy laden; *ask,* if you are evil; and everything that happens after that is of God. HGM. 148

If we have faith that the Lord Jesus will save us, we *are* saved, and we know it. When by the Spirit of God Jesus is made real to us, His presence makes everything as natural as breathing. His presence is the reality. OBH. 22

Our Lord came here for one purpose only—to bear away the sin of the world in His own Person on the Cross. He came to redeem men, not to set them a wonderful example. PR. 55

We belittle and misrepresent the love of God when we see it merely on the surface. It is easy to think imperially, easy to think big thoughts and dream big dreams. But Jesus Christ is not big thoughts and big dreams. He is a tremendously big Saviour for little insignificant creatures such as we are. SHL. 36

SCEPTICISM

Intellectual scepticism is good, but a man is to blame for moral scepticism. Every man believes in goodness and uprightness and integrity until he perverts his taste by going wrong himself. DI. 27

Our Lord was always stern with disbelief, i.e., scepticism, because there is always a moral twist about scepticism. MFL. 20

SCIENCE

There are no 'infallible' findings, and the man who bows down to scientific findings may be as big a fool as the man who refuses to do so. BFB. 82

A scientist can explain the universe in which common-sense men live, but the scientific explanation is not first; life is first. BFB. 91

Scientists reached the conclusion long ago that they dare not produce their 'experimental curve' into the inferential region beyond. They say, according to the record of common experience such and such is the case, and any isolated experience is put by itself. They do not say it cannot be, but that it does not come into their line of explanation. No true scientist says because the majority of human beings have never had a particular experience, therefore it is untrue. BP. 257

Science is an understanding of life and the universe. If a man said he had no use for science, we should reckon him to be a fool. It is the same with regard to the Christian religion. The important thing is to be a born-again man. SA. 21

SELF

Self-denial and self-sacrifice are continually spoken of as being good in themselves; Our Lord never used any such affectation. He aimed a blow at the mistake that self-denial is an end in itself. He spoke of self-denial and self-sacrifice as painful things that cost and hurt. AUG. 52

We start out with the notion that God is an almighty piece of ourselves, but God can never be on the side of any individual; the question to ask is—'Am I on God's side?' BFB. 48

The great peril is the peril within, which men never think of as a peril. My right to myself; self-pity, self-conceit, consideration for my progress, my ways of looking at things, those things are the Satanic perils which will keep us in perfect sympathy with Satan. BP. 23

We are far too complex to understand ourselves; we must hand over the keeping of our hearts to God. If we think that we are simple and easy to understand, we shall never ask God to save us or keep us; but if we have come to the condition of the Psalmist, we will hand the keeping of our souls right over to Him and say, "Search me, O God, and know my heart: try me, and know my thoughts." BP. 133

The true centre for self is Jesus Christ. BP. 180

The reason self-interest is detected in us is because there are whole tracts of our nature that have never been fused by the Spirit of God into one central purpose. DI. 31

My self is my conscious personality, the sum-total of all I call 'me' and 'mine.' Our Lord never taught the annihilation of self, He revealed how self might be rightly centred, viz., in love to God.

Love is the highest moral issue—*'God is love.'* GW. 39

'For the whole law is fulfilled in one word, even in this: Thou shalt love thy neighbour as thyself.' The love of self that Jesus not only justified but distinctly enjoined, is the direct product of the indwelling Holy Spirit; its perversion is the deification of my self. GW. 39

All the teaching of Jesus is woven around self; I have a moral self-love to preserve for God; not, 'Oh, I'm of no account,' 'a worm,' that would spell self-less-ness. GW. 40

The Redemption deals not only with moral imperfections, but with every phase of self-interest. Self-interest in the spiritual domain is a demoralizing force, it keeps me an individual, all 'elbows'; keeps me looking after my 'rag rights' and if anyone drags them aside I am mortally offended. The only way self-interest can be effaced is by presenting my body to God as a 'living sacrifice,' that is, self-interest must be put to death, by my most deliberate wish, or it will never be put to death. As long as self-interest is there and has to be suppressed, the Holy Spirit will reveal that something else has to go. GW. 42

I surrender myself—not because it is bad, self is the best thing I have got, and I give it to God; then self-realization is lost in God-realization. There is a subtle form of pride which is set on *my* holiness; in sanctification there is no pride. Go to the death of independence of God and you will never be bothered about yourself because you and God are one. GW. 41

The word translated 'soul' or 'life' may be equally well translated 'himself,' and the verses mean just what they say. Jesus is not defining the great fundamental doctrine of personality, He is talking about the man himself, the person who lives, and with whom we come in contact. Jesus says if a man gains himself, he loses himself; and if he loses himself for His sake, he gains himself. HG. 62

God can do nothing for me if I am sufficient for myself. HGM. 16

Self-pity is taking the wrong standpoint, and if self-pity is indulged in, before long we will take part in the decaying thing instead of in that which grows more and more into the glory of God's presence. LG. 86

Jesus Christ said it was impossible for the man who is self-centred in his particular impression of himself to believe in Him. MFL. 14

If my ruling disposition is self-interest, I perceive that everything that happens to me is always for or against my self-interest; if, on the other hand, my ruling disposition is obedience to God, I perceive Him to be at work for my perfecting in everything that happens to me. MFL. 50

Self is not sinful; if it were, how could Jesus say "I sanctify Myself"? Jesus Christ had no sin to deny, no wrong self to deny; He had only a holy Self. It was that Self He denied all the time, and it was that Self that Satan tried to make Him obey. MFL. 107

It was the denying of His holy Self that made the marvellous beauty of our Lord's life. MFL. 108

Many of us are after our own ends, and Jesus Christ cannot help Himself to our lives. MUH. 55

The first thing to do in examining the power that dominates me is to take hold of the unwelcome fact that I am responsible for being thus dominated. If I am a slave to myself, I am to blame because at a point away back I yielded to myself. Likewise, if I obey God I do so because I have yielded myself to Him. MUH. 74

The little "I am" always sulks when God says *do*. Let the little "I am" be shrivelled up in God's indignation—"I AM THAT I AM hath sent thee." He must dominate. Is it not penetrating to realize that God knows where we live, and the kennels we crawl into! He will hunt us up like a lightning flash. No human being knows human beings as God does.
MUH. 278

Determinedly take no one seriously but God, and the first person you find you have to leave severely alone as being the greatest fraud you have ever known, is yourself. MUH. 327

We have to get rid of all notions about ourselves and our own standards, and keep in front what God puts in front, viz., Our Lord Himself, then we will not be tempted to delusion about ourselves. Our eye must be on God, not on ourselves. NKW. 89

Whenever self comes into the ascendant, the life of the Son of God in us is perverted and twisted; there is irritation, and His life suffers. We have to beware of every element in human nature which clamours for attention first.
OBH. 75

If you indulge in self-pity and the luxury of misery, it means that you have forgotten God, forgotten that you have been purged from your old sins, and that you have to put on the new man, in accordance with the life of the Son of God in you. OBH. 76

"If any man would come after Me, let him deny himself." Our Lord is referring to the natural self which must be denied in order that it may be made spiritual. Our Lord does not teach 'Deeper Death to Self'; He teaches death right out to my self, death right out to self-realization and self-seeking. OBH. 115

The reason so few of us see the hosts of God is that we have never let go of things as they are, never let go of our small parochial notions, of the sense of our own whiteness and respectability, consequently there is no room for God at all. OPG. 55

A self indwelt by Jesus becomes like Him. PH. 81

Self-assertion is an indication that there is a struggle going on and we have to decide who is going to rule. We rarely take the standard of the Christian life laid down in the New Testament, viz., Jesus Christ; we make excuses. If I am yearning to recover God I have to come to the place where this disposition of self-assertion is located in me. One of the reasons we lose fellowship with God is that we will explain and vindicate ourselves; we will not let God hunt through us and chase out the interests of self-will and self-assertion. PH. 168

We cannot go on spiritually if we are self-assertive. PH. 169

Beware of the pious fraud in you which says—"I have no misgivings about Jesus, only about myself." No one ever had misgivings about himself! RTR. 53

The problem of the universe is not mine but the Almighty's; the problem I am up against is the muddle inside. SA. 68

We have no business to be ignorant about ourselves. If any of us have come to manhood or womanhood with the idea that we have a holy innocence on the inside, we are desperately deluded. SHL. 48

People say, 'Oh, I can't understand myself!' Of course you cannot. 'No one else understands me!' Of course they don't; if they did, we would not be worth understanding. There is only one Being Who understands us, and that is our Creator. SHL. 54

To say, 'Oh, I'm sick of myself,' is a sure sign that we are not. When we really are sick of ourselves we will never say so, but will gladly come to the end of ourselves. So long as we say, 'I'm tired of myself,' it is a sign that we are profoundly interested in ourselves. SHL. 79

The way God brings us to know ourselves is by the kind of people He brings round us. What we see to condemn in others is either the discernment of the Holy Ghost or the reflection of what we are capable of ourselves. We always notice how obtuse other people are before we notice how obtuse we ourselves are. If we see meanness in others, it is because we ourselves are mean. SHL. 81

There is no pain on earth to equal the pain of wounded self-love. Unrequited love is bad enough, but wounded self-love is the cruellest thing in human life because it shifts the whole foundation of the life. SHL. 82

The Holy Spirit continually urges us to sign away our right to our individual self to Jesus. SHL. 84

The little 'I am' always sulks when God says Do. And the Almighty's reply to Moses is full of stirring indignation—'I AM THAT I AM hath sent thee.' The big 'I am' and the little 'I am' have to go until there is no 'I am' but God, He must dominate. Let the little 'I am' be shrivelled up in God's indignation. SSY. 30

The real centre of the disciple's devotion is watching with Jesus. When once we have learned to watch with Him, the thought of self is not kept down because it is not there to keep down; self-effacement is complete. Self has been effaced by the deliberate giving up to another self in sovereign preference, and the manifestation of the life in the actual whirl of things is—'I am not my own, but His.' SSY. 169

. . . never believe what people tell you about themselves. There is only one person in a thousand who can actually tell you his or her symptoms; and beware of the people who can tell you where they are spiritually. I mean by that, never be guided by what people tell you; rely on the Spirit of God all the time you are probing them. WG. 15

SELF-REALIZATION

Self-realization is a modern phrase—'Be moral, be religious, be upright, in order that you may realize yourself.' Nothing blinds the mind to the claims of Jesus more effectually than a good moral life based on the disposition of self-realization. BE. 81

From man's standpoint, self-realization is full of light and wisdom; from God's standpoint, it is the dark night of the soul. BE. 81

Our Lord never denounced wrong-doing and immorality so strongly as He denounced self-realization. BE. 82

Our Lord's teaching is always *anti*-self-realization. BE. 82

The teaching of self-realization is the great opponent of the doctrine of sanctification—'I have to realize myself as a separate individual, educate and develop myself so that I fulfil the purpose of my being.' BE. 88

There is nothing in the nature of self-realization or self-consciousness in our Lord. BE. 88

Wherever there is self-realization, the voice of God is a continual embarrassment. HGM. 51

Apart from Jesus Christ, conscious self-realization is the great thing—the desire to develop myself. My natural self may be noble, but it is a moral earthquake to realize that if I pursue the conscious realization of myself it must end in losing my ideal of life. It is a tremendous revelation when I realize that self-realization is the very spirit of anti-christ. HGM. 75

The great characteristic of our Lord's life is not self-realization, but the realization of God's purposes. HGM. 75

Self-realization may keep a man full of rectitude, but it is rectitude built on a basis that ultimately spells ruin, because man is not a promise of what he is going to be, but a magnificent ruin of what human nature once was. If we go on the line of conscious self-realization, there will be an aftermath of bitterness. HGM. 75

Jesus did not say—"he that believeth in Me shall realize the blessing of the fulness of God," but—"he that believeth in Me out of him shall escape everything he receives." Our Lord's teaching is always *anti*-self-realization. His purpose is not the development of a man; His purpose is to make a man exactly like Himself, and the characteristic of the Son of God is self-expenditure. MUH. 246

Jesus Christ's attitude is always that of *anti*-self-realisation. His purpose is not the development of man at all; His purpose is to make man exactly like Himself, and the characteristic of the Son of God is not self-realisation but self-expenditure. PH. 132

Nothing blinds the mind to the claims of Jesus Christ more effectually than a good, clean-living, upright life based on self-realisation. PR. 105

It is a painful process becoming conscious of one's self; we are not conscious of ourselves at the beginning of life. A child has no realization of himself as distinct from those round about him, consequently he is in complete harmony. PS. 32

The critical moment in a man or woman's life is when they realize they are individually separate from other people. When I realize I am separate from everyone else, the danger is that I think I am different from everyone else. Immediately I think that, I become a law to myself; that means I excuse everything I do, but nothing anyone else does. PS. 33

The first thing conscience does is to rouse up self-consciousness, and that produces embarrassment. A little child is full of winsome beauty because he is utterly free from self-consciousness; when he begins to be conscious of himself he becomes awkward and shy and does all kinds of affected things; and when once the conscience of man is roused by the presence of God, it produces a consciousness of self that makes us scuttle out of His presence like bats out of the light. PS. 62

The great cry to-day is, 'Fulfil yourself, work out what is in you.' If you do, you will work out your own condemnation. But if you let God deal with what is wrong, let Him 'presence you with Divinity,' you will be able to work *out* what He works *in*, which is a totally different thing. The cry to realize ourselves is the cry to keep God out. SHL. 49

The modern jargon is all for self-realization; we educate ourselves for the purpose of self-realization, we select our friendships for self-realization purposes. Jesus says, 'Whosoever will lose his life for My sake'—deliberately fling it away—'shall find it.' SHL. 78

Self-realization must be renounced in order that Jesus Christ may realize Himself in us. SHL. 86

Jesus bases everything on God-realisation, while other teachers base everything on self-realisation. SSM. 16

The three main sensibilities in a man's life are sex, money and food. SA. 73

When God created the Federal Head of the race He required him to take part in his own development by a series of moral choices, whereby he was to sacrifice his natural sensibilities to the will of God and transform them. SA. 73

SELF, RIGHT TO

Whatever the Holy Ghost detects in you, trace it down, and you will find the whole disposition of sin, i.e., my claim to my right to myself, is at the basis of that infinitesimal thing of which our mind says, 'But it cannot be that.' AUG. 61

God's right to me is killed by the incoming of my self-conscious right to myself—'I can do without God.' BE. 82

Any man would have known without His coming that it was wrong to take life, the law is written in him; any man would have known that immorality was wrong; but no man apart from Jesus Christ would believe that 'my right to myself' is the very essence of sin. BSG. 12

Naturally, a man regards his right to himself as the finest thing he has, yet it is the last bridge that prevents Jesus Christ having His way in a life. DI. 34

I may be under conscious apprehension for discipleship, and I go through the form of being willing to give up my right to myself, but the Holy Spirit reveals that I have never really done it—'I will spend myself for Jesus,' 'I will do everything He asks me to do'—but not one thing, and it is the only thing I can do, viz., give up my right to myself to Him. GW. 42

If I am going to know Jesus Christ as Lord and Master I must realize what I have to forgo, viz., the best thing I know, my right to myself. It is easy to say, 'Yes, I am delighted to be saved from hell and put right for heaven, but I don't intend to give up my right to myself.' HGM. 74

Sin is a thing I am born with and I cannot touch it; God touches sin in Redemption. In the Cross of Jesus Christ God redeemed the whole human race from the possibility of damnation through the heredity of sin. God nowhere holds a man responsible for having the heredity of sin. The condemnation is not that I am born with a heredity of sin, but if when I realize Jesus Christ came to deliver me from it, I refuse to let Him do so, from that moment I begin to get the seal of damnation. "And this is the judgment" (the critical moment), "that the light is come into the world, and men loved the darkness rather than the light." MUH. 279

When we are told we must give up our right to ourselves to Jesus Christ, we are bound to ask—if we do not ask, we have not grasped the situation thoroughly— 'Who is it that asks this tremendous devotion? Is there any principle, any cause, any enterprise on the face of the earth of such importance that a man has to give the very highest he has, viz., his right to himself, for it?' The only Being Who dare ask of me this supreme sacrifice is the Lord Jesus Christ. PH. 16

"If any man will come after Me, let him deny himself," i.e., let him give up his right to himself. No one can bring us to this denial, even God Himself cannot, we must come there of our own accord, and the length of time it takes to do so depends entirely on whether we want to come or not. If we give way to the play of our emotions and do not intend deliberately to come to the point of identification, we will get off on to spiritual sentimentality and end nowhere. PH. 158

There are myriads of right things in this world that our Lord would not touch, relationships which He described by the 'eye,' and the 'right arm.' Our right arm is not a bad thing, it is one of the best things we have, but Jesus said, 'If it offends you in your walk with Me, cut it off.' Most of us baulk this; we do not object to being delivered from sin, but we do not intend to give up the right to ourselves to Him. PR. 103

The disposition of sin is not immorality or wrongdoing, but my claim to my right to myself. SA. 104

It may take four minutes or forty years to be identified with Jesus Christ; it depends on whether I am willing to face the music, i.e., forgo my hereditary right to my claim to myself and let Him take His claim to me. SA. 108

If you have to calculate what you are willing to give up for Jesus Christ, never say that you love Him. Jesus Christ asks us to give up the best we have got to Him, our right to ourselves. There is only this one crisis, and in the majority of lives it has never been reached, we are brought up to it again and again, and every time we go back. SHL. 86

SENSUALITY

The sign that the Holy Spirit is being obeyed by me is that I am not dominated by my sensualities. "And they that are of Christ have crucified the flesh with the passions and the lusts thereof." DI. 24

We use the term rational when we should say 'sensual.' Sensuality is a word that has lost its meaning in the higher realm to us, we only talk of sensuality on the grovelling line, but sensuality reaches higher, it means that bodily satisfaction is taken as the source of life— what I possess, what I feel, that is not rationalism but sensuality, and when it is allowed to dominate it works out as Paul says—they "became vain in their reasonings, and their senseless heart was darkened." IWP. 73

All fanaticism and the things that are foreign to the teachings of Jesus Christ start from spiritual sensuality, which means I have images in my mind of what I want to be, and what I am, and what I have experienced. IWP. 75

We mean by 'sensuality,' the life that draws its sustenance from natural surroundings, guided by a selfishly appointed purpose. We used to mean by sensuality gross awful and shocking sins; the world means that but a great deal more. Sensuality may be refined down to the thinness of a cloud. It is quite possible to be grossly sensual and spiritual. It is possible to say, 'I have one desire in being good, in being saved and sanctified, a particular end of my own'; that is sensuality. PS. 14

Sensuality is not sin, it is the way my body works in connexion with external circumstances whereby I begin to satisfy myself. Sensuality will work in a man who is delivered from sin by Jesus Christ as well as in a man who is not. I do not care what your experience may be as a Christian, you may be trapped by sensuality at any time. SA. 70

"Mortify the deeds of the body," mortify means to destroy by neglect. One of the first big moral lessons a man has to learn is that he cannot destroy *sin* by neglect; sin has to be handled by the Redemption of Jesus Christ, it cannot be handled by me. SA. 70

Whenever I utilize myself for my own ends, I am giving way to sensuality, and it is done not only physically, but mentally also, and one of the most humiliating things for a Christian is to realize how he does it. The impertinence of mental sensuality lies in the refusal to deny the right of an undisciplined intelligence that is contrary to Jesus Christ. SA. 71

Never attempt to solve outside problems first. If sin is to be destroyed in my personal life on the basis of Redemption, it is to be destroyed outside me also; if sensuality is to be mortified in my personal life, it is to be mortified outside me also. SA. 76

SEPARATION

All through the Bible the separation of a people by God is revealed, and the individual members of that people have to separate themselves to God's service. We are set apart that we may set ourselves apart. God Who requires the separation requires also that the person be sanctified intrinsically too. IYA. 66

Separation unto God is the first characteristic—separation unto God for food, for clothing, for money, for the next step. It is a 'going out' of all your 'kindred' and 'house' ways of looking at things, a 'going out' with nothing in view, but being perfectly certain that you are separated unto God. LG. 146

Jesus Christ knew and tasted to a fuller depth than any man could ever taste what it is to be separated from God by sin. PS. 18

SERMON ON THE MOUNT (BEATITUDES)

The Sermon on the Mount is not a set of principles to be obeyed apart from identification with Jesus Christ. The Sermon on the Mount is a statement of the life we will live when the Holy Spirit is getting His way with us. PR. 34

Jesus Christ does not lay down the statements in the Sermon on the Mount as principles and say, 'Now work them out,' He is describing what the new life is in its working from His standpoint. PR. 34

There is no cunning in the Sermon on the Mount. As long as we deal on the line of craft and cunning, Jesus Christ is no good to us. We can easily make a fool of goodness. SHH. 43

The motive at the back of the precepts of the Sermon on the Mount is love of God. Read the Beatitudes with your mind fixed on God, and you will realise their neglected side. Their meaning in relationship to men is so obvious that it scarcely needs stating, but the Godward aspect is not so obvious. "Blessed are the poor in spirit"—towards God. Am I a pauper towards God? Do I know I cannot prevail in prayer; I cannot blot out the sins of the past; I cannot alter my disposition; I cannot lift myself nearer to God? Then I am in the very place where I am able to receive the Holy Spirit. No man can receive the Holy Spirit who is not convinced he is a pauper spiritually. "Blessed are the meek"—towards God's dispensations. "Blessed are the merciful"—to God's reputation. Do I awaken sympathy for myself when I am in trouble? Then I am slandering God because the reflex thought in people's minds is—How hard God is with that man. It is easy to slander God's character because He never attempts to vindicate Himself. "Blessed are the pure in heart"—that is obviously Godward. "Blessed are the peacemakers"—between God and man, the note that was struck at the birth of Jesus. SSM. 15

To treat the Sermon on the Mount merely as an ideal is misleading. It is not an ideal, it is a statement of the working out of Jesus Christ's disposition in actuality in the life of any man. SSM. 92

The teaching of the Sermon on the Mount produces despair only in a man who is not born again. SSM. 93

As we study the Sermon on the Mount we find that we are badgered by the Spirit of God from every standpoint in order to bring us into a simplicity of relationship to Jesus Christ. The standard is that of a child depending upon God. SSM. 99

The Sermon on the Mount is not an ideal, because an ideal must have as its working power the possibility of its realization in the disposition obsessed by it. 'Love your enemies'; 'Give to him that asketh thee'; these things have no place in the natural disposition of a man. Jesus Christ is the only One Who can fulfil the Sermon on the Mount. SSY. 64

SERVICE

This Loneliness in Service is so subtle that if we try and state it in words we almost lose it. It is so easy to coarsen this sublime theme by a word misunderstood, so difficult to put it in any language saving when the heart is in profoundest communion with God. CD. VOL. 2, 111

Remember you are accountable to no one but God; keep yourself for His service along the line of His providential leading for you, not on the line of your temperament. AUG. 25

The only way to be sent is to let God lift us right out of any sense of fitness in ourselves and place us where He will. AUG. 26

The Cross is the great opening through which all the blood of Christian service runs. AUG. 55

Beware of the tendency of trying to do what God alone can do, and of blaming God for not doing what we alone can do. BP. 119

. . . our service is not to be that of pity, but of personal, passionate love to God, and a longing to see many more brought to the centre where God has brought us. BP. 184

The greatest service you can render God is to fulfil your spiritual destiny. DI. 86

Whenever we go into work for God from any standpoint saving that of the dominance of God, we begin to patronize at once; unless we go as the bondservants of Jesus Christ we have no business to go at all. Jesus Christ became the towel-girt Servant of His own disciples. GW. 74

We have a way of saying—'What a wonderful power that man or woman would be in God's service.' Reasoning on man's broken virtues makes us fix on the wrong thing. The only way any man or woman can ever be of service to God is when he or she is willing to renounce all their natural excellencies and determine to be weak in Him—'I am here for one thing only, for Jesus Christ to manifest Himself in me.' That is to be the steadfast habit of a Christian's life. MFL. 106

Beware of anything that competes with loyalty to Jesus Christ. The greatest competitor of devotion to Jesus is service for Him. It is easier to serve than to be drunk to the dregs. The one aim of the call of God is the satisfaction of God, not a call to do something for Him. We are not sent to battle for God, but to be used by God in His battlings. MUH. 18

Jesus Christ calls service what we are to Him, not what we do for Him. MUH. 171

Jesus Christ says, in effect, Don't rejoice in successful service, but rejoice because you are rightly related to Me. MUH. 243

Jesus Christ has no tenderness whatever toward anything that is ultimately going to ruin a man in the service of God. Our Lord's answers are based not on caprice, but on a knowledge of what is in man. If the Spirit of God brings to your mind a word of the Lord that hurts you, you may be sure that here is something He wants to hurt to death. MUH. 271

The measure of our service for God is not our usefulness to others. We have nothing to do with the estimate of others, nor with success in service; we have to see that we fulfil our ministry. "As Thou has sent Me into the world, even so have I also sent them into the world." PR. 108

We are here with no right to ourselves, for no spiritual blessing for ourselves; we are here for one purpose only—to be made servants of God as Jesus was. PS. 17

. . . "to serve the living God." This means a life laid down for Jesus, a life of narrowed interests, a life that deliberately allows itself to be swamped by a crowd of paltry things. It is not fanaticism, it is the stedfast, flint-like attitude of heart and mind and body for one purpose—spoilt for everything saving as we can be used to win souls for Jesus. PS. 22

My contact with the nature of God has made me realize what I can do for God. Service is the outcome of what is fitted to my nature; God's call is fitted to His nature, and I never hear His call until I have received His nature. When I have received His nature, then His nature and mine work together; the Son of God reveals Himself in me, and I, the natural man, serve the Son of God in ordinary ways, out of sheer downright devotion to Him. SSY. 12

Be ready for the sudden surprise visits of Our Lord, and remember there is no such thing as prominent service and obscure service; it is all the same with God, and God knows better than ourselves what we are ready to do.   SSY. 39

We are not here for successful service, but to be faithful.   SSY. 170

God grant that His choice may fall on everyone of us, and that we may learn with patience and discipline how He is going to teach us to be patient, to be powerful and to be passionate in His service! Never losing heart, never being discouraged, never being excited over a big catch. Many a worker has rendered himself useless to God by his undue hilarity over a big revival for God. "Notwithstanding in this rejoice not, that the spirits are subject to you," said Jesus; "but rather rejoice, because your names are written in heaven."   WG. 85

SHALLOW/PROFOUND

Beware of posing as a profound person; God became a Baby.   MUH. 327

We are all so abominably serious, so interested in our own characters, that we refuse to behave like Christians in the shallow concerns of life. Our safeguard is the God-given shallowness. It is the attitude of a spiritual prig to go about with a countenance that is a rebuke to others because you have the idea that they are shallower than you. Live the surface common-sense life in a common-sense way, and remember that the shallow concerns of life are as much of God as the profound concerns.   NKW. 68

It is not our devotion to God or our holiness that makes us refuse to be shallow, but our wish to impress others that we are not shallow, which is a sure sign that we are prigs. We are to be of the stamp of Our Lord and Master, and the prigs of

His day called Him a glutton and a wine-bibber, they said He was not dealing with the profound things. Beware of the production of contempt for others by thinking that they are shallow.   NKW. 69

To be shallow is not a sign of being wicked: the ocean has a shore. The shallow amenities of life are appointed of God and are the things in which Our Lord lived, and He lived in them as the Son of God. It is easier for personal pride not to live in them.   NKW. 69

Right views on profound subjects will always be the spring of right relationships in shallow matters.   NKW. 139

Our lives are lived in two compartments, the shallow and the profound, and both domains are to be God's. There is always the temptation to live only in the profound, and to despise others for not understanding our profundity. We are apt to forget that God is in the shallow as well as in the profound. We have to see that we live our shallow life in as godly a manner as we live the profound.   PH. 120

The majority of us are shallow, we do not bother our heads about Reality. We are taken up with actual comforts, with actual ease and peace, and when the Spirit of God comes in and disturbs the equilibrium of our life we prefer to ignore what He reveals.   PR. 122

SHOW BUSINESS

There was no 'show business' with the Son of God, and there is to be no 'show business' with the saints.   BSG. 32

The 'show business' belongs to the pagan order of things; devotion to God in actual human conditions belongs to the Redemptive order. A Christian is one who has learned to live the life hid with Christ in God in human conditions. NKW. 132

SIGHT

You must do what you see, or become blind in that particular. BE. 58

Our eyes record to the brain what they look at, but our disposition makes our eyes look at what it wants them to look at, and they will soon pay no attention to anything else. When the disposition is right, the eyes, literally the body, may be placed wherever you like and the disposition will guard what it records. BP. 73

Seeing is never believing: we interpret what we see in the light of what we believe. HGM. 70

When I commit myself to Jesus I begin to see properly. No man believes what he sees unless he believes before he sees. "Because thou hast seen Me, hast thou believed? Blessed are they who have not seen, and yet have believed." HGM. 98

We long for something that is not and shut our eyes to the thing that is. When the Lord Jesus awakens us to reality by new birth and brings us in contact with Himself, He does not give us new fathers and mothers and new friends; He gives us new sight, that is, we focus our eyes on the things that are near and they become wonderfully distant. "Put thy distance on the near." This craving to go somewhere else, to see the things that are distant, arises from a refusal to attend to what is near. MFL. 62

The eye records exactly what it looks at, and conscience may be called the eye of the soul. A 'single eye' is essential to correct understanding spiritually. MFL. 114

Jesus says that if our eye is evil, we shall misjudge what He does. If our spirits are untouched by God's Spirit, unillumined by God, the very light we have will become darkness. MFL. 115

In human sight we soon lose the innocence of sight; we know what we see, but instead of trusting the innocence of sight we confuse it by trying to state what we ought to see. Jesus restores the spiritual innocence of sight—"Except a man be born again, he cannot *see* the kingdom of God." Paul said that he was sent by God *'to open men's eyes.'* OBH. 76

We can enter into His Kingdom whenever the time comes for us to see it. We cannot see a thing until we do see it, but we must not be blind and say we don't see it when we do, and if we are enthusiastic saints we must not be too much disturbed about the fellow who does not see. At any second he may turn the corner of an agony and say, "I thought those other fellows were mad, but now I am prepared to see as they do." SA. 41

Jesus Christ says, "Come unto Me, and I will give you rest," i.e., I will put you in the place where your eyes are open. And notice what Jesus Christ says we will look at—lilies, and sparrows, and grass. What man in his senses bothers about these things! We consider aeroplanes and tanks and shells, because these demand our attention, the other things do not. SHH. 75

We see our friend, the other man sees a fellow in a tunic, we *perceive* the man inside the tunic. SHH. 75

The salvation of Jesus Christ enables a man to see for the first time in his life, and it is a wonderful thing. SHH. 75

'Verily, verily, I say unto thee, except a man be born again, he cannot see the kingdom of God.' The power of vision which the new birth gives refers to perception by the personal spirit, and the characteristic of being born from above is that you begin to discern the rule of God. God's rule was there all the time, but true to His nature; now you have received His nature, you can perceive His rule. SSY. 11

Jesus never tells us what to see, but when His touch is upon our eyes, we know that we see what He is seeing, He restores this pristine innocence of sight. 'Except a man be born again, he cannot *see* the kingdom of God.' SSY. 90

It is a great thing to have our spiritual sight tested by the Celestial Optician, to watch the way in which He rectifies and readjusts our sight. SSY. 134

SILENCE

It is only when our lives are hid with Christ in God that we learn how to be silent unto God, not silent about Him, but silent with the strong restful certainty that all is well, behind everything stands God, and the strength of the soul is that it knows it. IWP. 91

Because Jesus Christ keeps silence it does not mean that He is displeased, but exactly the opposite, He is bringing us into the great run of His purpose, and the answer will be an amazing revelation. IYA. 52

SIMPLICITY

There is nothing simple under heaven saving a man's relationship to God on the ground of the Redemption. BFB. 17

God is never subtle in His revelations, but always elemental and simple. The 'simple Gospel' does not mean simple to understand, but simple in the way God Himself is simple. BFB. 80

The restoration of a man by our Lord gives him simplicity and simplicity always shows itself in actions. Do not mistake simplicity for stupidity. By 'simplicity' is meant the simplicity that was in Jesus Christ. BP. 206

There is nothing simple under heaven saving the personal relationship to Jesus Christ, and Paul is concerned lest any philosophy should come in to corrupt that simplicity, the simplicity of an understanding relationship between God and our own soul. BSG. 66

I believe our Lord is repeatedly astounded at the stupidity we display. It is notions of our own that make us stupid; when we are simple we are never stupid, we discern all the time. 'Lord, shew us the Father'; 'Shew me Thy face'; 'Expound this thing to me'; and His answer comes straight back to our heart: 'Have I been so long time with you, and yet hast thou not known *Me*?' GW. 25

Beware of making simple what the Bible does not. The line of our simplicity is in Christ—'I am the Way, the Truth, and the Life.' The way the simplicity that is in Christ is corrupted is by trying to live according to a statement made by men's heads. It must be the relationship of a child all through. GW. 108

We shall never see God's point of view as long as we bring our own ideas to Him and dictate to God what we expect Him to do. We must become as little children, be essentially simple, keep our minds brooding on what God tells us to brood on, and let God do as He likes.

The difficulties come because we will not be simple enough to take God at His word. MFL. 68

The essential element in life of a saint is simplicity—"thy whole body shall be full of light." MFL. 114

The only simplicity there is, is a simplicity of life which is true to Jesus, not to a theory about Him. RTR. 22

The only simple thing in human life is our relationship to God in Christ. SA. 67

The essential element in the life of a saint is simplicity, and Jesus Christ makes the motive of godliness gloriously simple, viz., Be carefully careless about everything saving your relationship to Me. SSM. 16

Notice the essential simplicity of our Lord's teaching all through—right towards God, right towards God. SSM. 60

When we transacted business with the sovereign Christ, the misgiving in our heart was that it was too simple. The simplicity is the very thing that is of Jesus; anything that is not simple is not of Him. Anything that is complicated is not of His sovereignty, but of our self-interest, our self-will, our self-consideration. SSY. 134

'If ye abide in me, and my words abide in you.' We have continually to pull ourselves up short and recognize the amazing simplicity of Jesus Christ's counsel. SSY. 136

We live in a complex world, amid such a mass of sensibilities and impressionabilities that we are apt to imagine that it is the same with God. It is our complicated rationalism that makes the difficulty. We have to beware of every

simplicity saving the simplicity that is in Christ. SSY. 157

The key to missionary devotion is put in our hand at the outset, 'For His name's sake they went forth.' The key is amazingly simple, as is everything connected with Our Lord. Our difficulties arise when we lose the key, and we lose the key by not being simple. SSY. 157

SIN, BODY OF

There are two Mystical Bodies, the Body of Christ and the body of sin, both are outside me. The disposition of sin inside me, called the 'old man,' connects me with the body of sin; when I am born from above I have the disposition of holiness imparted to me, and this connects me with the Body of Christ and I go to the death of the 'old man,' and in this way the body of sin is going to be destroyed. BE. 69

The Bible refers to two mystical bodies—the Body of Christ and the body of sin; the Head of the one is God, the head of the other is the devil. GW. 84

The body of sin stands as the counterpart of the Mystical Body of Christ. The fountain head of the body of sin is the devil; the Fountain Head of the mystical body of Christ is God. IWP. 27

Christ became identified not only with the disposition of sin, but with the very "body" of sin. He had not the disposition of sin in Himself, and no connection with the body of sin, but, "Him who knew no sin, He made *to be sin.*" Jesus Christ went straight through identification with sin so that every man and woman on earth might be freed from sin by His atonement. He went through the depths of damnation and came out more than conqueror; consequently every one of us who is willing to be identified with Him is freed from the disposition of sin, freed from the connection with the body of sin, and can come out more than conqueror too because of what Jesus Christ has done. SA. 120

The Bible reveals that there is a solidarity of sin, a bond of union, that keeps men together known as 'the body of sin'; it is the mutual inheritance of the human race. SHL. 44

SIN, CLEANSING FROM

Cleansing from all sin by the blood of Jesus is far deeper than we can be conscious of, it is cleansing from all sin in the sight of God because the disposition of His Son is working out in every particular, not to our consciousness, but deeper than our consciousness. We are not cleansed more and more from all sin, if we walk in the light, as God is in the light, we *are* cleansed from all sin. In our consciousness it works with a keen poignant knowledge of what sin is. SHL. 50

SIN, CONVICTION OF

Conviction of sin and being guilty of sins are not the same thing. Conviction of sin is produced by the incoming of the Holy Spirit because conscience is promptly made to look at God's demands and the whole nature cries out, in some form or other, "What must I do to be saved?" BE. 76

When a man gets convicted of sin (which is the most direct way of knowing that there is a problem at the basis of life), he knows that he cannot carry the burden of it; he also knows that God dare not forgive him; if He did, it would

mean that man's sense of justice is bigger than God's. BFB. 42

The Holy Spirit convicts of sin, man does not. BP. 37

A man says—'My heart is not bad, I am not convicted of sin; all this talk about being born again and filled with the Holy Spirit is so much absurdity.' The natural heart needs the Gospel of Jesus, but it does not want it, it will fight against it, and it takes the convicting Spirit of God to make men and women know they need to experience a radical work of grace in their hearts. BP. 139

A sinner, i.e., one convicted of sin, is the only one who is in a fit state to understand why Jesus came. When God became Incarnate in Jesus Christ for the purpose of removing sin, men saw nothing in Him to desire. Jesus Christ is 'disadvantaged' in the eyes of everyone not convicted of sin. BSG. 46

A man does not need the Holy Spirit to tell him that external sins are wrong, ordinary culture and education will do that; but it does take the Holy Spirit to convict us of sin as our Lord defined it— *"because they believe not on Me."* HG. 107

What one longs to see more often is a soul shattered under the convicting blast of the Holy Ghost. It means that Jesus Christ has seen of the travail of His soul in that one, and it is one of the rarest sights. HG. 108

When the Spirit of God convicts of sin it is not like a detective convicting a criminal, it is sin finding out a man's own nature and making him say, 'Yes, I recognize it.' When once your sin does find you out, the exquisite pain of confessing acts like the sweetest medicine—"a broken and a contrite heart, O God, Thou wilt not despise." HGM. 132

Talk about conviction of sin! I wonder how many of us have ever had one five minutes' conviction of sin. It is the rarest thing to know of a man or woman who has been convicted of sin. IWP. 25

I am not sure but that if in a meeting one or two people came under the tremendous conviction of the Holy Ghost, the majority of us would not advocate they should be put in a lunatic asylum, instead of referring them to the Cross of Christ. IWP. 25

... when once the Spirit of God convicts a man of sin, it is either suicide or the Cross of Christ, no man can stand such conviction long. IWP. 26

In the spiritual domain when a man is convicted of sin, he realises that there are deeper depths in himself than he has ever known, and the things that can be clearly explained become utterly shallow, there is no guidance whatever in them. MFL. 43

If I build my life on the things which God did not form He will have to destroy them, shake them back into chaos. That is why whenever a man, moral or immoral, sees for the first time the light of God in Jesus Christ it produces conviction of sin, and he cries out, "Depart from me; for I am a sinful man, O Lord." OPG. 2

When the Holy Spirit gets hold of a man and convicts him of sin, he instantly gets to despair, for he recognises that the holiness of Jesus Christ is the only thing that can ever stand before God, and he knows there is no chance for him.
PR. 122

No man can have his state of mind altered without suffering for it in his body, and that is why men do anything to avoid conviction of sin. SHL. 41

When a man is convicted of sin he knows how terrific is the havoc sin has wrought in him and he knows with what a mighty salvation he has been visited by God; but it is only by obedience to the Holy Spirit that he begins to know what an awful thing sin is. SHL. 62

SIN/SINS

For a long while we can ignore sin and dwell on the fact that God is our Father, but if we mean by that that He forgives sin because He is loving, we make the Atonement a huge blunder and Calvary a mistake. AUG. 100

... in the Cross God "condemned *sin* in the flesh," not sins. Sins I look after; sin God looks after. The Redemption deals with sin. BE. 68

Sin is not a creation, it is a relationship set up between the devil (who is independent entirely of God) and the being God made to have communion with Himself. BE. 82

If you are not struggling, you don't need to bother your head; but if it is a struggle worthy of the name, remember the only way out is by coming to Jesus. So long as I have no struggle, no sense of sin, I can do well enough without Him. BE. 93

The trouble with the modern statements regarding sin is that they make sin far too slight. Sin according to the modern view simply means selfishness, and preachers and teachers are as dead against selfishness as the New Testament is. BE. 115

Sin is not wrong doing, it is wrong *being,* deliberate and emphatic independence of God. That may sound remote and far away from us, but in individual experience it is best put in the terms of 'my claim to my right to myself.' BE. 115

The characteristic of sin is to destroy the capacity to know we sin, and the Bible talks about unregenerate men as 'dead,' not dead physically, but dead towards God. BE. 116

The Bible distinctly states that sin is not the natural result of being a finite being, but a definite stepping aside from what that finite being knew to be right. BE. 116

The New Testament says Jesus became literally identified with the sin of the human race. "Him who knew no sin," (here language almost fails) *"He made to be sin on our behalf,"* for one purpose only—"that we might become the righteousness of God in Him." BSG. 26

The essence of sin is my claim to my right to myself. BSG. 50

During the ages human history proves that sin in man makes his heart naturally atheistic. CD. VOL. 2, 136

Sin is mutiny against God's rule; not vileness of conduct, but red-handed anarchy. CHI. 17

Whenever you talk about sin, it must be 'my' sin. So long as you speak of 'sins' you evade Jesus Christ for yourself. DI. 62

God deals with every bit of sin in the light of the purest justice. GW. 86

We shall find over and over again that God will send us shuddering to our knees every time we realize what sin is,

and instead of it increasing hardness in us towards the men and women who are living in sin, the Spirit of God will use it as a means of bringing us to the dust before Him in vicarious intercession that God will save them as He has saved us. HG. 89

Sin is not measured by a law or by a social standard, but by a Person. The Holy Spirit is unmistakable in His working: "and He, when He is come, will convict the world in respect of sin, . . . *because they believe not on Me."* That is the very essence of sin. HG. 107

As long as Jesus Christ will remain the 'meek and mild and gentle Jesus' I will listen to Him, but immediately He sets His face against my particular sin, my un-righteousness, my self-indulgence, I am going to have no more of Him; then the nemesis comes, and I realize that I am siding with the forces which are against Jesus Christ. HGM. 40

Any deflection in obedience to God is a sin. MFL. 46

Sin is the disposition of my right to myself, and it is also independence of God. These two aspects of sin are strikingly brought out in the Bible. Sin has to be dealt with from the ethical and intellectual aspect as well as from the spiritual aspect. MFL. 122

Many people are never guilty of gross sins, they are not brought up in that way, they are too refined, have too much good taste; but that does not means that the disposition to sin is not there. The essence of sin is my claim to my right to myself. I may prefer to live morally because it is better for me: I am responsible to no one, my conscience is my god. That is the very essence of sin. MFL. 22

To be born of God means that I have the supernatural power of God to stop sinning. In the Bible it is never—Should a Christian sin? The Bible puts it emphatically—*A Christian must not sin.* The effective working of the new birth life in us is that we do not commit sin, not merely that we have the power not to sin, but that we have stopped sinning. 1 John iii. 9 does not mean that we *cannot* sin; it means that if we obey the life of God in us, we *need not* sin.
MUH. 228

Sin is a fundamental relationship; it is not wrong doing, it is wrong *being,* deliberate and emphatic independence of God. The Christian religion bases everything on the positive, radical nature of sin. Other religions deal with sins; the Bible alone deals with sin. MUH. 281

No man knows what sin is until he is born again. MUH. 361

Divorce stands for apostasy. We must be *divorced* from sin, not separated from sin. NKW. 104

Sin belongs to hell and the devil; I, as a child of God, belong to heaven and God, and I must have nothing to do with sin in any shape or form. NKW. 105

Remember, we cannot touch sin.
NKW. 149

Sin is nothing but a big bully. Sin was killed at the Cross of Christ; it has no power at all over those who are set free by the Atonement of Jesus and are prosecuting their life in Him. OBH. 113

A doctrine which has insinuated itself right into the heart of Christianity and has a hold on it like an octopus, is the inveterate belief that sin is in matter, therefore as long as there is any 'matter'

about me there must be sin in me. If sin were in matter it would be untrue to say that Jesus Christ was "without sin" because He took on Him our flesh and blood, "becoming in the likeness of men." OPG. 4

Sin is not part of human nature as God designed it, it is extraneous. OPG. 7

The Bible always speaks of sin as it appears in its final analysis. Jesus does not say, 'You must not covet because it will lead to stealing'; He says, 'You must not covet because it *is* stealing.' He does not say, 'You must not be angry with your brother because it will lead to murder"; He says, 'You must not be angry with your brother it is murder." "Whosoever hateth his brother is a murderer." When the climax of these things is reached we begin to see the meaning of Calvary.
OPG. 70

There is a difference between sin and sins; sin is a disposition, and is never spoken of as being forgiven, a disposition must be cleansed. Sins are acts for which we are responsible. Sin is a thing we are born with, and we cannot touch it; God touches sin in redemption. PR. 35

By His bearing away the sin of the world, the way is opened up for every human being to get to God as if there had been no sin. PR. 48

The revelation in the Bible is not that Jesus Christ was punished for our *sins;* but that He took on Him the *sin* of the human race and put it away—an infinitely profounder revelation. PR. 49

Watch how our Lord faced men, He always faced this disposition of sin, He never summed men up by their external conduct. He was not driven into panics by immorality and fleshly sordidness, that sort of sin never seemed to bother Him half as much as the respectable pride of men and women who never were guilty of those things. PS. 14

It is only the right view of sin and right thinking about sin that ever will explain Jesus Christ's Life and Death and Resurrection. It is sin that He came to cope with; He did not come to cope with the poor little mistakes of men, they cope with their own mistakes; He came to give them a totally new stock of heredity, that is, He came to implant into them His own nature, so that Satan's power in the soul is absolutely destroyed, not counteracted. PS. 16

The possibility of sin and the inclination to sin are different things. Every man has the possibility of committing murder, but the inclination is not there. The inclination is as the deed, whether it is carried out or not. PS. 54

Sin is a relationship between two of God's creations. SA. 46

'Let your loins be girded about.' It is impossible to run in the loose Eastern garments unless they are girt up. The writer to the Hebrews counsels us to 'lay aside every weight, and the sin which doth closely cling to us.' He is not speaking of inbred sin, but of the circumambient sin, the spirit of the religious age in which we live, which will entangle the feet of the saint and hinder his running the race. SSY. 36

SINLESSNESS

Beware of the people who teach that though a man's body may sin, his soul does not. BP. 51

The doctrine of sinless perfection and consequent freedom from temptation runs on the line that because I am sanctified, I cannot now do wrong. If that is so, you cease to be a man. If God put us in such a condition that we could not disobey, our obedience would be of no value to Him. But blessed be His Name, when by His redemption the love of God is shed abroad in our hearts, He gives us something to do to manifest it. CHI. 89

The life of God in me does not sin. If I am based on the Redemption, this standard will manifest itself in the actual moments of my life, viz., I must not sin. It is not something I set myself to do, but something I know I never can do, therefore I let God do it. HG. 116

Born from above, I realize that the life of God has entered into me. God gives me 'Himself.' "The gift *of God* is eternal life" and 'eternal life' consciously in me is to know God. The life of God cannot commit sin, and if I will obey the life of God, which has come into me by regeneration, it will manifest itself in my mortal flesh. It is only when I disobey the life of God that I commit sin; then I must get back again into the light by confession. If I walk in the light as God is in the light, sin is not. HG. 117

According to that statement of the Apostle John no one is free from sin unless he is possessed of all the virtues. The Apostle is not teaching sinless perfection; he is teaching perfect sinlessness, which is a different matter. IWP. 59

The one thing that will enable us to stop sinning is the experience of new birth, i.e., entire sanctification. When we are born into the new realm the life of God is born in us, and the life of God in us cannot sin. That does not mean that we *cannot* sin; it means that if we obey the life of God in us, we *need not* sin. PR. 35

The sinless perfection heresy arises out of this confusion—it says that because the disposition of sin is removed, it is impossible to sin. The inclination to sin, thank God, is removed, but never the possibility. PS. 55

No good man is impeccable, that is, he never arrives at the place where it is impossible to sin. A man is able not to sin, but it never becomes impossible for him to sin. "Whosoever is born of God doth not commit sin; for his seed remaineth in him; and he cannot sin, because he is born of God." SHH. 100

SINNER

The sinner is absolutely solitary on God's earth, and as long as he remains proud in his solitariness he goes against everything that is anything like God; he goes against man, who is like God, and against the earth, which is also like God, and both man and earth cry out to God against him all the time. BE. 28

The Garden of Eden was closed, not to naughty children, but to sinners, and is never again opened to sinners. "The way of the tree of life" is guarded, preventing man getting back as a sinner; he only gets back, and thank God he does get back, in and through the Redemption. CHI. 65

The Cross of Christ spells hope for the most despairing sinner on the face of the earth. ". . . the Son of man hath power on earth to forgive sins." CHI. 97

'God loves the man, but hates the sinner,' although not scriptural, conveys the idea. God dare not love the sinner. When God saves a sinner, profoundly speaking, and only profoundly speaking, He does not save the sinner: He saves the man who is a sinner by removing the sinner out of him. GW. 85

A sinner can never stand in the presence of God; there is no justification whatever for sin in His presence, that is why a man convicted of sin has such a desperate time, he realizes with the Psalmist—'Against Thee, Thee only, have I sinned, and done this evil in Thy sight.' GW. 85

The surest evidence that the nature of God has come into me is that I know I am a sinner—"I know that in me (that is, in my flesh,) dwelleth no good thing." When God has made me know what I am really like in His sight, it is no longer possible for me to be annoyed at what others may tell me I am capable of; God has revealed it to me already. OBH. 58

When once we have had a dose of the plague of our own heart, we will never want to vindicate ourselves. The worst things that are said about us may be literally untrue; but we know that whatever is said is not so bad as what is really true of us in the sight of God. OBH. 58

Nothing associates itself with the sinner saving his sin. Once sin enters in, you are out of gear with God morally and with the universe physically. OPG. 11

It is impossible for a man to go wrong easily; he may drift a tremendously long way easily, he may come to have different standards easily; but if a man has known better than he does now, he has not arrived there easily. "The way of transgressors is hard." PH. 227

Jesus Christ came to save us so that there should be no 'sinner' left in us. PS. 25

Nowadays we have come to the conclusion that a man must be a down-and-out sinner before he needs Jesus Christ to do anything for him; consequently we debase Jesus Christ's salvation to mean merely that He can save the vile and sensual man and lift him into a better life. We quote our Lord's statement that 'the Son of Man came to seek and to save that which was lost' and misinterpret His meaning by limiting 'the lost' to those who are lost in our eyes.   SHL. 40

SLEEP

The deepest concerns of our souls, whether they be good or bad, are furthered during sleep. It is not merely a physical fact that you go to bed perplexed and wake clear-minded; God has been ministering to you during sleep. HG. 39

Sometimes God cannot get at us until we are asleep.   HG. 39

Often when a problem or perplexity harasses the mind and there seems no solution, after a night's rest you find the solution easy, and the problem has no further perplexity. Think of the security of the saint in sleeping or in waking, "Thou shalt not be afraid for the terror by night, nor for the arrow that flieth by day."   HG. 39

SOCIAL REFORM (SOCIABILITY)

Our Lord insists on the social aspect of our lives; He shows very distinctly that we cannot further ourselves alone. BP. 165

The social worker who does not know what Jesus Christ came to do will end in absolute despair before long, because the social worker more than anyone else begins to see the enormous havoc that sin has made of human nature, and if he does not know the Saviour from sin, all his efforts will meet with as much suc-

cess as attempting to empty the Atlantic Ocean with a thimble.   HG. 88

The external character of the life of our Lord was that of radiant sociability; so much so, that the popular scandal-mongering about Him was that He was "a gluttonous man and a winebibber, a friend of publicans and sinners!" The fundamental reason for our Lord's sociability was other than they knew; but His whole life was characterised with a radiant fulness, it was not an exhausted type of life. "Except ye become as little children . . ."   PH. 197

Jesus Christ is not a social reformer; He came to alter *us* first, and if any social reform is to be done on earth, we will have to do it.   PR. 65

Social reform is part of the work of ordinary honourable humanity and a Christian does it because his worship is for the Son of God, not because he sees it is the most sensible thing to do. The first great duty of the Christian is not to the needs of his fellow-men, but to the will of his Saviour.   PR. 65

God won't clear up our social conditions; Jesus Christ is not a social Reformer, He came to alter us first, and if there is any social reform done on earth, we will have to do it.   SA. 90

To-day the great craze is socialism, and men are saying that Jesus Christ came as a social reformer. Nonsense! We are the social reformers; Jesus Christ came to alter us, and we try to shirk our responsibility by putting our work on Him. Jesus alters us and puts us right; then these principles of His instantly make us social reformers.   SSM. 87

SOLITUDE

Solitude is bad unless the life is driven there by God. BSG. 29

... the main characteristic of Christianity is to drive us out of solitude; other religions earn it as a reward. BSG. 29

The monks in the early ages shut themselves away from everything to prove they were dead to it all, and when they got away they found themselves more alive than ever. Jesus never shut Himself away from things, the first place He took His disciples to was a marriage feast. He did not cut Himself off from society, He was not aloof, so much was He not aloof that they called Him, "a gluttonous man, and a wine-bibber!" But there was one characteristic of Jesus—He was fundamentally dead to the whole thing, it had no appeal to Him. IWP. 80

SONSHIP

Adam is called the son of God. There is only one other "Son of God" in the Bible, and He is Jesus Christ. Yet we are called "sons of God, " but how? By being reinstated through the Atonement of Jesus Christ. BP. 6

God shielded His Son from no requirements of a son, and when we are rightly related to God He will not shield us from any requirements of sons. BSG. 21

Jesus Christ is the 'only begotten Son'; His whole personality is Son-ship. GW. 30

On the basis of the Redemption God expects us to erect characters worthy of the sons of God. He does not expect us to carry on 'evangelical capers,' but to manifest the life of the Son of God in our mortal flesh. LG. 122

Why does God take such a long time? Because of what He is after, viz., "bringing many sons unto glory." It takes time to make a son. PH. 100

He has undertaken to take the vilest piece of stuff that humanity and the devil have put together, and to transform this into a son of God. SA. 41

Jesus Christ is bringing many *sons* to glory, and He will not shield us from any of the requirements of sonship. He will say at certain times to the world, the flesh, and the devil, "Do your worst, I know that 'greater is He that is in you than he that is in the world.' " God's grace does not turn out milksops, but men and women with a strong family likeness to Jesus Christ. Thank God He does give us difficult things to do! A man's heart would burst if there were no way to show his gratitude. "I beseech you therefore, brethren," says Paul, "by the mercies of God, that ye present your bodies *a living sacrifice.*" SSM. 96

'. . . though he was a Son, yet learned he obedience by the things which he suffered.' Our Lord was not a servant of God, He was His Son. The Son's obedience as Redeemer was *because He was* Son, not in order *to be* Son. SSY. 88

SORROW

Once grief touches a man he is full of reaction, he says spiteful things because he is hurt, but in the end grief leads a man to the right point of view, viz., that the basis of things is tragic. BFB. 40

In times of deep sorrow it is not the people who tell you why you are suffering who are of any use; the people who help you are those who give expression to your state of mind, often they do not speak at all, they are like Nature. Nature is never heartless to the one who is bereaved, but it takes a revelation to make us know this. HGM. 90

We can fathom our own natures by the things we sorrow over. HGM. 117

Those who sorrow over their own weakness and sins and stop short at that, have a sorrow that only makes them worse, it is not a godly sorrow that works repentance. HGM. 117

Godly sorrow not only works a positive godliness, but grants us the mark of the Cross in winning souls, an unsleeping sorrow that keeps us at it night, day and night, "filling up that which is behind of the afflictions of Christ." HGM. 118

SOUL

In the Old Testament the word 'soul,' i.e., animal soul, the soul that is present only in this order of beings, is mentioned about 460 times. In the New Testament the word 'soul' is mentioned about fifty-seven times, with the same meaning. When the Bible mentions a thing over five hundred times, it is time that Christians examined the teaching about it with care. BP. 44

. . . you can cut off a piece of a plant and the cut-off part will grow; but if you cut off the limb of an animal and plant it, it will not grow, the reason being that a plant has no soul, but an animal has. BP. 45

Soul . . . is something peculiar to men and animals, that God has not, that angels have not, and that plants have not. Man has soul, and brute has soul. BP. 45

Soul in fallen man is the expression of his personality, either in morality or in immorality. When Jesus Christ judges men He judges them according to the spirit, not according to soul, i.e., the fleshly presentation of their personality. He saw what we do not see, viz., the spirit behind. BSG. 76

Jesus Christ never attracts us by the unspeakable bliss of Paradise; He attracts us by an ugly beam. We talk about getting down to the depths of a man's soul: Jesus Christ is the only One Who ever did. IWP. 61

Jesus Christ told His disciples that they must lose their soul, i.e., their way of reasoning and looking at things, and begin to estimate from an entirely different standpoint. MFL. 34

Soul is my way of reasoning and looking at things, it is the expression of my personal spirit in my body. PH. 131

Beware of believing that the human soul is simple, for it is not true. SHL. 38

We befool ourselves into moral imbecility if we believe those who tell us the human soul is simple. As long as we think we understand ourselves we are in a lamentable state of ignorance. The first dose of conviction of sin, or of the realization of what the Psalmist states, viz., the unfathomable depths of our own souls, will put an end to that ignorance. SHL. 38

The only One who can redeem the human soul is the Lord Jesus Christ and He has done it, and the Holy Spirit brings the realization of this to us experimentally. SHL. 38

All this vast complex 'me' which we cannot begin to understand, God knows completely, and through the Atonement

He invades every part of our personality with His life. SHL. 38

Soul is my personal spirit manifesting itself in my body, the way I reason and think and look at things. Jesus says that a man must lose his soul in order to find it. SSM. 95

One of the greatest difficulties in most of our colleges for training ministers, who are supposed to work for the cure of souls, is that they are never taught how to deal with souls. There is hardly a college anywhere for training ministers where the question of dealing with souls is ever mentioned. Ministers will bear me out in this, that everything they have learned they have had to learn out of their own experience. They are trained in everything but how to deal with the facts they have to deal with. WG. 12

SOUL WINNING

Whenever the passion for souls obscures the passion for Christ, Satan has come in as an angel of light. AUG. 57

The socialist has a passion for souls, but the saint's passion for souls is not for man's sake primarily, but for the sake of the Lord Jesus Christ. This is the source of all evangelical missionary enterprise. PH. 19

God grant we may understand that the passion for souls is not a placid, scientifically worked-out thing, it compresses all the energy of heart and brain and body in one consuming drive, day and night from the beginning of life to the end—a consuming, fiery, living passion. WG. 82

Jesus Christ told the disciples He would make them "fishers of men," catchers of men. Unless we have this divine passion for souls burning in us because of our personal love for Jesus Christ, we will quit the work before we are much older. WG. 83

Oh, the skill, the patience, the gentleness and the endurance that are needed for this passion for souls; a sense that men are perishing don't do it; only one thing will do it, a blazing, passionate devotion to the Lord Jesus Christ, an all-consuming passion. Then there is no night so long, no work so hard and no crowd so difficult, but that love will outlast it all. WG. 83

The only way to learn how to fish is to fish! WG. 84

SPEECH

It is damnably easy to be kind in speech and cruel in heart. HGM. 133

There are those who talk like angels, yet they smudge the soul; there are others who may not talk sweetly yet they exhilarate the soul. NKW. 141

When you go into the presence of God, remember it is not to be in a passing mood; everything a man says to God is recognised by God and held clear in his record. Solomon indicates that it is better to have nothing to do with religious life than to talk religion in rashness only. SHH. 53

Practise the speech that is in accordance with the life of the Son of God in you, and slowly and surely your speech and your sincerity will be in accord. SSM. 40

'See that your speech is edifying'—good building-up stuff, not sanctimonious talk, but real solid stuff that makes people stronger in the Word of God, stronger in character, stronger in practical life. WG. 96

SPIRIT

The spirit within a man accounts for the way he interprets what he sees outside; and if I have not the Spirit of God, I shall never interpret the world outside as God interprets it; I shall continually have to shut my eyes and deny certain facts. BP. 228

To be saved and sanctified means to be possessed by the Spirit, not only for living but for thinking. BP. 234

The Bible points out that man's spirit is immortal, whether or not he is energized by the Spirit of God; that is, spirit never sleeps. Instead of the spirit sleeping at what we call death, at the breaking away of spirit from the body, the spirit is ten thousand-fold more awake. With the majority of us our spirits are half-concealed while we are in this body. BP. 259

Remember, spirit and personality are synonymous, but as long as a man is in the body his personality is obscured. Immediately he dies his spirit is no more obscured, it is absolutely awake; no limitations now, man is face to face with everything else that is of spirit. BP. 259

We can never know Jesus 'after the flesh' as the early disciples did, we know Him only after the Spirit, hence the insistence on receiving the Spirit. PH. 72

The spirit in man, however religious, however sweet and delightful it may appear to men, if it is not the Spirit of God, must be "scattering" away from Jesus. "He that gathereth not with Me scattereth." SA. 118

SPIRITUALISM

Beware of using the phrase 'Yield, give up your will.' Be perfectly certain to whom you are yielding. No one has any right to yield himself to any impression or to any influence or impulse; immediately you yield, you are susceptible to all kinds of supernatural powers and influences. There is only one Being to whom you must yield, and that is the Lord Jesus Christ; but be sure it is the Lord Jesus Christ to Whom you yield. BP. 162

Thought takes up no room, spirit partakes of the nature of thought, and there is no limit to the number of spirits a man's body may hold during demon possession. BP. 47

The Bible reveals that the unseen world has rulers and majesties and tremendous beings with whom man can get into communication and be possessed by, but God pronounces His curse on the man or woman who dares to communicate with them. SHL. 29

The good angels are a host and the bad angels are a host. To-day spiritualism is having tremendous vogue; men and women are getting into communication with departed spirits and putting themselves in league with the unseen powers. If you have got as far as reading fortunes in tea-cups, *stop*. If you have gone as far as telling fortunes by cards, *stop*. I will tell you why—the devil uses these apparently harmless things to create a fearful curiosity in the minds of men and women, especially young men and women, and it may bring them into league with the angelic forces that hate God, into league with the principalities and the rulers of this world's darkness. Never say, 'What is the harm in it?' Push it to its logical conclusion and ask— 'Where will this end?' SHL. 29

Drunkenness and debauchery are child's play compared with the peril of spiritualism. There is something uncannily awful about tampering with these super-natural powers, and in the speeding up of these days the necromantic element is increasing. Be on the look-out for the manifestations that are not of God; all have the one sign, they ignore Jesus Christ.   SHL. 55

If we turn to necromancy even in such seemingly ridiculous ways of telling fortunes in teacups or by cards or planchette, we commit a crime against our own souls, we are probing where we have no right to probe. People say, 'There's no harm in it.' There is all the harm and the backing up of the devil in it. The only One who can open up the profound mysteries of life is God, and He will do it as He sees we can stand it.   SHL. 57

SPIRITUALITY

"Without Me ye can do nothing." If we are not spiritual we will say that is not true, but if we are spiritual we know it is true. Our Lord said many things that are only true in the domain in which He spoke them.   IWP. 18

Spirituality is what God is after, not religiosity.   IWP. 64

The test of spiritual life is the power to descend; if we have power to rise only, there is something wrong.   LG. 51

The characteristic of the spiritual life is the delight of discerning more and more clearly the end God has in view for us.
MFL. 30

The last reach of spirituality is the thinking power, i.e., the power to express what moves our spirit.   MFL. 111

If you realize you are lacking, it is because you have come in contact with spiritual reality.   OBH. 93

Spiritual grit is what we need. We become spiritual whiners and talk pathetically about 'suffering the will of the Lord.' Where is the majestic vitality and might of the Son of God about that!
OBH. 102

Spiritual realities can always be counterfeited.   PH. 41

The spiritual life can never be lived in religious meetings, it can only be lived on sordid earth, where Jesus lived, amongst the things that make human life what it is.   PH. 175

Spiritual life is attained, not by a necromantic magic pill, but by moral choices, whereby we test the thing that presents itself to us as being good.   PS. 59

We have to beware of the notion that spirituality is something divorced from contact with sordid realities. The one and only test of a spiritual life is in practical reality.   SSY. 119

STRENGTH AND WEAKNESS

The realization that my Lord has enabled me to be a worker keeps me strong enough never to be weak. Conscious obtrusive weakness is natural unthankful strength; it means I refuse to be made strong by Him. When I say I am too weak it means I am too strong; and when ever I say 'I can't,' it means 'I won't.' When Jesus Christ enables me, I am omnipotently strong all the time.
AUG. 11

There is a difference between the weakness of refusing to think and the weakness that comes from facing facts as they really are. BFB. 42

It is a crime for a saint to be weak in God's strength. BE. 97

The 'strong man' idea is the one that appeals to men, the strong man physically, morally, strong in every way; the kingdoms of men are to be founded on strong men and the weakest are to go to the wall. History proves, however, that it is the strongest that go to the wall, not the weakest. GW. 100

I call upon my soul to remember what God has done and it makes me bold to entreat Him to do it again. It is a crime to give way to self-pity, to be weak in God's strength when all this God is ours. HG. 35

No one can remain under and endure what God puts a servant of His through unless he has the power of God. We read that our Lord was "crucified through weakness," yet it took omnipotent might to make Him weak like that. LG. 95

"He was crucified through weakness." Jesus Christ represents God limiting His own power for one purpose: He died for the weak, for the ungodly, for sinners, and for no one else. "I came not to call the righteous, but sinners to repentance." No chain is stronger than its weakest link. MFL. 106

Until we are rightly related to God, we deify pluck and heroism. We will do anything that is heroic, anything that puts the inspiration of strain on us; but when it comes to submitting to being a weak thing for God, it takes Almighty God to do it. "We are weak in Him." PH. 56

In all trade and commerce there is oppression, and we try to justify it by saying that the weakest must go to the wall. But is that so? Where are the mighty civilisations of other days? Where are the prehistoric animals, those colossal powerful creatures? It is they that have gone to the wall. The great blunder in all kingdoms amongst men is that we will demand strong men, consequently each kingdom in its turn goes to the wall because no chain is stronger than its weakest link. SHH. 46

The source of physical strength in spiritual life is different from what it is in natural life. In natural life we draw our strength direct from without; in spiritual life we draw our physical strength, consciously or unconsciously, from communion with God. SHL. 108

STUDY

Study to begin with can never be easy; the determination to form systematic mental habits is the only secret. Don't begin anything with reluctance. DI. 67

It is better for your mental life to study several subjects at once rather than one alone. What exhausts the brain is not *using* it, but abusing it by nervous waste in other directions. As a general rule, the brain can never do too much. DI. 68

To learn a thing is different from thinking out a problem. The only way to learn a thing is to keep at it uninterruptedly, day after day, whether you feel like it or not, and you will wake up one morning and find the thing is learned. DI. 68

Beware of mental lounging. Whenever we see notebooks for study, or work of any kind waiting to be done, we either go into dreamland, or we gather everything around us in an enormously bustling style, but we never do good solid work. It is nothing in the world but a habit of nerves which we have to check, and take time to see that we do.   DI. 68

A subject has never truly gripped you until you are mentally out of breath with it.   DI. 68

In the beginning to study a new subject you do it by repeated starts until you get your mind into a certain channel, after that the subject becomes full of sustained interest.   DI. 68

We infect our surroundings with our own personal character. If I make my study a place of stern industry, it will act as an inspiration every time I go into it; but if I am lazy there, the place will revenge itself on me.   DI. 69

If we have no system of work we shall easily come to think we are working when we are only thinking of working, that we are busy when we are only engaged.   DI. 69

SUBSTITUTION

The idea of substitution popularly understood is that Jesus Christ was punished for me, therefore I go scot-free. The doctrine of substitution in the Bible is always two-fold: Christ for me, that He might be substituted in me. There is no Christ *for* me if there is no Christ *in* me. The doctrine of substitution is the most practical, radically working thing in the world; it is the very essence of our Lord's teaching. "Except ye eat the flesh of the Son of man and drink His blood, ye have not life in yourselves."   BE. 120

That Christ is the substitute for me and therefore I go scot-free, is never taught in the New Testament. If I say that Christ suffered instead of me, I knock the bottom board out of His sacrifice. *Christ died in the stead of me.* I, a guilty sinner, can never get right with God, it is impossible. I can only be brought into union with God by identification with the One Who died in my stead.   NKW. 125

SUCCESS AND FAILURE

Spiritually, we cannot measure our life by success, but only by what God pours through us, and we cannot measure that at all.   MUH. 246

If you are drawing your life from God and begin to take a wrong line, God will withdraw His life. This is also true with regard to money. We have only one Source, and that is God. One of the biggest snares is the idea that God is sure to lead us to success.   NKW. 31

The test of the life of a saint is not success, but faithfulness as a steward of the mysteries of God in human life as it actually is.   NKW. 132

We will put up success as the aim in Christian work; the one thing glorifying to God is the glory of God manifested in human lives unobtrusively.   NKW. 132

The prosperity of the wicked remains a problem to everyone who is outside the life hid with Christ in God. It is only from that centre that we come slowly by faith to a solution. The problem persists, and it cannot be answered intellectually or psychologically.   PH. 74

We are determined to be successful; the Apostle Paul says we are called upon to be faithful.   SHL. 92

The great cry of modern enterprise is success; Jesus says we cannot be successful in this age. This is the age of the humiliation of the saints, that means we have to stand true to Jesus Christ while the odds are crushingly against Him all the time.   SHL. 117

SUFFERING

The problem in connection with suffering arises from the fact that there is seemingly no explanation of it.   BFB. 7

When I suffer and feel I am to blame for it, I can explain it to myself; when I suffer and know I am not to blame, it is a harder matter; but when I suffer and realize that my most intimate relations think I am to blame, that is the limit of suffering.   BFB. 14

There are some kinds of suffering and temptation and sorrow no one can sympathizē with, and by means of them a man gets on to the solitary way of life. It is not the suffering of a man who has done wrong and knows it; it is an isolation in which no one can sympathise, God alone can come near.   BFB. 61

Beware of the teaching that makes out that Jesus Christ suffered because He was so noble, so pure, so far beyond the age in which He lived, that men put Him to death; it is not true. No martyr ever said what He said—'I lay down My life of Myself.'   BSG. 39

The awful problem of suffering continually crops up in the Scriptures, and in life and remains a mystery.   CD. VOL. 1, 61

To suffer because of meekness is an exalting, refining and God-glorifying suffering. And mark this and mark it well, to suffer "as a Christian" is a shameful thing in the eyes of the societies of this world. The friends who in your hour of trial and slander, gather round to support and stand with you, are first amazed, then dazed, and then disgusted, when they find that you really do not mean to stand up for yourself, but meekly to submit.   CD. VOL. 1, 68

This spring of suffering, suffering 'according to the will of God,' is a great deep. Job did not know the preface to his own story, neither does any man. Job was never told that God and the devil had made a battleground of his soul. Job's suffering was not for his own sake, not for his perfecting or purifying, that was incidental; Job suffered *"according to the will of God."*   CD. VOL. 1, 73

After all that can be said, is said, the sufferings of the saint arise, not from inbred sin, but from obedience to the will of God, which can rarely be stated explicitly.   CD. VOL. 2, 105

When things go well a man does not want God, but when things get difficult and suffering begins to touch him, he finds the problem of the world inside his own skin. The slander of men is against God when disasters occur. If you have never felt inclined to call God cruel and hard, it is a question whether you have ever faced any problems at all.   CHI. 110

The thing that moves us is the pathos arising from physical suffering; the anguish of a soul trying to find God we put down to lunacy. The only way traditional belief can be transformed into a personal possession is by suffering. Look at what you say you believe, not an atom of it is yours saving the bit you have proved by suffering and in no other way.   CHI. 112

We do not know the preface to our own story any more than Job did; we suffer, and God alone knows why. It is beside the mark to say that it is because we deserve to suffer; Job did not deserve to suffer for he was a man 'perfect and upright, and one that feared God and eschewed evil.' Neither is it at all satisfying to say that suffering develops character. There was more in Job's suffering than was required to develop his character, and so it is with the sanctified soul. GW. 129

Suffering was inevitable to our Lord before God could make His Saviourhood a fact; He 'learned obedience by the things which He suffered.' Jesus Christ is not our Example, He is the Captain of our salvation; His position is unique. We do not suffer in order that we may become saviours; we suffer in order to enable God to fulfil His idea of saintship in us. GW. 130

We are called to fellowship with His sufferings, and some of the greatest suffering lies in remaining powerless where He remained powerless. LG. 56

To choose to suffer means that there is something wrong; to choose God's will even if it means suffering is a very different thing. No healthy saint ever chooses suffering; he chooses God's will, as Jesus did, whether it means suffering or not. MUH. 223

A man may be perfected through suffering or be made worse through suffering, it depends on his disposition. PH. 53

How did Jesus Christ suffer in the flesh? Not because He was diseased or because He was more delicately strung than we are, but because He was differently related to God, He suffered "according to the will of God," that is, He let Almighty God do His whole will in and through Him without asking His permission; He did not live His life in the flesh from the point of view of realising Himself. PH. 213

Beware of the line of thinking which has sympathy with your sufferings but has no sympathy with Jesus Christ. "Arm yourself with the mind of Christ," and the very suffering you go through will benefit others. PH. 214

The sufferings of Jesus Christ were not an accident, they are what He came for; He knew that His life was to be a ransom for many. The men who do not suffer in this world are not worth their salt. PR. 112

The finest men and women suffer, and the devil uses their sufferings to slander God. God is after one thing—bringing many sons to glory, and He does not care what it costs us, any more than He cared what it cost Him. PR. 113

God has taken the responsibility for the possibility of sin, and the proof that He did so is the Cross. He is the suffering God, not One Who reigns above in calm disdain. PR. 113

SURRENDER

Submission, for instance, means etymologically, surrender to another, but in the evangelical sense it means that I conduct myself actually among men as the submissive child of my Father in heaven. CD. VOL. 2, 28

Let me stake my all, blindly, as far as feelings are concerned, on the Reality of the Redemption, and before long that Reality will begin to tell in my actual life, which will be the evidence that the transaction has taken place. But there must be the deliberate surrender of will, not a surrender to the persuasive power of a personality, but a deliberate launching forth on God and what He says. CHI. 29

Belief in the Redemption is difficult because it needs self-surrender first.   DI. 56

It means more to surrender to God for Him to do a big thing than to surrender a big thing to God. We have to surrender our mean little notions for a tremendous revelation that takes our breath away.   LG. 147

We have dragged down the idea of surrender and of sacrifice, we have taken the life out of the words and made them mean something sad and weary and despicable; in the Bible they mean the very opposite.   LG. 148

We blunder mostly on the line of surrender, not of conceit, in the continual reminders we give to God that we are small and mean. We are much worse than small and mean: Jesus said—*"Without Me ye can do nothing."* Let us surrender all thinking about ourselves either for appreciation or depreciation, cast ourselves confidently on God and go out like children.   LG. 149

The whole of the life after surrender is an aspiration for unbroken communion with God.   MUH. 257

In every degree in which you are not real, you will dispute rather than come, you will quibble rather than come, you will go through sorrow rather than come, you will do anything rather than come the last lap of unutterable foolishness—"Just as I am." As long as you have the tiniest bit of spiritual impertinence, it will always reveal itself in the fact that you are expecting God to tell you to do a big thing, and all He is telling you to do is to "come."   MUH. 282

God pays no respect to anything we bring to Him. There is only one thing God wants of us, and that is our unconditional surrender.   MUH. 297

We are much more ready to celebrate what Jesus Christ has done than to surrender to Him. I do not mean the initial surrender to God of a sinner, but the more glorious surrender to God of a saint.   PH. 86

Many people lose their lives, but not for Christ's sake. "For My sake,"—that is the supreme surrender. God does not transform a man's life by magic, but through the surrender of the man to Himself.   PH. 133

To surrender to God is not to surrender to the fact that we have surrendered. That is not coming at all. To come means that we come to God in complete abandonment and give ourselves right over to Him and leave ourselves in His hands.   PR. 23

Spiritual reality is what is wanted. 'I surrender all'—and you feel as if you did, that is the awkward thing. The point is whether, as God engineers your circumstances, you find that you really have surrendered. Immediately you do surrender, you are made so much one with your Lord that the thought of what it cost never enters any more.   PR. 104

Over and over again the Holy Spirit brings us to the place which in evangelical language is called 'full surrender.' Remember what full surrender is. It is not giving up this thing and that, but the deliberate giving up of my right to my individual self.   SHL. 85

SUSPICION

When God brings a burden to you, never allow it to develop into carnal suspicion.   GW. 21

Always beware of suspicion, it comes from the devil and ends there. The Holy Spirit never suspects. HGM. 134

Adam's sin was not a conscious revolt against God; it worked out ultimately through the race as a revolt against God, but Adam's sin instead of being at the summit of all sin is at the foundation of all sin. Consequently whatever sin you take, you will get the characteristics that were in this first sin, viz., the principle and the disposition of this infused suspicion, "Yea, hath God said . . ." PS. 13

Absolute devastation awaits the soul that allows suspicion to creep in. Suspicion of God is like a gap in a dyke, the flood rushes through, nothing can stop it. The first thing you will do is to accept slanders against God. Because it is peculiar to you? No, because it is according to the stock that runs right straight through the human race, from this first sin of infused suspicion in the intelligence, in the innermost part of man. PS. 13

Once allow suspicion of God and of His goodness and justice to enter into a man's mind and the floodgates of sensuality are opened. PS. 14

SWORD

"A sword shall pierce through thy own soul also," a sword we should never have known if we were not born of God; a type of suffering we should have known nothing about if the Son of God had not been formed in us. PR. 45

A sword had to go through the heart of Mary because of the Son of God, and because of the Son of God in us, a sword must go through our natural life, not our sinful life. PR. 45

In a hundred and one ways we can prefer that the sword should go through the Son of God in us rather than through our natural life, and that our natural impressions should have the ascendency rather than the Son of God. PR. 51

If sin only needed to be corrected, the symbol would have been a lash, not a sword; but God uses the symbol for killing. Beware of getting into your mind ideas which never came from God's word, the idea, for instance, that we sin a little less each day; if we do, the salvation of Jesus Christ has never touched us. PS. 27

SYMBOLISM

"Opened heaven" to Our Lord means opened heaven to every man. The Holy Ghost descending as a dove is symbolical of the Holy-Spirit life that Jesus can communicate to every man. BSG. 25

The cloudy pillar, the fiery pillar, the ark, the man, the dove, are all God's symbols. This way of Divine guidance by symbols is a deep and blessed one. God does not leave us to the vague, ungraspable intuitions of the mind of some great man for guidance, or to our own vain imaginings. He has made a world of things, other than ourselves, the safeguard and inspiration of our common-sense reasonings; and He has made a world of spiritual realities the safeguard and inspiration of our discernment. CD. VOL. 1, 21

SYMPATHY

The sympathy which is reverent with what it cannot understand is worth its weight in gold. BFB. 66

In some ages, as with some people, the tendency is strong to make an essential out of what is a mere accompaniment. In our day this tendency is marked in the emphasizing of our Lord as a sympathizer, and the direct practical effect of this is to turn spirituality into sentimentality, and to make our Lord simply a kind brother-man. GW. 72

If I feel sympathy with anyone because he cannot get through to God, I am slandering God; my fundamental view is not the evangelical one, but a point of view based on mere human sympathy. Trace where your sympathies arise, and be sympathetic with God, never with the soul who finds it difficult to get through to God. God is never to blame. "Remember the people." Don't! Remember the Christ Who saves you. HG. 101

If you can help others by your sympathy or understanding, you are a traitor to Jesus Christ. MUH. 355

It is on 'Adam' sympathies that much of our Christian work is based, not on sympathy with Jesus Christ, the last Adam. Satan's temptations of our Lord were based on sympathy with the first Adam—'Put men's needs first.' Jesus Christ says—'Do not think first of the needs of the people; think first of the commands of God.' PR. 17

Never sympathise with a soul who finds it difficult to get through to God. It is perilously easy to sympathise with Satan instead of with God. No one can be more tender to men and women than God. PR. 113

Some people do not like to get saved all of a sudden, they do not like to have their problems solved in a lightning flash, they prefer to be spiritual sponges and mop up all the sympathy they can. SSY. 84

. . . never sympathise with a stupid soul. Sympathise with the sick soul; sympathise with the abnormal soul—sympathy is needed for nearly every soul but the stupid soul, but never sympathise with stupidity in the approach of a soul to God. WG. 75

T

TEACHER/TEACHING

As a product of shallow evangelical teaching, people are led to 'cod' themselves into believing that they are what they know perfectly well they are not; whereas the New Testament says if a man has the Holy Spirit it will show itself in fruit—"Wherefore by their fruits ye shall know them." There are any number of men who suddenly realize the shallowness of persuading themselves that they are what they are not, and they long for Reality.   BFB. 57

Never judge a man by the fact that he has good ideas; and never judge yourself by the fact that you have stirring visions of things. We are told that a man cannot teach the doctrine of entire sanctification unless he is entirely sanctified himself, but he can. The devil can teach entire sanctification if he pleases.   BP. 49

A teacher is simply meant to rouse us up to face the truths revealed in the Bible and witnessed to by the Holy Ghost. Watch the tendency which is in us all to try and safeguard God's truth.   CHI. 48

It is a slow business teaching a community living below the Christian level, I have to act according to the Christian ethic while not ignoring the fact that I am dealing with a community which lives away below it. The fact that I live with a degenerate crowd does not alter my duty, I have to behave as a disciple of Jesus.   DI. 74

One of the most despairing things of our day is the shallow dogmatic competence of the people who tell us they believe in the teachings of Jesus but not in His Atonement. The most unmitigated piece of nonsense human ears ever listened to! Believe in the teachings of Jesus—what is the good of it? What is the good of telling me that I have to be what I know I never can be if I live for a million years—perfect as God is perfect? What is the good of telling me I have to be a child of my Father in heaven and be like Him? We must rid our minds of the idea that is being introduced by the modern trend of things that Jesus Christ came to teach. The world is sick of teachers. Teachers never can do any good unless they can interpret the teaching that is already here.   HG. 59

Jesus Christ is not a great Teacher alongside Plato and other great teachers; He stands absolutely alone. "Test your teachers," said Jesus; the teachers who come from God are those who clear the way to Jesus Christ, and keep it clear. We are estimated in God's sight as workers by whether or not we clear the way for people to see Jesus.   HGM. 125

The one test of a teacher sent from God is that those who listen see and know Jesus Christ better than ever they did.   IWP. 111

The interests of a child are altogether in the senses, and in teaching a child you must begin by interesting him. The teacher who succeeds best with children is the one who does things before them; it is no use teaching children abstract stuff. That is why it is necessary in teaching a young life, whether young in years of the flesh or the spirit, for a teacher to attend more to what he does than to what he says.   MFL. 97

The test for apostles and teachers is not that they talk wonderful stuff, not that they are able to expound God's word, but that they edify the saints.   OBH. 42

God brings His own particular teachers into our lives, and we have to watch that we do not slack off in our loyalty to them. Loyalty to teachers is a very rare thing.   OBH. 126

The test of any teaching is its estimate of Jesus Christ. The teaching may sound wonderful and beautiful, but watch lest it have at its centre the dethroning of Jesus Christ.   PR. 76

Jesus Christ did not come primarily to teach; He came to make it possible for us to receive His heredity, to have put into us a new disposition whereby we can live totally new lives.   SA. 37

TEMPERAMENT

The 'gospel of temperament' works very well if you are suffering only from physical neuralgia, so to speak, and all you need is a cup of tea; but if you have a real deep complaint, the injunction to 'Cheer up' is an insult.   BFB. 32

We breed our temperament out of the disposition that is in us.   IWP. 53

One of the greatest hindrances to our coming to Jesus is the talk about temperament. I have never seen the Spirit of God pay any attention to a man's temperament, but over and over again I have seen people make their temperament and their natural affinities a barrier to coming to Jesus. We have to learn that Our Lord does not heed our selective natural affinities. The idea that He does heed them has grown from the notion that we have to consecrate our gifts to God. We cannot consecrate what is not ours.   OBH. 104

It is easy to have the attitudes of religion, but it is the temper of our mind we have to watch. It is not the wrong things, but our temper of mind in serving God that will turn us from Him.   PH. 228

When God makes a saint He plants a new disposition in him, but He does not alter his temperament; the saint has to mould his temperament according to the new disposition.   PS. 79

TEMPTATION

The first Adam did not stand the strain for very long; but the last Adam did not begin to give way under the strain. Adam was innocent, not holy; that is, he had no wrong disposition in him, yet he was tempted. Jesus was holy, yet He was tempted. It was impossible to tempt Jesus with evil.   BSG. 34

We imagine that when we are sanctified we are delivered from temptation; we are not, we are loosened into it; we are not free enough before to be tempted. Immediately we are sanctified, we are free, and all these subtleties begin to work. God does not shield us from any requirements of a full-grown man or woman, because His aim is to bring many "sons to glory"; not emotional, hysterical people, but men and women who can withstand and overcome and manifest not only innocence, but holiness.   BSG. 34

When we are born again we get our first introduction into what God calls temptation. When we are sanctified we are not delivered from temptation, we are loosened into it; we are not free enough before either morally or spiritually to be tempted. Immediately we become His "brethren" we are free, and all these subtleties are at work. CHI. 57

When temptation comes, stand absolutely true to God no matter what it costs you, and you will find the onslaught leaves you with affinities higher and purer than ever before. CHI. 57

Wherever there is moral responsibility there is temptation, i.e., the testing of what a man holds in his own person.
DI. 75

The old Puritan idea that the devil tempts men had this remarkable effect, it produced the man of iron who fought; the modern idea of blaming his heredity or his circumstances produces the man who succumbs at once. DI. 75

Every temptation of Satan is the acme of human wisdom, but immediately the Spirit of God is at work in a man the hollow mockery at its heart is recognized.
DI. 75

The moments of severest temptation are the moments of His divinest succour.
DI. 76

In the temptation the devil antagonized the same thing that he antagonized in the first Adam, viz., oneness with God. HGM. 60

If after a season of temptation a saint retains the power that draws the purest spirits to him, he may feel assured that the temptation has been gone through with successfully. HGM. 114

The word "temptation" has come down in the world; we are apt to use it wrongly. Temptation is not sin, it is the thing we are bound to meet if we are men. Not to be tempted would be to be beneath contempt. Many of us, however, suffer from temptations from which we have no business to suffer, simply because we have refused to let God lift us to a higher plane where we would face temptations of another order.

A man's disposition on the inside, i.e., what he possesses in his personality, determines what he is tempted by on the outside. The temptation fits the nature of the one tempted, and reveals the possibilities of the nature. Every man has the setting of his own temptation, and the temptation will come along the line of the ruling disposition.

Temptation is a suggested short cut to the realization of the highest at which I aim—not towards what I understand as evil, but towards what I understand as good. Temptation is something that completely baffles me for a while, I do not know whether the thing is right or wrong. Temptation yielded to is lust deified, and is a proof that it was timidity that prevented the sin before.

Temptation is not something we may escape, it is essential to the full-orbed life of a man. Beware lest you think you are tempted as no one else is tempted; what you go through is the common inheritance of the race, not something no one ever went through before. God does not save us from temptations; He succours us in the midst of them. MUH. 261

The temptations of Jesus do not appeal to us, they have no home at all in our human nature. Our Lord's temptations and ours move in different spheres until we are born again and become His brethren. The temptations of Jesus are not those of a man, but the temptations of God as Man. By regeneration the Son of God is formed in us, and in our physical life He has the same setting that He had on earth. Satan does not tempt us to do wrong things; he tempts us in order to make us lose what God has put into us by regeneration, viz., the possibility of being of value to God. He does not come on the line of tempting us to sin, but on the line of shifting the point of view, and only the Spirit of God can detect this as a temptation of the devil. MUH. 262

Temptation is a short cut to what is good, not to what is bad. PH. 35

The way steel is tested is a good illustration of temptation. Steel can be 'tired' in the process of testing, and in this way its strength is measured. PR. 60

Temptation is the testing by an alien power of the possessions held by a personality in order that a higher and nobler character may come out of the test. PR. 60

The temptations of our Lord have no home at all in our human nature; they do not appeal to us because they are removed from any affinity with the natural. Our Lord's temptations and ours move in different spheres until we become His brethren, by being born again. PR. 61

The temptations of Jesus are not those of Man as man, but the temptations of God as Man. The statement that our Lord was tempted as ordinary men are is readily accepted, but the Bible does not say that He was so tempted. PR. 61

Jesus Christ was not born with a heredity of sin; He was not tempted in all points as ordinary men are, but tempted like His brethren, those who have been born from above by the Spirit of God and placed in the Kingdom of God by supernatural regeneration. PR. 61

The records of our Lord's temptations are given not that we might fathom Him, but that we might know what to expect when we are regenerated. When we are born again of the Spirit of God and enter into fellowship with Jesus Christ, then the temptations of our Lord are applicable to us. PR. 61

We are apt to imagine that when we are saved and sanctified we are delivered from temptation; we are not, we are loosened into it. Before we are born again, we are not free enough to be tempted, neither morally nor spiritually. PR. 61

Immediately we are born into the Kingdom of God, we get our first introduction into what God calls temptation, viz., the temptations of His Son. PR. 61

In His temptation our Lord does not stand as an individual Man; He stands as the whole human race vested in one Personality, and every one of us when regenerated can find his place and fellowship in those temptations. PR. 64

Our Lord's temptations are carefully presented so that we may know the kind of temptation to expect when His life is formed in us. PR. 67

Temptation yielded to is lust deified. PR. 69

The practical test for us when we have been through a season of temptation is whether we have a finer and deeper affinity for the highest. PR. 70

Temptation must come, and we do not know what it is until we meet it. When we do meet it, we must not debate with

God, but stand absolutely true to Him no matter what it costs us personally, and we will find that the onslaught will leave us with higher and purer affinities than before. PR. 70

Temptation is not something we may escape; it is essential to the full-orbed life of a son of God. We have to beware lest we think we are tempted as no one else is tempted. What we go through is the common inheritance of the race, not something no one ever went through before. It is most humiliating to be taken off our pedestal of suffering and made to realise that thousands of others are going through the same thing as we are going through. PR. 71

Temptation is something that exactly fits the nature of the one tempted, and is therefore a great revealer of the possibilities of the nature. Every man has the setting of his own temptation. PS. 54

Temptation and sin are profoundly different. Temptation is a pathway to the end desired, but it leads to a perplexing situation, inasmuch as it makes a man decide which factor he will obey in the dilemma. PS. 54

Our Lord Jesus Christ had the possibility of disobedience, but when the temptation producing the dilemma came to Him, it found no inclination to disobedience; and everyone that is saved by Him is put in the position He was in when He was tempted. PS. 55

The devil does not tempt to wrong things, he tries to make us lose what God has put into us by regeneration, viz., the possibility of being of value to God. PS. 59

There is a limit to temptation. "God is faithful who will not suffer you to be tempted above that ye are able." God does not save us from temptations, but He succours us in the middle of them. PS. 59

TENACITY

The greatest fear a man has is not that he will be damned, but that Jesus Christ will be worsted; that the things He stood for—love and justice, forgiveness and kindness among men, won't win out in the end. Then comes the call to spiritual tenacity, not to hang on and do nothing, but to work deliberately and tenaciously with the certainty that God is not going to be worsted. GW. 135

We all have our problems, something about which we say, 'Now, why is it?' Never take an explanation which is too slight. A materialistic explanation or an evolutionary explanation cannot be final. The great thing is to remain absolutely confident in God. 'Be still, and know that I am God.' GW. 135

TESTIMONY

Our Lord insists that we begin at Jerusalem for the sake of our own character, and our 'Jerusalem' is unquestionably among the bounties of our own particular flesh and blood relations. It is infinitely easier to offer the 'sacrifice of praise' before strangers than amongst our own flesh and blood. That is where the '*sacrifice* of praise' comes in, and that is what young converts want to skip. It is by testifying to our own flesh and blood that we are confirmed in our own character and in our relationship to Jesus Christ. BP. 169

To testify is part of the life of every Christian, but because you have a personal testimony it does not follow that you are called to preach. DI. 77

To say what God has done for you is testimony, but you have to preach more than you have experienced—more than anyone has ever experienced; you have to preach Jesus Christ. Present the Object of your faith, the Lord Jesus, lift Him up, and then either give your testimony, or know you have one to give. DI. 77

Whenever you meet a man who is going on with God you find his testimony explains your own experience. A true testimony grips everyone who is after the Truth. DI. 77

The danger of experience-meetings when they get outside the new Testament standard is that people don't testify to anything that glorifies God, but to experiences that leave you breathless and embarrassed. It is all on the illuminated line, on the verge of the hysterical. DI. 78

When we talk to a soul, we talk like a tract! When Jesus talked to the woman of Samaria He did not use a prescribed form of address, He told her Divine truth and made her aware of her sin. When He talked to the disciples on the road to Emmaus, their hearts burned within them. The characteristic of the man of God's method is that he can speak to a sinner and win him before the sinner knows where he is; he can speak to saints and make their hearts burn. GW. 48

The weakness of many a testimony is that it is based on what the Lord has done—'I have to testify to what God has done for me in order that other people may have the same thing done for them.' It sounds all right, but it is not the New Testament order of testimony. Jesus Christ never sent out a disciple on the ground that He had done something for

him, but only because he had seen the Lord after He had done something for him. HGM. 55

People testify to conversion and to the grace of God in their lives, but plainly they do not know Him. There is no question about His having emancipated them from sin and done a mighty work in them, but the great passion of the life is not Jesus Christ. HGM. 55

As soon as we see Jesus and perceive who He is by His Spirit, He says 'Go'— 'Go out into actual life and tell My brethren, not what I have done for you, but that I am risen.' HGM. 57

If our testimony is hard, it is because we have gone through no crisis with God, there is no heartbroken emotion behind it. If we have been through a crisis in which human feeling has been ploughed to its inner centre by the Lord, our testimony will convey all the weight of the greatness of God along with human greatness. NKW. 136

In the Bible confession and testimony are put in a prominent place, and the test of a man's moral calibre is the "say so." I may try and make myself believe a hundred and one things, but they will never be mine until I "say so." PH. 209

There are some people we are always the better for meeting, they do not talk piously, but somehow they give us a feeling of emancipation, they have a larger horizon. The reason is that they have opened the door for themselves by their "say so," and now the Word of God becomes spirit and life through them to others. PH. 212

It is easier to stand true to a testimony which is mouldy with age because it has the dogmatic ring about it that people agree with, than to talk from your last moment of contact with God. RTR. 74

Sometimes it is cowardly to speak, and sometimes it is cowardly to keep silence. SHH. 27

. . . we are losing sight of the real meaning of testimony; it is not for the sake of others, but for our own sake. It makes us know we have no one to rely on but God. SHL. 15

TEXTUALISM

Never use your text as a title for a speculation of your own, that is being an impertinent exploiter of the word of God. AUG. 21

Exegesis is not torturing a text to agree with a theory of my own, but leading out its meaning. DI. 9

An absurd thing to say is—"Give me a text to prove it." You cannot give a text to prove any one of God's revelations, you can only give a text to prove your simplification of those revelations. A text-proof is generally used to bolster up a personal spiritual affinity of my own. DI. 9

Learn to get into the quiet place where you can hear God's voice speak through the words of the Bible, and never be afraid that you will run dry, He will simply pour the word until you have no room to contain it. It won't be a question of hunting for messages or texts, but of opening the mouth wide and He fills it. IWP. 93

The Holy Spirit does not bring text after text until we are utterly confused; He simply brings back with the greatest of ease the words which we need in the particular circumstances we are in. MFL. 31

Do we come to the Bible to be spoken to by God, to be made "wise unto salvation," or simply to hunt for texts on which to build addresses? There are people who vagabond through the Bible, taking out of it only sufficient for the making of sermons; they never let the word of God walk out of the Bible and talk to them. RTR. 58

THEOLOGY

It is possible to build logical edifices on a theological position and at the same time to prove in practical life that the position is wrong. BFB. 49

Never be afraid if your circumstances dispute what you have been taught about God; be willing to examine what you have been taught, and never take the conception of a theologian as infallible; it is simply an attempt to state things. BFB. 54

Theology is the science of Christianity; much that is wrongly called theology is mere psychological guess-work, verifiable only from experience. Christian theology is the ordered exposition of revelation certainties. If our teaching and preaching is not based on a recognition of those things that cannot be experienced it will produce parasites, people who depend on being fed by others. HGM. 146

Theology is the science of religion, an intellectual attempt to systematize the consciousness of God. Intellect systematizes things to a man's mind, but we do not reach reality through intellect. Theology comes second, not first, and ought always to be open to dispute. SA. 22

THINKING

"I am the Way," not only the way to be saved and sanctified and to live as a Christian, but the way to think as a Christian. BP. 231

We have not only to be good lovers of God, but good thinkers, and it is only along this line that we can "try the spirits whether they are of God." BP. 234

There is a wonderful symbolism about the place of the crucifixion; Jesus was crucified at "a place called Golgotha, that is to say, The place of a skull." That is where He has always been put to shame, in the thinking part of man, and only when the thinking part of a man is swayed by the Holy Ghost will he find an answer to every one of the temptations that Satan brings. BSG. 34

Until a man is born again his thinking goes round and round in a circle and he becomes intoxicated with his own importance. When he is born again there is a violent readjustment in his actual life, and when he begins to think along Jesus Christ's line there is just as tremendous a revolution in his thinking processes. BSG. 67

We are called upon not only to be right in heart, but to be right in thinking. When we have become personally related to Jesus Christ we have to do the thing that is in our power to do, viz., think aright. BSG. 69

'I can't alter my thinking.' You can. It is actually possible to identify your mind with the highest point of view, and to habituate yourself by degrees to the thinking and the living in accordance with it. DI. 79

If I make my life in my intellect I will certainly delude myself that I am as good as I think I am. "As a man thinketh *in his heart*,"—that means 'me,' as I express my thinking in actual life, *"so is he."* DI. 79

We know that we are not perfect yet in outer manifestation, but in thinking we have to remember what we received Jesus for, to be absolute Lord, absolute Saviour. GW. 13

If my actual life is not in agreement with my thinking the danger is that I exclude myself from actualities which bring home to me the knowledge of what I am, in spite of what I think. GW. 17

A child does not work from a conscious ambition, it obeys the law of the life that is in him without thinking. When we are born again and rightly related to God we will live the right kind of life without thinking. IWP. 21

As long as the devil can keep us terrified of thinking, he will always limit the work of God in our souls. IWP. 52

The only way to progress in spiritual matters is to think voluntarily. A great amount of stuff we call thinking is not thinking, but merely reverie or meditation. Thinking is a voluntary effort, and in the initial stages it is never easy; voluntary effort must be made to keep the mind on some particular line. MFL. 18

When we become spiritual we have to exercise the power of thinking to a greater degree than ever before. MFL. 18

We starve our mind as Christians by not thinking. MFL. 18

. . . when you begin to use a muscle in a particular way, it hurts badly, but if you keep on using that muscle judiciously it will get beyond hurting until you are able to use it with mechanical precision. The same thing is true in regard to thinking. It is a difficult matter to begin with. MFL. 19

The first moment of thinking alters our life. MFL. 20

We are so extraordinarily fussy that we won't give ourselves one minute before God to think, and unless we do we shall never form the habit of abiding. We must get alone in secret and think, screw our minds down and not allow them to wool-gather. Difficult? Of course it is difficult to begin with, but if we persevere we shall soon take in all the straying parts of our mental life, and in a crisis we shall be able to draw on the fact that we are one with Jesus in God's sight. MFL. 38

We begin by thinking we know all about ourselves, but when a man gets a dose of 'the plague of his own heart,' it upsets all his thinking. MFL. 43

If we do not base all our thinking on the presupposition of the Atonement, we shall produce a faith conscious of itself, hysterical and unholy, that cannot do the work of the world. OBH. 110

We starve our minds as Christians by not thinking, and we cannot think as Christians until we are born from above. So many of us have a good spiritual experience, but we have never thought things out on Christian lines. It is just as true that a man may *live* a Christian life without thinking as that a man may *think* a Christian life without living it. We have to learn to combine the two,

and to do this we must build up our minds on these great truths. PR. 116

We have not been taught to *think* as Christians, and when an agony reaches us we are knocked to pieces, and only hang on by the skin of our teeth. We may have faith enough to keep us going, but we do not know where to put our feet or to tell anyone else where to put theirs. We have been taught to think as pagans, and in a crisis we act as pagans. It is a great thing to have a spiritual experience, but another thing to think on the basis of it. SA. 19

God can impart to a man the power to select what his mind thinks, the power to think only what is right and pure and true. SHL. 11

THOUGHTS

'Think proper thoughts.' *Live proper lives!* and you will think proper thoughts. AUG. 59

To bring every thought into captivity is the last thing we do, and it is not done easily; in the beginning we have to do violence to our old ways of thinking just as at sanctification we had to do violence to our old ways of living. Intellect in a saint is the last thing to become identified with Jesus Christ. BSG. 67

Thought is not the sum-total of a man's personality, it is simply the garment personality wears. Think, for instance, of the beautiful things you write in your essays, and think of the mean scrubs you are outside your essays! proving that your beautiful thinking is not the garment that fits you yet. GW. 17

God has not the remotest opportunity of coming to some of us, our minds are packed full with our own thoughts and conceptions; until suddenly He comes in like the wind and blows all our thoughts right away, and thoughts come sauntering in from the Word of God. We can never get those thoughts for ourselves. They are the free gift of God for anyone and everyone who is learning to pay attention to Him.   MFL. 66

Beware of saying you cannot help your thoughts; you can; you have all the almighty power of God to help you. We have to learn to bring every thought into captivity to the obedience of Christ, and it takes time. We want to reach it in a moment like a rocket, but it can only be done by a gradual moral discipline, and we do not like discipline, we want to do it all at once.   MFL. 86

God will not make me think like Jesus, I have to do it myself; I have to bring every thought into captivity to the obedience of Christ. "Abide in Me"—in intellectual matters, in money matters, in every one of the matters that make human life what it is. It is not a handbox life.   MUH. 166

TIME AND ETERNITY

What an unspeakably wonderful day the Day of Pentecost was! There is only one Bethlehem, one Calvary, one Pentecost; these are the landmarks of Time and Eternity, everything and everyone is judged by them.   HGM. 20

How many of us spend our time expecting that we will be something we are not. 'Oh the time is coming when I am going to be so and so.' It never will come; the time is always *now*.   MFL. 60

Spend plenty of time with God; let others things go, but don't neglect Him. And beware of practical work.   NKW. 137

We can choke God's word with a yawn; we can hinder the time that should be spent with God by remembering we have other things to do. 'I haven't time!' Of course you have not time! *Take* time, strangle some other interests and make time to realize that the centre of power in your life is the Lord Jesus Christ and His Atonement.   OBH. 124

In the spiritual domain the passing of the years counts for nothing.   PR. 39

The Cross is the centre of Time and of Eternity, the answer to the enigmas of both.   PR. 99

Let us examine ourselves the next time we say, 'I have not time,' or 'I give all the time I can to the study of God's Word,' 'I give all the time I can to praying.' God grant we may be put on the alert on these lines that we may not be found lying to the Holy Ghost.   WG. 103

TITHING

The giving of the tenth is not a sign that all belongs to God, but a sign that the tenth belongs to God and the rest is ours, and we are held responsible for what we do with it. To be "not under the law, but under grace" does not mean that we can do as we like.   SSM. 22

TONGUE/TONGUES

The tongue in our Lord Jesus Christ got to its right place because He never spoke from the spirit of His right to Himself; and our tongue and our brain will only be in the right place when we learn to obey the Spirit of God in thinking.   BP. 236

When you are brought face to face with a case of happy indifference, pray for all you are worth, but let him alone with your tongue—the hardest thing for an earnest Christian to do. DI. 89

The Bible reveals the tongue to be the worst enemy a man has—"Sharp arrows of the mighty"—they never miss their mark. HG. 10

Never testify with your lips what your life does not back up. HGM. 41

There are miraculous dealings which lure to destruction, the tongues movement, the seeking for signs and wonders. Almost without exception the people who are lured on this wrong road are those who have been told to fast and concentrate for something for themselves whereby the Lord may show how marvellous He is. IYA. 25

It sounds right to ask God to produce signs and wonders, and all through the twenty centuries of the Christian era this temptation has been yielded to, every now and again, in the most wild and inordinate manner. For the past ten years or more it has been in our midst in the Tongues movement, and hundreds of those who were really enlightened by the Spirit of God have gone off on the line of this temptation. PR. 67

TOUCH

Touch has more power than even speech to convey the personality. If some people touch us, we feel the worse for it for days; if others touch us, we live a transfigured life for days. That is an experience recognizable by us all, but we may not have realized that it is because the touch conveys the dominating personality behind. A caress from a bad personality is incarnated hypocrisy. It is at grave peril to our own souls that we ignore these subtle indications of warning.

When once the barriers that God creates around His children are broken down and His warnings ignored, we shall find that the enemy will break through at the places we have broken down. If we keep in touch with the Master, He will keep us out of touch with baldness. SSY. 88

TRANSFIGURATION

We say, 'No cross, no crown'; in the life of Our Lord the crown of the glory of the Transfiguration came before the Cross. You never know Jesus Christ, and Him crucified, unless you have seen Him transfigured in all His transcendent majesty and glory; the Cross to you is nothing but the cross of a martyr. BSG. 38

Between the Baptism and the Transfiguration there is no mention made of Jesus Christ being made sin; during that time He was perfecting holiness, i.e., living the kind of life God requires us to live. After the Transfiguration we see Him dealing with sin—He "put away sin *by the sacrifice of Himself."* BSG. 40

The completion of the Transfiguration is the Ascension, not the Resurrection. The Transfiguration is a glimpse of glory—but not yet. BSG. 41

Our Lord emptied Himself of His glory when He became Incarnate, and here on the Mount the glory which He had with the Father before the world was suddenly burst through; the material part of Him was shot through with glory, that is, God and matter became one. That is what would have happened to the human race if Adam had not sinned, there would have been no death, but transfiguration. The counterpart of the Transfiguration is not the Resurrection, but the Ascension. HGM. 93

All the events in our Lord's life to which we have no corresponding experience happened after the Transfiguration. From then onwards our Lord's life was altogether vicarious. Up to the time of the Transfiguration, He had exhibited the normal perfect life of a man; from the Transfiguration onwards, everything is unfamiliar to us. Gethsemane, the Cross, the Resurrection— there is nothing like these experiences in our human life. PR. 118

When our Lord as a Man had fulfilled all God's demands of Him, and when by obedience He had transformed His natural life into a spiritual life, He reached the place where it was all spiritual, earth had no more hold on Him, and on the Mount of Transfiguration His real nature, viz., His essential Deity, broke all through the natural and He was transfigured. He had fulfilled all the requirements of His Father for His earthly life, and God's presence, symbolised in the cloud, waited to usher Him back into the glory which He had with the Father before the word was. But He turned His back on the glory, and came down from the Mount to identify Himself with fallen humanity, because through Calvary there was to issue the newly constructed humanity. If Jesus Christ had gone to heaven from the Mount of Transfiguration, He would have gone alone. He would have been to us a glorious Figure, One who manifested the life of God's normal man and how wonderful it is for God and man to live as one, but what good would that have been to us? We can never live in the power of an ideal put before us. What is the use of Jesus Christ telling us we must be as pure in Heart as He is when we know we are impure? But Jesus Christ did not go to heaven from the Mount. Moses and Elijah talked with Him, not of His glory, nor of His Deity, but of His *death,* the issue which He was about to accomplish at Jerusalem. By His death on the Cross Jesus Christ made the way for every son of man to get into communion with God. PR. 119

TREASURE

We have to lay up treasure for ourselves, it is not laid up for us; and we have to lay it up in heaven, not on earth. MFL. 111

Whatever we possess in the way of treasure on earth is liable to be consumed by moth and rust. MFL. 112

When we lay up treasure on earth it may go at any moment, but when we learn to lay up treasure in heaven, nothing can touch it—"therefore will not we fear, though the earth be removed . . ."; it is perfectly secure. MFL. 112

Our Lord kept all His treasure of heart and mind and spirit in His oneness with the Father; He laid up treasure in heaven, not on earth. Our Lord never possessed anything for Himself. MFL. 112

In the degree that we possess anything for ourselves we are separated from Jesus. So many of us are caught up in the shows of things, not in the way of property and possessions, but of blessings, and all our efforts to persuade ourselves that our treasure is in heaven is a sure sign that it is not. MFL. 113

"But lay up for yourselves treasure in heaven," i.e., have your banking account in heaven, not on earth; lay up your confidence in God, not in your commonsense. SSM. 62

'Treasure in heaven' is faith that has been tried, otherwise it is only possible gold. 'Oh yes, I believe God can do everything.' But have I proved that He can do *one* thing? If I have, the next time a trial of faith comes I can go through it smilingly, because of the wealth in my heavenly banking account. SSY. 61

TRIBULATION

God allows tribulation and anguish to come right to the threshold of our lives in order to prove to us that His life in us is more than a match for all that is against us. SHL. 11

It does not matter where a man may get to in the way of tribulation or anguish, none of it can wedge in between and separate him from the love of God in Christ Jesus. SHL. 37

Jesus said that in the lives of the saints there will be tribulation, not difficulties, but tribulation. SHL. 117

TRINITY

The great Triune God has 'form,' and the term that is used for describing that form is 'glory.' BP. 12

Our word 'Trinity' is an attempt to convey the externally disclosed Divine nature, and 'glory' is the Bible term for conveying the idea of the external form of that Triune Being. BP. 12

... what is true of God the Father is true also of God the Son and of God the Holy Ghost, because They are one. The main characteristics which are the same in the Father and in the Son and in the Holy Ghost are Will, Love and Light. BP. 213

The term 'Trinity' is not a Bible word, but a term that arose in the throes of a great conflict of minds, and is the crystallised attempt to state the Godhead in a word. One element of the Godhead be-

came, through the Word of God, the Incarnate Son of God. PR. 130

The doctrine of the Trinity is not a revelation, it is an attempt to put into scientific language the fact of God. SA. 36

TROUBLE

Trouble always arises when men will not revise their views of God. BFB. 39

There is no bright side to some troubles. BFB. 68

Compare your life with the life of one who has never known God—"they are not in trouble as other men; neither are they plagued like other men." PH. 228

No matter what actual troubles in the most extreme form get hold of a man's life, not one of them can touch the central citadel, viz., his relationship to God in Christ Jesus. SHL. 98

TRUST

It is not easy to say that God is love when everything that happens actually gives the lie to it. Everyone's soul represents some kind of battlefield. The point for each one is whether we will hang in, as Job did, and say 'Though things look black, I will trust in God.' BFB. 100

It is very easy to trust in God when there is no difficulty, but that is not trust at all, it is simply letting the mind rest in a complacent mood; but when there is sickness in the house, when there is trouble, when there is death, where is our trust in God? CD. VOL. 1, 111

God has to deal with us on the death side as well as on the life side. It is all very well to know in theory that there are things we must not trust in, but another thing to know it in fact. When God deals with us on the death side He puts the sentence of death on everything we should not trust in, and we have a miserable time until we learn never any more to trust in it, never any more to look anywhere else than to God. It sometimes happens that hardly a day passes without God saying, 'Don't trust there, that is dead.' GW. 14

The reason our Lord tells us to beware of men is that the human heart is "deceitful above all things, and desperately wicked," and if we put our trust in men we shall go under, because men are just like ourselves, and none of us in our wits before God would ever think of trusting ourselves; if we do it is a sign that we are ignorant of ourselves. HG. 24

There is nothing so secure as the salvation of God; it is as eternal as the mountains, and it is our trust in God that brings us the conscious realization of this. HG. 28

Never trust the best man or woman you ever met, trust only the Lord Jesus. HGM. 139

"Though He slay me, yet will I trust Him." That is the most sublime utterance of faith in the Old Testament. MFL. 87

Our Lord trusted no man yet He was never suspicious, never bitter; His confidence in what God's grace could do for any man was so perfect that He never despaired of anyone. MFL. 89

Trust no one, not even the finest saint who ever walked this earth, ignore him, if he hinders your sight of Jesus Christ. MUH. 89

If I put my trust in human beings first, I will end in despairing of everyone; I will become bitter, because I have insisted on man being what no man ever can be—absolutely right. Never trust anything but the grace of God in yourself or in anyone else. MUH. 132

You cannot lay up for a rainy day if you are trusting Jesus Christ. MUH. 187

Before us there is nothing, but overhead there is God, and we have to trust Him. NKW. 12

Suppose Job had said—'If I were trusting in God I should not be treated like this'; he *was* trusting in God, and he *was* treated like that. NKW. 60

Beware of the thing that makes you go down before God and sway from side to side spiritually—'I don't know what to do'; then don't do anything. 'I don't see anything'; well, don't look for anything. 'I thought by this time I should see something'; if you don't, be foolish enough to trust in God. NKW. 61

When Jesus says, 'Come unto Me,' I simply come; when He says, 'Trust in God in this matter,' I do not try to trust, I *do* trust. An alteration has taken place in my disposition which is an evidence that the nature of God is at work in me. NKW. 127

It is always easier not to trust; if I can work the thing out for myself then I am not going to trust in God. OPG. 34

. . . trust in God does not mean that God will explain His solutions to us, it means that we are perfectly confident in God, and when we do see the solution we find it to be in accordance with all that Jesus Christ revealed of His character. OPG. 36

Whenever we begin to note where we are successful for God, we do trust in ourselves. PH. 45

When we are standing face to face with Jesus, and He says, "Believest thou this?" our faith is as natural as breathing, and we say—'Yes, Lord,' and are staggered and amazed that we were so stupid as not to trust Him before. PH. 226

Quiet trust in God is the state of mind and heart that is fittest to do the duty that lies nearest without any fluster. RTR. 22

Experiences of what God has done for me are only stepping-stones; the one great note is—I trust in the Lord Jesus, God's providence can do with me what it likes, make the heavens like brass, earth like hell, my body loathsome (as Job's was), but my soul that is trusting in Jesus gets where Job got, "Though He slay me, yet will I trust Him." RTR. 79

Live your life as a labouring man, a man rightly related to mother earth, and to the providential order of tyranny; trust in God whatever happens, and the result will be that in your heart will be the joy that every man is seeking. SHH. 64

TRUTH

No man ever puts a stumbling-block in the way of others by telling the truth; to tell the truth is more honouring to God than to tell a lie. BFB. 41

The only way we get at Truth is by life and personality. When a man is up against things it is no use for him to try and work it out logically, but let him obey, and instantly he will see his way through. BFB. 102

Truth is moral, not intellectual. We perceive Truth by doing the right thing, not by thinking it out. 'If any man will do His will, he shall know of the doctrine . . .' BFB. 102

Jesus Christ talked rugged unmitigated truth, He was never ambiguous, and He says it is better to be maimed than damned. BE. 49

Amid all the whirling contentions and confusions produced in men's minds by what is called truth, again our Lord's word to Thomas abides, "I *am the truth.*" CD. VOL. 1, 138

We do not create truth, we receive it. CHI. 30

Every partial truth has so much error in it that you can dispute it, but you can't dispute 'truth as it is in Jesus.' DI. 3

Whenever a truth comes home to me my first reaction is to fling it back on you, but the Spirit of God brings it straight home, 'Thou art the man.' We always want to lash others when we are sick with our own disobedience. DI. 73

The Personality of Truth is the great revelation of Christianity—'I am the Truth.' Our Lord did not say He was 'all truth' so that we could go to His statements as to a text-book and verify things; there are domains, such as science and art and history, which are distinctly man's domains and the boundaries of our knowledge must continually alter and be enlarged; God never encourages laziness. GW. 33

When once you take any one of the great works of God as an end, or any one of the truths which depend on Jesus Christ, as *the* truth, you will go wrong, you are outside the guard of God. The safeguard is the Highest—*'I* am . . . the Truth.' *'I,* if *I* be lifted up . . .' Allow nothing to take you away from Jesus Himself, and all other phases of truth will take their right place. GW. 106

It is perilous to listen to the truth of God unless I open my will to it. HG. 102

"But ye have an unction from the Holy One, and ye know all things," and, "the same anointing teacheth you of all things." The meaning of that is very practical and sane—Test all you hear, all you read, by this inner anointing, by the indwelling Spirit; He will test all the truth of God. IYA. 79

You can never be the same after the unveiling of a truth. MUH. 364

Truth is a Person. *"I am the Truth,"* said Jesus. OPG. 1

If we refuse any one way of getting at the truth because we do not like that way, we are dishonest. PR. 21

Truth is not discerned intellectually, it is discerned spiritually. PR. 116

Beware of making God's truth simpler than He has made it Himself. RTR. 39

Beware of turning your back on what you know is true because you do not want it to be real. SHL. 60

Let people do what they like with your truth, but never explain it. Jesus never explained anything; we are always explaining, and we get into tangles by not leaving things alone. SSM. 40

The central truth is not Salvation, nor Sanctification, nor the Second Coming; the central truth is nothing less than Jesus Christ Himself. "I, if I be lifted up from the earth, will draw all men unto Me." Error always comes in when we take something Jesus Christ does and preach it as the truth. It is part of the truth, but if we take it to be the whole truth we become advocates of an idea instead of a Person, the Lord Himself. SSM. 83

U

UNDERSTANDING

If ever we are going to understand God, we must receive His Spirit, then He will begin to expound to us the things of God. We understand the things of the world by our natural intelligence, and we understand the things of God by "the spirit which is of God." BP. 212

The word 'understanding' does not mean anything necromantic; it means that we understand with a responsible intelligence that which comes from God; and God holds us responsible for not knowing it. It is not a question of any uncanny spiritual influence, or of a flashing spiritual intuition, but of having the nous, our responsible intelligence, so obedient to the Holy Spirit that we can understand what is of God and what is not. BP. 244

We must continually take stock of what is ours in Christ Jesus because only in that way will we understand what God intends us to be. DI. 4

Watch what you say you don't understand—you understand only too clearly. DI. 80

Learn to be glad when you feel yourself a chaos that makes you bitterly disappointed with yourself, because from that moment you will begin to understand that God alone can make you 'order' and 'beauty.' DI. 80

We must be prepared to be led, and the way we come to an understanding is by the relationship of our personal life to the Person of Jesus Christ, then bit by bit we begin to understand. GW. 108

To understand means we can reconstruct a thing mentally and leave no element out. When we come to try and understand the Highest Good of our Lord, we must take it in His language, and it will take all time and eternity to understand what that Good is. Whether we live for the Highest Good does not depend on our understanding, but on whether we have the life of the Highest Good in us. HG. 50

The only One Who understands us is God. MUH. 12

To understand where I am in the sight of God means not only to listen but to obey promptly all He says. I can always know where I am. NKW. 114

Never be afraid because you do not understand yourself, and never be sour because no one else understands you. There is only One Who understands us, and that is God. PH. 120

UNIVERSE

Every type of superstition pretends it can rule the universe, the scientific quack proclaims he can control the weather, that he has occult powers and can take the untameable universe and tame it. God says it cannot be done. BFB. 98

The Bible distinctly states that our universe is pluralistic, not monistic; that means there are other forces at work besides God, viz., man and the devil. These are not God, and never will be. Man is meant to come back to God and to be in harmony with Him through Jesus Christ, the devil will be at enmity with God for ever. BP. 31

. . . in all probability there was a former order of things, which was ruined by disobedience, thereby producing the chaos out of which God reconstructed the order of things which we know, and which we so differently interpret. BP. 227

God keeps open house for the universe. HGM. 29

Those who deal with the great secrets of the universe imply that our planet is such a tiny spot in the tremendous universe that it is a piece of stupid conceit on our part to think that God watches over us. And to make our planet the centre where God performed the marvellous drama of His own history of the Incarnation and Atonement is absurd, they say. But watch a simple-minded person, one who is right with God and is not terrified by the reasonings of men, as he looks at the stars and exclaims, 'when I consider Thy heavens, the work of Thy fingers, the moon and the stars, which Thou hast ordained; what is man, that Thou are mindful of him?' It is said not in despair, but in adoring wonder. SHL. 34

Look at the world either through a telescope or a microscope and you will be dwarfed into terror by the infinitely great or the infinitely little. Naturalists tell us that there are no two blades of grass alike, and close inspection of a bee's wing under a microscope reveals how marvellously it is made. What do I

read in the Bible? I read that the God of heaven counts the hairs of our heads. Jesus says so. I read that the mighty God watches the sparrows so intimately that not one of them falls on the ground without His notice. I read that the God who holds the seas in the hollow of His hand and guides the stars in their courses, clothes the grass of the field. Through the love of God in Christ Jesus we are brought into a wonderful intimacy with the infinitely great and the infinitely little. SHL. 35

USEFULNESS

Unless we have the right matter in our minds intellectually and in our hearts affectionately, we will be hustled out of usefulness to God. AUG. 7

The intensity of the moments spent under the shadow of the Almighty is the measure of your usefulness as a worker. AUG. 27

Don't get dissipated; determine to develop your intellect for one purpose only—to make yourself of more use to God. AUG. 36

We constantly ask, 'Am I of any use?' If you think you are, it is questionable whether you are being used by the Holy Spirit at all. It is the things you pay no attention to that the Holy Spirit uses. DI. 86

The only way we can be sent is by God deliberately lifting us out of any sense of fitness in ourselves; I realize I am utterly weak and powerless, and that if I am to be of any use for God, He must do it in me all the time. GW. 48

If I am going to be of any use to Jesus Christ I must spend a great deal of time with Him as my Lord and Master, then

He can reveal Himself through me to others. GW. 55

If you are right with God, you will be amazed at what other people get in the way of real spiritual help out of what you say; but never think about it. The temptation comes all along to say, 'It is because I brooded that God gave me that thought.' The right attitude is to keep the mind absolutely concentrated on God and never get off on the line of how you are being used by Him. IWP. 45

If we are paying attention to the Source, rivers of living water will pour out of us, but immediately we stop paying attention to the Source, the outflow begins to dry up. We have nothing to do with our 'usability,' but only with our relationship to Jesus Christ, nothing must be allowed to come in between. IWP. 45

. . . if we are to be of use to God in the world we must be useful from God's standpoint, not from our own standpoint or the standpoint of other people. LG. 55

The people who are of absolutely no use to God are those who have sat down and have become overgrown with spiritual mildew; all they can do is to refer to an experience they had twenty or thirty years ago. That is of no use whatever, we must be vitally at it all the time. With Paul it was never 'an experience I once had,' but *"the life which I now live."* MFL. 99

The tendency to-day is to put the emphasis on service. Beware of the people who make usefulness their ground of appeal. If you make usefulness the test, then Jesus Christ was the greatest failure that ever lived. The lodestar of the saint is God Himself, not estimated usefulness. It is the work that God does through us that counts, not what we do for Him. MUH. 243

Being taught of God is a delightful life, it means the discernment is exercised. God does not put us in His 'show room,' we are here for Him to show His marvellous works in us and to use us in His enterprises. OBH. 113

If we are going to be used by God, He will take us through a multitude of experiences that are not meant for us at all, but meant to make us useful in His hands. PH. 34

Our Lord's first obedience was not to the needs of men, not to the consideration of where He was most useful, but to the will of His Father, and the first need of our life is not to be useful to God, but to do God's will. PR. 108

If you want to be of use to God, get rightly related to Jesus Christ and He will make you of use unconsciously every minute you live. RTR. 47

Our Lord pays not the remotest attention to natural abilities or natural virtues; He heeds only one thing—Does that man discern Who I am? Does he know the meaning of My Cross? The men and women Jesus Christ is going to use in His enterprises are those in whom He has done everything. SSY. 49

V

VENGEANCE

Vengeance is probably the most tyranni-
cal passion of the carnal mind. BP. 101

The deepest-rooted passion in the human soul is vengeance. Drunkenness,
sensuality, and covetousness go deep,
but not so deep as vengeance. BP. 117

There is no element of the vindictive in
our great and good God. GW. 50

Confess before God that you have been
distracted away from faith in Him; don't
vindicate yourself. The lust of vindica-
tion is a state of mind that destroys the
soul's faith in God—'I must explain myself'; 'I must get people to understand.'
HG. 22

VICTORY

It is a shameful thing for a Christian to
talk about getting the victory. The Vic-
tor ought to have got us so completely
that it is His victory all the time, and we
are more than conquerors through
Him. MUH. 298

If you say, 'My goal is God Himself' before you have been to school, it is merely
a nursery rhyme; but say it after winning a victory that tells for God, and the
victory does not seem such a glorious
thing after all, until you find that the
goal is not a prize, but the fulfilment of a
decree of God in and through you.
NKW. 44

It is the presence of God that is the secret of victory always. OPG. 71

VIRTUE

The inspiration of God does not patch
up my natural virtues; He re-makes the
whole of my being until we find that
'every virtue we possess is His alone.'
God does not come in and patch up our
good works, He puts in the Spirit that
was characteristic of Jesus; it is His patience, His love, and His tenderness and
gentleness that are exhibited through
us. BP. 145

The things from which we have to loose
ourselves are the good things of the old
creation as well as the bad, e.g., our natural virtues, because our natural virtues
can never come anywhere near what
Jesus Christ wants. CHI. 106

If you are in danger of building on the
natural virtues, which are a remnant of
the former creation, the Holy Spirit will
throw a searchlight and show you things
that cause you to shudder. He will reveal
a vindictiveness, a maliciousness, you
never knew before. DI. 23

Our Lord can never be spoken of in
terms of the natural virtues, they don't
apply to Him, and they don't apply to
the new man in Christ, all that is taken
knowledge of in those possessed by
Christ is that they have been with Jesus,
the dominating personality that tells is
that of the Son of God, it is His life that
is being manifested. GW. 64

Faith, hope, love, the three supernatural virtues, have a two-fold aspect in the saint's life. The first is seen in the early experiences of grace when these virtues are accidental; the second, when grace is worked into us and these virtues are essential and abiding.   IWP. 83

When we experience what technically we call being born again of the Spirit of God, we have 'spurts' of faith, hope, love, they come but we cannot grip them and they go; when we experience what technically we call sanctification those virtues abide, they are not accidental any more.   IWP. 83

The power of God was exhibited in Jesus Christ—that insignificant Nazarene Carpenter whom Roman paganism did not notice. In the eyes of the world pagan virtues are admirable: Christian virtues are contemptible.   LG. 74

'If there is any virtue anywhere in the world, think about it,' because the natural virtues are remnants of God's handiwork and will always lead to the one central Source, Jesus Christ.   MFL. 92

No man is virtuous because he cannot help it; virtue is acquired.   MUH. 339

The way the Holy Spirit corrupts our natural virtues when He comes in is one of the most devastating experiences. He does not build up and transfigure what we possess in the way of virtue and goodness by natural heredity; it is corrupted to death, until we learn that we *'. . . dare not trust the sweetest frame, But wholly lean on Jesus' name.'*   OBH. 98

No one is virtuous naturally, we may be innocent naturally, but innocence is often a hindrance because it is nothing in the world but ignorance. Virtue can only be the outcome of conflict. Everything

that does not partake of the nature of virtue is the enemy of virtue in us. Immediately we fight we become moral in that particular. Spiritually it is the same, everything that is not spiritual will make for our undoing.   OBH. 102

Drudgery is the touchstone of character. It is a 'drudging' thing to be virtuous. Necessity is not virtue; virtue can only be the outcome of conflict. The virtuous man or woman is the one who has gone through the fight and has added virtue, added it on the basis of the Divine nature, not on the basis of human determination.   OBH. 106

There is no virtue that has not gone through a moral choice. A great many of us make virtues out of necessity.   OPG. 68

Jesus Christ does not patch up our natural virtues. He creates a new man, "Wherefore if any man is in Christ, he is a new creature: the old things are passed away, behold, they are become new," and we find that 'every virtue we possess, is His alone.'   PH. 55

Virtue is not in the man who has not been tempted, neither is purity. When a man is tempted and remains steadfastly unspotted, then he is virtuous.   PH. 148

We must be re-made on the inside and develop new virtues entirely, 'a new man in Christ Jesus.' This is one part of the problem which no teacher outside the Bible deals with. Books on ethics and morals take the natural virtues as promises of what a man is going to be; the Bible indicates that they are remnants of what man once was, and the key to these virtues is Adam, not Jesus Christ.   PS. 69

The majority of people are not blackguards and criminals, living in external sin, they are clean-living and respectable, and it is to such that the scourge of God is the most terrible thing because it reveals that the natural virtues may be in idolatrous opposition to God. SHL. 72

Natural virtues are lovely in the sight of Jesus, because He sees in them remnants of His Father's former handiwork. SSY. 57

VISION

If the Holy Spirit has given you a vision in your private Bible study or during a meeting which made your heart glow, and your mind expand, and your will stir itself to grasp, you will have to pay to the last farthing in concentration along that line until all you saw in vision is made actual. CHI. 58

It is all very well to preach, the easiest thing in the world to give people a vision of what God wants; it is another matter to come into the sordid conditions of ordinary life and make the vision real there. DI. 44

Vision is an inspiration to stand us in good stead in the drudgery of discipline; the temptation is to despise the discipline. DI. 70

A vision puts enthusiasm into you, a thrilling understanding of God's Word and you soar above in a tremendous ecstasy; then you come down and run without being weary, and then you come to the grandest days and walk without fainting. IYA. 45

When we are born again we all have visions, if we are spiritual at all, of what Jesus wants us to be, and the great thing is to learn not to be disobedient to the vision, not to say that it cannot be attained. MUH. 24

Always distinguish between what you see Jesus to be, and what He has done for you. If you only know what He has done for you, you have not a big enough God; but if you have had a vision of Jesus as He is, experiences can come and go, you will endure "as seeing Him Who is invisible." MUH. 71

If we lose the vision, we alone are responsible, and the way we lose the vision is by spiritual leakage. If we do not run our belief about God into practical issues, it is all up with the vision God has given. The only way to be obedient to the heavenly vision is to give our utmost for God's highest, and this can only be done by continually and resolutely recalling the vision. The test is the sixty seconds of every minute, and the sixty minutes of every hour, not our times of prayer and devotional meetings. MUH. 71

A man with the vision of God is not devoted to a cause or to any particular issue: he is devoted to God Himself. MUH. 123

The healthiest exercise for the mind of a Christian is to learn to apprehend the truth granted to it in vision. Every Christian with any experience at all has had a vision of some fundamental truth, either about the Atonement or the Holy Spirit or sin, and it is at the peril of their souls that they lose the vision. By prayer and determination we have to form the habit of keeping ourselves soaked in the vision God has given. The difficulty with the majority of us is that we will not seek to apprehend the vision, we get glimpses of it and then leave it alone. PS. 40

Let me plead with you, "as though Christ besought you," do not be disobedient to the heavenly vision. There is only one purpose for your life, and that is the satisfaction of the Lord Jesus Christ. RTR. 13

Visions are great things, but it is useless to tell a man about the vision of God on earth unless you can get down into the mire he is in and lift him up; and the marvel is that if you have got hold of the vision of God and are working it out by moral obedience in your own life, you can do the lifting. SA. 90

VOWING

'*Come unto Me,*' said Jesus. The thing that keeps us from coming is religious self-idolatry; we will not let God make a covenant with us, we will make vows with God. Vowing means I can do it if I pledge myself to do it. NKW. 64

Don't pile up vows before men, and certainly not before God. SHH. 55

W

WANT

Want is a conscious tendency towards a particular end. My wants take shape when something awakens my personal life. MFL. 9

If you tell half a dozen clean-living, upright, sterling men that God so loved them that He gave His Son to die for them, only their good breeding will keep them from being amused—'Why should Jesus Christ die for me?' It is not a living proposition to them, not in the sphere of their life at all. Their morality is well within their own grasp, they are clean-living and upright, all that can be desired; they will never be awakened in that way; but present them with Jesus Christ, or with a life that is like His life, and instantly there will awaken in them a want they were not conscious of before. That is why Jesus said, "If I had not come . . . , they had not had sin: but now they have no cloke for their sin." MFL. 10

You can never tell from a man's life to date what he is going to want next, because the real element of want is not logical. MFL. 11

When I see Jesus Christ I simply want to be what He wants me to be. A wish is more definite than a want, which is inarticulate, something I am conscious of and that is all. MFL. 12

We must always get to the point of acting on the want and the wish born in us when we are in the presence of Jesus Christ. MFL. 17

WAR

There is one thing worse than war, and that is sin. The thing that startles us is not the thing that startles God. We get tremendously scared when our social order is broken up, and well we may. We get terrorised by hundreds of men being killed, but we forget that there is something worse—sinful, dastardly lives being lived day by day, year in and year out, in our villages and towns—men without one trace of cleanness in their moral lives. That is worse. CD. VOL. 1, 109

'Is war of the devil or of God?' It is of neither, it is of men, though both God and the devil are behind it. War is a conflict of wills, either in individuals or in nations. LG. 29

WAY/TRUTH/LIFE

Beware of the tendency of asking the way when you know it perfectly well. MUH. 131

"I am the Way." If a man will resign himself in implicit trust to the Lord Jesus, he will find that He leads the wayfaring soul into the green pastures and beside the still waters, so that even when he goes through the dark valley of the shadow of some staggering episode, he will fear no evil. Nothing in life or death, time or eternity, can stagger that soul from the certainty of the Way for one moment. PH. 8

The Way is used by everyone who has not the childlike heart; we have to go humbly lest we miss the way of life just because it is so simple. God has hidden these things from the wise and prudent and revealed them unto babes. PH. 8

When a man has been found by the Lord Jesus and has given himself to Him in unconditional surrender, the fact that he has found The Way is not so much a conscious possession as an unconscious inheritance. PH. 9

One of the significant things about those who are in The Way is that they have a strong family likeness to Jesus, His peace marks them in an altogether conspicuous manner. The light of the morning is on their faces, and the joy of the endless life is in their hearts. Wherever they go, men are gladdened or healed, or made conscious of a need.
PH. 9

Jesus Christ is not the way to God, not a road we leave behind us, a fingerpost that points in the right direction; He is the way itself. PR. 137

Let Plato or Socrates, for instance, say, "I am the Way, the Truth, and the Life," and we see what it involves. Jesus Christ is either mad or what He claims to be, viz.: the only revelation of God Almighty that there is. SA. 36

Jesus Christ says neither the Church nor the Bible is the authority, but "I am the Way, the Truth, and the Life"; the Church and the Bible are secondary.
SA. 63

WEARINESS

There is no such thing as weariness in God's work. If you are in tune with the joy of God, the more you spend out in God's service, the more the recuperation goes on, and when once the warn-ing note of weariness is given, it is a sign that something has gone wrong. NKW. 37

Spiritual fatigue comes from the unconscious frittering away of God's time. When you feel weary or are exhausted, don't ask for hot milk, but get back to God. NKW. 37

The secret of weariness and nervous disease in the natural world is the lack of a dominating interest, and the same is true in spiritual life. NKW. 37

When I get my eyes off Him I begin to get weary. I am kept from wasting in the way only as I abide under the shadow of the Almighty and stake my all in confidence in God. I have nothing to do with the results, but only with maintaining my relationship to Him. PH. 239

When I only do what God wants me to do, He will recuperate me all the time. Watch the things that exhaust you.
RTR. 49

WILL

Man's spirit has not 'life in itself,' i.e., man cannot will pure will, or love pure love. The Holy Spirit has life in Himself, and when He comes in He energizes our spirit and enables us "to will and to do of His good pleasure." BP. 254

Remember, you must urge the will to an issue; you must come to the point where you *will* to believe the Redeemer, and deliberately wash your hands of the consequences. CHI. 29

The great impelling power of the Holy Spirit is seen in its most fundamental working whenever an issue of will is pushed. It is pleasanter to listen to poetical discourses, more agreeable to have your affinities appealed to, but it is not good enough, it leaves you exactly as you were. The Gospel appeal comes with a stinging grip—'Will you?" or "Won't you?'; 'I will accept,' or, "I'll put it off,'—both are decisions, remember. DI. 25

It is never our wicked heart that is the difficulty, but our obstinate will. DI. 31

Modern ethical teaching bases everything on the power of the will, but we need to recognize also the perils of the will. The man who has achieved a moral victory by the sheer force of his will is less likely to want to become a Christian than the man who has come to the moral frontier of his own need. GW. 132

There is no limit to what God can make us are we but willing. His great love is ever overshadowing us and He waits to visit us with His saving life. GW. 146

We have rigorously to push an issue of will, and when the issue is put you find the obstruction; men resent it, and that is the barrier to God. Immediately that barrier is down God comes in like a torrent, there is nothing to keep Him back; the one thing that keeps Him back is anarchy and rebellion, the essential nature of Satan—I won't give up my right to myself; I won't yield, and God is powerless. Immediately a man removes the barriers it is as if God romped into his soul with all His almightiness, it is a flood of blessing quite overwhelming. HG. 102

The will is not a faculty, will is the whole man active—body, soul and spirit. IWP. 92

Let a man get right with God through the Atonement and his activity becomes in that manner and measure akin to Jesus Christ. The whole of my will

free to do God's will, that means a holy scorn of putting my neck under any yoke but the yoke of the Lord Jesus Christ. IWP. 92

Beware of thinking of will as a faculty. Will simply means the whole nature active. We talk about people having a weak will or a strong will, it is a misleading idea. When we speak of a man having a weak will, we mean he is without any impelling passion, he is the creature of every dominating influence; with good people he is good, with bad people he is bad, not because he is a hypocrite, but because he has no ruling passion, and any strong personality knits him into shape. MFL. 9

Always let the instinct that rules you in the presence of Jesus lead. That is why it is so necessary in an evangelistic meeting to push people to an issue of will. It is a terrible thing to awaken people up to a certain point and never give them the chance to act in the same atmosphere. MFL. 15

Whatever rouses your will is an indication of the bias of your personality. MFL. 29

Never look upon the will as something you possess as you do a watch. Will is the whole man active. MFL. 126

The profound thing in man is his will, not sin. Will is the essential element in God's creation of man: sin is a perverse disposition which entered into man. In a regenerated man the source of will is almighty. "For it is God which worketh in you both to will and to do of His good pleasure." MUH. 158

Will is the whole man active. I cannot *give up* my will, I must exercise it. I must *will* to obey, and I must *will* to receive God's Spirit. When God gives a vision of truth it is never a question of what He will do, but of what we will do. MUH. 190

Surrender is not the surrender of the external life, but of the will; when that is done, all is done. There are very few crises in life; the great crisis is the surrender of the will. God never crushes a man's will into surrender, He never beseeches him, He waits until the man yields up his will to Him. MUH. 257

The moments when I truly live are the moments when I act with my whole will. MUH. 309

God's command is—Take *now*, not presently. It is extraordinary how we debate! We know a thing is right, but we try to find excuses for not doing it at once. To climb to the height God shows can never be done presently, it must be done now. The sacrifice is gone through in will before it is performed actually. MUH. 316

When God draws me, the issue of my will comes in at once—will I react on the revelation which God gives—will I come to Him? Discussion on spiritual matters is an impertinence. Never discuss with anyone when God speaks. Belief is not an intellectual act; belief is a moral act whereby I deliberately commit myself. Will I dump myself down absolutely on God and transact on what He says? If I will, I shall find I am based on Reality that is as sure as God's throne. MUH. 357

We cannot remain boss by the sheer power of will; sooner or later our wills must yield allegiance to some force greater than their own, either God or the devil. NKW. 52

Make your will let Jesus do everything, make no conditions, and He will take you home with Him not only for a day but for ever; self-interest will be done with, and the only thing left will be the real interest that identifies you with Jesus. OBH. 104

'Ask what you *will*,' i.e., what your will is in. There is very little our wills are in, consequently it is easy to work up false emotions. PR. 124

Christian evidences don't amount to anything; you can't convince a man against his will. SA. 32

The oppression of tyranny means that I drive my will on other people, and if they do not do what I want, I break them. It is an oppression in which one power crushes another. SHH. 44

Will is not a thing I possess; will is the whole man active. SHH. 89

The profound thing in man is his will, not sin. Will is the essential element in God's creation of man; sin is a perverse disposition which entered into man. At the basis, the human will is one with God; it is covered up with all kinds of desires and motives, and when we preach Jesus Christ the Holy Spirit excavates down to the basis of the will and the will turns to God every time. We try to attack men's wills; if we lift up Jesus He will push straight to the will. SSM. 85

WISDOM

A philosopher is a lover of wisdom, and spiritual philosophy means the love of wisdom not only in our heart life, but in our heads—the last place a Christian gets to. IWP. 42

The whole wisdom of God has come down to the shores of our lives in a flesh and blood Man, and John says, we have seen Him and we know Him. PR. 23

Books of Wisdom: Job—how to suffer; Psalms—how to pray; Proverbs—how to act; Ecclesiastes—how to enjoy; Song of Solomon—how to love. SHH. 2

The wisdom of to-day concerns itself chiefly with the origin of things and not with God, consequently neither the philosopher nor the mystic has time for actual life. SHH. 58

The wisdom of God is arrant stupidity to the wisdom of the world, until all of a sudden God makes the wisdom of the world foolish. SHH. 83

The world of wisdom is to bank all on God and disregard the consequences. SHH. 91

We are not Christians at heart, we don't believe in the wisdom of God, but only in our own. We go in for insurance and economy and speculation, everything that makes us secure in our own wisdom. SHH. 143

WISH

To tell a man who is down and out to get up and do the right thing can never help him; but when once Jesus Christ is presented to him there is a reflected wish to be what Jesus wants him to be. MFL. 13

The wish ought to be followed by immediate obedience. I must take the wish and translate it into resolution and then into action; if I don't, the wish will translate itself into a corrupting power in my life instead of a redeeming power. MFL. 13

WITNESSES

God will never answer our prayer to be baptized by the Holy Ghost for any other reason than to be a witness for Jesus. "Ye shall receive power, after that the Holy Ghost is come upon you: and ye shall be witnesses unto Me." Not witnesses of what Jesus can do, that is an elementary witness, but "witnesses unto Me," 'you will be instead of Me, you will take everything that happens, praise or blame, persecution or commendation, as happening to Me.' No one can stand that unless he is constrained by the majesty of the personal power of Jesus. AUG. 31

Remember, weariness in work which is attended by spiritual weakness means you have been using your vital energy without at the same time witnessing. Natural weariness in work while you witness, produces steady and wonderful rejuvenescence. DI. 87

A witness means that just as Jesus was made broken bread and poured-out wine for our salvation, so we are to be broken bread and poured-out wine in sacrificial service. HGM. 23

"and ye shall be My witnesses"—not witnesses of what Jesus can do or of His gospel, but witnesses unto Him, that is, He is perfectly satisifed with us wherever we are. HG. 29

Christianity is a personal history with Jesus. "and ye shall be My witnesses." HGM. 38

The baptism of the Holy Ghost makes us witnesses to Jesus, not witnesses to what he can do, that is an elementary witness, but 'witnesses unto Me.' HGM. 138

'*Ye shall be witnesses unto Me.*' This great Pentecostal phrase puts the truth for us in unforgettable words. Witnesses not so much of what Jesus Christ can do, but *Witnesses unto Me*, a delight to the heart of Jesus, a satisfaction to Him wherever He places us. LG. 132

Concentrate on God, let Him engineer circumstances as He will, and wherever He places you He is binding up the brokenhearted through you, setting at liberty the captives through you, doing His mighty soul-saving work through you, as you keep rightly related to Him. Self-conscious service is killed, self-conscious devotion is gone, only one thing remains—"witnesses unto Me," Jesus Christ first, second and third.
MFL. 108

Whenever you make a transaction with God, it is real instantly and you have the witness; when there is no witness, no humility, no confidence or joy, it is because you have made a transaction with your religious self and you say—I must wait for God's witness. That is self-idolatry; there is no trust in God in it, but just the mewling of a sick infant.
NKW. 64

You can never give other people what you have found, but you can make them homesick for the same thing. That is the meaning of these words of Our Lord— "Ye shall be My witnesses"—you will exhibit a oneness with Jesus Christ whilst He carries out His will in your life in every detail. OBH. 94

". . . and ye shall be My witnesses." Literally, 'the Holy Ghost coming upon you will make you witnesses unto Me, not witness of what I can do, not recorders of what you have experienced, but witnesses who are a satisfaction to Me.'
PH. 174

'Ye shall be my witnesses'; 'not witnesses to what I can do, but witnesses who satisfy Me in any circumstances I put you in.' 'I reckon on you for extreme service, with no complaining on your part and no explanation on Mine.' SSY. 96

A witness is one who has deliberately given up his life to the ownership of another, not to a cause, and death will never make him swerve from his allegiance. SSY. 147

'Ye shall be my witnesses.' Many a man is prevented from being a witness to Jesus by over-zealousness for His cause. SSY. 147

Bible training and missionary training is not meant to train men for a purpose for which human nature can train itself. Religious institutions start out on the right line of making witnesses to Jesus, then they get swept off on to the human line and begin to train men for certain things, to train for a cause, or a special enterprise, or for a denomination, and the more these training places are multiplied, the less chance is there of witnesses to Jesus being made. Nowadays we are in danger of reversing Jesus Christ's order. There stands the eternal word of Christ—'As the Father hath sent me, *even so send I you.*' SSY. 147

WOMAN

There are only two beings a woman is not too much for, one is God, the other is the devil. OPG. 52

The Bible reveals that the essentially feminine is meant to be the handmaid of God; but if the essentially feminine is prostitute, no man on earth can withstand her. SHH. 108

WONDER

Has the sense of wonder been dying down in your religious life? If so, you need to get back to the Source. If you have lost the fervour of delight in God, tell Him so. The old Divines used to ask God for the grace of trembling, i.e., the sense of wonder. When wonder goes out of natural love, something or someone is to be severely blamed; wonder ought never to go. With a child the element of wonder is always there, a freshness and spontaneity, and the same is true of those who follow Jesus Christ's teaching and become as little children. HG. 34

Satisfaction is too often the peace of death; wonder is the very essence of life. Beware always of losing the wonder, and the first thing that stops wonder is religious conviction. HGM. 143

WORD AND DEED

The expression of our lips must correspond with our communion with God. It is easy to say good and true things without troubling to live up to them; consequently the Christian talker is more likely to be a hypocrite than any other kind of worker. AUG. 27

The Holy Spirit will bring us to the practical test, it is not that I *say* I am righteous, but that I prove I am in my deeds. BE. 22

I can 'mouth' my salvation, I can thank God for it, but if I do not produce 'goods up to sample' my religious life is a travesty. BE. 62

If you have a time of real devotion before God and see what God wants you to do and you do not work it out in your practical life, it will react in secret immorality. That is not an exceptional law, it is

an eternal law, and I wish it could be blazed in letters of fire into the mind of every Christian. BE. 73

The Apostle James will have nothing to do with pious talk that is not backed by the life. Pious words without works are so much wind. RTR. 10

The best way you and I can help our fellow-men is to work out the thing in our own lives first. Unless it is backed up by our life, talking is of no use. We may talk a donkey's hind leg off, but we are powerless to do any lifting. If we look after the vision in our own life, we shall be a benediction to other people. SA. 91

There is a tendency in all of us to appreciate the sayings of Jesus Christ with our intellects while we refuse to *do* them; then everything we build will go by the board when the test comes. SSM. 109

WORDS

The power of the spoken word accounts for the prominent place given in the Bible to prophesying and preaching. BFB. 69

Can Jesus Christ speak to me to-day? Certainly He can, through the Holy Spirit; but if I take the words of Jesus without His Spirit, they are of no avail to me. I can conjure with them, I can do all kinds of things with them, but they are not "spirit and life." When the Holy Spirit is in me, He will bring to my remembrance what Jesus has said and make His Words live. The Spirit within me enables me to assimilate the words of Jesus. BP. 231

A child is not responsible, but the statements of persons of mature intelligence are responsible; consequently we are judged by our words. It is quite true that there are times when we have to say, 'answer my meaning, not my words,' but those times are exceptional. The things we express, the statements we make, and the thoughts we form, are all stamped with responsibility. BP. 239

The stupendous profundities of God's will, surging with unfathomable mysteries, come down to the shores of our common life, not in emotions and fires, nor in aspirations and vows, and agonies and visions, but in a way so simple that the wayfaring men, yea fools, cannot make a mistake, viz., in words.
CD. VOL. 1, 16

The revelation of God's will has been brought down to us in words. GW. 70

It is not always the cross mood that leads to the cross speech, but the cross word that makes the cross mood. If in the morning you begin to talk crossly, before long you will *feel* desperately cross. Take to God the things that perturb your spirit. HG. 21

When the words of the Bible come home to us by the Holy Spirit, the supernatural essence of the Redemption is in those words and they bring forth new life in us. HG. 96

My spiritual life is based on some word of God made living in me; when I transact on that word, I step into the moral frontier where Jesus works. LG. 119

Our Lord crowned the words that the powers of this world detest—'servant,' 'obedience,' 'humility,' 'service.' MFL. 105

Jesus Christ says a great deal that we listen to, but do not hear; when we do hear, His words are amazingly hard. MUH. 230

When we take Jesus Christ's words about His Cross, the least thing we can do is to endeavour to get at His mind behind His words. Jesus says things from a different point of view from ours, and unless we receive His Spirit, we do not even begin to see what He is driving at.
PH. 218

"Depart from Me," the most appallingly isolating and condemning words that could be said to a human soul. SSM. 106

WORK

The impatience of modern life has so crept into Christian work that we will not settle down before God and find out what He wants us to do. AUG. 27

We try to save ourselves, but God only can do that; and we try to sanctify ourselves, but God only can do that. After God has done these sovereign works of grace in our hearts, we have to work them out in our lives. ". . . work out your own salvation with fear and trembling. For it is God which worketh in you both to will and to do of His good pleasure."
BP. 119

The great snare in Christian work is this—'Do remember the people you are talking to.' We have to remain true to God and His message, not to a knowledge of the people, and as we rely on the Holy Spirit we will find God works His marvels in His own way. DI. 44

The more we talk about work, the less we work, and the same with prayer.
DI. 70

The value of our work depends on whether we can direct men to Jesus Christ. DI. 85

This fundamental principle must be borne in mind, that any work for God before it fulfils its purpose must die, otherwise it 'abides alone.' The conception is not that of progress from a seed to full growth, but of a seed dying and bringing forth what it never was. That is why Christianity is always 'a forlorn hope' in the eyes of the world.   DI. 85

We take on a tremendous amount of stuff which we call work for God, and God puts the sentence of death on it for we are exhausted by it without being recuperated, because our strength is drawn from somewhere other than the Highest. The sign that what we are doing is God's work is that we know the supernatural recuperation.   GW. 106

The people who tell are those who don't know they are telling, not the priggish people who worship work.   HGM. 76

Unless God has worked in us we shall hinder Him all the time by trying to be His children; we cannot, we have to be born from above by the will of God first, be regenerated; then our working is not working to help God, it is working to let God express through us what He has done in us so that we may prove we are the children of our Father in heaven.   IWP. 63

The times God works most wonderfully are the times we never think about it. When we work of ourselves we always connect things with time.   IWP. 67

We need a spiritual vision of work as well as a spiritual vision of truth. It is not that we go through a certain curriculum and then we are fit to work; preparation and work are so involved that they cannot be separated.   LG. 90

We are in danger of forgetting that we cannot do what God does, and that God will not do what we can do. We cannot save ourselves nor sanctify ourselves, God does that; but God will not give us good habits, He will not give us character, He will not make us walk aright. We have to do all that ourselves, we have to work out the salvation God has worked in.   MUH. 131

This is a day when practical work is overemphasized, and the saints who are bringing every project into captivity are criticized and told that they are not in earnest for God or for souls. True earnestness is found in obeying God, not in the inclination to serve Him that is born of undisciplined human nature.
MUH. 253

We can ever remain powerless, as were the disciples, by trying to do God's work not in concentration on His power, but by ideas drawn from our own temperament. We slander God by our very eagerness to work for Him without knowing Him.   MUH. 277

In the beginning we do not train for God, we train for work, for our own aims, but as we go on with God we lose all our own aims and are trained into God's purpose. Unless practical work is appointed by God, it will prove a curse.   NKW. 128

I must beware of the tendency to become dissipated in my conception by false notions of Christian work, or by ideas as to what I ought to be doing. I ought to be nothing but a disciple of Jesus Christ; He will be doing through me all the time.   PH. 112

There are saints who are being rattled out of holiness by fussy work for God, whereas one five minutes of brooding on

God's truth would do more good than all their work and fuss. RTR. 38

Work is often taken up with the absurd deification of pluck—"this thing has got to be done, and I must do it," and men damage their souls in doing it because God is not there to protect them. But when a man or a woman is called of God, the facts he or she has to face never upset the equilibrium of the life garrisoned by the presence of God. RTR. 60

When a man is not well he is always doing things, an eternal fidget. Intense activity may be the sign of physical weariness. When a man is healthy his work is so much part of himself that you never know he is doing it; he does it with his might, and that makes no fuss. We lose by the way we do our work the very thing it is intended to bring us.
SHH. 129

God works in us to do His will, only we must do the doing; and if once we start to do what He commands we find we can do it, because we work on the basis of the noble thing God has done for us in Redemption. SSM. 95

God demands of us our utmost in working out what He has worked in. We can do nothing towards our redemption, but we must do everything to work it out in actual experience on the basis of regeneration. SSM. 96

The New Testament never asks us to *believe* the Holy Spirit, it asks to *receive* Him; He makes the appearance and the reality one and the same thing. He *works in* our salvation and we have to *work it out*, with fear and trembling lest we forget to. Thank God, He does give us the sporting chance, the glorious risk. SSM. 104

No Christian has a special work to do. A Christian is called to be Jesus Christ's own, one chosen by Him; one who is not above His Master, and who does not dictate to Jesus as to what he intends to do. Our Lord calls to no special work; He calls to Himself. Pray to the Lord of the harvest, and He will engineer your circumstances and thrust you out. SSY. 129

In the active work we do for God we do not really believe that Jesus Christ is sovereign Lord; if we did, we should fuss less and build more in faith in Him. We cannot do the Saviour's work by fuss, but only by knowing Him as the supreme sovereign Lord. SSY. 134

There is a time to smite and a time to smile; a time to slay and thrust straight home when the true, sterling worth of your own repentance and the true, sterling worth of God's work of grace in your heart is put to the test. WG. 54

WORKER

God puts His workers where He puts His Son. AUG. 8

Never choose to be a worker, but when once God has put His call on you, woe be to you if you turn to the right hand or to the left. AUG. 9

My life as a worker is the way I say 'Thank you' to God for His unspeakable salvation. AUG. 18

A worker for God must be prepared to endure hardness; he must learn how to 'sop up' all the bad and turn it into good, and nothing but the supernatural grace of God and his sense of obligation will enable him to do it. As workers we will be brought into relationship with people for whom we have no affinity; we have to stand for one thing only, "That I might by all means save some." AUG. 30

The one mastering obligation of our life as a worker is to persuade men for Jesus Christ, and to do that we have to learn to live amongst facts: the fact of human stuff as it is, not as it ought to be; and the fact of Bible revelation, whether it agrees with our doctrines or not. AUG. 31

The discipline of a worker is not in order to develop his own life, but for the purposes of his Commander. The reason there is so much failure is because we forget that we are here for that one thing, loyalty to Jesus Christ; otherwise we have no business to have taken the vows of God upon us. AUG. 64

As soon as we become rightly related to God, the prince of this world has his last stake in the flesh, he will suck every bit of your physical life out of you if he can. Many Christian workers do not know this, and Satan will seek to wear them out to the last cell; but if they know this 'trick' of his and also know God's grace, every time they are exhausted in work for God, they will get supernatural physical recuperation, and the proof that it is God's work is the experience of this supernatural recuperation. BP. 263

If you become exhausted in doing work in the world, what have you to do? You have to take an iron tonic and have a holiday, but if you are exhausted in God's work, all the iron tonics in the world will never touch you, the only thing that will recuperate you is God Himself. BP. 263

Remember, Satan's last stake is in the flesh, and when once you know that all your fresh springs are in God, you will draw on Him. Beware of laying off before God tells you to; if you lay off before

God tells you to, you will rust, and that leads to 'dry rot' always. BP. 264

Beware of any cleverness that keeps you from working. No one is born a worker; men are born poets and artists, but we have to make ourselves 'labourers.' DI. 67

The worker for God must live among the common-sense facts of the natural world, but he must also be at home with revelation facts. DI. 84

"Lovest thou Me?. . . Feed My sheep." That means giving out my life-blood for others as the Son of God gave His life-blood for me. DI. 85

You cannot be too severe with self-pity in yourself or in others. Be more merciless with yourself than you are with others. DI. 87

If we realize the intense sacredness of a human soul in God's sight we will no longer romp in where angels fear to tread, we will pray and wait. DI. 88

"We then, as workers together with Him . . . ," the One referred to is Almighty God, "the Creator of the ends of the earth." Think of the impregnable position it gives the feeblest saint to remember that he is a fellow-worker with God. DI. 90

The thing that staggers the worker is that men will not believe. How can they believe, when every spring of life is impure? The great need is to have a channel through which the grace of God can come to men and do something in their unconscious life, then slowly as that breaks into the conscious life there will come an expression of belief, because they see Jesus; but the way they see Him is through the worker who is a sacramental personality. GW. 109

The centre of life and of thinking for the Christian worker is the Person of Jesus Christ. We get deadly respectable when we face only the problems we have been used to facing; but if we will obey the Holy Spirit He will bring us to face other problems, and as we face them through personal relationship to Jesus Christ we shall go forth with courage, confident that whether it be in the domains of heathendom or in our own land, Jesus Christ is never nonplussed, never worsted. GW. 109

There is no royal road to becoming a worker for God. The only way is to let God in His mighty providence lift the life by a great tide, or break it from its moorings in some storm, and in one way or another get the life out to sea in reckless abandon to God. GW. 125

When we see evil and wrong exhibited in other lives, instead of awakening a sickening despair, it awakens a joyful confidence—I know a Saviour who can save even that one. One worker like that is of priceless worth, because through that one life the Son of God is being manifested. HG. 88

Our Lord was in no wise a hard worker; He was an intense reality. Hard workers are like midges and mosquitoes; the reality is like the mountain and the lake. Our Lord's life was one of amazing leisure, and the presentation of His life as one of rush is incorrect. HG. 111

The life of a worker is not a hop, skip and a jump affair, it is a squaring of the shoulders, then a steady, stedfast tramp straight through until we get to understand God's way. LG. 90

It takes the energy of God Himself to prepare a worker for all He wants to make him. LG. 90

Look at the laborious way of a scientist in finding out the secrets of Nature, and then look at our own slipshod ignorance with regard to God's Book. If the worker will obey God's way he will find he has to be everlastingly delving into the Bible and working it out in circumstances, the two always run together. LG. 92

An exclusive worker is excluded by God, because God does not work in that way. LG. 92

The worth of a worker to God is just the worth of a man's own fingers to his brain. LG. 92

It is not the tones of a man's speech, or the passion of a man's personality, it is the pleading power of the Holy Ghost coming through him; consequently the worker has no sympathy with things with which God's Spirit has no sympathy. We are in danger of being stern where God is tender, and of being tender where God is stern. LG. 93

If a worker is tripped in private life, the world strikes against that at once and makes it the excuse for not accepting the Gospel. The perilous possibility of being an occasion of stumbling is always there. LG. 94

If you are a worker for God, Satan will try to wear you out to the last cell; but if you know God's grace you will be supernaturally recuperated physically. MFL. 33

As Christian workers, worldliness is not our snare, sin is not our snare, but spiritual wantoning is, viz.: taking the pattern and print of the religious age we live in, making eyes at spiritual success. MUH. 115

It is never the consecration of our gifts that fits us for God's service. Profoundly speaking, we are not here to work for God. Absorption in practical work is one of the greatest hindrances in preventing a soul discerning the call of God. Unless active work is balanced by a deep isolated solitude with God, knowledge of God does not grow and the worker becomes exhausted and spent out. Our Lord said that the only men He will use in His enterprises are those in whom He has done everything; otherwise we would serve our own ends all the time. NKW. 119

Many of us who call ourselves Christian workers ought to be learners in God's school of Calvary. PH. 72

Insist on taking the initiative for God in every place you are in. As a worker, always determine to give God "the first foot." RTR. 17

If you talk about the need for personal sanctification to an aggressive Christian worker, he will say—'You are a dreamer of dreams, we have to get to work and *do* something'; whereas it is not a question of doing things, but a question of realizing deep down until there is no shadow of doubt about it, that if we are going to do anything, it must be by the supernatural power of God, not by our own ingenuity and wisdom. SSY. 122

Holiness people are not unpractical, they are the only ones who are building on the great underlying ideal of God. Our business as workers for God is to find out what God's ideal is, to ask ourselves on what line we are doing our duty; whether we are progressing along the line of God's ideal, and working that out, or being caught up in the drift of modern views and evolving away from God's ideal. SSY. 122

. . . we must keep ourselves in touch, not with theories, but with people, and never get out of touch with human beings, if we are going to use the word of God skilfully amongst them, and if the Holy Spirit is to apply the word of God through us as workmen needing not to be ashamed. WG. 12

If you are a worker, He will constantly surround you with different kinds of people, with different difficulties, and He will constantly put you to school amongst those facts. He will keep you in contact with human stuff, and human stuff is very sordid; in fact, human stuff is made of just the same stuff as you and I are made of; do not shut yourself away from it. Beware of the tendency to live a life apart and shut away. Get amongst men. WG. 13

Let me emphasise these three things again: First, the Christian worker who is right with God must rely every moment on the Holy Spirit when dealing with another soul. Second, the worker must live among human facts, men and women, not theories. Do not let us tell ourselves what men and women are like, let us find out what they are like. One of the greatest mistakes in the world is to tell yourself what a man is like; you do not know what he is like. The only One Who can teach you how to deal with the various specimens around you is the Holy Spirit. The third thing is, ransack this old Book from cover to cover in the most practical way you know—by using a concordance, by rewriting the Psalms, or by any other immediate practical method. WG. 14

Keep these three things in mind—reliance on the Holy Spirit of God, keeping in contact with people, and above all, keeping in contact with the revelation facts in God's Book; live amongst

them, and ask God how to apply them.
WG. 15

. . . do live among human facts! Thank God He has given the majority of us the surroundings of real, definite, sordid human beings; there is no pretence about them, the people we live among and come in contact with are not theories, they are facts. That is the kind of thing God wants us to keep among. WG. 20

. . . the first thing the worker must do is to keep his heart always believing in Jesus. WG. 25

Do remember that it is the most practical thing on this earth to be a worker for the cure of souls. WG. 27

There is only one Being Who understands us all and that is the Holy Spirit, and He understands the Lord Jesus Christ too, and if you keep the avenues of your soul open to Him and get your messages from Him and see that you allow nothing to obscure Him, you will find He will locate the people. For every new message you give, God will give you human beings who have been convicted by it, and you will have to deal with them, whether you like it or not; and you will have not only to deal with them, but you will have to take them on your heart before God. God will make you work for the cure of the souls He has wounded by your message. If the wounding has come along His line, the line of the faithful proclamation of His message, He will let you see Him healing that soul through you as a worker, as you rely on the Holy Spirit. WG. 27

. . . the Spirit of God will not work for the cure of some souls without you, and God is going to hold to the account of some of us the souls that have gone uncured, un-healed, un-touched by Jesus

Christ because we have refused to keep our souls open towards Him, and when the sensual, selfish, wrong lives came around we were not ready to present the Lord Jesus Christ to them by the power of the Holy Spirit. Workers for God, let us believe with all our heart these Divine revelations, and never despair of any soul under heaven. WG. 28

If the worker for God is going to go all lengths for God for the cure of souls, he has to allow God to examine deep down the possibilities of his own nature.
WG. 52

Set a thief to catch a thief, that is the method of the world; but when God Almighty sends a worker He sends one whom He has literally turned inside out, in a spiritual sense, one whose disposition He has altered and allowed the man or woman to know what He has done. There is no false knowledge in that worker's life. That worker goes straight for one purpose, the condemnation of the sinner, not to show his discernment, but that he may bring the soul out of its duplicity, out of its hypocrisy, into the light of God. WG. 54

God grant we may understand that working for the cure of souls is not a babe's work; it is a man's work, requiring man's power, grasped and transformed by God Almighty, so that God can get straight through the worker to the man He is waiting for. WG. 56

If you think you know how to present Jesus Christ to a soul, you will never be able to do it. But if you will learn how to rely on the Holy Ghost, believing that Jesus Christ can do it, then I make bold to state that He will do it. If you get your little compartment of texts, and search them out and say, 'I know how to deal with this soul,' you will never be able to deal with it; but if you realise your absolute helplessness and say, 'My God, I cannot touch this life, I do not know where to begin, but I believe that Thou canst do it,' then you can do something. WG. 66

The majority of workers are in the road with their convictions of how God is going to work, there is no real, living, stirring, vital reliance on the Holy Ghost which places straight before the tortured, stricken soul the Mighty Lord Jesus. God grant we may so rely on the Holy Spirit that we may allow Him to introduce through the agony of our intercession—that is the point, through the agony of vicarious intercession—the Living, Mighty Christ! WG. 68

Ignorant souls we can deal with, they need knowledge; the stupid soul does not need knowledge; the stupid soul needs to have the word of God until it is worried by it. The difficulty is how the worker is to get the word of God into its right place. Jesus Christ says the stupid soul is the one that hears the word and does not understand it. WG. 73

The only safeguard for the Christian worker is, 'Holiness unto the Lord.' If we are living rightly with God, living holy lives in secret and in public, God puts a wall of fire round about us. Beware of calling anything holiness that is only winsome and sweet to the world. God grant we may never lose the touch of God that produces the holy dread.
WG. 105

WORLD

Look at the world through either a microscope or a telescope and you will be dwarfed into terror by the infinitely minute or the infinitely great; both are appalling. BFB. 38

The world is the system of things which man has erected on God's earth. BE. 24

When Our Lord said, "Be of good cheer; I have overcome *the world*," He obviously did not mean the world in the material physical sense, the rocks and trees, the seasons, and the beautiful order of Nature, the sea and sky; it was not these He overcame, but the world in its ordered system of religion and morality, with all its civilizations and progress, which system reveals in the final analysis that it is organized absolutely apart from any consideration of God. A clean cut from everything that savours of the world in this sense is essential for the Christian. BE. 34

The hatred of the world is its intense objection to the principles exhibited by the saint, and frequently it is the best specimens of the worldly spirit who positively hate and detest the otherworldly spirit of the saint. It is not that they hate you personally, they may be very kind to you, but they hate what you represent of Jesus Christ. BE. 36

When you meet the hatred of the whole world-system unspiritual people around you will laugh to scorn the idea that you have a struggle on hand, but you realize that you are wrestling not against flesh and blood, but against the spiritual hosts of wickedness in the heavenly places. BE. 36

Both Jesus Christ and Paul were unquestionably mad, according to the standard of the wisdom of this world; they were related to affairs differently from the majority of other men, consequently, for the sake of self-preservation, they must be got rid of. Our Lord was crucified, and Paul was beheaded. When we are imbued with Jesus Christ's Spirit and are related to life as He was, we shall find that we are considered just as mad according to the standard of this world. BP. 160

The constructed world of man is not the created world of God. GW. 44

The popular evangelical idea that we are to be against the world in the sense of a pitched battle with it, is simply an expression of the spirit of the world dressed up in a religious guise. Our Lord was not against the world in that sense; He submitted to its providential order of tyranny, but there was no compromise in His spirit, and the model of the Christian's spirit is Christ Himself. GW. 56

It is by our spiritual choices that we maintain a right relation to the world. When a man ceases conflicting the world by spiritual choices, he succumbs to it and becomes part of the world that needs saving instead of being a saviour in the world. GW. 56

When we pray, "Thy Kingdom come," we have to share in the pain of the world being born again; it is a desperate pain. God's servants are, as it were, the birth-throes of the new age. "My little children, of whom I travail in birth again until Christ be formed in you." Many of us receive the Holy Ghost, but immediately the throes begin we misunderstand God's purpose. We have to enter into the travail with Him until the world is born again. The world must be born again just as individuals are. HG. 25

"The meek shall inherit the earth," not the world; the world is not God's; the world is the name given to the system of things men have placed on God's earth, and the Bible foretells the time when these shall pass away; they are going into the crucible just now. HGM. 93

Every forgiven soul will love the world so much that he hates to death the sin that is damning men; to love the world in any other sense is to be "an enemy of God": to love the world as God loves it is to spend and be spent that men might be saved from their sins. HGM. 118

The sign for the world without God is a circle, complete in and for itself; the sign for the Christian is the Cross. The Christian knows by bitter yet blessed conviction of sin that no man is sufficient for himself, and he thereby enters into identification with the Cross of Calvary, and he longs and prays and works to see the sinful, self-centred world broken up and made the occasion for the mighty Cross to have its way whereby men may come to God and God come down to men. HGM. 118

There are no nations in Jesus Christ's outlook, but *the world*. MUH. 290

The genius of the Spirit of God is to make us pilgrims, consequently there is the continual un-at-home-ness in this world. NKW. 135

Immediately Jesus Christ comes in, He produces havoc, because the whole world system is arrayed against His Redemption. It was the world system of His day, and particularly the religious system, that killed the Son of God. PR. 95

The world is that system of things which organises its life without any thought of Jesus Christ. PR. 105

In the eyes of the world the way a saint trusts God is always absurd, until there is trouble on, then the world is inclined to kneel down and worship the saint. PS. 80

Our Lord told His disciples over and over again that they must lay their account with the hatred of the world. SSY. 97

WORLDLINESS

"My Kingdom is not of this world," said Jesus, and yet we are more inclined to take our orders from the world than from Jesus Christ. AUG. 17

It is easy to denounce wrong in the world outside me—anyone without a spark of the grace of God can do that; easy to denounce the sins of others while all the time I may be allowing all sorts of worldly things in my own religious life. BE. 34

To be 'of' the world means to belong to the set that organizes its religion, its business, its social life and pleasures without any concern as to how it affects Jesus Christ, as to whether He lived or died matters nothing at all. BE. 34

The counsel of the Spirit of God to the saints is that they must allow nothing worldly in themselves while living among the worldly in the world. Those who live otherworldly in this world are the men and women who have been regenerated and who dare to live their life according to the principles of Jesus. BE. 35

Instead of being pilgrims and strangers on the earth, we become citizens of this order of things and entrench ourselves here, and the statements of Jesus have no meaning. NKW. 135

The line where the world ends and Christianity begins alters in every generation. What was worldliness in Paul's day is not worldliness in our day; the line is altering all the time. To-day the

world has taken on so many things out of the Church, and the Church has taken on so many things out of the world, that it is difficult to know where you are. SHL. 17

If we give the best we have got to worldliness we shall one day wake up to the revelation of what we have done and shall experience the wrath of God, mingled with ungovernable despair—'I gave the best I had got, not to God, but to the world, and I can't alter now.' SHL. 91

Prosperous worldliness is unspiritual and those who do not pray and who are not at all holy get on well. SHL. 93

WORLDLING

Never have the idea that the worldling is unhappy; he is perfectly happy, as thoroughly happy as a Christian. BE. 32

The people who are unhappy are the worldlings or the Christians if they are not at one with the principle which unites them. BE. 32

A worldling is not immoral, he is one who wisely keeps within the bounds of the disposition which the Bible alone reveals as sinful, viz., my claim to my right to myself. BE. 33

When a worldly man who is happy, moral and upright, comes in contact with Jesus Christ, his 'beauty,' i.e., the perfectly ordered completeness of his nature, is destroyed and that man must be persuaded that Jesus Christ has a better kind of life for him; otherwise he feels he had better not have come across Him. SHL. 41

When a worldling is not a worldling at heart, he is miserable; and when a Christian is not a Christian at heart, he is miserable, he carries his religion like a headache instead of something that is worth having. SHL. 44

WORRY

If we have really had wrought into our hearts and heads the amazing revelation which Jesus Christ gives that God is love and that we can never remember anything He will forget, then worry is impossible. BP. 143

Jesus Christ says, in effect, that when as His disciples we have been initiated into the kind of life He lives, we are based on the knowledge that God is our heavenly Father and that He is love. Then there comes the wonderful working out of this knowledge in our lives; it is not that we *won't* worry, but that we have come to the place where we *cannot* worry, because the Holy Spirit has shed abroad the love of God in our hearts, and we find that we can never think of anything our heavenly Father will forget. Although great clouds and perplexities may come, as they did in the case of Job, and of the Apostle Paul, and in the case of every saint, yet they never touch 'the secret place of the Most High.' BP. 219

If all power is given to Jesus Christ, what right have I to insult Him by worrying? If we will let these words of Jesus come into our heart, we shall soon see how contemptible our unbelief is. Jesus Christ will do anything for us in keeping with His own character; the power that comes from Him is stamped with His nature. BSG. 57

Fussing generally ends in sin. We imagine that a little anxiety and worry is an indication of how wise we really are; it may be an indication of how wicked we really are. GW. 80

Our Lord never worried, nor was He ever anxious, because He was not 'out' to realize His own ideas, He was 'out' to realize God's ideas. GW. 81

There is no use sitting up late or rising up early, I must do the work that lies before me, and avoid worry as I would the devil. "It is vain for you to rise up early, to sit up late . . ." HG. 38

Think of the unspeakable marvel of the remaining hours of this day, and think how easily we can shut God right out of His universe by the logic of our own heads, by a trick of our nerves, by remembering the way we have limited Him in the past—banish Him right out, and let the old drudging, carking care come in, until we are a disgrace to the name of Jesus. LG. 150

When once we see Jesus, He does the impossible thing as naturally as breathing. Our agony comes through the wilful stupidity of our own heart. We *won't* believe, we *won't* cut the shore line, we prefer to worry on. MUH. 60

"Take no thought . . ."; don't take the pressure of forethought upon yourself. It is not only wrong to worry, it is infidelity, because worrying means that we do not think that God can look after the practical details of our lives, and it is never anything else that worries us. Have you ever noticed what Jesus said would choke the word He puts in? The devil? No, the cares of this world. It is the little worries always. I will not trust where I cannot see, that is where infidelity begins. The only cure for infidelity is obedience to the Spirit. MUH. 144

Are we irritable and worried? Then do not let us say we are born from above, because if what Jesus says is true, how can we worry? Worry means one of two things—private sin, or the absence of new birth. PR. 33

The man who trusts Jesus Christ in a definite practical way is freer than anyone else to do his work in the world. Free from fret and worry, he can go with absolute certainty into the daily life because the responsibility of his life is not on him but on God. SSM. 72

If once we accept the revelation of Jesus Christ that God is our Father and that we can never think of anything He will forget, worry becomes impossible.
SSM. 72

In order to keep a stout heart to the difficult braes of life, watch continually against worry coming in. *"Let not your heart be troubled,"* is a command, and it means that worrying is sinful. SSM. 97

It is not the devil who switches folk off Christ's way, but the ordinary steep difficulties of daily life, difficulties connected with food, and clothing, and situations. The "cares of this world, . . . choke the word," said our Lord. We all have had times when the little worries of life have choked God's word and blotted out His face from us, enfeebled our spirits, and made us sorry and humiliated before Him, even more so than the times when we have been tempted to sin. SSM. 97

WORSHIP

The supreme lesson of the perfectly actual life of faith is to learn how to worship. Faith brings me into personal contact with God before Whom I must ever bow. I have to maintain a worshipful relationship to God in everything, and in the beginning this is difficult. NKW. 41

When we take the initiative we put our wits on the throne, we do not worship God. God never guides His children by their own initiative. The only initiative we have to take is the initiative of worshipping God. PH. 93

The only thing that will keep us watching and praying is continuing to worship God while we do our duty in the world as ordinary human beings. PR. 66

Worshipping is greater than work in that it absorbs work. SSY. 82

We must remember to take time to worship the Being Whose Name we bear. SSY. 135

'I beseech you, . . . present your bodies a living sacrifice . . . , which is your spiritual worship.' Worship of God is the sacramental element in a saint's life. We have to give back to God in worship every blessing He has given to us. SSY. 171

WORTHINESS

'Oh, but I don't feel worthy.' Of course you are not worthy! Not all your praying or obedience can ever make you worthy. Leave yourself absolutely in His hands, and see that you plunge yourself deep down in faith on the revelation that you are made one with God through the Redemption of Jesus Christ. AUG. 72

The worthiness of our Lord Jesus Christ is moral worth in the Divine and in the human sphere, and our moral worth is to be of the same order. BP. 266

Y

YIELDING

. . . it is so perilous to tell people to yield. *Don't* yield! Keep as stiff a neck as ever you had, and yield to nothing and to no one, unless you know it is the Lord Jesus Christ to Whom you are yielding. MFL. 22

Once you go on the yielding line, on the surrendering line and you do not know that it is the Lord Jesus Who is calling for the yielding, you will be caught up by supernatural powers that will wield you whether you like it or not. MFL. 23

If a man has difficulty in getting through to God we are apt to imagine it is an indication of a fine character, whereas the opposite is true; he is refusing to yield and is kicking, and the only thing God can do is to cripple him. OPG. 62

The Lord Jesus Christ is the one Person to Whom we ought to yield, and we must be perfectly certain that it is to Himself that we are yielding. PR. 23

Do not be sorry if other appeals find you stiff-necked and unyielding; but be sorry if, when He says "Come unto Me," you do not come. The attitude of coming is that the will resolutely lets go of everything and deliberately commits all to Him. PR. 23

If anyone has a difficulty in getting through to God, it is never God who is to blame. We can get through to Him as soon as we want to, there is nothing simpler. PR. 125

One life yielded to God at all costs is worth thousands only touched by God. SHL. 79

YOKE

Always keep your own life measured by the standard of Jesus Christ; bow your neck to His yoke alone and to no other yoke whatever; and see that you never bind any yoke on others that Jesus Christ Himself does not place. It takes a long time to get us out of imagining that unless people see as we do they must be wrong. AUG. 60

We are made sons and daughters of God through the Atonement and we have a tremendous dignity to maintain; we have no business to bow our necks to any yoke saving the yoke of the Lord Jesus Christ. BP. 39

Where are Christians putting their necks nowadays? Why, nine out of every nine and a half of us are absolute cowards, we will only put our necks under the yoke of the set we belong to. IWP. 92

A new delight springs up in any saint who suffers the yoke of Christ. Beware of dissipating that yoke and making it mean the yoke of a martyr. It is the yoke of a person who owes all he has to the Cross of Christ. Paul wore the yoke when he said, "For I determined not to know anything among you, save Jesus

Christ, and Him crucified." "Take My yoke upon you"—it is the one yoke men will not wear. IWP. 96

Jesus Christ cannot give me a meek and quiet spirit, I have to take His yoke upon me; that is, I have to deliberately discipline myself. NKW. 103

If we have been brought into a right relationship with God by the Redemption of Jesus Christ, He expects us to put on His yoke and to learn of Him. PR. 96

"It is good that man should both hope and quietly wait for the salvation of the Lord"; quietly wait, submit to the yoke, sit silent. All these are characteristics the world ridicules. RTR. 25

If we have taken His yoke upon us, we shall never say when things are difficult—'Why should this happen to me?' We shall be meek toward God's dispensations for us as Jesus was meek towards His Father. SSY. 85

YOUTH

A precocious young life rarely ends well, it becomes ordered too soon. God holds us responsible for the way we judge a young life; if we judge it by the standards by which we would judge a mature life, we will be grossly unjust. BE. 19

Much misjudgment of young life goes on in the religious domain. There is a stage when a young life manifests a sudden interest in everything to do with religion, but never bank on these awakenings because they are not necessarily awakenings by the Spirit of God, and when the intense stage passes—and it certainly will pass if it is not born of the Spirit—the one who is judging is apt to say that the boy or girl has backslidden. BE. 19

. . . we would never think of judging a boy or girl by the same standard of judgment we would pass on them when they are mature, because a boy or a girl is not in full grip of a character; but when once a soul is matured, the character which is manifested meets with severe judgment. BP. 66

. . . no man thinks so clearly or has such high ideals as in his teens, but unless our ideals find us living in accordance with them they become a mockery. OPG. 69

When we are young in the spiritual life we do practically exactly what we want to do, then there comes a time when we have to face this question of moral death to self-will. PH. 161

When a young life passes from early childhood into girlhood or boyhood, there is a new birth of the mind, and the boy or girl becomes interested in literature, in poetry, and usually in religion; but that is not spiritual new birth, and has nothing to do with the working of the Spirit of God; it has to do with the ordinary natural development of the life. At this stage great devotion to God and to Christian service may be manifested, and this is apt to be looked on as an evidence of the work of the Spirit of God, whereas it is the mere outcome of the natural life beginning to unfold itself in the process of development. These things always go together—physical development, an alteration in bodily organs, and mental, moral, and spiritual development. The boy or girl sees more purely and clearly than the man or woman. No man thinks so clearly at any time or is ever so thrilled as he is in his 'teens.' PR. 38

There are many signs of religiosity in a young life that arise simply from natural physical development and are not spiritual at all. A boy or girl in their teens often show amazingly religious tendencies and these are mistaken for the real work of the Spirit of God; they may or may not be. The need for spiritual discernment on this point in those of us who are workers is intense. PS. 34

It is a disastrous thing for a man never to be ragged, an appalling thing to be a privileged young man! A lad who has been his mother's pet and has been brought up like a hothouse plant is totally unprepared for the scathing of life as it is, and when he is flung out into the rugged realities of life, he suffers intolerably. Conceive the suffering of a lad who has been sheltered, never had anything to go against him, never been thwarted, when the tension does come. It is better to be a wise youth who can stand being ragged and taken down. One can always recognise the lad who has not been with others, he will not be admonished, consequently you cannot warn him. SHH. 49

The lad who is exceptionally clever at school very often becomes nothing afterwards; he attained too early. No boy has any right to attain too early or mature too quickly. By the time he comes to the age of twenty or thirty the power that ought to mature is not there, he has ripened too soon. The boy who gives the grandest promise does not always become what you expect, while the lad who is stodgy to begin with may come out top. SHH. 130

It is an appalling thing to see a young man with an old head on his shoulders; a young man ought not to be careful but to be full of cheer. "Rejoice, O young man, in thy youth." SHH. 146

God gives us all things richly to enjoy, and in youth and early manhood heaps rich precious bounties upon us, God must be remembered then, else we shall grievously hurt Him, and defraud ourselves. SHH. 149

Only the cynic will despise the loveliness and allurement of youthful days; but the saint will learn that even that bears the fatal hall-mark of "vanity." It too must pass. The happy delights of youth slip through our fingers as we hold them. SHH. 150

The only way youth can save itself from being despised is by the life being in keeping with the profession, the teaching backed by it, the conversation, the manner of life, the purity, the clean, vigorous, upright manhood; not only a worker sent from God, but an ensample of what God can do. WG. 100

Index